Deaf Studies *Today*

A Kaleidoscope of Knowledge, Learning, and Understanding

CONFERENCE PROCEEDINGS
UTAH VALLEY STATE COLLEGE • OREM, UTAH
APRIL 12–14, 2004

Edited by Bryan K. Eldredge, Doug Stringham,
and Minnie Mae Wilding-Diaz

Deaf Studies *Today*
A Professional Conference
at Utah Valley State College
www.deafstudies.org

The biennial Deaf Studies *Today!* conference brings together the best and brightest minds in the inter-disciplinary field of Deaf studies. Over three days, scholars from around the country present the latest research and thinking in the field in an environment conducive to the open exchange of ideas. Open to everyone interested in Deaf studies, including scholars, educators, students, Deaf people, and parents of deaf children, Deaf Studies *Today!* also aims to provide networking opportunities and promote Deaf-World interests.

Deaf Studies *Today!* includes presentations and papers that cover a broad range of topics related to Deaf people, their language, culture, and issues. Presentations are based on original work and present current research/thinking relevant to the field of Deaf Studies, including but not limited to perspectives from anthropology, history, linguistics, interpretation and translation, education, psychology, sociology, public administration, political science, social work, philosophy, ethics, art, literature, American Sign Language instruction, audiology, and any number of other allied disciplines.

Proceedings of Deaf Studies *Today!* are published by the American Sign Language and Deaf Studies Program at Utah Valley State College. Opinions expressed by the authors of these papers are their own and do not necessarily reflect those of the editors or of Utah Valley State College. Authors are responsible for the accuracy of the references cited. Use of the words Deaf or deaf in each paper also follows the authors' original manuscripts. ASL glosses are represented by small caps (e.g. DEAF, not 'deaf').

Deaf Studies *Today!* takes no responsibility for copyright infringements made by or in behalf of presenters or authors, and presenters agree to indemnify the publishers of Deaf Studies *Today!* against any illegal use of original artwork or creation.

Copies of Deaf Studies *Today!* procedings are available to anyone interested in perspectives on the field of Deaf studies; individual copies can be purchased for $11.00 (plus $3.00 for shipping and handling; allow two to four weeks for delivery). Address purchase requests to the address below:

Deaf Studies *Today!*
ASL and Deaf Studies Program—167
Utah Valley State College
800 West University Parkway
Orem, Utah, 84058-5999

Orders must include the following information: name, mailing address, phone number, e-mail address, relation to the field of Deaf studies (instructor, student, professional, etc.) and a check or money order made out to Utah Valley State College. Requests for permission to reprint material found in these proceedings should be sent in writing to the address above.

Editors:
Bryan Eldredge, Ph.D.
Co-Chair, Deaf Studies *Today!*
Program Coordinator, ASL and Deaf Studies
Utah Valley State College

Minnie Mae Wilding-Diaz, M.A.
Co-Chair, Deaf Studies *Today!*
Associate Professor, ASL and Deaf Studies
Utah Valley State College

Editing, Design, and Layout:
Doug Stringham
Adjunct Instructor, ASL and Deaf Studies
Utah Valley State College

Table of Contents

About the Conference

The first Deaf Studies *Today!* Conference was held at Utah Valley State College, Orem, Utah, April 12–14, 2004. The Conference was timed to immediately precede the 2004 USA Deaf Basketball national basketball tournament, also held at the college. Deaf Studies *Today!* was born out of a desire to bring scholars from the many disciplines comprising the field of Deaf Studies to a single academic conference.

Some six hundred and eleven registered participants, along with a number of other invited guests and college personnel, attended the conference. Highlighting the conference were addresses from Dr. Harlan Lane, Northeastern University; Dr. Ben Bahan, Boston University; Dr. Carol Padden, University of California at San Diego; and Dr. Douglas Baynton, University of Iowa. The conference also featured the presentation of nearly thirty papers on topics ranging from ASL sociolinguistics to Deaf history and art. (Most of these papers are included in these proceedings; Dr. Padden's address was not available at press time.)

In addition to paper presentations, Deaf Studies *Today!* included tradeshow-like exhibitors, live entertainment from internationally renowned actors Howie Seago and Nat Wilson, as well as local entertainers Bobby Giles and Reid Simonsen. Participants also viewed Deaf films on loan from the Chicago Institute for the Moving Image. In addition, the conference featured the premiere of a documentary film created by Deaf Studies faculty and students at Gallaudet University. This film, *Audism Unveiled,* examines the prejudices and animosity that confront Deaf people today. It also explores the hegemonic practices that maintain inequality between Deaf and hearing people. Following the screening, H. Dirksen Bauman and Ben Jarashaw, some of the film's creators, fielded questions in an open forum on the topics addressed in the film.

Tribute: Dr. Clayton Valli
At Deaf Studies *Today!* 2004, we paused at a luncheon in honor of Dr. Valli to remember not only his contributions to the academic community, but also to the lives of so many of us in the field. In addition to being one of the most well-known ASL poets, Dr. Valli was a pioneer. He was among the first to delve into the nuances of ASL poetry, and, as the recipient of the Stokoe Scholarship in 1983 (awarded to graduate students doing research on sign language or the Deaf community), he focused on the technical and linguistic aspects of ASL poetry. Eventually, his doctoral dissertation explored the intracacies of ASL poetry, and Dr. Valli became the first person to ever receive a degree in this field. Armed with the awareness of how ASL poetry is—and can be—produced, Valli went on to create a wide range of ASL poetry, from fun ("Cow and Rooster") to proud ("Deaf World") to political ("Pawns").

Dr. Clayton Valli was not only known for his poetry, he was also recognized for his work in linguistics, and in particular, sociolinguistics. He presented workshops all over the country and consulted various groups in terms of their ASL goals. He was the author and editor of several books on ASL and the Deaf community. More importantly, Dr. Valli's work affected almost every scholar in Deaf Studies in one way or another. Clayton's research enlightened us; his art inspired us; and his friendship changed us.

Dr. Clayton Valli passed away at age 51 on March 7, 2003 in Miami, Florida. This luncheon was our tribute to him. Thank you, Clayton!

Sponsors
Deaf Studies *Today!* extends our thanks to the organizations that made this conference and these proceedings possible through their generous support:

Gold-Level Sponsors: Dawn Sign Press; Stephen Hales Creative

Silver-Level Sponsors: Sprint; MCI; DeafNation

Keynote Address Sponsors: Salt Lake Community College; Brigham Young University

Institutional Sponsors: Utah Valley State College, Office of the Academic Vice President, The School of Humanities, Arts, and Social Sciences, The Department of Foreign Languages, Conferences and Workshops Department, The Center for the Study of Ehtics; The Gallaudet University Regional Center at Ohlone College in Fremont, California.

Volunteers
Deaf Studies *Today!* would simply not exist were it not for the hours and hours of work volunteered by the students of Utah Valley State College. They inspire us, and we give them our heartfelt thanks.

"The signing of the charter of Gallaudet College," National Association of the Deaf, 1915.
Gallaudet mathematics professor and faculty secretary, Amos G. Draper, tells of the historic event
in 1864 when the charter for the college was signed by President Abraham Lincoln.

Courtesy Gallaudet University Archives

Ethnicity, Ethics, and the Deaf-World

HARLAN LANE, PH.D.

Harlan Lane is a University Distinguished Professor at Northeastern University, Boston, Massachusetts. This address was given as a keynote address at Deaf Studies Today!, 13 April 2004.

IT HAS BECOME WIDELY KNOWN that there is a Deaf-World in America, some million citizens whose primary language is American Sign Language and who identify as members of that minority culture. The English terms *Deaf, hearing-impaired,* and *Deaf community* are commonly used to designate a much larger and more heterogeneous group than the members of the Deaf-World. Most of the 20 million Americans who are in this larger group communicate primarily in English or one of the spoken minority languages; they do not identify themselves as members of the Deaf-World, nor do they participate in its organizations, profess its values or behave in accord with its mores; rather, they consider themselves hearing people with a disability.

My topic today concerns the smaller group, the Deaf-World. I aim to show that it qualifies as an ethnic group, not a disability group, and that a failure to understand this is at the root of major ethical issues in the relation of the majority with this minority—issues such as genetic counseling and screening, gene therapy, and pediatric cochlear implants.

First I will present the case that the Deaf-World in America is an ethnic group and then I will examine the ethical issues from that perspective.[1]

- Collective name
- Feeling of community
- Norms for behavior
- Values
- Knowledge
- Customs
- Social structure
- Language
- Art forms
- History
- Kinship

Figure 1: Is the Deaf-World an Ethnic Group? Distinct Properties of Ethnic Groups

Figure 1 lists criteria that social scientists use to characterize ethnic groups.

Collective name: The Deaf-World has one.

Feeling of community: Self-recognition, and recognition by others, is a central feature of ethnicity. Americans in the Deaf-World do indeed feel a strong identification with that world and show great loyalty to it. This is not surprising: the Deaf-World offers many Deaf Americans what they could not find at home: easy communication, a positive identity, a surrogate family. The Deaf-World has the highest rate of intermarriage of any ethnic group, some ninety percent.

Norms for behavior: In Deaf culture, there are norms for relating to the Deaf-World; for decision-making, consensus is the rule, not individual initiative; for managing information; for constructing discourse; for gaining status; for managing indebtedness; and many more such norms.

Distinct values: Deaf people actively value their Deaf identity, which the hearing world stigmatizes; they value their sign language and act to protect and enrich it; they value cultural loyalty; the residential schools; physical contact; and much more.

Knowledge: Deaf people have culture-specific knowledge such as who their leaders are (and their characteristics); what's up with rank-and-file members of the Deaf-World; important events in Deaf history; how to manage in trying situations with hearing people. They know Deaf-World values, customs, and social structure.

Customs: The Deaf-World has its own ways of doing introductions and departures; of taking turns in a conversation; of speaking frankly and of speaking politely; it has its own taboos.

Social structure: There are numerous organizations in the American Deaf World: athletic, social, political, literary, religious, fraternal, leisure, ethnic, senior citizen and more.

Language: Competence in American Sign Language is a hallmark of Deaf ethnicity in the United States and some other parts of North America. A language not based on sound demarcates sharply the Deaf-World from the Hearing-World. The signed language of the Deaf-World is the core of Deaf-World authenticity.

The Arts: Language arts: ASL narratives, storytelling, oratory, humor, tall-tales, wordplay, pantomime, and poetry. Theatre arts and the visual arts address Deaf culture and experience.

History: The Deaf-World has a rich past recounted in stories, books, films, etc. Members of the Deaf-World have a particular interest in their history. That's because "[T]he past is a resource in the collective quest for meaning."[2] A sense of common history unites successive generations.

Kinship: Some scholars maintain that the core of ethnicity lies in the cultural properties we have examined, so kinship is not necessary for the Deaf-World or any other group to qualify as an ethnic group.[3] Others say kinship should be taken in its social meaning as "those to whom we owe primary solidarity."[4] Certainly there is a strong sense of solidarity in the Deaf-World; the metaphor of family goes far in explaining many Deaf-World norms and practices.

What kinship is really about, other scholars contend, is a link to the past; it's about "intergenerational continuity." The Deaf-World does pass its norms, knowledge, language, and values from one generation to the next: first, through socialization of the Deaf child by his or her Deaf parents and, second, through peer socialization of Deaf children who do not have Deaf parents. When we think of kinship, yet other scholars maintain, what is really at stake is biological resemblance; in that case, members of the Deaf-World are kin since Deaf people resemble one another biologically in that they are visual people.[5] Finally, many students of ethnicity would insist that ethnic groups have at least a claimed bond of blood—hereditary links among its members. And indeed most culturally Deaf people, born Deaf or early become so, are Deaf for hereditary reasons.[6]

Many scholars in the field of ethnicity believe that these "internal" properties of the ethnic group that we have just reviewed must also be accompanied by an "external" property, a boundary separating the minority from other ethnicities, in particular, the majority ethnicity.[7] Does the Deaf-World in the United States occupy its own ecological niche? Does it look to itself for the satisfaction of certain needs, while looking to the larger society for the satisfaction of other needs—and conversely?

In the second figure I have identified on the left activities that are primarily conducted by Deaf people for Deaf people, while I have listed on the right activities in the hearing world that impact Deaf people; in the middle are areas of overlap.

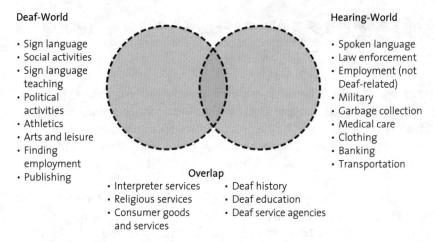

Deaf-World

- Sign language
- Social activities
- Sign language
  teaching
- Political
  activities
- Athletics
- Arts and leisure
- Finding
  employment
- Publishing

Hearing-World

- Spoken language
- Law enforcement
- Employment (not
  Deaf-related)
- Military
- Garbage collection
- Medical care
- Clothing
- Banking
- Transportation

Overlap

- Interpreter services   • Deaf history
- Religious services   • Deaf education
- Consumer goods   • Deaf service agencies
  and services

Figure 2: Deaf-World/Hearing-World Boundaries

I start with language—always a powerful creator of boundaries between ethnic groups, but especially so in the case of Deaf people, since hearing people are rarely fluent in visual language and Deaf people are rarely fluent in spoken language. Next, Deaf-World social activities are organized and conducted by Deaf people with little or no hearing involvement. On the other hand, law enforcement is a hearing world activity. Religious services overlap the Deaf and hearing worlds—there are missions to the Deaf, Deaf pastors, and signed services but the operation of the house of worship is generally in hearing hands. There's a lot in this table we could discuss but the important point is this: The Deaf-World keeps to itself for many of its activities; it collaborates in a few with the hearing world; and it leaves the really broad responsibilities such as law enforcement to the larger society; in this it is like other ethnic groups.

The American Deaf-World today meets the criteria put forth for ethnic groups and thus it is appropriate to view the Deaf-World as an ethnic group.[8] Thus we will apply the label _ethnic group_ to Deaf people and that will lead us to do appropriate things: learn their language, defend their heritage against more powerful groups, study their ethnic history, etc. Laws and treaties protecting ethnic groups then apply to the Deaf-World.

Is it also appropriate to label the Deaf a disability group? I do not ask, "do Deaf people in fact have a disability?" because it is not a matter of fact; disability, like ethnicity, is a social construct, not a fact of life. And it is a property of such constructs they appear misleadingly to be a fact of life. Yet we know that membership in the disability category comes and goes. Alcoholism went from moral flaw to crime to disability. Homosexuality went from moral flaw to crime to treatable disability to a minority group seeking civil rights. Shortness became a disability of childhood when growth enzyme was discovered, not before. Mild mental retardation became a disability with the arrival of the IQ test.

So we understand that disability is a label and, further, we recognize with the leaders of the disability community that disability is not in the individual but in society, that it is a shared oppression among people whose bodies differ in ways that general social customs do not accommodate. Shall we then label, and encourage the labeling of Deaf people as a disability group?

Some reasons have been advanced for Deaf people to embrace the disability label. Deaf people, like people with disabilities, suffer oppression because their bodies differ in ways that general social customs do not accommodate. However, consider some groups that suffer shared oppression because social custom does not accommodate their bodily difference: blacks; women—especially in the third world; people who are relatively short or tall; homosexuals. These groups among others suffer oppression because their bodies differ in ways that general social customs do not accommodate. Does their physical difference affect how they function in the world? Indeed it does. In much of the world, gays are rarely parents; women are not free to engage in activities reserved for men; many ethnic groups are restricted in their activities and some even targeted for genocide; large people and short people are often devalued and daily battle with an unaccommodating physical environment. And yet we would not class gays, women, blacks, large, or short people with groups said to have a disability. Thus the fact that a group suffers oppression because of its bodily difference from the norm is not a sufficient reason to label it a disability group.

One might well ask: Why not? Why not acknowledge the many things that physically different people share by using a common label. After all, some disability activists make a claim for disability culture; many oppose mainstreaming as do many Deaf activists. Both groups pay the price of social stigma. Both struggle with the troubled-persons industries for control of their destiny. Both endeavor to promote their construction of their identity in competition with the efforts of professionals to promote their constructions.

At one level, oppressed minorities do indeed share important traits and a common struggle for the defense and valuing of their diversity. At another level, however, many practical truths apply only to individual minorities, with their own make-up, demographics, histories, and cultures. To minimize that diversity would be to provide wrong answers to wrong questions and to undermine the most cherished goal of each group—to be respected and valued for its difference.

Another argument advanced for Deaf people to embrace the disability label is that it might assist Deaf people in gaining more of their rights. For example, interpreters are not normally provided in the classroom for members of ethnic groups; Deaf people have them in many places under a disability umbrella. However, some things important to Deaf people have come through an understanding of them as an ethnic group. I am thinking of the burgeoning of ASL in America's high schools and colleges and its increasing acceptance to meet the foreign language and culture requirement. I am thinking of the mushrooming of scholarship in the last 40 years concerning Deaf ethnicity—history, arts, social structure, culture and language. I am thinking of the birth of the discipline of Deaf Studies, of the reforms in Deaf education—all these gains are predicated on Deaf ethnicity.

Although the disability label seems inappropriate for the Deaf-World, its members have not aggressively promoted an understanding of its ethnicity and of the poor fit of the disability label. As a result, the majority's accommodation of the Deaf has come under a disability label and Deaf people must in effect subscribe to that label in order to gain their rights in access to information, in education, and other areas.

There are numerous professions that have an economic interest in promoting the disability understanding of the Deaf. To cite three: the American Speech-Language-Hearing Association, the National Institute on Deafness and Other Communication Disorders, and the American Academy of Otolaryngology—Head and Neck Surgery. Several of these organizations and others like them have paid lobbyists, control over federal funding, and large budgets. The Deaf-World has none of these advantages in seeking to promote an ethnic understanding of being Deaf.

The overwhelming reason to refuse to view culturally Deaf people as members of a disability group concerns **how Deaf people see themselves.** People who have grown up Deaf and have become integrated into Deaf culture do not, as a rule, see themselves as a disability group. This is an extremely strong argument for rejecting the disability label: Deaf people speak from intimate knowledge of what it is to be Deaf and there is no higher authority on how a group should be regarded than the members of the group themselves. Some disability scholars have impugned the Deaf point of view by saying that to have a disability is to be stigmatized and Deaf people are simply denying the truth of their disability to avoid stigma. However, people of all kinds do not wish to acquire disabilities; surely that cannot be a reason to judge that all those groups are in denial about their own disability. The Deaf-World is small and thus quite familiar with its members who have a disability; indeed it gathers them in and often makes special accommodation. Most Deaf people know Deaf people with disabilities—indeed, they are in their households. Furthermore, most Deaf people have heard a lot about the oppression encountered by the Deaf-blind, the Deaf mentally retarded, the Deaf motorically impaired, and so on. When Deaf people say they do not have a disability, they are often speaking from more knowledge than their hearing counterparts.

Deaf scholars like Humphries and Bienvenu in the U.S. and Ladd in England are not, I believe, rejecting the disability label because to be seen as having a disability is to be stigmatized. Rather they are rejecting it because as Humphries has said so well, "It doesn't compute." In ASL, the sign whose semantic field most overlaps that of the English "disability" can be glossed in English LIMP-BLIND-ETC. I have asked numerous Deaf informants to give me examples from that category: they have responded by citing people in wheelchairs, blind people, mentally retarded people, and people with cerebral palsy, but no informant has ever listed Deaf and all reject it as an example of a disability group when asked.

One further example of how the disability label doesn't compute: Deaf parents want children like themselves; they would like to see more Deaf people in the world. Leaders of the disability rights movement, on the other hand, call for ambivalence about their impairment. Individually they want it valued, as a part of who they are; at the same time, they ask that we regret the impairment and try to prevent it.[9] Parents who believe they have a disability generally do not want children like themselves or more adults like themselves, quite unlike culturally Deaf people. But then, do not all ethnic groups value their physical difference? Of course they do, so it is perfectly expected that culturally Deaf people positively value the Deaf difference. Culturally Deaf people do not see themselves as disabled.

Thus, embracing the disability label in hopes it might assist Deaf people in gaining more of their rights is fundamentally flawed because Deaf people don't believe it. For Deaf people to surrender anyway to how others define them is to misrepresent themselves. And that is the first reason to reject the disability label.

There are many penalties for misrepresenting, for allowing the disability label, and that brings me to the second argument for rejecting the disability label for Deaf people. It concerns the **risk to the Deaf child**. All children whose bodies differ from their parents in ways that age alone does not explain are at **medical and surgical risk**. Parents want children like themselves and, if they are unlike, they will listen to the doctors who say they can reduce or eliminate the difference, often mutilating the child in the process. It is very tempting to locate the source of the social stigma with the child rather than the society; after all, the child is right there and much more manageable than an entire society; moreover the technologies of normalization are knocking at the door. When children who have undergone surgical normalizing become adults, they frequently decry what was done to them as children.

Thus it has been the practice in America to operate on children with ambiguous genitalia, most often carving a vagina in male children because the surgical methods are not available to create a penis. As adults, these and other intersexuals have been campaigning to dissuade urologists from continuing to perform this maiming surgery.[10] Little People, when their parents are not dwarfs, are frequently subjected as children to bone breaking surgery for limb lengthening. It is painful, it is risky, it is incapacitating, it places the child in a no-man's-land, neither short as a dwarf nor average size, and most adult dwarfs are utterly opposed to the surgery.[11] There are many more victims of the medical-surgical imperative. One thinks of the horrors visited on the mentally ill, like frontal lobotomy,[12] and those visited on homosexuals such as deconditioning.[13]

Now to label the Deaf child as having a disability places that child at risk for interventions like cochlear implant surgery; speech training at the cost of effective education; a muddled identity. The surgery itself has dangers such as infection, occasionally fatal, and many implanted children have about the same limited command of English after the surgery and training that they had before.[14] We know that early acquisition of American Sign Language facilitates later mastery of English.[15] This linguistic intervention may rival or exceed the effect on English of implant surgery; the comparison study has not been done. Indeed, the surgeons are more interested in auditory sensation than in long-term language, social, and psychological outcomes.

Concerning the ethics of these medical-surgical interventions, it is profoundly troubling to realize that the child, too young to give informed consent, would in all likelihood refuse that consent if he or she were old enough to be asked. For example, Deaf adults, who were once Deaf children but are now old enough to make a considered decision, are overwhelmingly opposed worldwide to pediatric implant surgery. If medical and surgical procedures used with children who are Deaf, or intersexuals, or dwarfs, or gays, required informed consent from adults like the child—they would almost never take place! And when the parents are like the child, in fact they rarely take place.

Further ethical problems confront implant surgery on children. It is innovative, but optional innovative surgery on children is ethically problematic.[16] There is scant research on language benefit and no studies of the effects of the implant on educational achievement, social identity, or psychological adjustment. Fifty percent of implanted children in a special education survey have stopped using their implants; others use them but report little benefit.[17]

Finally, audiologists agree that implanted children remain "severely hearing-impaired" and comparisons with hearing-aid users place them in the category of "profoundly hearing-impaired."[18] To compound the harm of ineffective surgery, special educators who work with the surgical team urge oral educational programs on the parents and discourage sign language use.[19] If implanted children are unable to learn spoken English and are prevented from mastering American Sign Language, they will remain languageless for many years. There are cognitive and linguistic penalties for delayed language acquisition. It is inexcusable to leave a child without language for years on end; it is child abuse.[20]

Deaf parents raise Deaf and hearing children perfectly well without any surgery or other intervention by professionals. In fact, they do a better job on the average than hearing parents of Deaf children do, often with professional intervention. So it is clear that it would be a needless error to place Deaf children at risk of the medical-surgical imperative by labeling the Deaf as a disability group. Granted there are many self-described disability groups that protest excessive surgical and medical intervention. But why place Deaf children among them? Why run the risk?

My third argument against the disability label for the Deaf-World concerns **the risk to the Deaf-World as a whole.** A majority of people in the Deaf-World have inherited their ethnicity, as it is with other ethnic groups. Deaf inheritance and a failure to understand the ethnic status of culturally Deaf people have long led hearing people to promote eugenic efforts to regulate childbearing by Deaf parents. Alexander Graham Bell was the leading figure in the last century in efforts to stop Deaf reproduction through model sterilization laws, campaigns to dissuade Deaf adults from marrying and procreating, and efforts to discourage Deaf people from socializing and education in the company of other Deaf people.[21]

In principle, we could search for the genetic bases of being African or Asian, say. We do not. But federally funded programs today search for the genetic bases of being Deaf and they hold the promise, they proclaim, of creating a society in which there are no more Deaf people. When researchers at Boston University announced that they had identified a gene found in many people born Deaf, the director of the National Institute on Deafness and Other Communication Disorders called the finding a "major breakthrough that will improve diagnosis and genetic counseling and ultimately lead to substitution therapy or gene transfer therapy."[22] The goal of such efforts as gene transfer therapy is, of course, to reduce Deaf births, ultimately altogether.[23]

Imagine the uproar if medical scientists trumpeted a similar break-through for any other ethnic minority, promising a reduction in that ethnic group's children—promising fewer Navajos, fewer Jews, whatever ethnic group. The Australian government undertook a decades-long eugenic program to eliminate its aboriginal peoples by placing their children in white boarding houses in the city where it was hoped they would marry white and have white children. The Australian government has acknowledged that it is guilty of genocide and has launched a program of reparations.[24] Under international law, an activity that has the foreseeable effect of diminishing or eradicating a minority group, even if it is undertaken for other reasons and is not highly effective, is guilty of genocide.[25] Why do Americans fail to see that a program with the foreseeable effect of diminishing or eradicating the Deaf minority is indeed genocide? Americans fail to see the danger of allowing a genocidal program in this instance because most Americans see Deaf people as having a disability. And the goal of eradicating a disability, although it may be in some circumstances unwise and unethical, is not seen as genocide.

If culturally Deaf people were understood to be an ethnic group, they would have the protections offered to such groups. It is widely held as an ethical principle that the preservation of minority cultures is a good. The variety of humankind and cultures enriches all cultures and contributes to the biological, social and psychological well-being of humankind. Laws and covenants, such as the United Nations Declaration of the Rights of Persons Belonging to National or Ethnic, Religious, and Linguistic Minorities, are founded on a belief in the value of protecting minority cultures. The Declaration calls on states to foster their linguistic minorities and ensure that children and adults have adequate opportunities to learn the minority language.

It further affirms the right of such minorities to enjoy their culture and language and participate in decisions on the national level that affect them. Programs that substantially diminish minority cultures are engaged in ethnocide and may constitute crimes against humanity.

Because they are an ethnic group whose language and mores were long disparaged, Deaf people commonly feel solidarity with other oppressed groups, the more so as the Deaf-World includes such groups as people with disabilities, seniors, women, blacks, and so on. Deaf people have special reasons for solidarity with people with hearing impairments; their combined numbers have created services, commissions, and laws that the Deaf-World alone probably could not have achieved. Solidarity, yes, but when culturally Deaf people allow their ethnic identity to be subsumed under the construct of disability they set themselves up for wrong solutions and bitter disappointments. The risks to the future of the Deaf-World of embracing the disability label are grave.

This is my fourth argument against the disability label, **wrong solutions.** If the Deaf were to chose to align with disabled people, it would urge upon Americans an understanding from which grow solutions that Deaf people oppose. It is because disability advocates think of Deaf children as disabled that they want to close the special schools and absurdly plunge Deaf children into hearing classrooms in a totally exclusionary program called inclusion. It is because government is allowed to proceed with a disability construction of the culturally Deaf that the United States Office of Bilingual Education and Minority Language Affairs has refused for decades to provide special resources for schools with large numbers of ASL-using children although the law requires it to do so for children using any other non-English language. A committee of the National Association of the Deaf that worked diligently to gain Deaf children's language rights from that Office was in the end sent down the hall to the Office of Education for the Handicapped, but since handicapped people are not a language group they got nowhere.

There are landmark court rulings under the Civil Rights Act and the Equal Educational Opportunities Act that require schools with children who do not speak English to provide instruction initially in the children's best language. It is because of the disability construction of Deaf people that those laws have not been applied to ASL-using children. It is because of the disability construction that the teachers most able to communicate with America's Deaf children are excluded from the profession on the pretext that they have a disqualifying disability. It is because lawmakers see Deaf people as disabled that, following the Gallaudet Revolution, the United States Congress passed a law, not recognizing ASL or the Deaf-World as an ethnic minority, but a law establishing another institute of *health*, The National Institute on Deafness and Other Communication Disorders [sic], operated by the Deafness troubled-persons industry, and sponsoring research to reduce the numbers of Deaf people.

I have presented the case that culturally Deaf people are best viewed as an ethnic group and I have cited four obstacles in the way of understanding the Deaf-World as a disability group: Deaf people themselves do not believe they have a disability; the disability construction brings with it needless medical and surgical risks for the Deaf child; it also endangers the future of the Deaf-World. Finally, the disability construction brings bad solutions to real problems because it is predicated on a misunder-standing. The ethically troubling practices in which doctors and surgeons are engaged—operating on perfectly healthy Deaf children, seeking the means to eradicate the Deaf-World—exist because this ethnic group is misunderstood as a disability group.

How we ultimately resolve these ethical issues goes well beyond Deaf people; it will say a great deal about what kind of society we are and the kind of society in which we wish to live. Difference and diversity not only have evolutionary significance but, we would argue, are a major part of what gives life its richness and meaning.

There is reason for hope: society can adopt a different understanding of a people. Native Americans were once seen as savages; black Ameri-cans as property; women as utterly dependent.

The case for Deaf ethnicity built by the social sciences is powerful. Increasingly, linguists take account of ASL, sociologists of the social structure of the Deaf-World, historians of its history, educators of its culture and so on. It remains to reform those other professions that simply have an outdated understanding. It has been done before. It can be done again.

ENDNOTES

1. In the United States, the idea of classifying the Deaf-World with the nation's ethnic groups has been around for a long time—more than 25 years, during which it was discussed repeatedly by scholars. (Padden & Markowicz, 1976; Markowicz & Woodward, 1978; Erting, 1978, 1982; Johnson & Erting, 1982, 1984, 1989.)

2. Nagel, 1994, p. 163.

3. One scholar writes: "Some groups are defined by their genetic heritage, others by their language or religion or other criteria" (Petersen, 1980, p. 235; see also Sollors, 2001; Schneider, 1972, p. 59; Barth, 1998, p. 5). Another writes: "It does not matter whether an objective blood relationship exists" (Weber quoted in Sollors 2001, p. 4815).

4. Schneider, 1969.

5. Johnson & Erting, 1989.

6. Considering first Deaf people in general, the figure 50 percent Deaf for genetic reasons is often cited (Reardon et al., 1992). But the general figure is probably an underes-timate for the Deaf-World in particular for two reasons: first, the general figure does not include members of the Deaf-World who are Deaf for hereditary reasons but also have what otologists view as an illness associated with being Deaf (such as "Waardenburg's syndrome"); second, some hereditarily Deaf people are not aware of having Deaf relatives and so they are mistakenly excluded from the category of hereditarily Deaf. Smith, 1995.

7. Barth, 1998.

8. It is probably more precise to say that the Deaf child in America today has mul-tiple ethnicities, Deaf ethnicity among them. For example, a Deaf Asian American might be Chinese-American with respect to other Asian Americans, Asian American with respect to

mainstream American ethnicity, Deaf in relation to all of the above, Deaf Asian-American in relation to other Deaf Americans, and American with respect to foreign ethnicities.

9.   Abberley, 1987; Lane, 1995.
10.   Dreger, 1998.
11.   Kennedy, 2003.
12.   Valenstein, 1986.
13.   Conrad & Schneider, 1980
14.   Lane & Bahan, 1998; Lane, 1999, 239–261.
15.   Padden & Ramsey, 2001.
16.   Lane & Grodin, 1997.
17.   Rose, 1994; Rose, Vernon & Pool, 1996.
18.   Osberger et al., 1991; Boothroyd, 1993; Geers and Brenner, 1994; Horn, Nozza and Dolitsky, 1991. Miyamoto et al., 1995.
19.   Tye-Murray, 1992.
20.   Petitto, 1993; Maybery & Eichen, 1991.
21.   Lane 1984.
22.   BU team, 1992.
23.   BU team, 1992; Gene that causes, 1992.
24.   National Inquiry, 1997.
25.   National Inquiry, 1997.

REFERENCES

Abberley, P. (1987). The concept of oppression and the development of a social theory of disability. *Disability, Handicap and Society*, 2:5–19.

Barth, F. (1998). *Ethnic groups and boundaries*. Prospect Heights IL: Waveland.

Boothroyd, A. Profound Deafness. (1993). In: Tyler R. (ed.) *Cochlear implants: Audiological foundations*. San Diego, California: Singular. pp. 1–33.

BU Team Finds Genetic Cause of Waardenburg Syndrome. (1992). *Deaf Community News*, March, p. 6.

Conrad, P., & Schneider, J. (1980). *Deviance and medicalization*. (Columbus, Ohio, Merrill).

Dreger, A. (1998). *Hermaphrodites and the medical invention of sex*. Cambridge: Harvard University Press.

Erting, C. (1978). Language policy and Deaf ethnicity in the United States. *Sign Language Studies*, 19:139–152.

Erting, C. (1982). *Deafness, communication and social identity: An anthropological analysis of interaction among parents, teachers and deaf children in a preschool*. Unpublished doctoral dissertation, American University, Washington, DC.

Geers, A. and Brenner, C. (1994) Speech perception results: Audition and lipreading enhancement. *Volta Review* 96:1–11.

"Gene that Causes Waardenburg's Syndrome." (1992). *New York Times* 141, B7, C2.

Horn, R. M., Nozza, R. J. & Dolitsky, J. N. (1991). Audiological and medical considerations for children with cochlear implants. *American Annals of the Deaf* 136:82–86.

Johnson, R. E. & Erting, C. (1982). Linguistic socialization in the context of emergent deaf ethnicity. In C. Erting & R. Meisegeier (Eds.), *Working Papers No. 1: Deaf children and the socialization process*. Washington, DC: Gallaudet College, Sociology Dept.

Johnson, R.E., & Erting, C. (1984). Linguistic socialization in the context of emergent Deaf ethnicity. *Wenner-Gren Foundation Working Papers in Anthropology*. (ed.) Keith Kernan. New York: Wenner-Gren.

Johnson, R.E., & Erting, C. (1989). Ethnicity and socialization in a classroom for Deaf children. In: C. Lucas (Ed.), *The sociolinguistics of the Deaf community.* New York: Academic Press. pp. 41–84.

Kennedy, D. (2003). *Little people.* New York: St. Martin's Press

Lane, H. (1984). *When the mind hears: A History of the Deaf.* New York: Random House.

Lane, H. (1995). Constructions of deafness. *Disability and Society* 10:171–89.

Lane, H., and B. Bahan. (1998). Effects of cochlear implantation in young children: A review and a reply from a DEAF-WORLD Perspective. *Otolaryngology: Head and Neck Surgery* 119:297–308

Lane, H. (1999). *Mask of benevolence.* 2nd. Ed. San Diego: DawnSignPress.

Lane, H., and M. Grodin. (1997). Ethical Issues in cochlear implant surgery: An Exploration into disease, disability, and the best interests of the child. *Kennedy Institute of Ethics Journal* 7:231–251.

Markowicz, H., & Woodward, J. (1978). Language and the maintenance of ethnic boundaries in the Deaf community. *Communication and Cognition* 11: 29–37.

Mayberry, R., & Eichen, E. (1991). The long-lasting advantage of learning sign language in childhood: another look at the critical period for language acquisition. *Journal of Memory and Language* 30:486–512.

Miyamoto, R. T., Kirk K. I., Todd, S. L., Robbins, A. M. & Osberger, M. J. (1995). Speech perception skills of children with multichannel cochlear implants or hearing aids. *Annals of Otology Rhinology and Laryngology* 104 (Suppl)I: 334–337.

Nagel, J. (1994). Constructing ethnicity: Creating and recreating ethnic identity and culture. *Social problems,* 41(1): 152–176.

National Inquiry into the Separation of Aboriginal and Torres Strait Islander Children from Their Families. (1997). *Bringing them home.* New South Wales: Sterling Press.

Osberger, M. J., Miyamoto, R. T., Zimmerman-Phillips, S., Kemink, J. L., Stroer B., Firszt, J. B., Novak, M.A. (1991). Independent evaluations of the speech perception abilities of children with the Nucleus 22-channel cochlear implant system. *Ear and Hearing* 12(4) (Suppl): 66S–80S.

Padden, C., & Markowicz, H. (1976). Cultural conflicts between hearing and deaf communities. In F. B. Crammatte & A. B. Crammatte (Eds.), *VII World Congress of the World Federation of the Deaf.* Silver Spring, Maryland: National Association of the Deaf. pp. 407–411.

Padden, C., & Ramsey, C. (2001). American Sign Language and reading ability in Deaf children. In: Chamberlain, C. Morford, J. & Mayberry, R. (eds.), *Language acquisition by eye.* Maway, New Jersey: LEA. pp. 165–189.

Petersen, W. (1980). Concepts of ethnicity. In S. Thernstrom (ed.), *Harvard Encyclopedia of American Ethnic Groups.* Cambridge MA: Harvard University Press. pp. 234–242.

Petitto L. (1993). On the ontogenetic requirements for early language acquisition. In: E. de Boysson-Bardies, S. de Schonen, P. Jusczyk, & J. Morton (eds.), *Developmental neurocognition: speech and face processing in the first year of life.* New York: Kluwer Academic Press. pp. 365–383.

Reardon, W., Middleton-Price. H., Malcolm. S., Phelps. P., Bellman. S., Luxon. L., Martin. J., & Bumby. A. (1992). Clinical and Genetic Heterogeneity in X-Linked Deafness. *British Journal of Audiology* 26: 109–114.

Rose D. E. (1994) Cochlear implants in children with prelingual deafness: Another side of the coin. *American Journal of Audiology* 3:6.

Rose D., Vernon, M. and Pool A. (1996). Cochlear implants in prelingually deaf children. *American Annals of the Deaf* 141: 258–261.

Schneider, D.M. (1969). Kinship, nationality, and religion in American culture: toward a definition of kinship. In R. F. Spencer (Ed.), *Forms of symbolic action* Seattle: University of Washington Press. pp. 116–125.

Schneider, D.M. (1972). What is kinship all about? In P. Reining (Ed.), *Kinship studies in the Morgan centennial year.* Washington DC: Anthropological Society of Washington. pp. 32–64.

Smith, A.D. (1986). *The ethnic origin of nations.* Cambridge: Blackwell.

Smith, S. (1995). Overview of genetic auditory syndromes. *Journal of the American Academy of Audiology:* 6, 1–14.

Sollors, W. (2001). Ethnic groups/ethnicity: Historical aspects. In N. J. Smelser & P. B. Baltes (eds.), *International Encyclopedia of the Social Sciences.* New York: Elsevier. pp. 4813–4817.

Tye-Murray N. (1992). *Cochlear implants and children: A handbook for parents, teachers and speech and hearing professionals.* Washington, DC: Alexander Graham Bell Association for the Deaf.

Valenstein, E. (1986). *Great and desperate cures.* New York: Basic Books.

ABOUT THE AUTHOR

A specialist in the psychology of language with a focal interest in Deaf people, Harlan Lane was a visiting professor of linguistics at the Sorbonne and then at the University of California San Diego. In 1974, he founded Northeastern University's program of instruction in American Sign Language (ASL) and his own continuing program of sponsored research on ASL and Deaf culture. Dr. Lane is the author of numerous articles in professional journals concerning speech, hearing, and deafness, and of several books, among them, The Wild Boy of Aveyron: Foundations of Special Education; When the Mind Hears: A History of the Deaf; The Mask of Benevolence: Disabling the Deaf Community; *and (with R. Hoffmeister and B. Bahan)* A Journey into the Deaf-World.

Dr. Lane's honorary awards include the International Social Merit Award of the World Federation of the Deaf; the John D. and Catherine T. MacArthur Foundation Fellowship, the Distinguished Service and Literary Achievement Awards of the National Association of the Deaf, and the Order of Academic Palms from the French government.

"Coffin Door"

Memoir Upon the Formation of a Visual Variety of The Human Race[1]

BENJAMIN BAHAN, PH.D.

Ben Bahan is professor and director of the graduate program in the Department of Deaf Studies at Gallaudet University. This address was given as a keynote address at Deaf Studies Today!, *14 April 2004.*

IN NEW YORK CITY, A father and daughter sat in a café people watching out the window and drinking coffee.

"Look across the street," signed the father.

His daughter quickly scoped the busy street packed with people hustling to and fro before quizzically looking back at her dad.

"One of them is deaf...which one is it?" he asked.

She scanned the crowd. She noticed one man's eyes glancing from side to side. "The one with the brown overcoat," she guessed.

"I agree. Let's watch and see," he suggested.

The man in the brown overcoat was about to cross the street, but sensed the sudden shift in the crowd of people around him as they simultaneously looked in the same direction. He decided he too should check in that direction and saw sirens and flashing lights accompanying a speeding ambulance. After the commotion subsided, he crossed the street and continued walking past the cafe. The father waved his hands in the man's periphery. In the middle of a bustling city, the man in the brown overcoat noticed a flutter of hands through the window and quickly turned to see the father and his daughter.

"You deaf?" signed the father.

The man was astounded and asked, "How did you know?"

PEOPLE OF THE EYE

The characters in this short story are unique in that they inhabit a highly visual world. They use a visual language to communicate and have developed a visual system of adaptation to orient them in the world that defines their way of being.[2]

This is not an unusual story. Episodes like this have been shared and reported all over the world. The claim that deaf people are highly visual and tactile is not a new concept. It has been stated time and time again in various sources—both in writing and through the air ("orally"). The most notable statement came from George Veditz, who eloquently commented at the National Association of the Deaf convention in Colorado in 1910, "...[Deaf people] are first, last and of all time the people of the eye" (Veditz, 1910).[3]

The strongest support for the notion put forward by Veditz (and others) is the emergence of a visual-gestural language. Since the dawn of time, whenever and wherever there were deaf people[4] on earth, a visual communication system (using gestures, mime, and home signs) would be developed to convey thoughts, feelings, desires, and ideas. Although there is no written record of this phenomenon from the ancient times, one of the earliest recorded observations of deaf people using gestures and signs are found in Plato's *Cratylus*. In ensuing dialogue between Socrates, Hermogenes, and Cratylus on issues of names and language, Socrates made an observation in reference to deaf people using gestures/signs in Athens around 400 to 350 BCE:

> Suppose that we had no voice or tongue, and wanted to communicate with one another. Should we not, like the deaf and dumb, make signs with the hands and head and the rest of the body? (Plato, 1961, 457)

Observations of deaf people creating visual-gestural communication do not only occur in major metropolitan areas but also in isolated places around the globe from the jungles of the Amazons[5] to the many islands scattered all over the world's oceans.[6, 7] In essence this discussion highlights what Veditz also said in 1913, "As long as we have deaf people on earth, we will have signs" (National Association of the Deaf, 1913).

The desire and drive to create signs is deeply rooted in our fundamental human need for communication. The truth is "we cannot be truly human apart from communication...to impede communication is to reduce people to the status of things" (Freire quoted in M.J. Wheatley (2002). Deaf people, being of a human variety, have refused to be reduced to the status of things and found ways to communicate visually and developed visual languages.[8] That is the essence of their being. All other things are constructed around this, channeled through and by vision.

The roots in visual-gestural languages have pushed the boundary of vision far beyond other human groups known.[9] This paper will draw from various bodies of research and observations to further demonstrate the significance of "vision" to the Deaf-World.

THE USE OF EYES IN LANGUAGE AND CULTURE

Before looking at the role that vision and the use of eyes play in the language and culture of deaf people, we need to realize two things: 1) there are people who are not deaf but are highly visual in the way they think, behave, and express themselves and 2) unlike the ears, human eyes have communicative functions, which play a role in sending and receiving information. Almost all humans are able to display this duality. The size of pupils sends information on whether one is scared, interested and so on. Droopy eyes indicate drowsiness.[10] However, among signing deaf people, the role vision and the use of eyes expands exponentially.

We must bear in mind that when using signed languages signers manifest many different kinesthetic features which are depicted visually: the body, head, hands, arms, facial expressions, and the physical space surrounding the signer and his/her eyes. The focus here will be on the role the eyes and vision have in linguistic and discourse exchanges and ways they are extended to other cultural and literary functions.

Various Eye Behaviors in Language. When signing, the signer's eyes are always moving in saccadic manner—rapid eye movements to and from fixation points—to signal various linguistic information in different layers. The eye movement may occur over a single word[11] to convey specific meaning, appear in sentences to indicate the spatial position of the object, signal constituent boundaries, bring the addressee in and out of a story world, and/or play a role in turn-taking. All saccadic movement happens in one brief exchange.

At the lexical level, the eye gaze may shift to correlate with the manual portion of a sign and convey additional meaning to the word. Sentence 1 shows an example of this co-occurrence with an adjective. In this sentence the signer looks at the addressee then quickly shifts his gaze to the hands where the shortness of the cute boy is conveyed and shifts his gaze back to the addressee:

Sentence 1:

gaze down

BOY CUTE SHORT.

Translation: The boy is short and cute.

(Note: No eye gaze transcription over a sign means the signer is looking at the addressee).

At the syntactic level, the eyes play a critical role in relations to syntactic constituents, such as noun phrases and verb phrases in simple sentences. They have different functions depending on where in the sentence the eyes are being used. In noun phrases, the eyes can have function to convey the location and distance of an entity.[12] Eye gaze frequently accompanies the indexical sign that expresses definite determiners in ASL. The eye gaze to the same location in space where the finger points: the location in space associated with the referent that is being referred back to, as seen in sentence 2:

Sentence 2:

___*gaze left*___

IX-left MAN WANT BUY YOUR CAR

Translation: The man (over there) wants to buy your car.

Indefinite reference in ASL is associated with a broader region in space than just a single point. So, for example, the indefinite determiner, SOME-THING/ONE is articulated by an upward pointing index finger moving in quick circles within a small region in space. The eye gaze that accompanies the indefinite determiner is also more diffused within that region of space. So, sentence 3 illustrates the distinction in the definiteness/indefiniteness of the noun is reflected in the different types of eye gaze used:

Sentence 3:

___*diffused gaze*___

SOMEONE MAN WANT BUY YOUR CAR

Translation: A man wants to buy your car.

In the verb phrase, the eyes used in transitive constructions serve as non-manual markers of syntactic object agreement.[13] In sentence 4, the direction of the eye gaze (to the left) marks the location associated with the object and augments the sentence by functioning as a non-manual object agreement marker as it spreads across the verb phrase.

Sentence 4:

___*gaze left*___

JOHN LOVE MARY.

Translation: John loves Mary.

When engaging in discourse, the listener usually fixes and maintains his gaze on the signer's face—particularly the eyes—thus creating a conversational partnership in regulating different discourse functions. As previously mentioned, the signer's eyes are constantly moving in a saccadic manner to convey various linguistic purposes. This eye movement continues throughout the exchange. The signer gazes away from the addressee (- gaze) for various linguistic and discourse related reasons and gazes back to the addressee (+ gaze) to check on him/her, to keep him/her involved, and/or to give a turn.[14]

This "checking mechanism" often happens at points that are identified as constituent boundaries or lines.[15] In a situation where the addressee wants to initiate a turn, he will place his hands in the signer's visual field, wait until the signer is gazing at him (+ gaze), and then start signing. In a heated exchange, the signer can maintain his role by minimizing the number of times he performs + gaze. By doing this he minimizes the chances of being interrupted.[16]

The dynamics of a classroom involves more complex turn-taking strategies where the teacher usually assumes the role of a regulator. In the case of signing classrooms, this equation has been observed: the more fluent the teacher is with visual communication signals, the more fluid classroom discourse will be. These teachers maintain a clear distinction between two forms of gazes: individual gaze (I-gaze) and group gaze (G-gaze).[17]

In a classroom, the two different gazes serve different functions; for instance, when the teacher wants to address a particular student, he employs the I-gaze at that student by keeping his eyes transfixed to that student (with allowance for saccadic linguistic markers) and maintaining mutual eye contact while engaging in questions and answers. When the teacher wants to talk to the class as a whole, his gaze is less transfixed and more diffused as he addresses the whole group. The teacher will also sweep his gaze and head around the group to address all of the students.

Handling this distinction between the two types of classroom eye gaze has been problematic for non-fluent signing teachers and has caused misunderstandings between teachers and students. For example, a teacher used an I-gaze at one particular student when he was actually addressing the whole class. Signing "Please pay attention when I am talking," with the eye gaze at one particular student will likely result in the student responding, "I have been paying attention; why are you picking on me?"[18]

While telling a story, a signer typically does not relinquish his/her turn to the audience. Instead, the expectation is that the storyteller maintains his/her turn until the story is completed. Thus, the role of eye gaze, while still vital to engaging the listener/audience, takes a somewhat different form. In addition to the constant saccadic shifts that fall within the categories described above (e.g. using eye gaze for lexical and syntactic purposes), the teller uses eye gaze in constructed action/dialogue to present information from the point of view of a character in the story.

This type of eye gaze serves a major function in storytelling. The teller assumes various characters' gazes while signing his/her actions and incorporates reciprocal gazes to clearly represent dialogues between two or more characters in a story. On a more global level, the teller brings the story world up right before the addressees' eyes, and eye gaze serves to modulate between the narrator's perspective, the story world, and the more "direct" depiction of events through the eyes of a character.[19] In addition, closer scrutiny allows one to see that the teller's rhythmic gaze from the story world to the audience serves as a device for demarcating narrative units in a formulaic sense.[20]

There are eye behaviors, other than gaze directions or saccadic movements, which play additional roles in the language that are worth mentioning here. While accompanying various spatial related signs, the aperture of the eyelids can also convey a sense of nearness or farness. When the eyelids widens in association with a lexical item it conveys closeness, whereas the squinting of the eyelids convey distance. Another behavior includes the way the closure of the eyes with a word conveys an emphasis; this has been identified as emphatic eye closure.[21]

Another type of eye behavior involves eye blinks in sentences. If one looks at the site where eye blinks occur with regularity, one will find signers blink their eyes in constituent boundaries that are between the NPs and VPs and at the end of sentences as shown in sentence 5:

Sentence 5:

blink   *blink*

LAST–NIGHT JOHN   VISIT   MARY.

Translation: Last night John visited Mary.

The proposition that the role of eyes used for signaling communicative function among signing deaf people is expanded exponentially is thus confirmed. The essence of what may appear as simple eye-gazing behavior is in fact part of a complex multi-layered linguistic system in American Sign Language. That is, the signer's eyes are always moving in a saccadic manner to signal various linguistic information in different layers from a single word to interactions with a large group.

Visual language and the brain.[22] Oliver Sacks, a renowned neurologist and author, was astounded at the complexity and multi-layered role that eyes play in conjunction with sign production. He commented:

> "One can have a dozen, or a dozen-and-a-half, grammatical modifications, done simultaneously, one on top of the other, and when this came home to me, the neurologist in me was aroused. I thought: "that's impossible. How the hell can the brain analyze eighteen simultaneous visual patterns?" I was filled with a sort of neurological awe. The answer to this, briefly, is that the normal brain can't make such visual analysis, but it can learn to do so."[23]

There are a number of neurological studies examining the interactive function of signed language, vision, and the brain that support Sacks' observation. In this paper, the focus is on three research areas that portray this learned visual way of being: 1) peripheral vision, 2) spatial processing tasks, and 3) rapidly presented visual information tasks.

Since the 1980s, several studies have looked at peripheral vision and deaf people through electroencephalograms (EEGs) and functional magnetic resonance imaging (fMRIs) tests. The results have consistently shown that signers have superior attention to the peripheral visual space.[24] This scientific proof gave legitimacy to what has been known in the Deaf community for a long time. The story in the beginning of this paper showed how the man in the brown overcoat was able to use his peripheral vision to "navigate" his way in the world of sound. This attention to the periphery develops at a very early age in children.

One personal observation concerns my daughter when she was three-and-a-half years old. She was engaged in a conversation with an adult seated across from her at the dining room table. I was seated to her right (in her periphery). They were going over the names of her preschool classmates. I supplied a name sign hoping to clarify and help out the adult. My daughter quickly looked away from the adult and corrected the way I produced that particular classmate's name. I was astonished that at *age three-and-a-half*, she was able to recognize the name sign error I made out of her *peripheral* line of vision. Her facility using peripheral vision is further evidence in support of the claim that signers have superior attention in this area.

Several spatial processing tasks were also done comparing native signers of ASL with non-signers. The tasks required subjects to recall, compare, and identify various mental and visual images. They include being able to quickly identify, generate and transform mental and mirror images.[25] Tests include spatial cognition tasks in non-verbal IQ tests such as block designs, a subtest of the Wechsler Intelligence Scale for Children[26] and recognition and matching an array of six faces oriented and shadowed differently with the target face.[27] These spatial processing tasks show that native signers of ASL performed better than non-signers.[28]

Another task focused on the ability of deaf people to recognize rapidly presented visual information. Researchers created a videotaped test of invented Chinese characters written in the air with tiny light bulbs attached to a hand. The videotape was shown to a group of deaf and hearing Chinese first graders. The tasks required students to maintain in memory the path traced rapidly, analysis into component strokes and finally reproduction on paper. The Deaf signing first graders significantly outperformed their hearing counterparts.[29]

The perception tasks discussed above do not require knowledge or use of signed languages. However, comparative results show that the native signers had a consistent advantage when performing the tasks. These studies reinforce the notion that signing Deaf people make better use of vision.

In Culture and Literature. The visual way of being in the world discussed thus far is carried over into the cultural lives, values, consciousness, social spaces, and literatures of signers.[30] Recall the story in the beginning of this paper, where the father and daughter were able to identify the man in the brown overcoat as deaf out of thousands of people on the bustling city street. They noticed the subtleties that only members of this culture (those who share the visual experience) can see.

The first visual cue was the way the man in the brown overcoat was orienting himself in the streets of New York City by executing saccadic eye and head movements. The father and daughter knew from observing the synchrony of these movements that there was something uniquely familiar about this man; something this is visual only to deaf people. This man had what is known in the community as "deaf eyes." The daughter's guess that the man in the brown overcoat was "the" deaf man was confirmed by observing how he read the world.

Visual-cultural adaptions. There are different sets of learned behaviors and adaptive systems that are passed on with respect to "reading the world." One learns to engage in observing, looking and eventually seeing that sound has ways of bouncing off visual cues. I remember my father's advice as I was growing up. He would sign, "Observe others around you; if you notice them looking in one direction, something is happening over there. This is not limited to people walking, but also driving. If cars in front of you slow down or stop at an intersection when the light is green, do not attempt to pass without checking around you because this is a telltale sign of an oncoming ambulance or police in the intersection." My father also noted that pets and/or other animals are able to broadcast auditory cues. My wife and I are able to "hear" our kids coming down the stairs or playing upstairs when they are supposed to be in bed by noticing our pets (cats and dog) perk up from their sleep and glance at the space behind us.

When I walk my dog in the woods, I often "hear" things by noticing her glances in particular directions. Another "visual rule" my father hammered into me was the necessity of looking back every time you leave a room or place. "You never know if someone may need your attention, so it is a courtesy to look behind you to check with others before you leave." I also learned the significance of periphery as an integral part of reading the world. The man in the overcoat used it to respond to the father through the café window just as my three-and-a-half year old daughter used it to correct me when I incorrectly produced her friend's name sign.

When we look at social spaces, we see that the proxemics or social distance between interlocutors is at a distance that is comfortable for the eyes. When more than two people are involved, the spacing arrangement between signers becomes circular. When additional signers join the conversation the circle becomes larger, and always maintains visual sight lines of one another. At conferences or sporting events it is common to see many circles forming throughout the lobby. The proxemics are regulated by visual needs.

When participating and/or joining a circle, signers need to be in synchrony with each other's body rhythms.[31] Listeners need to be in sync with the signer's pace of signs, body, and saccadic movements in order to take a turn. To join a conversation already underway, the newcomer needs to be in sync with the established interlocutors. When deftly done it appears as if the person was part of the initial conversation.

There appears to be symbiosis between native members of the signing community. Whenever native signers go to a location for the first time, whether it is a national or international site, they meet new people and hang out with new friends. Invariably these new friends are also native signers. It is remarkable that without actively seeking them out they naturally connect with other native signers. There is clearly a rapport, a synchronicity, and a subjective way of being that binds them. Having grown up in visual environments they learn to use the eyes and body for various functions related to language, discourse, and culture. When they meet someone else who has acquired and emits this ways of being, synchronicity happens and a connection results.

Another related area is how signers naturally create or modify their habitat as exemplified by the notorious phrase "this is a deaf house." This comment indicates that the particular house has earned the "seal of approval" for the way it is structured for vision. The floor plan of a "deaf house" is usually open, has fewer walls and many windows in the common area.[32] Additionally the line of sight to the second floor is not obstructed and there are visual extensions of auditory signals such as flashing doorbell lights, phone, and baby-cry signals. Some homes also have strategically placed mirrors to allow for visual access in other parts of the house that are obstructed. The significant features of this type of habitat—a "deaf house"—create minimal visual obstructions and enhance visual communication pathways.

VISUAL SYMBOLISM IN ARTS & LITERATURE

In the preface of Charles-Michel de l'Epee's[33] 1776 book on methods of educating the deaf through sign language he wrote, "The book will show, as clearly as possible, how to go about bringing in through the window what cannot come in through the door; namely, to insinuate into the minds of the deaf through the visual channel what cannot reach them through the auditory channel" (p. 51).[34] The dichotomy of a window and a door is a metaphor.

Fast-forward two centuries. This section will show the two symbols percolating into the consciousness of the community as ways disclosing visual experiences in arts and literature.[35] Although the signing community shares many established symbols in various arts and literary works with the majority culture, there are some idiosyncratic representations that are only shared among signers. Examination of these two symbols provides insight into the consciousness of the community.

The attributes of doors and windows are often tied to visual permeability, which for our purpose is connected to language modality. A large number of "Deaf" narratives, especially narratives of personal experiences, have recurrent themes of protagonists being caught, shut in or locked out behind doors. Conflicts arise because of the opaqueness of doors, which make them inaccessible transporters of visual elements and language modalities. In seeking resolution, the protagonists try various visual extensions of sound to get the attention of the party "on the other side."[36]

More conflicts arise when these extensions fail and the ultimate solution is almost always found through a window of some sort. Windows are permeable; protagonists wave through windows, throw objects at windows, and climb up to windows in order to communicate. As conveyors of light, windows are conveyors of visual communication.

In terms of communication permeability, doors are to hearing people what windows are to deaf people. Though they do impede the process, hearing people can communicate through closed doors because they allow the transmission of sound. Otherwise, there would be no "knock-knock" jokes. Their prevalence in the hearing community speaks volumes. There is even a website devoted exclusively to knock-knock jokes *(www.knock-knock-joke.com)*. Here is an example of conversations happening through doors:

> Knock, knock!
> Who's there?
> Doris.
> Doris, who?
> Doris locked, that's why I had to knock!

Knock-knock jokes are almost non-existent in the deaf signing community; for Deaf people, the exchange stops at "knock-knock."[37] Windows, on the other hand, silence hearing people. Generally, hearing people have difficulty carrying on conversations through closed windows. One scene in the mockumentary film, "This is Spinal Tap," about a heavy metal band in decline, effectively demonstrates this point. There is a scene involving the heavy metal band riding in the back of a limousine whose driver incessantly and fanatically rambles about Frank Sinatra to them. An annoyed member of the band presses the button closing the power window behind the driver in order to shut him up. The impermeability and divisiveness of windows as a conductor of speech communication is echoed in "The Ebony Tower," by John Fowles: "The cruelty of glass: as transparent as air, as divisive as steel."[38]

Thus, even though non-deaf people can see each other, communication is assumed to be blocked, if the auditory channel is reduced as in the case with a closed window. In comparison, windows allow visual communication for signers as this story demonstrates:[39]

> A Deaf couple stops by a supermarket to pick up a few items on their way home. As they pull into the shopping center, they realize that their two-year-old child has fallen asleep. Rather than waking up the child, they agree that the mother should stay in the car and the father goes in for the items they need. As he shops, the father realizes he is not sure which type of herbal tea his wife wanted. So, he goes to the front of the store, past the cashier and waves through the window to get the answer to his question. The mother notices someone waving in side the store and looks up. Through two sets of windows (the store window and car window) they clarify exactly the kind of tea she wants. As he turns to go back

to the aisle where teas are shelved, he notices all the people around the cashier staring at him wondering what he was doing.

The following story[40] further illustrates the differences in the way a deaf man and a hearing man deal with windows and communication:

> At a stoplight a deaf man noticed out of his periphery that the driver of the car to his left had rolled down the passenger window. The deaf man turned to find the driver asking, "May I have the time?" Which the deaf man was able to lip-read.
>
> The deaf man glanced at his wristwatch and gestured (by holding up five fingers on one hand and an index finger on the other hand), "six."
>
> The hearing driver shook his head and said, "Roll down the window."
>
> The deaf man rolled down his window and repeated the gesture "six."
>
> The hearing man finally got it.

The humorous tale above is a spoof on hearing people and their helplessness when it comes to communicating through windows. There was no change in the way the deaf person expressed himself. The visual message was the same; it only became "louder" to the hearing person when the gesture was done through an open window.

There are also several poems that incorporate the use of doors and/or windows. Consider Ella Lentz's poem "The Door."[41] This creative work describes deaf people breaking free from the bondage of oralism, sheltering themselves in a room with a heavily secured door. Later in the poem, someone bangs on the door and the deaf people in the room wonder who it could be. Finally, one person goes to open the door, but the other cautions this person saying, "You don't know who it could be!" The role of the door as "a passage" takes on additional meaning here. In this case, as in other literary works, it represents taking a risk, opening the door to an inaccessible unknown.[42]

In a performance entitled "Doors for Sale: Audism in the Deaf World" (St. Paul College, Minnesota, May 7, 2004), I told various stories and talked about doors as a metaphor for oppression and barriers in the Deaf World and proposed their elimination. After all, unless you can hear, one never knows who stands on the other side. Soon after my presentation I received this email from John Lee Clark.

> I recalled a 1921 obituary in the Minnesota State Academy for the Deaf's school paper, "The Companion." You know, in those days deaf families would have hearing neighbors who they'd go to if they needed important calls made. Well, late one night this fellow's wife became very sick and urged her husband to go over to the next house to have the widow there

call the doctor. He goes over there and knocks on the door. No reply. More knocking. Still no reply. More kno—BOOM!—The guy is shot dead. The widow was calling "Who's there?" and grew panicky when she got no response and she got the rifle and simply shot through the door. So you can say that at least one door killed a deaf person. A window would've saved his life. Even a small window, bullet-hole sized like a peephole, would've been enough to save his life. I've thought about that story now and then, but now it has a new significance for me." (John Lee Clark, personal communication, May 7, 2004)

A similar application of these literary analyses to visual arts adds new perspectives on several paintings by the late Harry R. Williams. In these paintings, doors are featured in the middle of landscapes.[43] The "Coffin Door," (see page 16) is one example.

In this picture, we see a door shaped like a coffin (resembling one at Gallaudet University) directly in the middle of beautiful seascape blocking its visual continuity and obstructing the view. A hand enfolds (from behind) the top of the door suggesting that someone is behind it. This demystifies the situation, yet we never know who it is. To the left of the door in the distance is a picture window of the city of Los Angeles. In the foreground is a rowboat, presumably ready to travel towards the window suggesting an orientation towards the visible.[44]

As we further extend the symbols it is important to note that doors and windows are parts of a dwelling. If we consider the human body "a dwelling" it creates an interesting metaphor related to particular signs that closely resemble doors and windows. The sign DOOR (figure 1) is done with the same "B" hand shape and palm orientation as the formal sign DEAF (figure 2).[45]

The sign for WINDOWS (figure 3) is made with the same hand shape and

Figure 1: The ASL sign DOOR   Figure 2: The formal ASL sign DEAF

palm orientation as the signs EYES–SHUT and EYES–OPEN[46] shown in figure 4 and 5 respectively.

It is doubtful whether the association is intentional, but the natural rela-

Figure 3: The ASL sign WINDOW

Figure 4: The ASL sign EYES–SHUT

Figure 5: The ASL sign EYES–OPEN

tionships of these parallels are worth pursuing. It is beyond question that they further contribute to a pattern of symbolic representations of visual communication and opacity. But, interestingly, unlike real windows, the sign WINDOW cannot be seen through. Thus the abstract representation loses something that is in the real world.

REFLECTION

The evidences presented in this paper—though not comprehensive—demonstrate that signing Deaf people see well beyond the capacity of ordinary eyes. They inhabit a highly visual sensory world and appear to be pushing the boundaries of vision beyond limits known by other human groups. The push results from the innate human need to communicate. This desire is essential and powerful enough to cause a domino effect in the following areas:

- In language: We have seen the emergence and flourishing of visual languages (using space and physical phonological building blocks) as well as the role of eye gaze inside the linguistic system. These all impact discourse patterns and how visual language relates to the brain.
- In culture: We have witnessed various systems of adaptations, and

a history of solutions to real obstacles. As a result there has been an evolution of various social behaviors and belief systems tied to maximizing this visual way of being.

- In literature: We have appreciated the recurrent themes of vision demonstrated through rich symbols in the arts and in literature.

This just scratches the surface of the potential for vision and visuality. We have come so far yet there is so much further to go. And in terms of examining Deaf people's sensory world, we have not yet explored what has lived in countless anecdotes—the way deaf people develop tactile minds.

In retrospect, I can't help but wonder about the "what-ifs," because it has taken society so long to acknowledge the role of vision and signed languages in the lives of Deaf people. So many generations of signers have been handcuffed in a society intoxicated by the ideology that speech is language and vice versa. It is amazing that with these impositions, deaf people have developed into one of the most visual groups of people on the face of the Earth. One wonders what the possibilities would be if they were allowed to proceed in life unbounded...how far would this human variety push the boundaries of vision?

REFERENCES

Bahan, B. (1996) *Non-manual Realization of Agreement in American Sign Language.* Doctoral dissertation, Boston University

Bahan, B. and S. Supalla (1995) Line Segmentation and Narrative Structure: A Study of Eye Gaze Behavior in American Sign Language. In K. Emmorey and J. Reilly (eds.), *Sign, Gesture, and Space*, Hillsdale, New Jersey: Lawrence Erlbaum Associates, 171–191.

Baker, C. & Padden, C. (1978). Focusing on nonmanual components of American Sign Language. In P. Siple (Ed.), *Understanding language through sign language research.* (pp. 27–57). New York: Academic Press.

Baker, C. (1976) *Eye-openers in ASL.* Paper presented at the California Linguistic Association Conference, San Diego State University.

Baker, C. (1977). Regulators and turn-taking in American Sign Language discourse. In L. Friedman (Ed.), *On the other hand: New perspectives on American Sign Language.* (pp. 215–236). New York: Academic Press.

Bavelier, D., Tomann, A., Hutton, C., Mitchell, T., Corina, D., Liu G., & Neville, H. (2000) Visual Attention to the Periphery is Enhanced in Congenitally Deaf Individuals. *The Journal of Neruoscience*, 20.

Baynton, D. (1996) *Forbidden Signs: American Culture and the campaign against sign language.* Chicago: University of Chicago Press.

Bellugi, U., O'Grady, L., Lillo-Martin, D., O'Grady-Hynes, M., van Hoek K. & Corina, D. (1994) Enhancement of Spatial Cognition in Deaf Children. In V. Volterra & C. Erting (Eds.) *From gesture to language in hearing and deaf children* (p. 278–298) Berlin: Springer Verlag.

Chamberlain, C. (1994) *Do the Deaf "See" Better? Effects of Deafness on Visuospatial*

Skills. MS Thesis, McGill University, Montreal.

Emmorey, K. (1993). Processing a dynamic visual-spatial language: Psycholinguistic studies of American Sign Language. *Journal of Psycholinguistic Research,* 22(2), 153–188.

Epee (1776). "Institution des sourds et muets par la voie des signes méthodiques." In Lane, H. (1984) *The Deaf Experience: Classics in Language and Education.* Cambridge: Harvard Press.

Farb, P. (1993) *Word Play: What Happens When People Talk.* New York: Vintage.

Fowles, J (1974) *The Ebony Tower.* Boston: Little, Brown & Company.

Goldin-Meadow, S. (2003) *The Resilence of Language: What gesture creation in deaf children can tell us about how all children learn language.* New York: Psychology Press Inc.

Groce, N. (1985) *Everyone Here Spoke Sign Language: Hereditary deafness on Martha's Vineyard.* Cambridge: Harvard Press.

Hall, E.T. (1982) *The Hidden Dimension.* New York: Anchor Books.

Hall, R.Y. (1994) Deaf Culture, Tacit Culture, and Ethnic Relations. In C.J. Erting, R.C. Johnson, D.L. Smith, & B.D. Snider (editors) *The Deaf Way: Perspectives from the International Conference on Deaf Culture.* p. 31–39.

Jay, M. (1993) *Downcast Eyes: The Denigration of Vision in Twentieth-Century French Thought.* Berkeley: University of California Press.

Kakumasu, J. (1968) Urubu Sign Language. *International Journal of American Linguistics* 34 (4), 275–281.

Klima, E.S., O. Tzeng, A. Fok, U. Bellugi, D. Corina, & J. Bettger (1999). From sign to script: Effects of linguistic experience on perceptual categorization. In O.J. L. Tzeng, The Biological Bases of Language, Monograph series, 13, *Journal of Chinese Linguistics,* 96–129.

Lane, H., Hoffmeister, R., and Bahan, B. (1996) *A Journey into the DEAF-WORLD.* San Diego: DawnSignPress.

Lentz, E (1995) *The Treasure: Poems by Ella Mae Lentz.* In Motion Press.

Liddell, S (2003) *Grammar, Gesture, and Meaning in American Sign Language.* Cambridge: Cambridge University Press.

MacLaughlin, D. (1997) *The Structure of Determiner Phrases: Evidence from American Sign Language.* Doctoral dissertation, Boston University.

Mather, S.A. (1987) Eye gaze and communication in a deaf classroom. In *Sign Language Studies* 54, Spring 1987. pp. 11–30. Silver Spring, Maryland: Linstok Press.

Mathers, S.A. (1989). Visually oriented teaching strategies with deaf preschool children. In C. Lucas (Ed.), *The sociolinguistics of the deaf community.* pp. 165–187. San Diego: Academic Press.

Neidle, K., J. Kegl, D. MacLaughlin, B. Bahan, & R. Lee (2000) *The Syntax of American Sign Language: Functional Categories and Hierarchical Structure.* Cambridge: MIT Press.

Neville, H. (1988) Cerebral organization for spatial attention. In J. Stiles-Davis, M. Kritchevsky & U. Bellugi (eds.), *Spatial cognition: Brain bases and development* (p. 327–341) Hillsdale, New Jersey: Lawrence Erlbaum Associates.

Plato (1961) Cratlyus. In Hamilton, E. & H. Cairns (Eds.) *The Collected Dialogues of Plato Including the letters.* Princeton: Princeton University Press. p. 457.

Poole, J. (1979) *A Preliminary Description of Martha's Vineyard Sign Language.* Unpublished manuscript, Boston University. Paper also presented at the 3rd International Symposium on Sign Language Research, Rome, Italy, June 1983.

Sacks, O (1990) Seeing Voices: Lecture at Durham University, January 31, 1990. Video transcript. Deaf Studies Research Unit, Durham, England.

Sisco, F.H. & R.J. Anderson (1980) Deaf children's performance on the WISC-R relative to hearing status of parents and child-rearing experiences. *American Annals of the Deaf,* 125, 923–930.

Thoutenhoofd, E. (1997) Vision | Deaf: Vision as a constitutive element of 'Deaf communities.' In *Deaf Worlds,* 1:13.

Veditz, G. (1910) *Proceedings of the Ninth Convention of the National Association of the Deaf and the Third World's Congress of the Deaf*, 1910. Philadelphia: Philocophus Press, 1912, p. 30.

Veditz, G. (1913) *The Preservation of Sign Language in The Preservation of American Sign Language: The Complete Historical Collection*. Burtonsville, Maryland: Sign Media, Inc. 1997.

Washbaugh, W. (1986). *Five fingers for survival*. Ann Arbor: Karoma Publishers.

Wheatley, M.J. (2002) "The power of talk." In *Utne Reader*, July–August 2002, p. 54–58.

Wilbur, R. (1994) Eye Blinks and ASL Phrase Structure. *Sign Language Studies* 84: 221–240

Woodward, J. (1978a). Attitudes toward deaf people on Providence Island, Columbia. *American Anthropologist* 63: 49–68.

ENDNOTES

1.   A lot of thoughts and discussions with the following colleagues have lead their way into this paper, I thank: Dirksen Bauman, MJ Bienvenu, Todd Czubek, Janey Greenwald, John Lee Clark, Robert Lee, Flavia Fleischer, Sue Burnes, Steve Nover, Carol Neidle, Laura Petitto, Bob Hoffmeister, and Harlan Lane. I want to particularly thank Janey Greenwald, Robert Lee, and Dirksen Bauman for their editorial assistance. And Sue Burnes for appearing as sign model in this paper.

2.   Edward Hall pointed out that "people of different cultures not only speak different languages but, what is possibly more important inhabit different sensory worlds." (Page 2, 1982).

3.   George Veditz used the phrase "people of the eye" at least twice. The first can be found in his president's message to the congress, "...all-wise Mother Nature designed for the people of the eye, a language..." (p. 22.)

4.   The discussion here refers to those who were born deaf or became deaf in their infancy.

5.   Kakumasu, 1968; Farb, 1973

6.   Woodward, 1978; Poole, 1979; Groce, 1985; Washbaugh, 1986 to name a few.

7.   For further information on the development of home signs and gestures among deaf children in contemporary world, see Goldin-Meadow, (2003) and others.

8.   Over the course of human history, the social perception of gestures and sign language swayed from being acceptable to not acceptable. In the later part of western civilization (from the mid-19th century to today) many have held that the uses of gestures and sign language were not language per se or have no significant social value; and have imposed restrictions on its development and use (see Baynton (1996) and others).

9.   See Chamberlain's (1994) thesis "Do deaf people see better?" which argues that being deaf alone is not enough to see enhanced visual processing skills. The research suggests that it is the inclusion and use of sign language that enables this enhancement.

10.   For more discussion see Martin Jay (1993) and Edward T. Hall (1982).

11.   The term 'word' is used in this paper instead of 'sign' to reduce the need for such distinction because there is no difference. A human utterance is a human utterance whether signed or spoken.

12.   MacLaughlin (1997), Bahan (1996), Neidle, Kegl, MacLaughlin, Bahan and Lee (2000)

13.   In case of first person object, the eye gaze will mark the subject. For more information see Bahan (1996), Neidle, Kegl, MacLaughlin, Bahan, and Lee (2000).

14   Baker, 1976, 1977; Baker & Padden, 1978; Bahan & Supalla, 1995

15.   Bahan & Supalla, 1995; Baker, 1976, 1977; Baker & Padden 1978

16.   Baker, 1976, 1977; Baker & Padden 1978

17.   Mather, 1987 and 1989

18.   See Mather, 1987 and 1989 for more details about this phenomenon.

19.   Bahan and Supalla, 1995

20.   Bahan and Supalla, 1995

21.   Baker, C., 1976

22.   Most information in this section draws from Lane, Hoffemister and Bahan (1996).

23.   Sacks 1990:16.72. Thoutenhoofd's video transcript of Sack's lecture as reported in Thoutenhoofd (1997) p. 26.

24.   Neville, 1988; Bavelier, Tomann, Hutton, Mitchell, Corina, Liu and Neville, 2000.

25.   Emmorey, 1995; Lane, Hoffmeister and Bahan, 1996

26.   Bellugi, O'Grady, Lillo-Martin, O'Grady-Hynes, van Hoek & Corina, 1994; Sisco & Anderson, 1980; Lane, Hoffmeister, and Bahan, 1996

27.   Bellugi, O'Grady, Lillo-Martin, O'Grady-Hynes, van Hoek & Corina, 1994; Emmorey, 1993; Lane, Hoffmeister, and Bahan, 1996.

28.   With exception of several studies on non-verbal IQ tests which showed deaf children scoring higher than hearing children.

29.   Klima, Tzeng, Fok, Bellugi, Corina & Bettger, 1999 and Lane, Hoffmeister, and Bahan, 1996.

30.   Most of the observations discussed in this section are based personal experience as a native member of this visual culture.

31.   For some examples of synchrony of body rhythms see Edward Hall (1994) _Deaf Culture, Tacit Culture, and Ethnic Relations._ In C.J Erting, R.C Johnson, D.L Smith, and B.D. Snider (editors) _The Deaf Way: Perspectives from the International Conference on Deaf Culture._ pp. 31-39.

32.   One should take a look at houses or buildings designed by Olof Hanson.

33.   He is credited as being the founder of the first public school for the deaf in history in Paris, France in the 1760s.

34.   Epee (1776) _"Institution des sourds et muets par la voie des signes méthodiques."_ I thank Ben Jarashow for bringing this to my attention.

35.   The connection between Epee's statement and the current analysis may be a coincidence but it is intriguing, nevertheless.

36.   In narratives of personal experiences persons are deaf by default, unless mentioned for emphasis. Those non-deaf are usually be identified, e.g. hearing person.

37.   There are some people who enjoy these jokes and translate them into ASL, but this is not widespread.

38.   I thank John Lee Clark for bringing this to my attention.

39.   This composite was told at several storytelling events by Ben Bahan.

40.   This composite was told at several storytelling events by Ben Bahan.

41.   _The Treasure_ (1995) In Motion Press.

42.   A hearing person would have simply asked, "Who's there?"

43.   HRW, as he is known, has done several paintings that feature doors, one is featured on the cover of the text _Journey into the DEAF-WORLD._ Near the end of his life he has painted a series of coffin doors, which may have foreshadowed his coming demise.

44.   Like all artworks, there may be different interpretations on this. I am merely applying what I have learned from various literary works to the painting. Unfortunately, I cannot confirm this analysis with HRW.

45.   I thank Dirksen Bauman for this insight.

46.   There are other signs used to depict the same concept.

ABOUT THE AUTHOR

Ben Bahan is a professor and director of the graduate program in the Depart-ment of Deaf Studies at Gallaudet University. Dr. Bahan has published dozens of articles related to the field of Deaf Studies and ASL linguistics and co-authored such important books as Journey into the DEAF-WORLD, *and* The Syntax of American Sign Language. *He prefers to be known as an ASL storyteller and has produced and appeared in several videotapes. In addi-tion, Dr. Bahan is Vice President of DawnSignPress, a leading publisher of American Sign Language and Deaf Studies books and videos. (Editor's note: Dr. Bahan's keynote address was sponsored by the ASL Program, Department of Linguistics and English Language, and College of Humanities at Brigham Young University.)*

"Graduation At The New York Institution For The Instruction Of The Deaf And Dumb,"
Frank Leslie's Illustrated Newspaper, July 12, 1879

Courtesy Douglas C. Baynton

Beyond Culture: Deaf Studies and the Deaf Body

DOUGLAS BAYNTON, PH.D.

Douglas Baynton is a associate professor of History and American Sign Language at the University of Iowa, Iowa City, Iowa. This address was given as a keynote address at Deaf Studies Today!, 14 April 2004.

THE CONCEPT OF DEAF CULTURE is fundamental to the field of Deaf Studies. In recent decades, the distinctive cultural attributes of the American Deaf community have been documented and described at length, among them a shared history, a rich literary culture, rules of etiquette and naming practices that differ from those of the larger hearing society, a strong tendency to marry within the group, a unique means of transmitting cultural knowledge between generations, and, of course, a complex visual language. In addition, like other cultural minority groups, Deaf people have established a variety of social, political, and economic organizations, as well as a periodical press, dating from the mid-nineteenth century. Perhaps most important, Deaf people share fundamental values that differ from those of the hearing Americans around them, in particular having to with the value of American Sign Language and the Deaf world. The existence of a deep, rich, and longstanding culture of American Deaf people is now beyond reasonable dispute.[1]

As important and useful as it has been, however, the concept of Deaf culture increasingly appears inadequate by itself as an explanation of the Deaf community and the experiences of Deaf people. For example, recent research has shown that Deaf people process visual information differently than hearing people, and in some ways more efficiently. This has complemented a growing emphasis in recent years on the centrality of vision to Deaf experience, with some Deaf people suggesting that they instead be referred to as "seeing people" or "visual people."[2] The statement by George Veditz that Deaf people "are facing not a theory but a condition, for they are first, last, and all the time the people of the eye," has become a popular aphorism among Deaf activists.[3] Deaf people now often speak of "deaf eyes," a characteristic and recognizable way Deaf people have of using the eyes. Under an exclusively cultural model, how do we discuss such phenomena? What, moreover, is the implication of arguing, as Deaf people long have argued, that it is in the nature of deaf people to use signed languages, a view that has been given support by linguistic research into language acquisition and development among Deaf children? All of these suggest that Deaf people differ from hearing people in physical (or, more precisely, sensory) ways that are not explained by culture.

This is not to say that sensory difference by itself is sufficient to explain Deaf identity. For example, many people identify themselves as hearing impaired, hearing disabled, deaf, or hard of hearing who are not culturally Deaf: they do not share the values of Deaf people, they are not (or only partially) fluent in the language of the community, they do not identify as Deaf and are not seen as Deaf. The cultural distinction between deaf and Deaf, while sometimes ambiguous, is nevertheless a crucial one.

Consider, however, another kind of outsider to Deaf identity: hearing people who grow up within a Deaf family, marry into the Deaf community, or for whatever reason immerse themselves in the Deaf world. They may be as fluent in ASL, cognizant of Deaf cultural beliefs and etiquette, familiar with Deaf folklore, and involved in the social life of the Deaf community as any Deaf person. They may be accepted, respected, well-liked, included in the community "as if" they were Deaf, and they may even be referred to as "Deaf" in certain circumstances. Yet they are recognized as not really Deaf. As Padden and Humphries note in *Deaf in America,* "Hearing children of Deaf parents represent an ongoing contradiction in the culture: they display the knowledge of their parents—skill in the language and social conduct—but the culture finds subtle ways to give them an unusual and separate status." Cultural explanations by themselves are insufficient to explain Deaf identity.[4]

The cultural model also fails to adequately account for the stories Deaf people commonly tell of their first weeks at the residential school, of feeling that they had found their true home. Culture cannot explain that experience, for they are not yet "Deaf" when they arrive. Similarly, many young deaf people grow up in oral schools or in mainstream programs who do not encounter ASL or Deaf culture until adulthood, yet as young adults (often as students at Gallaudet University) choose to learn ASL as best they can, to principally associate with Deaf people, and to identify themselves as culturally Deaf. This includes many people who were considered to be "oral successes" by their teachers and parents. Under a simple cultural model, this ought not to happen with such frequency. Children raised in the hearing world are culturally hearing, not Deaf, yet in large numbers choose to join the Deaf world. An explanation of why they make this choice must point beyond culture.

Moreover, how do we explain the strong connections that Deaf people often feel to other Deaf people from outside their own country, to people from very different and distant cultures? Deaf cultures, like hearing cultures, vary a great deal from country to country.[5] Carol Padden is currently studying the Bedouin deaf, who are fully integrated in a hearing community where everyone signs, and who consequently have not created a distinct Deaf culture. Yet Padden sees her research as part of Deaf studies and of interest to American Deaf people. Why should that be, if culture alone is what defines Deaf people and binds them together? Indeed, in spite of major cultural differences, Padden tells me that upon meeting the Bedouin deaf, she felt the same sense of commonality and connection that Deaf people typically feel upon meeting.[6] The cultural model needs a great deal of stretching to cover such phenomena. A more plausible and straightforward alternative is to posit that Deaf people are different from hearing people in ways other than cultural.

It has become standard practice in Deaf studies to speak of the Deaf community as an ethnic group. While that term fits in many ways, in other ways it can be misleading. As Jeffrey Nash pointed out in 1987, "in conventional ethnic groups, members of the first generation have the ethnic mother tongue as native, and...second and third generations shift from the ethnic to the dominant language."[7] In other words, ethnic groups in American typically assimilate during the second and third generations. Deaf people do not. Nor do Deaf people tend to marry outside the group, as do second and third generation children of ethnic groups. Furthermore, ethnicity is typically an identity shared within familes, while deafness is typically not. Recent research estimates that only about three percent of Deaf people have two Deaf parents. Ethnicity, then, offers a misleading model for the childhood experiences of 97 percent of Deaf people (and of that three percent, a majority have hearing siblings, again an experience unlike that of most ethnic groups).[8]

When I wrote my book, *Forbidden Signs: American Culture and the Campaign Against Sign Language*, I worked within the cultural model. One of the criticisms I encountered from a historians who read my early drafts, however, was that I argued that deafness was a cultural construction while simultaneously contending that oralism was necessarily harmful to deaf people. They pointed out to me that if deafness was truly just a cultural construction, there were no grounds for taking the position that deaf people everywhere in all times needed signed language. In making that claim I was necessarily making a claim about the nature of deafness. In response to that criticism, I wrote the following in my introduction to the book:

> Deafness is...very much a cultural construction that changes over time. But it is also a physical reality. The hearing people who have traditionally made most of the decisions concerning the education of deaf children can spend entire careers contented within these constructions of deafness, unconstrained by physical reality, but deaf people cannot. When the cultural climate of the nineteenth century changed to make sign language objectionable, hearing people could simply say, "Away with sign language," and imagine that this could be accomplished. Deaf people could not, for they are both members of a species that by nature seeks optimal communication, and inhabitants of a sensory universe in which that end cannot be achieved by oral means alone.[9]

In the book's conclusion, I added that being deaf "is more than a cultural construction. It means most fundamentally that one occupies a different sensory world from those who hear, and this has certain consequences that cannot be constructed away. This physical reality (upon which culture works, certainly, and with which culture intertwines and interacts) transcends culture." I did not pursue the matter any further, however. Constrained by the cultural model, I simply did not know what to do with these ideas. Increasingly, I have become convinced that if the field of Deaf studies is to progress, it must move beyond the culture model to talk about the body, about the significance of living in a different sensory world.

There is an understandable resistance among Deaf people and Deaf studies scholars to focusing on the physical aspect of deafness. In the past, such a focus has meant defining deafness in terms of defect and deficiency. It has meant talking about what Deaf people have in common with other disabled people, which has seemed a dangerous path to start down, given that most people think of disability in terms of inability, absence, and loss. Many Deaf people have tried to distance themselves from this image by distancing themselves from any notion of disability and insisting that their identity is based on cultural rather than physical difference from the hearing majority. They explain that being Deaf is not a defect, that being Deaf offers no less rich and rewarding a life than being hearing, and that being Deaf is neither a pathology nor a medical matter. Most of us in Deaf studies have correspondingly defined our work as a branch of ethnic studies, separate and distinct from disability studies.

However, what most people have in mind when they think of disability is a medical model (a.k.a. the functional limitations or pathological model).

According to this model, disability is simply a physical, mental, or sensory impairment. It resides solely or largely in the individual with the impairment. Prevention, cure, and rehabilitation are of primary importance. When Deaf people say that "disabled" does not describe them, it is generally this model that they reject.[10]

It is precisely this model, however, that disability studies scholars (and disability rights activists) also reject. In recent decades they have advanced a social model that locates disability not in individual bodies but rather in social structures and practices that do not take account of normal human variation. Just as gender and race are not merely matters of bodily difference, so is disability not simply inherent in bodies but rather a way of interpreting human differences. People with particular physical differences from the majority are disabled by the prejudicial beliefs and actions of the majority. When buildings, technology, and media are designed for certain types of people but not others, when communication is carried out in ways accessible to certain types of people but not others, or when school curricula are designed for certain types of learning but not others, disability results. Disability, in short, is a product of oppression.[11]

In this, disabled people have followed a trajectory similar to other oppressed groups. It was once also generally accepted that the bodies of women and members of "inferior races" limited their capacity to participate in social and economic life. As Harlan Hahn has noted, "unlike other disadvantaged groups, citizens with disabilities have not yet fully succeeded in refuting the presumption that their subordinate status can be ascribed to an innate biological inferiority." They have made considerable progress in recent years, however. People with physical differences from the majority have increasingly moved away from the notion that they have a disability, or are persons with a disability, and instead refer to themselves as disabled people to indicate its centrality to their identity, and speak of "disablement" to refer to the social process of becoming disabled. Many people find it difficult to understand that anyone would willingly embrace the identity of "disabled person," since disability in our culture seems self-evidently a personally discrediting label. Just as most hearing people simplistically translate 'deaf' into 'cannot hear,' so do most people equate 'disabled' with 'unable.' By claiming disability as an identity, however, disabled people name the oppression under which they live, declare solidarity with others similarly oppressed, and set themselves in opposition to it.[12]

Our bodies matter because they shape how we experience, understand, and interact with the world, and because they affect how others view us. On both counts, the body is intensely relevant to Deaf people. The appropriate vocabulary is that of difference, however, not loss. Just as deafness brings into being new ways of using the other senses, so does any physical difference result in a new configuration of abilities. Merely equating disability with impairment reduces a way of life, a complex relation to the environment, and a web of social relationships and cultural meanings to a simple and concrete absence. It fails utterly to account for the human experience of disability. Like Deaf people, disabled people experience disability in terms of social relations rather than as personal deficiency, and it becomes just one aspect of the world in which they live, in all its complexity.

This does not mean that disabled people experience no limitations, but rather that the experience of limitation is a universal one, not characteristic merely of a subset of humanity. Relative to most of the animal kingdom, after all, humans live in a flat and unvariegated scent world. Their vision is severely impaired by the standards of, say, a hawk, and their night vision is abysmal compared to an owl or a cat. They are deaf to frequencies heard well by dogs, bats, whales, and elephants. They are poor swimmers, slow runners, and incapable of flight absent assistive technology. The list of abilities that other creatures enjoy and that humans lack is long indeed, yet somehow the human species manages to limp along without nursing feelings of grief or loss. The reason we do not consider ourselves disabled is that the term is relative to notions of normality around which we structure our societies. Radio programs do not employ frequencies beyond normal human hearing, jobs do not demand the eyesight of an eagle, and schools do not require students to stand all day like horses without sitting. We establish expectations based on what is normal for the majority and design our built environment to serve that norm— and to exclude, often, any who fall outside it. Deaf people are disabled in the sense that they fall outside most cultures' notions of normality and are on that basis denied equal access to social and economic life.

PRAGMATIC CONSIDERATIONS

Considered as a purely practical matter, what good and what harm comes from Deaf people aligning themselves with disabled people and the concept of disability? This is by no means a simple question. In the past, the emphasis of the disability rights movement on educational inclusion or mainstreaming has been a point of serious contention. Disability rights activists have increasingly come to understand and respect the Deaf position on this question, in addition to increasingly questioning the often ideologically rigid, one-size-fits-all approach of the early years of the movement. Disability Watch, the periodic assessment of the status of disabled people in the United States published by Disability Rights Advocates, pointed out that while inclusion has been good for most disabled people, it "is proving disastrous for deaf children." It went on to describe how "the Deaf community has vigorously opposed these ill-considered practices, but its cogent dissent has gone largely unheeded" by school authorities.[13]

Of course, as with any coalition made up of groups with diverse interests and experiences, disagreements are unavoidable. Still, cooperation between Deaf and disability rights groups has accomplished much good, most notably the Americans with Disabilities Act. The constant refrain heard from the Deaf community that "we are not disabled," however, threatens to undermine the basis for that cooperation. Disabled and nondisabled people alike increasingly respond that if Deaf people really don't want to be considered disabled, then they ought not to claim the protections of that designation.

In any case, alignment with disabled people clearly holds more promise than one with ethnic groups. If there are differences among disabled groups, they pale in comparison with the distance between Deaf and other ethnic communities. Can we imagine the Chinese-American community agitating in favor of Deaf teachers? What reason would hearing Spanish speakers have for supporting residential schools for Deaf children? (After all, in California a majority of Hispanic-American voters recently joined other citizens in voting to end bilingual education). In battling the resurgence of eugenics, are disabled people or Cuban Americans going to be more steadfast allies? Who have been powerful allies of Deaf people in the past, ethnic Americans or disabled Americans?

If the disability model tends to have a bias toward assimilation, contrary to the interests of the Deaf community, the ethnic model in the United States does as well, but with no accommodations for physical differences from the majority. The rights and services that Deaf people demand are of the kind demanded by disabled people not ethnic groups. Interpreters, for example, are provided to linguistic minorities in the United States only in a limited number of unusual situations, such as court appearances and medical emergencies. Those who wish to attend college or take up a profession are expected to master and use the national language. College instructors and graduate students whose first language is not English must pass an exam demonstrating their ability to make themselves clearly understood in spoken English before they are permitted to teach. Deaf people, on the other hand, rightly demand subsidized interpreting services that allow them to participate in cultural, social, and economic life on an equal basis with hearing people. The demand for captioning and relay services is even less compatible with the ethnic group model. To the extent that these services are provided, it is in the name of disability rights, not ethnic group rights, since no other minority requests, let alone asserts a right to, such services. The principle at work in the provision of these services is that it is wrong to construct, for example, a phone system that serves some people and excludes other, or to offer a college education that is accessible to some but not others, merely on the basis of physical, sensory, or mental differences. As far as I am aware, every useful law in the United States protecting Deaf rights has been based on this principle, rooted in the demand for disability rights rather than in protections for ethnic minorities. Furthermore, aside from the pragmatic considerations of political efficacy, the ethnic model fails conceptually even to explain the kinds of rights that Deaf people assert.

In the struggle to provide a decent education for deaf children, the cultural model also falls short, and in fact is counter productive. Hearing parents of deaf children are rarely persuaded of the value of ASL by being told about Deaf culture, and often resist the notion that their children ought to be part of a culture other than their own. In fact, they frequently express fears of "losing their children to the Deaf culture." More persuasive arguments stress the importance of ensuring linguistic input via the eyes while children are still very young, to achieve their fullest social and intellectual development. That is, it focuses on the ways in which their children's sensory needs differ from those of hearing children.[14]

The Deaf culture model by itself has always posed a troublesome incongruity when used to discuss deaf children. When we speak of deaf adults who are not culturally Deaf, no one objects to referring to them as disabled. However, when we speak of mainstreamed deaf children in hearing families, we often speak of them as Deaf even when they have had no contact with Deaf culture, in part because we think that they ought to be Deaf, and in part because they are likely to become Deaf at some point in the future. Some of them, however, will never be culturally Deaf, and it is clearly contradictory to speak of deaf children as Deaf, only to reclassify some of them as disabled when grown, when nothing substantive has changed other than their age. We are stuck with making this incoherent argument because, under the cultural minority model, there is no other logical way to assert their linguistic rights as children. To claim, however, that children who have no connection to or even knowledge of the Deaf community are culturally Deaf is unpersuasive to say the least. It is utterly unpersuasive to their hearing parents, who often view it presumptuous as well as absurd, and it is intellectually implausible to scholars to suggest that Deaf people, unlike any others in the world, might somehow be born with a culture inherent within them.

An alternative that resolves the incongruity, as well as offering a more plausible line of argument in favor of early ASL for all deaf children, is to take seriously the truism that (in Padden and Humphries words), "Deaf people are both Deaf and deaf."[15] That is, Deaf people are both a cultural minority and disabled. This allows us to say that a deaf child is physically different from hearing children, therefore has fundamentally different needs from hearing children, and therefore if denied access to effective bilingual education is disabled by that denial. It allows us to say, further, that both Deaf and hard-of-hearing persons are disabled by social practices designed to accommodate only hearing people, and to demand arrangements that accommodate them as well as hearing people.

Indeed, those writing within the Deaf culture model often do say that deaf children who are denied access to ASL and to the Deaf community by parents and schools are disabled by that denial.[16] This is precisely in line with the social model of disability. The disability studies model would go further, however, to argue that even Deaf children who attend bicultural/bilingual educational programs and are fully acculturated in the Deaf community continue to be disabled by discriminatory practices that extend beyond secondary school. It is disabling to be denied equal access to television, movies, theater, civic and public events. It is disabling to be denied reasonable accommodations, in higher education or on the job, such as competent interpreting services. According to the social model of disability, both deaf and Deaf people are disabled not because they do not hear, but because society is structured and everyday business is conducted in ways that exclude them: mass media and public services are often inaccessible; education is generally inferior; information in public places comes over aural but not visual channels; prejudice, demeaning stereotypes, and discrimination are widespread; and in general the hearing majority assumes a hearing norm and does accommodate those who deviate from it.

Thus when disability activists claim that Deaf people are in the same boat with them, they do not mean to suggest that Deaf people are afflicted with a defect which ought to be fixed or eliminated, or that they are not whole, or that something is wrong with them, as Deaf people often seem to assume. Rather, they mean that Deaf people have a sensory difference from the majority which requires a different way of life; that the majority hearing population often tries to obstruct or thwart that way of life, or at the least does not make reasonable accommodations for it; and that the hearing majority thereby disables Deaf people. It is understood that if Deaf people were to live entirely in a Deaf world they would not be disabled, just as it is understood that the same is true of many other—perhaps most—disabled people. This way of understanding disability does not seem to contradict in any fundamental way how Deaf people already view themselves.

The cultural model also has had little practical relevance to the debate over cochlear implants. Even if all hearing people were to become convinced that Deaf people are "not disabled" and constituted a cultural minority, would that affect the implanting of deaf children? After all, minority cultures in the United States come and go without much fanfare. There used to be strong Italian-American communities in many cities, for example, that have mostly disappeared. There were once thriving Scandinavian cultures across the rural upper Midwest and Polish-American communities in the cities. Asian Americans and Jewish Americans are increasingly assimilating today. A marked and distinct ethnic identity usually persists only to the extent that majority prejudice prevails over the tendency toward assimilation, as has been the case for most African Americans.

The charge of "ethnocide" sometimes raised in the case against cochlear implants is not a persuasive one in the United States, for the disappearance of minority cultures—whatever opinion one may hold about this—is not only commonplace but has often been held up as an ideal. Not only are Americans generally unwilling to offer bilingual education for the purpose of preserving ethnic cultures, opposition to the persistence of minority cultures is one of the main arguments deployed against bilingual education, which is on the defensive and in decline across the country. If it is true that implants threaten Deaf culture (which is a subject of debate within the Deaf community), hearing Americans seem unlikely to support the idea of preserving deafness in order to preserve Deaf culture when they have shown no widespread concern for preserving other minority cultures.

Medicalization of difference is as much an issue for disabled people generally as it is for Deaf people. Disabled people are equally concerned about the attitudes that lead to excessive, risky, and often ineffective surgeries performed on children in valiant attempts to restore "normal function"—for example, to enable someone to walk about with difficulty, rather than modifying public spaces in ways to enable them to roll about with ease. The problem Deaf people face is not that they are not recognized as an ethnic group, but rather, as Alice Dreger has written, that in the modern west "the most prevalent myth is that an unusual anatomy must be considered a medical pathology." It is equally a problem for deaf and all disabled people that "most children with unusual anatomies are born to parents who do not share the unusual trait, and so the parents' reaction often involves fear, confusion, shame, guilt, and distress....The parents often can't imagine living 'that' way."[7]

Like Deaf people, many disabled people see disability as central to their identity and have no desire whatsoever to join the nondisabled "other."[8] This is particularly true of those born disabled or disabled from an early age. Disabled people are, in fact, very similar to Deaf people in this way, and use similar language when they speak of disability as their norm, as something in which they have pride, as essential to their identity. The question is not so much whether one is Deaf, blind, or a wheelchair user, but rather whether that is an integral part of one's identity, which is in large part a question of time and life stage. People who grew up with an atypical body or set of senses tend to see themselves as "normal" and experience little or no desire to change. Those who experience a dramatic change in bodily or sensory configuration go through a period, some longer than others, of wishing they could return to their earlier norm.

Resistance to technological normalization flies in the face of powerful social forces and is an uphill battle no matter what arguments are deployed. Nevertheless, the disability critique of the modern tendency to homogenize human experience, to regulate human appearance and behavior, and to lessen human variation, is a broad and powerful argument. Claiming that implanting deaf children constitutes ethnocide is not, for the children who are implanted are neither culturally Deaf nor members of an ethnic group. As individuals, they possess no elements of a minority culture. What they do possess is a different sensory relationship to the world around them. It is the value of that difference that is at issue. If an effective counter-argument is to be constructed, it is more likely to be based upon the good that comes from preserving sensory and physical diversity rather than upon ethnic identity.

HISTORICALLY CREATED IDENTITIES

The statement that "Deaf people are not disabled" suggests that current definitions of Deaf and disabled are natural, timeless, and universal categories. These are not fixed definitions, however, but rather historically created and impermanent identities. Padden and Humphries put the matter more accurately when they wrote in Deaf in America that, "'disabled' is a label that historically has not belonged to Deaf people," but still they left open the question of which historical period they meant.[9]

My preliminary research suggests the possibility that the "Deaf people are not disabled" claim may be of fairly recent origin.

In the 19th century, it seems to have been common to talk of Deaf people as disabled. Laurent Clerc, one of the founders of the American School for the Deaf, in an 1818 address, spoke of "the infirmities of the bodily organization, such as deafness, blindness, lameness, palsy, crookedness, ugliness." In 1835, John Burnet wrote of his deafness as one of the "long catalogue of infirmities which flesh is heir to." He went on to explain that,

> [Our] misfortune is not that [we] are deaf and dumb, but that others hear and speak. Were the established mode of communication...by a language addressed not to the ear, but to the eye, the present inferiority of the deaf would entirely vanish; but at the same time the mental and social conditions of the blind would be far more deplorable, and their education far more impracticable, than that of the deaf is now."[20]

This seems a perfect an expression of the social model of disability, applied to deafness and blindness.

In 1855, John Jacob Flournoy argued that Deaf people should abandon the hearing world that oppressed them and establish their own state. At the same time, he saw no contradiction in describing Deaf people as disabled. Responding to William Turner's statement that a Deaf man was as unsuited to serve in a legislature as a blind man was to lead an army, Flournoy wrote (in his wonderful phrasing): "The old cry about the incapacity of men's minds from physical disabilities, I think it were time, now in this intelligent age, to explode!" He made his case by referring to great disabled military heroes and blind philosophers: "Have you ever heard how Muley Moloch had himself borne in a litter, when lamed by wounds, to the head of his legions...? So much for a lame man. Then, as for a blind one..." Flournoy described Deaf people as a distinct and oppressed community and as sharing a common oppression with other disabled people.[21]

Nor does it seem to have been common for Deaf people to reject the association with disability (at least in print) through most of the twentieth century. Bob Buchanan, in his book, *Illusions of Equality,* describes two instances, during the 1908 battle over the hiring of deaf people in the Civil Service, when Deaf community leaders objected to an association with disability. George Dougherty worried that being classed in Civil Service regulations with "the insane, the crippled, and criminals" would prejudice employers against them.

And George Veditz similarly warned, "Once let the government brand deafness as a disability that renders us ineligible for its service, and it will not be long before the prejudice will spread among the employers at large." This is significant, but both have to do specifically with employment rather than a general aversion to being thought of as disabled. The Veditz quotation is ambiguous in that he does not reject the idea that deafness is a disability, but specifically that deafness is a disability that renders "us ineligible" for employment. The term "disability" in the past was often used in this more specific sense to refer to a trait that disqualified a person for certain rights and privileges. Buchanan also documents occasions on which Deaf leaders decided against collaboration with disability groups, but while this may suggest a rejection of the concept of disability, it does not do so necessarily. The ethnic group model, after all, is not weakened by the fact that Deaf people do not typically collaborate with other ethnic groups.[22]

Susan Burch, in *Signs of Resistance,* suggests that Deaf people began to reject the association with disability in the early twentieth century. It is a plausible suggestion, but Burch provides only one significant source for the claim. An editorial in the *Empire State News,* supporting a proposal for a Labor Bureau for deaf people and responding to an argument that it ought to serve all disabled people, asserted that "the average deaf worker belongs in the classification of foreign-language groups rather than that of the physically handicapped." This would appear at first glance to be an endorsement of the cultural model and rejection of the disability model.

However, the editorial went on to explain that a worker's "deafness is sure to raise difficulties of communication which may hinder his effectiveness until he becomes accustomed to the routine of work in that particular place. Hence, some follow-up work would be necessary in a placement service for the deaf. This is an additional detail which the regular service cannot handle." That is, the editorial is focused entirely on the issue of what deaf people need from a labor bureau, not their identity in general. Deaf people have employment needs that are distinct from those of "other handicapped groups," the editorial continued, because "one has to have effective communication between the placement officer and the deaf applicant. No such difficulty exists in the case of the blind, the crippled, and other groups, for all of these possess in common with the director and his assistants the great blessing of combined hearing and speech, which facilitate the interview." The point is the specific employment needs of deaf people, nothing broader. Moreover, the editorial twice refers to "other groups of handicapped people," which suggests no aversion to being thought of as one of those groups.[23]

In my (admittedly not exhaustive) research so far, I have found no unambiguous and explicit examples of Deaf people rejecting association with disability before the 1970s. While it would not be surprising to find at least a few examples, it is suggestive that I've come across no published examples so far, while I have found numerous examples of Deaf people who freely referred to themselves as disabled or handicapped.

For example, in 1930, Albert Ballin, in *The Deaf Mute Howls*, referred to deafness as a "handicap," as did Thomas Ulmer, a Deaf contributor to the *American Annals of the Deaf* in 1945. In 1941, Tom Anderson, then president of the NAD, urged President Roosevelt to "give handicapped persons a break in working for the defense program," by which he clearly meant to include Deaf people. He was quoted in a New York Times opinion column by a disabled man writing in favor of greater employment opportunities for disabled people, and in 1942 the *Empire State News* approvingly reprinted that piece.[24]

The president of the California Association of the Deaf, Toivo Lindholm, in 1953 referred to Deaf people as handicapped. In 1970, NAD president Frederick Schreiber wrote of deaf people having a "disability." In 1974, in his book *A Deaf Adult Speaks Out,* Leo Jacobs described Deaf people as a minority group and simultaneously as people who have a "handicap."[25] In 1998, Tom Willard wrote of his own frustration with "the misconception that people with disabilities are not happy or whole until they have overcome their disability."[26]

Clearly more research is needed, but if what I have found is borne out, it may be that the argument that Deaf people are not disabled came to prominence alongside the Deaf rights movement and the rise of the culture model in the 1970s and 1980s. If so, the claim that Deaf people have long rejected identification as disabled might be an example of an "invented tradition," a common phenomenon in all cultures but particularly those reacting to rapid change. Historians have become increasingly interested in recent years in the ways that societies seek to reinforce the legitimacy of their values by projecting their origins back in time and defending them as longstanding cultural traditions.[27]

The rejection of disability since the 1970s seems mainly intended as a refutation of the demeaning focus on deafness as physical defect and medical problem. In their desire to avoid the focus on the ear to the exclusion of all other aspects of Deaf experience, and to emphasize the legitimacy of their culture, Deaf people increasingly denied that physical difference had any significance in the formation of Deaf identity.

Just as early ASL studies downplayed the importance of fingerspelling, iconicity, and any other element that seemed to make signed languages less like "true languages" (that is, conforming to definitions and standards derived from the study of spoken language), so also did early Deaf studies deny the importance of sensory difference in order to emphasize the cultural aspect of Deaf identity. Just as it was thought that a "true language" would not rely on iconicity or the spelling of borrowed words, a "true culture" could have nothing to do with physical difference.

However, just as ASL scholars now have enough confidence to explore the significant place of iconicity and fingerspelling in the language, so too has Deaf studies begun pointing toward the significance of physical difference in defining the Deaf community.

CONCLUSION

The common argument that Deaf people are a cultural and linguistic group and therefore are not disabled wrongly characterizes culture and disability as mutually exclusive. Saying that Deaf people share a culture says nothing about the usefulness or validity of speaking of Deaf people as disabled. "Disability" describes a particular kind of relationship between a majority and a minority, between socially constructed notions of normality and deviance. "Culture" describes a set of values and beliefs within a group. Saying that Deaf people share a culture says nothing about the usefulness or validity of speaking of Deaf people as disabled. Not only is it entirely possible for Deaf people to be both a distinct cultural group and disabled, it is necessary if Deaf and disability studies scholars are to provide a coherent account of the Deaf community.

Nothing I have written here should be construed as an argument against the cultural model. It has been and continues to be a powerful tool in Deaf studies, as well as in the struggle for Deaf rights and community pride. Ethnicity is a crucial concept because it provides a framework for exploring the ways in which Deaf Americans have maintained distinct community institutions and have passed down, over many generations, a common history, language, and culture. As Ella Mae Lentz recently pointed out to me, it may also more closely reflect the way in which deaf people experience their relationships with hearing people. When encountering a nonsigner, she maintained, a Deaf person does not think, "I cannot hear and therefore cannot communicate with this person," but rather, "Our languages are different and therefore we cannot communicate with each other." In this way, the Deaf individual's experience is that of a linguistic minority.

However, the social model of disability can account for much that the cultural model cannot. The disability model allows us to explore how sensory differences between hearing and deaf people shape their worlds, as well as how the concept of normality shapes both the attitude of hearing people towards to Deaf people and the development of Deaf childrens' sense of identity. It provides an explanatory context for the medicalization of deafness, and a theoretical framework for the argument that Deaf people are not disabled by hearing impairment, but rather by the oppression of difference. It provides powerful arguments for ASL in Deaf education. It shows us that the response of hearing people to deafness is not unique but rather part of a larger response to disability. It makes sense of the fact that Veditz wrote not that Deaf people were people of sign language, but that they were people of the eye.

Moreover, the disability model should not pose a threat to Deaf people's sense of identity any more than does the ethnic model. After all, until fairly recently most Deaf people would have strongly objected to being identified with ethnicity. Once Deaf people in the 1970s and 1980s began to identify themselves as an ethnic group, they felt no less Deaf than they had before, and they felt no compulsion to merge their identities with Vietnamese Americans, Italian Americans, or other ethnic groups. Deaf Americans (or for that matter Chinese Americans) are not expected to feel a close affinity for Cuban Americans just because, for purposes of explaining their experiences as minorities, we describe both as ethnic groups. The same holds true for disability. Deaf people will doubtless always feel far more affinity for other Deaf people than for other disabled people (or for other ethnic groups). It is not a question about identity but rather about the need for a coherent category of analysis for scholars, for a unified, broad-based movement for effective activism, and for explanations that the general public, in particular the parents of deaf children, can find both plausible and persuasive.

Most groups who now identify themselves as disabled have done so only recently. Blind people in particular long resisted both the label and association with the larger universe of disabled people. People with mental disabilities and those with physical disabilities have long had an uneasy relationship. Those with acquired disabilities, such as disabled war veterans, often have resisted association with people who have lifelong disabilities. The tendency of those with lesser stigmatized disabilities to distance themselves from those with more highly stigmatized disabilities is a common phenomenon. Throughout American history, disabled people have been more likely to identify themselves in terms of a specific group than as disabled.

Only recently has the identity of "disabled person" been widely embraced. This is in part a conscious political decision, in part the product of a new consciousness of shared experience, and in good part is due to increasing awareness of the social model of disability. It was once common to hear wheelchair users say, "Just because I use a wheelchair doesn't mean you should treat me like I'm retarded." Today it is more common to hear something like, "Nobody, regardless of their disability, should be treated that way." Some disabled people are far more vulnerable to discrimination, institutionalization, and eugenic assault than others, but a tenet of disability solidarity is that those less threatened should not abandon the more vulnerable. Disabled people differ significantly from one another, but they share common experiences resisting the medicalization of their identity, coping with inferior "special" education, fighting for autonomy and self-determination—in short, they share a common experience of oppression and of struggle against it. Thus, sharing a common oppression, they have undertaken to forge a common liberation.

Indeed, one of the remarkable aspects of the pan-disability rights movement is its ability to bring together diverse groups of people into common action. It is a fractious coalition, riven by identity politics and conflicting agendas to be sure. Nevertheless, its very existence and dramatic growth is testament to a powerful idea—that the goal ought not to be for any one group to find liberation for itself, in effect merely reshuffling the deck, but rather to resist and disrupt the systematic translation of difference into structures of privilege and oppression.

ENDNOTES

1.   American Deaf culture has been described in a number of books and articles. See, for example, Carol Padden and Tom Humphries, *Deaf in America: Voices from a Culture* (Harvard University Press, 1988), John V. Van Cleve and Barry A. Crouch, *A Place of Their Own: Creating the Deaf Community in America* (Gallaudet University Press, 1989), Harlan Lane, Robert Hoffmeister, Ben Bahan, *A Journey into the DEAF-WORLD* (DawnSign Press, 1996), Robert Buchanan, *Illusions of Equality: Deaf Americans in School and Factory, 1850–1950* (Gallaudet University Press, 2002), Susan Burch, *Signs of Resistance: American Deaf Cultural History, 1900 to 1942* (New York University Press, 2002).

2.   Lane, Journey into the Deaf-World, 111–116. Brice Alden, "Visualist Theory 101," Tactile Mind (Spring 2002): 8. Ben Bahan, "Notes from a 'Seeing Person,'" in *American Deaf Culture: An Anthology*, ed. Sherman Wilcox (Linstock Press, 1989), 30, 31.

3.   *Proceedings of the Ninth Convention of the National Association of the Deaf and the Third World's Congress of the Deaf*, 1910 (Philadelphia: Philocophus Press, 1912), 30.

4.   Carol Padden and Tom Humphries, *Deaf in America: Voices from a Culture* (Harvard University Press, 1988), 3. Some Deaf people, most notably World Federation of the Deaf president, Markku Jokinen, and the editors of *The Tactile Mind*, have argued recently for thinking in terms of "sign language users" rather than "Deaf persons," as this would emphasize culture and language rather than lack of hearing. Paddy Ladd, in his recent and important book, *Understanding Deaf Culture: In Search of Deafhood* (Multilingual Matters LTD, 2003), suggests that in the absence of oppressive relations Deaf people would welcome culturally Deaf hearing people as full members of the community. I would maintain

that sensory differences matter, regardless of the cultural setting. Ladd, in another section of his book, suggests this point by arguing that "blindness, being a sensory impairment, might well involve certain psychological patterning which, when reinforced by time spent together, might add up to a phenomenon with some notable cultural features." Human beings are cultural beings, and they are also physical beings. To deny one or the other, to say that our fates are entirely decided by our bodies, or conversely that we are all culture and that our bodies do not shape who we are, are equally wrong.

5.   Arkady Belozovsky, for example, spoke at the 2004 Deaf Studies Today conference about cultural differences between Russian and American Deaf people, such as attitudes toward physical contact and ways of introducing people. Arkady Belozovsky, "Learning Foreign, Linguistically Related Sign Languages: What are the Benefits to ASL/Deaf Studies Instructors," *Deaf Studies Today*, Utah Valley State College, April 12–14, 2004.

6.   Carol Padden, "A New Language," presented at the "Deaf Studies Today" conference held at Utah Valley State College, April 12–14, 2004. Joseph Murray suggested to me that Padden's experience of a sense of connection could also be explained by her expectation that Deaf people should feel such a connection with one another. This indeed suggests an alternative explanation in general for Deaf experiences of kinship across national lines; genuine kin often feel a similar sense of connectedness and mutual responsibility in spite of cultural divides. Still, I would argue that the shared experience of deafness, of sensory difference from the majority and the knowledge that another's experiences of the world are in this fundamental way like one's own, would be unlikely not to produce a sense of commonality.

7.   Jeffrey E. Nash, "Policy and Practice in the American Sign Language Community," *International Journal of the Sociology of Language* 68 (1987): 11. Nash also points to important similarities between Deaf and other ethnic groups.

8.   Ross E. Mitchell and Michael A. Karchmer, "Chasing the Mythical Ten Percent: Parental Hearing Status of Deaf and Hard of Hearing Students in the United States," *Sign Language Studies* 4, (Winter 2004):138–163.

9.   *Forbidden Signs: American Culture and the Campaign Against Sign Language* (University of Chicago Press, 1996), 10.

10.   Paddy Ladd, in his recent and important book, *Understanding Deaf Culture: In Search of Deafhood* (Multilingual Matters Ltd, 2003), acknowledges the significance of the disability model, writing that Deaf people should be "seen as intrinsic 'dual-category members' —that is, that some of their issues might relate to issues of non-hearing whilst others relate to language and culture" (p 16). He notes that the concept of "access" has provided a rationale for important services to Deaf people such as interpreting services, text telephones, captioning and the like (while it has also created problems, as in the debate over separate versus mainstreamed education). On the whole, however, he downplays deafness and focuses almost entirely on what he aptly terms "Deafhood." The emphasis is understandable, given that he is trying to reach a public ignorant of Deaf culture and that views Deaf people simply as people burdened with nonfunctioning ears. Nevertheless, it leads him to understate the importance of sensory difference in constructing the Deaf community and determining its membership (pp 41–42, 74 n8) And while he gives a serviceable description of the social model of disability, he then goes on to equate recognition of "physical deafness" with "the medical concept," which is precisely the equation that the social model rejects (pp 16, 166–69).

11.   On the social model of disability, see Mike Oliver, *The Politics of Disablement* (Palgrave McMillan, 1990); J. Swain, et al, eds. *Disabling Barriers—Enabling Environments* (Sage Publications, 1993); Harlan Hahn, "Antidiscrimination Laws and Social Research on Disability: The Minority Group Perspective," *Behavioral Sciences and the Law* 14 (1996): 41–59; Tom Shakespeare and N. Watson, "Defending the social model," *Disability and Society* 12 (1997): 293–300; Len Barton and Mike Oliver, eds. *Disability Studies: Past Present and Future* (1997); Mark Priestley, "Constructions and Creations: Idealism, Materialism and Disability Theory,"

Disability and Society Vol. 13, No. 1 (1998): 75–94; Len Barton, et al, eds, *Disability Studies Today* (Polity Press, 2002). For recent examples of disability studies in the humanities, see Paul K. Longmore, *Why I Burned My Book and Other Essays on Disability,* (Temple University Press, 2003); Thomson, Rosemarie Garland, *Extraordinary Bodies: Figuring Physical Disability in American Culture and Literature* (Columbia University Press, 1997); Mitchell, David T., and Sharon L. Snyder, eds., *The Body and Physical Difference: Discourses of Disability* (University of Michigan Press, 1997); Davis, Lennard, *Enforcing Normalcy: Disability, Deafness, and the Body* (Verso Press, 1995); Longmore, Paul, Lauri Umansky, eds. *The New Disability History: American Perspectives* (New York University Press, 2000). For overviews of recent work in the field, see my essay, "Bodies and Environments: The Cultural Construction of Disability," *Employment, Disability and the Americans with Disabilities Act: Issues in Law, Public Policy and Research,* Peter Blanck, ed., (Northwestern University Press, 2000), pp 387–411, and Catherine J. Kudlick, "Disability History: Why We Need Another 'Other'," *American Historical Review* 108 (June 2003): 763–793.

12.   Harlan Hahn, "Antidiscrimination Laws and Social Research on Disability: The Minority Group Perspective," *Behavioral Sciences and the Law* 14 (1996): 43. Simi Linton defines disability as "a marker of identity" that has brought together a coalition of people stigmatized by physical, sensory, and mental differences from the majority, in *Claiming Disability: Knowledge and Identity* (New York University Press, 1998).

13.   Reprinted in Paul Longmore, *Why I Burned My Book,* 26.

14.   Jim Reisler "Technology-Improving Sound, Easing Fury," *Newsweek* (February 24, 2003).

15.   Carol Padden and Tom Humphries, *Deaf in America: Voices from a Culture* (Harvard University Press, 1988), 3.

16.   See for example, Harlan Lane, *The Mask of Benevolence: Disabling the Deaf Community* (Knopf, 1992), and Jan Branson and Don Miller, *Damned for Their Difference: The Cultural Construction of Deaf People as Disabled* (Gallaudet University Press, 2002).

17.   Alice Dreger, *One of Us: Conjoined Twins and the Future of Normal* (Harvard University Press, 2004), 77, 55.

18.   Joseph Shapiro, *No Pity: People with Disabilities Forging a New Civil Rights Movement* (Random House, 1994), 14).

19.   Carol Padden and Tom Humphries, *Deaf in America: Voices from a Culture* (Harvard University Press, 1988), 44.

20.   Laurent Clerc, "Address to the Connecticut Legislature," and John Burnet, "What the Deaf and Dumb are before Instruction," in *Krentz, A Mighty Change,* 17, 40.

21.   John Jacob Flournoy, "Mr. Flournoy's Plan for a Deaf-Mute Commonwealth," *American Annals of the Deaf* (1858), reprinted in *A Mighty Change: An Anthology of Deaf American Writing,* 1816–1864, Christopher Krentz, ed. (Gallaudet University Press, 2000), 166.

22.   Robert Buchanan, *Illusions of Equality: Deaf Americans in School and Factory, 1850–1950* (Gallaudet University Press, 2002), 42.

23.   Susan Burch, *Signs of Resistance: American Deaf Cultural History, 1900 to 1942* (New York University Press, 2002), 121. Burch cites two other issues of the Empire State News, but I could find nothing in them related to this question. The first briefly alludes to dissatisfaction with the work of the New York State Employment Service and endorses the idea of a deaf labor bureau. The other discusses concerns that the New York State Employment Service "claims to have 19 specially trained interviewers for the handicapped, but that none of these specially trained interviewers are equipped by experience or training to deal intelligently with the problems of the deaf." Again, the point is to address the particular needs of deaf people, not to make any conceptual distinctions between them and other "handicapped" persons.

24.   Quoted in Jay McMahon, "Rehabilitation Urged," *New York Times* (April 28, 1941): section E, page 6; reprinted in a regular column by Charles Joselow, "For Your Record," *Empire*

State News (January–February, 1942): 3; both cited in Buchanan, *Illusions of Equality*, p 175 n 10.

25.   Albert Ballin, *The Deaf Mute Howls* (Gallaudet University Press, 1998 [1930]), 57. Toivo Lindholm, "Place of the Adult Deaf in Society," in *Deaf World: A Historical Reader and Primary Sourcebook*, Lois Bragg, ed. (New York University Press, 2001), 272. Frederick Schreiber, "What a Deaf Jewish Leader Expects," in *Deaf World*, 34. Leo M. Jacobs, *A Deaf Adult Speaks Out* (Gallaudet University Press, 1989 [1974]), 13, 23.

26.   Albert Ballin, *The Deaf Mute Howls* (Gallaudet University Press, 1998 [1930]), 57. Frederick Schreiber, "What a Deaf Jewish Leader Expects," in *Deaf World: A Historical Reader and Primary Sourcebook*, Lois Bragg, ed. (New York University Press, 2001), 34. Tom Willard, "What Exactly Am I Supposed to Overcome," in *Deaf World*, 273. Leo M. Jacobs, *A Deaf Adult Speaks Out* (Gallaudet University Press, 1989 [1974]), 13, 23.

27.   See for example, Eric Hobsbawm, Terence Ranger eds., *The Invention of Tradition*, (Cambridge University Press, 1983).

ABOUT THE AUTHOR

Douglas Baynton is the author of Forbidden Signs: American Culture and the Campaign Against Sign Language, *an exploration of the significance for American cultural history of the suppression of American Sign Language. He was one of the principal researchers and writers of the History Through Deaf Eyes museum exhibit. His recent works include an introductory essay to Albert Ballin's* The Deaf-Mute Howls, *originally published in 1930 and reissued in 1998 by Gallaudet University Press, and "The Curious Death of Sign Language Studies in the Nineteenth Century," published in* The Study of Signed Languages: Essays in Honor of William C. Stokoe, *edited by David Armstrong and others. An essay titled "Disabling Deaf Studies" will appear in a forthcoming collection,* Sightings: Explorations in Deaf Studies, *edited by Dirksen Bauman and Ben Bahan. His current project is a cultural history of the exclusion of Deaf and disabled people from immigration into the United States.*

De'VIA: Art Talk—
A History of Deaf Art

CHUCK BAIRD

Chuck Baird has been a painter since his teen years and was the official curator of Deaf Way II in Washington, D.C., in 2003.

In the summer of 1989, a month before Deaf Way held at Gallaudet University, Seven other Deaf artists and I gathered to discuss the future of deaf art. We defined it as Deaf Visual Image Art, or De'VIA, and developed a manifesto. For the Deaf Studies Today conference, I prepared a 45-minute, three-part presentation on the past, present and future of De'VIA. However, as soon as I entered the room, I realized I had to adjust my presentation quickly, since the participants weren't what I had envisioned. There were approximately 40 attendees, with the majority being young hearing students from the college where the conference was being held. De'VIA was a foreign concept to most of the participants. I have chosen to provide both versions for the reader. My presentations are a bit different from typical seminars or workshops; they are more of a narrative of what I have witnessed firsthand as a De'VIA artist. —Chuck Baird

RATHER THAN GIVE AN IN-DEPTH look at our art movement, I will give a basic description of Deaf View Image Art (De'VIA) and its brief history.

My presentation at the Deaf Studies Today conference included a tour of some artwork on exhibit there. Since gathering permission from artists to show variations of De'VIA would be a difficult task, I did not have the luxury of using a slide show or PowerPoint presentation to showcase artwork. Instead, I used a flipchart to illustrate some of my points. At the end of the presentation, we moved to another room where there was some artwork hanging for an exhibition. There we explored the exhibitions and held a question-and-answer session.

It seems prudent that I give a bit of history regarding the exhibition that the students and I explored. In October 2003, when I first learned of the [Deaf Studies *Today*] conference, there was no mention of plans for an art show like the 1999 conference in Oakland, California. The art show in Oakland, curated by volunteer Brenda Schertz, was a time-consuming but successful show. I contacted the conference committee to see about the possibility of finding a gallery near the conference site, thinking that I could inform both experienced and emerging artists about this show. However, UVSC's art gallery near the campus was unavailable, and there were no other options available. Deaf artists like myself no longer tolerate the use of inappropriate sites (such as a hotel ballroom or room) for the exhibition of our work, due to inappropriate lighting, set-up, and so on. I also felt that due to circumstances beyond the conference committee's control, time, and money did not really allow for a full-fledged art show.

One month to prior the conference, I decided to risk bringing my own works anyway, in the hopes that there would be a small space to exhibit. Much to my relief, there was a suitable location in the same building where the conference was held. This became the mini gallery that I took the participants to on the day of my presentation. This makeshift art exhibit consisted of two artists: my late sister, Elizabeth Lee Baird (a.k.a. Liz) and myself. I did not have the intentions of making it a family art show, but I have always considered Liz a true De'VIA artist. Upon her passing in 2003, my other deaf sister and I found Liz's paintings from 1984 and 1985 that she had stashed away in her shed. We agreed to ask the conference hosts if we could hang the paintings at the conference in honor of her pioneering work.

My art hanging next to Liz's was a relatively new discipline for me to explore. Originally untitled, my work was later named *Scrapbook of Deaf Americans: 1900–1950*. 45 pieces of 8" x 10" framed photographs were exhibited as part of the work. The conference goers who attended my presentation asked many questions, and we ended the hour by browsing the exhibitions.

PRE-DE'VIA

My first exposure to De'VIA came through Dr. Betty G. Miller. This was during the early 1970s, long before we gathered to create the name and manifesto of De'VIA. I was a transfer student at the National Technical Institute for the Deaf at Rochester Institute of Technology (NTID/RIT) at the time, but I often traveled to Washington, D.C. to visit my friends at Gallaudet University or to visit my late sister Liz, who was sharing a townhouse with Betty near Capitol Hill. It was at this townhouse that I first saw Betty's paintings with my naked eyes.

I was blown away by the awesome power of her artwork, such as *ASL Prohibited* and *A.G. Bell School*. It was the first time I ever saw De'VIA.

I returned to Rochester and created a couple of paintings for my studio course, including *Mechanical Ear* and *Why Me?* (available for viewing in *Chuck Baird: 35 Plates,* published by DawnSignPress). But I stopped painting like this because it wasn't really from my heart, and I didn't want to copy Betty's style when it didn't reflect my own feelings. She did influence me, though, and planted the seed of De'VIA in me.

This was in 1973, and I didn't paint Deaf-related artwork again for the next 19 years. I was worried about the quality of the forms in my works more than the contents. Meanwhile, I continued my studies at NTID/RIT aiming for a professional job in the mainstream to make my vocational rehabilitation counselor happy with the money she spent on my education. This was, unfortunately, the general mentality about young deaf artists' futures: that they needed "real" jobs to be successful. Making a living as an artist isn't always easy, and even more so for a Deaf person; this is what the old school of thinking was in these days.

I was not surprised to learn recently that my former classmates such as Harry Williams, Ann Silver, John Smith, and others who majored in art at Gallaudet, wanted to express the Deaf theme in their class art projects. It was, after all, the 1970s—an era of awakening for the Deaf community. But they, instead, had to focus on elements of art and design or they wouldn't pass their courses. Yet Betty shocked students and faculty alike in 1971 when she used the Deaf theme in her now-famous faculty show at Gallaudet University's Washburn Art Building. This exhibit truly was the shot that was heard (seen) around the world. She faced a lot of opposition, including deaf faculty who said her work was too raw and exposed her feelings too much; however, the Washington Post gave her a full-page review full of praise. Even the anger in her paintings was pure art.

The question, then, became: Who showed the Deaf Experience as visual art first? The students? The faculty? The beginning may be found as far back as deaf photographers like Theophilus H. d'Estrella (1851–1929), Frances Allen (1854–1941) and Mary Allen (1858–1942), Maggie L. Sayer (1920–2000). As Deborah Sonnenstrahl has written, photography was initially considered a part of science or technology, but later it became considered a form of fine art, showing souls like a painting.[1] Were these deaf photographers De'VIA artists?

Dennis Watson, a CODA, drew illustrations for a 1964 sign language book, *Talk With Your Hands.* His style was playful and his humor showed through. Some believe that the influence of growing up with deaf parents was apparent in his drawings. However, opponents insist that before the age of computer art, illustration was not in the same category as fine art.

Regardless of who was the first De'VIA artist, Betty holds the claim to being the first Deaf artist to expose the country to the genre. She had a strong and clear vision of what she was doing. Her exhibit was a bold step, just like Paul Cèzanne was ahead of his time. Cèzanne, the father of modern art, was perceived by European high society as crazy.

The 1970s were a time of cultural change, especially with the civil rights movement, the Vietnam War, and the discovery by William Stokoe that ASL was a true language. These changes—certainly influenced many deaf people like myself to become Deaf. We were becoming free from pure oralism, finally being accepted and feeling a sense of liberation, yet we deaf artists were not ready to express our experiences as Deaf people. But Betty was. We were impressed by her cutting edge artwork, and slowly began to follow her example—not necessarily through rage, but through our own various approaches.

I see a parallel between those days and the days after 9/11. I recently read an interesting article in the New York Times about artists living in New York City in the wake of 9/11. While the media ran 24-hour coverage of the terrorist attacks and the horrific deaths, the artists in the city responded slowly. They had to digest the events before attempting to express themselves in artistic form.

The writer of the article surveyed the artists about who responded first to the tragedies. The first were the musicians who quickly made albums or did benefits, such as Bruce Springsteen's *The Rising*. Next were poets, playwrights, choreographers, symphonists, and so on. The very last group to respond was the group of visual artists (with the exception of photographers, who were part of the media). The visual artists simply weren't ready, and needed to absorb different things before revealing their innermost feelings to the world.

This made me realize that in the Deaf community, visual arts, too, were the last to emerge. The 1960s and 1970s sparked social changes for Deaf people and performing artists, such as Good Vibrations, Hughes Memorial Deaf Theatre Group, National Theatre of the Deaf, Fairmount Theatre of the Deaf, Rock Gospel, and so on. But we Deaf visual artists were probably the last ones to respond to the social changes around us. We simply weren't ready. We slowly absorbed while watching the scenes of the Deaf community celebrating our Deaf culture and language being accepted and becoming stronger. As I mentioned earlier, Betty was ahead of our time, and that is a testimony to her courage as a frontrunner.

These days are what Paul Johnston, another deaf artist, and I recently agreed to call pre-De'VIA days.

Eventually, a few organizations advocating and spreading awareness about Deaf artists were formed, such as Spectrum, Focus on Deaf Artists (FODA) in Austin, TX (1976–1980), and Deaf Artists of America in Rochester (1985–1990).

In 1975, the 7th World Congress for the Deaf was held in Washington, D.C., and two hearing women from Austin, Texas asked my fellow artists and I what we desired or dreamed of. We answered: an art colony of our own. And this is how Spectrum was conceived.

The following summer, these women invited us to spend a week near Austin. In addition to harmonizing and sharing, we discussed our aspirations and goals for the expansion into a national organization. We wanted the organization to operate as a clearinghouse, archives, and so on. After signing the proposed constitution, Spectrum was born.

It was the first time ever that an art organization was available for Deaf people and run by Deaf people. Soon after, a highlight of the year was when the next summer conference was held, with almost 40 artists in attendance. Afterwards, about half stayed on to work for Spectrum, living in the area.

Let me skip over the history of Spectrum and focus on who was involved as Deaf/De'VIA artists. Betty had resigned from Gallaudet and started a masters program, along with Liz Baird and Carolyn Ball. The rest of us were working for the organization in various capacities. We had a weekly seminar on Wednesdays, discussing the uniqueness of Deaf visual artists. "De'VIA" was not yet coined at that time, but Betty was persistent in trying to pull us into something like De'VIA. Except for my sister Liz and few others, many of us failed to see why it was necessary for us to analyze ourselves as deaf artists and putting that into our art. We were simply not ready to show our bare souls. We were in denial. We were very slow to capture the concept and again, Betty was way ahead of us.

Spectrum expanded quickly, especially since we had an oil rancher donating on an annual basis almost half of our budget. Eventually, due to unforeseen circumstances, our benefactor had to discontinue her support. This created a crisis for us. With increasing demands and inadequate funds, many of us became unhappily strapped for money. Some of us had to leave in order to survive financially. I was one of the very last artists remaining in town.

Later, as I was recruiting Texas Visual Artists for an exhibition at the Texas capitol rotunda during Deaf Awareness Day, I met Tony Landon McGregor, who later became one of the stronger De'VIA leaders. We had our paintings hung in the rotunda. My painting was *Mechanical Ear* that I brought from my college days. I look back today and think how strange I painted it without having any intentions of it becoming De'VIA.

That was the first time I didn't feel shame in exhibiting the painting. It's also interesting that this painting was created with pathologists in mind, long before cochlear implants became widespread.

When Spectrum formally closed its doors in 1980, I left Austin and headed for the National Theatre for the Deaf, where I was for the next 10 years. I did paint in acrylics during my spare time, but I wish I had done much more than that. Although I painted sceneries for the NTD almost every year that had nothing to do with De'VIA, I only painted maybe three to five pieces a year for myself.

In 1985, I met Harry Williams, an extraordinary artist, again in Berkeley, California, when we exhibited our works at *Celebration,* sponsored by D.E.A.F. Media. I never have forgotten how I fell in love with his masterful art—very romantic and surrealistic. We were alone in the room with our works hanging. We spent hours discussing everything about art and our identities as Deaf persons. He was so brilliant and articulate. I was spellbound.

Let me tell you something important about Harry. He graduated from Gallaudet filled with Deborah Sonnenstrahl's art history teachings, especially fascinated with Baroque and surrealism and inspired by Betty's exhibit. He returned to his home in southern California, spending much time alone to develop a singular vision in painting. None of us knew what he was doing during that time. He brought his new works to Washington, D.C., delighting us all. His works were more poetic and celebratory, glorifying ASL and the blessings of the visual world.

We learned from him that De'VIA didn't have to be all about anger. He should be recognized as a pure De'VIA artist, one of the earliest next to Betty. He has influenced me, especially in my choice of approaches to my art. His death at the age of 42 from AIDS was sad for us all, and in one of my paintings, *Left and Right,* the calla lilies in it are my way of paying homage to him.

Allow me to return to 1985. Five years after Spectrum became inactive, Tom Willard, a late-deafened photographer, journalist and a NTID/RIT graduate, formed Deaf Artists of America (DAA) that focused on visual art only. The organization moved from New Jersey to Rochester into a rented space, apart from NTID. The Deaf community there gave DAA its full support. Deaf artists' works were curated and exhibited, with a careful balance between locals and out-of-towners, genders, Deaf and hard of hearing, and so on. We were thrilled with DAA's services, but we were still hungry for more Deaf Visual Artists out there unheralded. DAA lasted longer than Spectrum did, having learned from Spectrum's mistakes, though financial difficulties persisted.

In 1988, a well-attended art conference was held at NTID. There were full days of various seminars and lectures, and artwork was on display. The conference was fun, but at the roundtable discussion for Deaf artists, there were a lot of conflicting ideas and opinions about the future of DAA. Afterwards, many of us left feeling divided and headed nowhere. At this point, De'VIA still had not been devised. After one of the most memorable years in my life performing in *King of Hearts* for the National Theatre of the Deaf, I was summoned by Jane Norman, part of the first Deaf Way committee, and Paul Johnston, to paint a 10 x 30 foot mural at Gallaudet related to Deaf Way. When I went there to begin the huge project over Memorial Day weekend before the Deaf Way, I was suddenly pulled into a room where many deaf artists were present. I told them I didn't know what was going on, but they smiled and said, "You will see." We spent three days and nights debating, drawing, critiquing, laughing, videotaping, writing, and painting before we finally came up with Deaf View Image Art, or De'VIA. We created a manifesto and signed it:

(1) De'VIA represents Deaf artists and perceptions based on their Deaf experiences. It uses formal art elements with the intention of expressing innate cultural or physical Deaf experience. These experiences may include Deaf metaphors, Deaf perspectives, and Deaf insight in relationship with the environment (both the natural world and Deaf cultural environment), spiritual and everyday life.

(2) De'VIA can be identified by formal elements such as Deaf artists' possible tendency to use contrasting colors and values, intense colors, contrasting textures. It may also most often include a centralized focus, with exaggeration or emphasis on facial features, especially eyes, mouths, ears, and hands. Currently, Deaf artists tend to work in human scale with these exaggerations, and not exaggerate the space around these elements.

(3) There is a difference between Deaf artists and De'VIA. Deaf artists are those who use art in any form, media, or subject matter, and who are held to the same artistic standards as other artists. De'VIA is created when the artist intends to express their Deaf experience through visual art. Deafened or hearing artists may also create De'VIA, if the intention is to create work that is born of their Deaf experience (a possible example would be a hearing child of Deaf parents). It is clearly possible for Deaf artists not to work in the area of De'VIA.

(4) While applied and decorative arts may also use the qualities of De'VIA (high contrast, centralized focus, exaggeration of specific features), this manifesto is specifically written to cover the traditional fields of visual fine arts (painting, sculpture, drawing, photography, printmaking) as well as alternative media when used as fine arts such as fiber arts, ceramics, neon, and collage.

Drs. Betty G. Miller and Paul Johnston lead our session. Dr. Deborah M. Sonnenstrahl, Guy Wonder, Alex Wilhite, Sandi Inches, Lai-Yok Ho, Nancy Creighton, and I also participated.

When we came to the point where we discussed the third paragraph, about the difference between deaf artists and De'VIA, I said, "Hey, I know some artists who happen to be deaf here and there, especially those at DAA. Can't they be De'VIA?" I guess I was still naïve, and I often misunderstood people—I was exhausted from the long days of discussion. I saw that Betty was looking at me, Paul was saying "Come on!", and Deborah was being patient with me. I ended up signing the manifesto without completely agreeing with it. In reality, I had thought it was a huge mistake. I had no idea that I would be as solid De'VIA as I am today. Funny, when I reread the manifesto as I write this, I now support every word of the manifesto. One hundred percent.

After the gathering, I returned to the mural. It took me three long months to complete the mural. Perhaps that was my first De'VIA work, but I feel it was all from me. I saw the mural again after 12 years, and even if I feel I could have done it differently, I know it has had an impact on some people. That comforts me.

Let me fast forward to the time where I feel it important to see De'VIA as an art movement that changed our lives as visual artists. De'VIA has long remained the same, almost never changing. After Deaf Way and good feelings from the conference, we (Deaf artists) got responses from different places asking, "What is De'VIA? What's wrong with Deaf Art?"; "It sounds like a French word for nitwit or nut!"; and so on. One argument was that no one nor art critics would know what the heck De'VIA was. Rob Roth, a good friend of my from the Bay Area and a visual artist in printmaking, gave a presentation at one of the early Deaf Studies Conferences sponsored by Gallaudet. He said that it was essential for our artworks of Deaf experience to reach out larger audiences, that we are part of the mainstream thru art critics or reporters. He suggested that De'VIA would confuse the people we needed to reach.

We, as the creators of De'VIA, remained silent and waited until doubters' arguments faded out. We knew time would come when our critics would agree. We drew inspiration from the small group of artists that often met in salons in Paris at the turn of the 20th century. They would discuss what their paintings had in common, and others asked who they were trying to impress. With time, the artists created the label, "French Impressionism." The public reaction was "What is it?" Now it is one of the world's most beloved terms. I am a witness to the fact that the name of De'VIA is widespread, in almost every Deaf school and many mainstreamed programs. It has always been a topic in at the past few Deaf Studies conferences. The name has been used in Europe, Russia, Japan, and other countries. Paul Johnston is even now teaching De'VIA as part of the Deaf Studies curriculum at Gallaudet University. He will also lead the art department's De'VIA Studio as a major or elective course for the first time this semester.

Let me take you through quickly the important highlights of De'VIA exhibitions. There have been several one-person shows, but the group art shows are always thick with art and experience as we De'VIA artists gather and share new eloquent experiences among us. Every time we meet, there is always an addition of emerging De'VIA artists, which is truly an exciting thing. (These with asterisks have a list of participating artists at the end of this paper.)

1989, DEAF WAY ART EXHIBIT; WASHINGTON, D.C.

The exhibit at Deaf Way was held in the field house at Gallaudet University. We were very fresh from the first and historical De'VIA meeting. We met several more visual artists but the days flew by too quickly, and we never had a full day to ourselves.

1993, DEAF STUDIES CONFERENCE; CHICAGO

A few of us De'VIA artists brought our works there. My works were hung on display. Ann Silver and Betty Miller were also there, and we had a seminar on De'VIA. But the seminar became more like a debate between two artists with the third leaving feeling deadlocked.

1993, A PERSPECTIVE OF DEAF CULTURE THROUGH ART; ESSEX, MASSACHUSETTS*

Brenda Schertz, who majored in Art History and Museum Studies at the Massachusetts College of Art, took her first opportunity of setting a major exhibition of many De'VIA artists at Northern Essex Community College. The exhibit was a very impressive and well-publicized event, and Brenda also gave exhibit tours as a docent. Not only were Deaf people delighted at receiving rich and in-depth information about art and Deaf culture, but hearing people also learned about human values in the Deaf community.

1995, DEAF STUDIES CONFERENCE IV; BOSTON*

Again, Brenda, as curator, pulled off another successful exhibit. With pride, she made this well-organized exhibition special for the conference (a list of participating artists is below). Brenda trained several docents for the conference participants and local Deaf people and friends. The main attraction of the show was works of then-emerging artist Susan Dupor of Wisconsin who used both painting and freehand animation.

Susan's work was very powerful and evoking, especially her painting, *Family Dog* (available for viewing in Deborah Sonnestrahl's book). The interesting thing about her work was that she was similar to Betty in that she was raw and blunt in her art. Her works quickly became popular and were exhibited at many locations. Many years later, when I was part of the visual art committee for Deaf Way II in 2002, we invited 12 people to give ratings on works submitted as color slides. One wrote on his evaluation about the works of a young female from Mexico, Ixchel Solis Garcia, as "Duporseque." I considered that a major honor! Dupor's works have changed through time; she has passed her anger phase in her art, just like Betty did many years ago. However, her subject matter remains the same with the views of a feminist, ecologist, maybe psychologist, and of course, De'VIA. She currently works at the Wisconsin School for the Deaf as an art teacher, yet amazingly she finds time to paint.

1999, DEAF STUDIES CONFERENCE VI; OAKLAND*

The avid art-lover behind the success of the Oakland art exhibition was Dr. Susan Rutherford. Brenda was the curator with her amazing energy, and brought bright and bold works of De'VIA from 22 visual artists. The artworks were hung in a site two blocks from the conference site in a contemporary place with plenty of appropriate lighting. The opening reception was a phenomenal success, with a packed room of people in awe shoulder to shoulder. It was one of the best exhibitions ever.

On the next Sunday morning, we De'VIA artists (Ann Silver, Brenda Schertz, Guy Wonder, and myself) were part of a panel with Paul Johnston moderating. We shared our thoughts on this and that, all things De'VIA-related. One particularly interesting moment came when a conference goer asked whether or not a CODA artist could be part of De'VIA. After we discussed both sides of the issue, the audience was asked if they would vote for CODA works being included in the next exhibition. All of them raised their hands in support. We began to understand that De'VIA had not changed in ten years.

1998, DEAF ARTISTS RETREAT; HARRODSBURG, KENTUCKY*

One week prior to the third Deafestival in Louisville, Kentucky Commission on the Deaf and Hard of Hearing (KCDHH) executive director Bobbie Beth Scoggins, and her two right-hands, Virginia Moore and Rowan Hollaway (all who strongly believe in arts through visual mediums as an imperative foundation of Deaf Culture), found time and space in the country away from the hustle and bustle of daily life for us, the deaf artists, to meet and grow with each other.

It was a mind-blowing and spirit-lifting experience. The group consisted of five national artists and five local artists, and we learned about each other. We had in common our being Deaf and our passion for De'VIA. We created new works there and brought them in for display at the Deafestival at the Kentucky Art Center.

2000–2001, DEAF ART EXHIBIT ON TOUR: ELEMENTS OF A CULTURE VISION BY DEAF ARTISTS*

This exhibit was a gigantic step forward for De'VIA, and the credit goes to Brenda Schertz once again for her energy and hard work. The provost of a Boston college invited to a linguistic seminar at Northeastern University responded to Dupor's *Family Dog*. She said that the artwork should have a national tour. At Harlan Lane's prompting, Brenda wrote a grant, and received funding from the Knight Foundation for a Deaf Art tour consisting of 16 De'VIA artists that lasted a year and half. That was the first national touring of De'VIA.

After the selection of artists for the tour, they observed and wrote down into four categories: political expression, communication barrier, cultural affirmation, and visual sound. Read more at *www.deafart.org* and *www.artdeaf.com*.

2000, DEAFESTIVAL; COVINGTON, KENTUCKY

After the first three festivals hosted by KCDHH, a focus on Deaf visual artists was added since the festival organizers felt that we deserved audiences as much as performing artists or groups. We had our own space separate from the general exhibitions, known as the Deaf Visual Artists Studio. There, festival attendees could enjoy watching us as we worked on our crafts or paintings, and purchase our works from there. Brenda Schertz was there, and set up a small group show of artwork there next to the nooks and had a group discussion among visual artists. Half of us wondered about what De'VIA really meant. Some had mixed reactions about De'VIA, wondering if those who were not Deaf could still be considered part of De'VIA—for instance, those who were not raised using ASL and continued using spoken English, or those who weren't necessarily culturally Deaf. Tony Landon McGregor brought up a brilliant solution. He said that we could do whatever differently from others, and still consider our art part of De'VIA, by putting our art in a subcategory: Southwest De'VIA, Native American De'VIA Feminist De'VIA, Black De'VIA, CODA De'VIA, Late Deafened De'VIA, and so on.

At the same meeting, Brenda also surveyed us and found that we wanted to network and keep in touch with each other. She created a group mailing list, DeafArtTalk, and for the next eight months, about 50 people joined and contributed wonderful comments and questions.

2001, SEEING THROUGH DEAF EYES; NEW YORK CITY*

We who were selected to show our works there were overwhelmingly impressed by how they set up the show in two galleries next to each other on Prince Street and Blue Mountain in the heart of the Chelsea District, a hotbed for the galleries, and we were treated like royalty. The show was partly curated by Lesley Kushner, a deaf art teacher at Lexington School and Center for the Deaf. There was a benefit one evening where almost every one of the artists showed up. We were stunned and honored by the red carpet treatment we got. There was a mix of different mediums and yet a strong representation of the genre of De'VIA. This was the first time that De'VIA and Deaf artists were treated like real artists.

2002, DEAF WOMEN ART SHOW; NEW YORK CITY*

Lesley brought several female artists into the gallery for a group show focusing on the unique experience of being Deaf women. I wish I had seen the show, because when I learned about it, I was thrilled to see these artists getting this much-deserved privilege. Since I wasn't at the show, I should not write about it.

2002, DEAF WAY II ART EXHIBITION; WASHINGTON, D.C.*

Deaf Way II was unlike the exhibitions for the first Deaf Way, not better but quite different. In fact, they're incomparable. I worked on contract with the committee for the Visual Art Exhibition for sixteen months prior to the festival. It was a huge task and rewarding experience for me—I learned so many things while living on campus and painting commissioned art for Gallaudet as well.

I viewed slides of over 500 entries from around the world, which was a unique experience. It was interesting to see the mix of artworks—some incorporated the Deaf experience into their art; others didn't. Since Gallaudet was considered a setting for all Deaf and hard of hearing students, we had to be neutral in the selection process, and look for the best quality that would appease both Deaf and hearing audiences.

Unlike the first Deaf Way, Gallaudet president I. King Jordan wanted to have cultural art programs that would reach out to the Washington, D.C. metro area as our primary audience. With that in mind, we had to whittle the selections down to 70. 12 invited judges evaluated the works, with the committee remaining neutral. Out of 70 selected as featured artists, 22 were Americans, six were from Russia, eight were from the United Kingdom, 10 from China, and one or two from other countries, for a total of 21 countries,

Let me skip ahead to the very week of the international Deaf festival, which had over 10,000 registered attendees. Like many De'VIA artists there, I felt very fortunate to meet all 70 artists, both in honor and modesty, wishing we could have much more than 70. To be able to witness their skills and interact with them throughout three opening receptions and group discussions was such a rich and rare opportunity for us.

As I helped hang or set their works in 10 different venues (four on campus and six off campus), I saw that about 40 out of 70 artists expressed the Deaf experience in their works to varying degrees. That is something to consider. There would have been more but some countries like communist China train deaf artists never to reveal their culture as Deaf people. There was an exception: Hong Ze, a glass engraver. When Brenda Schertz and I saw his detailed painting that had deaf children wearing ancient clothing signing to each other, our eyes became wide. We were delighted to discover that there is no way to prevent deaf artists from expressing their own language or culture.

The group of painters from Russia amazed us with how advanced and disciplined they were. Out of six, all but one was culturally Deaf. I may be bold in claiming that we American Deaf or De'VIA artists would benefit in learning from them. We were amazed to learn that Russian Deaf people have a strong sense of Deaf culture just like here in America. We noticed fish always present in almost every painting by the Russians, and were floored to learn that they look at fish as similar to Deaf people: fish don't have ears, nor do they bark in the water.

2003, SECOND DEAF ARTISTS RETREAT; HARRODSBURG, KENTUCKY*

The second meeting of Deaf artists was held at the same location as the first. In attendance were 12 visual artists, two performers, and one poet. For the NAD conference in July 2004, KCDHH will host booths exclusively for Deaf artists, much like the Deaf Visual Artists Studio at Deafestival.

What I really enjoyed at this gathering was to see how warm and happy the artists were to share their arts and techniques with each other nonstop, almost as if there would be no other gathering again. Bobbie Beth Scoggins has said she believes that Deaf Americans in general have overlooked the gem of Deaf Culture. Not only do Deaf performers and actors deserve the spotlight, but also visual artists. We were truly grateful to the people at KCDHH who helped make this happen.

2004, "IMAGES AND VISIONS OF A CULTURE"; ST. PAUL, MINNESOTA*

There was a major group show by 14 Deaf/De'VIA artists held at the aND Gallery in St. Paul in April 2004. The gallery, run by a hearing owner who has a sister that works with deaf people, hosted the showing with the help of Brenda Schertz. I was not there nor was my artwork, so I must again abstain from commenting on the events. The show was part of a month-long celebration of Deaf/De'VIA artwork, including presentations by Deborah Sonnestrahl. Although the gallery presented the show in an impressively designed manner, there were a few art critics.

Mary Thornley, an artist who painted *Milan, Italy, 1880*, read an article which quoted deaf artists. The article (found at *http://news.minnesota. publicradio.org/features/2004/04/30_tundeln_deafart/*) was a preview rather than a review or critique. Thornley wrote in a weekly column, "Well, yawn, how many times have I read this or something like it in my many years as an artist? For the same number of years as I have yearned for a more sophisticated understanding, a treatment that does not address me as other or odd, that does not describe me as silent or my art works as a replacement for hearing, any more than a hearing artist's work is a replacement for deafness." Thornley added, "During Deaf Way II the Featured Artists Committee contacted art critics in the D.C. area and asked them to write up our exhibits. All refused. One said it would be like telling someone in a wheelchair how to walk!" (*The Tactile Mind Weekly*, Week #59, June 8, 2004).

THE FUTURE OF DE'VIA

The Art Critic. Why are we waiting for art critics to finally write about the work of a De'VIA artist (or artists)? We artists have discussed several times about why we couldn't ask an art critic to come to write about our shows. This would be a great help documents for supporting our manifesto, and we still have not accomplished this yet.

Betty recently has said that we are still not finished with making the definition clear of what or how De'VIA is. Paul Johnston once said something that I never thought of before: we don't have to wait for an art critic to volunteer in appearing at a show and writing it down—this would take forever before it'd happen. What we should do instead, Paul said, is to hire an art critic who would be glad to write whatever we want. We also can do critique ourselves, like the French Impressionists or any group did.

Let us, any of us—experts, artists, art lovers or De'VIA followers—start writing or saying about your or other artists' works. Don't wait for them to tell you. If you don't want to write, sign to someone and have him or her write for you! The shelf containing information on De'VIA is almost empty—there are too few resources. We need to fill that shelf so that someday, an art critic or two will pick them up and learn about De'VIA.

The De'VIA artists. I encourage artists to continue exploring and find ways to critique our work. I recommend that, for the future when artists meet for exhibitions, retreats, or workshops, they sit down and open up a more honest dialogue without fear about what common grounds we have in our works. We should be cautious not to discuss about marketing our work, which often creates possible divisions among us. Marketing could be discussed in a specific seminar, not mixed with the spiritual aspect of the arts. Let us focus on the spirit of De'VIA that will bring us further exploration into the center of creativity.

We should also be aware that considering English the superior language can create strong divisions. Being open-minded and sensitive, ASL will do perfectly fine, regardless of where artists are in fluency at English. Do not try to sign in English. If you want to communicate in English order, you may ask someone to write for you as you sign. English is best left to spoken or written methods.

The most optimal leader for a seminar would be a person like a Deaf art historian, art expert, or even a yoga teacher. Find a place far from civilization to harmonize with each other, and to realize that there is no harm around us. We can go beyond and have fun in new discoveries about our Deaf Culture and ourselves.

Last, but not least, for any of you who wish to expand on or learn more specifications about the De'VIA manifesto, I recommend that you study the similar genre of De'VIA in other countries more. We shall not focus on what we have here in America only. Like any scientific method, you will need to compare with others to define your own. You will be amazed at what you find, and will come to learn about and appreciate De'VIA so much more.

ACKNOWLEDGMENTS

I would be remiss if I did not mention individuals that I have been working with for years in ongoing discussions of what De'VIA really is.

Dr. Paul Johnston, artist, close colleague, and my old friend, who is now teaching Art and De'VIA at Gallaudet University.

Dr. Betty G. Miller, the Mother of De'VIA and an old friend of my deaf sisters, who has had a long artistic career in Washington, D.C.

Dr. Deborah (Sonnenstrahl) Meranski, who is beloved and remembered for her many years of teaching art history at Gallaudet. She is also the author of the newly published book by DawnSignPress, _Deaf Artists in America: Colonial to Contemporary_. She is currently enjoying retirement in Florida.

Brenda Schertz, curator of many exhibitions, especially the Deaf Art Exhibition on Tour in 2000–2001. She now works as an ASL instructor and lecturer on Deaf Culture at the University of Southern Maine, and continues her love of art.

And those, also, whom I am proud to have met and/or had our works displayed together—I consider them very important active hands in helping De'VIA shape up in America to be what it is today:
The late Harry William of Southern California
The late Frank Allen Paul of San Diego, California
Ann Silver of Seattle, Washington
Tony McGregor of Austin, Texas
Alex Wilhite of Pinehurst, North Carolina
William Spark of Winston-Salem, North Carolina
Susan Dupor of Delavan, Wisconsin
Iris Aranda of Kenosha, Wisconsin (originally from Panama)

Mary Thornley of Alexandria, Virginia
Guy Wonder of San Francisco, California
Ron Trumble of Berkeley, California
Jeff Carroll of Cincinnati, Ohio
Paula Grcevie of Rochester, New York
Rita Straubhaar of Rochester, New York
Morris Broderson of Los Angeles, California
Charles Wildbank of Long Island, New York
Joan Popovich-Kutscher of Orange County, California
Israeli Uzi Buzgalo of Boulder, Colorado

There are also so many new emerging De'VIA artists that I truly am excited to meet and see their works spread around. I wish I could name all but once again, please forgive me if I didn't name everyone that has eye-touched and hand-touched my life as an artist. We are like one big family, expressing our Deaf Experience in Visual Art forms. And those have given us a major awakening, the international Deaf Visual Artists, especially the United Kingdom and Russia artists, as I have mentioned above in my presentation. And special thanks goes to Trudy Suggs of T.S. Writing Service for editing this article.

LIST OF CONTRIBUTING ARTISTS

Perspective of Deaf Culture through Art, 1993: James Canning, Randy Dunham, Susan Dupor, Betty G Miller, Eddie Swayze, Mary Thornley, Sandi Inches Vasnick, Chuck Baird

Deaf Studies Conf. IV in Boston, 1995: Susan Dupor, Lee S. Ivey, Betty G. Miller, Ralph R. Miller, Elizabeth A. Morris, Ann Silver, Marjorie Stout, Eddie Swayze, Mary J. Thornley, Harry R. Williams, Chuck Baird

Deaf Studies Conf. VI in Oakland, 1999: Irene Bartok, Jeff Carroll, Connie Clanton, Susan Dupor, Paul Johnston, Tony Landon McGregor, Betty G. Miller, Victor Notaro,Joan Popovich-Kutscher,Tracey Salaway, Orkid Sassouni, Paul Setzer, Ann Silver, Ethan Sinnott, Dawn Skwersky, Robin Taylor, Mary J. Thornley, Ron Trumble Guy Wonder, Chuck Baird

Deaf Artists Retreat in Harrodabury, 1999: Betty G. Miller, Brenda Schertz, Steven Barabas, William Wombles, Jeff Carroll, Betty Taylor, Beulah Hester, Barbie Harris, Chuck Baird

Deaf Art Exhibit on Tour: Elements of a Culture Vision by Deaf Artists, 2000–2001: Irene Bartok, Uzi Buzaglo, Susan Dupor, Paul Johnston Thad C. Martin, Tony Landon McGregor, Betty G. Miller, Joan Popovich-Kutscher, Orkid Sassouni, Ann Silver, Marjorie Stout, Robin Taylor, Sandi Inches, Alex Wilhite, Harry R. Williams, and Chuck Baird.

Seeing Through Deaf Eyes, 2001: Susan Dupor, Paula Grcevic, Ann Silver, Charles Wildbank, Paul Johnson, Mary Kiejbus, Betty Miller, Alex Whilhite, Oleg Golovushkin, Tony Landon McGregor, Orkid Sassouni, Rita Straubhaar, Morris Broderson, and Chuck Baird

Dyer Arts Center Inaugural Invitational Exhibit, 2001–2002: Morris Broderson, Paula Grcevic, Rita Straubhaar, Ron Trumble, Charles Wildbank, Carl Zollo, and Chuck Baird.

"Works by Deaf Women" at Ceres Gallery in Soho, New York City: Janet Ahren, Irene Bartok, Claire Bergman, Susan Dupor, Lesley Kushner, Orkid Sassouni, *Dana Simon, Robin Taylor, Mary Thornley

Deaf Way II Art Exhibitions in Washington D.C. 2002: Beniam Afeworque, (Ethiopia) Hilary Allumaga, (Nigeria) Mitko Androv, (France) Iris Aranda, (USA) Rubbena Aurangzeb-Tariq, (UK) Andrey Averjanov, (Russia) Tesfaye Tsadik Bantiwalu, (Ethiopia) Ilya Barabulya, (Russia) Sander Blondeel (Beligium) Sergei Bondarenko, (Russia) Jeff B. Carroll, (USA) Yuri Chernuha, (Russia) Jose de la Cruz (Philippines) Susan Dupor, (USA) Carlo Fantauzzi, (Italy) Dietr Fricke (Germany) Gloria Amparo Gonzalez, (Columbia) Xiaodi Gao, (China) Ixchel Solis Garcia, (Mexico) Paula a. Grcevic, (USA) Johnston B. Grindstaff, (USA) Mingxia He and Xiaoning Zhou, (China) Paul Johnson, (USA) Abelardo Parra Jimenez, (Columbia) Victor Karepov, (Russia) Julia Keenan, (UK) Nam Ko, (China) Zhang Li, (China) Dennison Long, (USA) Jianyi Lu, (China) Stanislav Lubina, (Slovak) Yu Xiang Ma, (China) Gary Mayers, (USA) Michelle McAuliffe, (USA) Niall McCorkack, (UK) Tony Landon McGregor, (USA) Afework Mengesha, (Ethiopia) Anatoly Mikljaev, (Russia) Eiichi Mitsui, (Japan) Tommy Motswai (South Africa) Karim Nada, (Egypt) Kevin O'Connor, (UK) Jeannette Patrice (USA) M. Ramalingam, (India) Babara Rashid, (UK) Colin Redwood (UK) Damien Robinson, (UK) Cao Ruiqiang, (China) Christopher Sacre, (UK) Orkid Sassouni, (USA) MJ Seltzer, (USA) Paul Setzer, (USA) Yunhua Shi, (China) Ann Silver, (USA) Xiaoming Shu, (China) Rita Straubhaar, (USA) Alexei Svetlov, (Austria) Mary Thorney, (USA) Judith Treesberg and Betty G. Miller, (USA) Alexey Utkin, (Kazakhstan) Mary Weinberger, (UK) Alex Wilhite, (USA) Peter Zacsko, (Sweden) Hong Ze, (China) Han Dong, (China) Chuck Baird, (USA)

Second Deaf Artists Retreat in Harrodsburg, 2003: Betty Taylor, Beulah Hester, Barbie Harris, Juan Hoffman, Roy Ricco, Victor Notaro, Dick Moore, Paul Johnson, Jeff Carroll, Peter Cook, Pinky Aiello, Kevin Kreutzer, Anita Dowd, Alex Wilhite, Chuck Baird

"Image and Visions of A Culture" at aND Gallery in St. Paul, Minnesota, 2004: Iris Aranda, Loretta Bebeau, Morris Broderson, Susan Dupor, Marian Lucas, Tony McGregor, Orkid Sassouni, Ann Silver, Mary Silvesri, Rita Straubhaar, Mary Thornley, Cecily Whitworth, Charles Wildbank, Alex Wilhite

ABOUT THE AUTHOR

 *Chuck Baird has been a painter since his teen years and has led a distin-guished career, most notably as the official curator of Deaf Way II art exhibitions in the Washington D.C. area in 2003. He has served as artist in residency at over thirty schools, has been involved with the National Theatre for the Deaf for a total of ten years, has participated in dozens of exhibits, and has been commissioned many times. Having recently com-pleted his role in the play, "Nothing Sweet in my Ear," at the Mixed Blood Theatre in Minneapolis, MN, he is settling in Austin, Texas, rolling up his sleeves and getting his hands wet with paint.*

"Carousel Dragon"

Courtesy Sara Stallard

Deaf Narratives and 'Deaf Life': An Integrated Look

FRANK BECHTER

Frank Bechter is a PH.D. *candidate in sociocultural and linguistic anthropology at the University of Chicago, Chicago, Illinois.*

At the closing dinner for UVSC's Deaf Studies *Today!* conference, one of my tablemates told a striking story, a true story recounting an event from earlier that day. Namely, not only had Keith Gamache's presentation on the role of etymology in the study of ASL been jam-packed with people, but, in fact, the president of UVSC himself, William Sederburg, had even crouched down on his hands and knees to *crawl into the room!*

This kind of event is seldom narrated in the deaf community. In this essay, however, I wish to relate that event—Gamache's lecture—to deaf narrative in general, i.e., to the logic of deaf narrative as a "system of genres," in which each genre bears a definable set of formal and concep-tual relations to all other genres, and where the system is understood to function in the deaf community's sociocultural reproduction. Preliminar-ily, let me simply note that what made this event narratable is, of course, not the crawling alone (there were others who had crawled in, including me). Rather, implicitly in the telling, it was to be understood that the person doing the crawling was the hearing president of a major public institution. The most important official at UVSC, a hearing man having no extensive exposure to the deaf, did not hesitate to crawl into a deaf lecture, on deaf language, and delivered in masterful deaf language.

And he did this not because he had to, or because he had been tricked or beaten down into submission, but rather because of his own interest and excitement (so it readily seemed to us all at the table) about the content of the lecture, the skill of its presenter (an instructor at his university), and the momentum of the conference as a whole. Gamache's lecture, and the unstated logic of my tablemate's story, I will try to show here—although this suggestion may seem strange at first—is actually like the abstract compositional logic of an "ABC story."

TWO "FORMAL STUDIES": ABC AND PERSONIFICATION GENRES

In a forthcoming article, "The deaf convert culture, and its lessons for Deaf Theory" (following from Gallaudet's 2002 *Deaf Studies Think Tank*), I contrast ABC stories to "personification stories," a deaf narrative form which has not received focused attention in the literature. Bahan (2001) grants personification stories generic status, but personification is often mentioned in the literature simply as a technique of signing in general— "almost everything has a character," says a tip-sheet on ASL storytelling collected in my fieldwork at Gallaudet. Valli, in an overview of "Artistic Expression in ASL" (his categories are Storytelling, Creative Art, Deafsong, and Poetry), lists personification along with simile, metaphor, irony and symbols under his final subcategory for Poetry, "other elements" (n.d., one-page xerox). (Valli lists ABC stories under "creative art." He divides "storytelling" into personal stories, paraphrase of written stories, adapted stories, and original stories.)

Yet personification stories do comprise a distinct narrative genre. My corpus contains over 35 examples, the most paradigmatic being Paul Johnston's "The Pinball," performed at the 1998 TISLR conference. While the signer's stylistic prowess at personification is central to how this genre functions, I wish to show here that privileging this technique as the endpoint of analysis compromises our general understanding of the form as it relates to other genres, and as it functions in the ethical world of the deaf. The genre is stylistic, but rather than focusing on this stylistic aspect, it is more analytically productive to consider the personification genre in terms of its archetype protagonist. In this way, and perhaps surprisingly, this little-studied genre actually becomes the centerpiece of a systemic analysis of deaf narrative as a whole, following Bahan's call for a "systematic study that...collectively categorize[s] the various genres" (2001:13). While simple in abstract form, personification stories are a prism through which to conceptualize the structure of other deaf narrative genres, even complex forms.[1]

A personification protagonist can be a coffee cup, an airplane, a football, a table, a dish, a piece of chewing gum, a flower, or any number of objects. While the abstract characteristics attributed to these protagonists may vary to some degree—e.g., the golf ball personified by Bill Ennis on his *Live at SMI* video does seem to know that it is a golf ball, and, to some extent, can "speak," and even admonishes the golfer for cheating-nonetheless, the archetype protagonist for the genre is "the pinball," an entirely "voiceless" entity. The protagonist is trapped within a game it didn't design, and has no dialogue with any other character, nor with the entity controlling its fate. The dictator of the protagonist's fate, it is further to be understood, does not "recognize" it in terms of the pathos the storyteller's audience sees, nor, indeed, does the protagonist recognize itself. That is, unlike the golf ball in Ennis's story, Johnston's pinball does not realize that it is a pinball. It does not understand that it is a specific kind of thing in the world whose role is to play a part in someone else's coherent "system," in someone else's valued pursuit. Indeed, while the protagonist does not recognize itself, the *audience* of the genre has the specific task of recognizing it. The audience must guess the protagonist's identity based on the environment represented as moving around it and impacting it. Peter Cook (1998) prefaces his personification of a bowling ball simply with the title-card: "Guess what?" This differential between the pinball's recognition, and the player's, and the audience's, suggests that a fundamental property of the personification protagonist is "relative recognition."

Although the pinball is entirely constrained, without arms or legs or any ability to control its fate, it is possible to model a "relative" nature to this constraint by noting that the character's own boundaries impose a countervailing constraint against the game. Though fingers are shown to penetrate the "skull" of Cook's bowling ball, nonetheless, it would seem that these fingers do not fully penetrate the protagonist's "brain." The bowling ball never *thinks* like a bowler. In one sense, as discussed, this is a sign of the protagonist's own lack of self-recognition (it does not think like a bowler because it doesn't know it's a bowling ball). But, on the other hand, the differential between the bowling ball and the implied bowler indicates that the totalizing system in which the protagonist is trapped has itself been somehow constrained from completely defining it. There is "something" to the bowling ball, as it were, "before it is a bowling ball."

Political voice is thus framed as a "relative" concept at base-relating some pre-articulated state of existence to some possible individual capacity and social sphere wherein that state would be relatively articulable. When Cook's bowling ball "waves its hands" frantically in front of the bowling pins it finds itself rushing towards, exclaiming "no, no, no!" with its mouth, the presumption is that this expression is not actually a "shout," but merely the type of shout that a bowling ball would give if it only could. Though it does not think like a bowler (it has no desire to impact the pins), the bowling ball, as it were, does not really "have hands" to speak with. Similarly, though Ennis's golf ball does seem to have hands, scolding the golfer with a "tsk, tsk" gesture when the latter moves the ball, the golfer is not represented as having seen this. Thus, even when a personification protagonist can articulate its thoughts (even when they're in league with the game), it is not "heard." It has "no audience" in its own sphere of life. Indeed, though it would be possible—artistically speaking—for the pinball to make "asides" to the audience, it never does. In essence, it does not know that it has an audience, either the storytelling audience or any kind of transcendent audience.

The pinball's relative position along a continuum of constraint, recognition, and voice is best modeled by comparing this archetype protagonist to the ABC storyteller. Each ABC story's plot, of course, has its own protagonist. But considering the genre as a whole, it is actually the teller whose ordeal is the most relevant drama that the audience attends to, and who might therefore be considered the genre's real "protagonist." Via this perspective, the genres emerge as exact opposites, as summarized in the following table.

	Personification Genre	ABC Genre
relative constraint	• in game, trapped • playing piece • not penetrated • endures constraints	• in game, by choice • player • not penetrated (unless fails) • penetrates constraints
relative recognition	• no self-recognition • teller sees protagonist trapped in valued system; isn't blinded by received value-orientation • some audience members discern protagonist's identity • constraints made visible • audience discerns via story	• full self-recognition • teller sees ASL trapped in alphabet system; isn't blinded by received value-orientation • some audience members realize protagonist's identity • constraints made invisible • audience "fooled" via story
relative voice	• voiceless • no hands • mastered by constraints • never thinks like player • no audience	• voiced • signing hands • masters/transforms constraints • never thinks "with letters" • maximal "deaf" audience
companions	• alone	• center of community

Table 1: Emerging Personification and ABC Genres

The pinball and ABC storyteller both face constraints, but the ABC storyteller masters these constraints, and can do so precisely because he or she "has hands" and knows how to "speak" with them. While the pinball is trapped within a game it didn't design and has no audience in its sphere, the ABC storyteller is likewise confined, but it is in a game that the deaf community itself has designed, and he or she has chosen to engage with it. Meanwhile, the teller of a personification story has, beforehand, played the part of an "audience" to the entity he or she wishes to represent, "seeing it" where others in the world would not. Similarly, the ABC storyteller must "see ASL" trapped within the manual alphabet, and the audience of an ABC story must learn to see the ABC storyteller as such.

Over and against the narrative the storyteller skillfully provides, the audience must both see this narrative and see past it, such that, ultimately, their attention is not distracted from "the real drama" at issue—namely, a deaf protagonist's "transcendence" of the constraints it faces. Thus, while the pinball's audience guesses its identity by virtue of seeing the constraints of the "generic system" that defines it, the ABC storyteller, in contrast, actually makes constraints *invisible* to the audience. Audience members' consciousness is drawn into various "generic systems"—"typical" spheres of activity whose dramas and "values" we have internalized to the extent that they dictate what we perceive.

Thus, audiences of both genres must "see" their protagonists specifically "when others would not." Implicitly in the performance, there must be the possibility that some audience members will not decipher the personified object, or will not realize that the story they have just witnessed was, in fact, proceeding under radical formal constraint. If it is easy to see the alphabet, if it is easy to recognize every event affecting a personification protagonist (whose identity thus becomes "obvious"), the value of the achievement by both kinds of storytellers is made null. The value of an ABC story is similarly nullified if the storyteller skips letters. This is equivalent to the teller being "penetrated" by his or her constraints, rather than mastering them.

The productivity of this view is that it seems to account for properties of deaf representation that other views cannot. It is quite common, for example, for signers to account for the personification genre in terms of stylistic mastery. It is true that the form requires great signing skill, and, as just detailed, this skill is even intrinsic to the form (a poorly told personification story is hardly a personification story at all). And yet, when this stylistic reckoning of the genre is made central, the analysis cannot be applied to other forms of deaf representation. Pictured in the Autumn 2002 edition of *The Tactile Mind,* a deaf literary journal, Sara Stallard's photographic piece, "carousel dragon," (page 38) is essentially a personi-fication story. And yet there is no signing involved in the representation. Putting the dragon in central focus while the rest of the carousel blurs by is a challenge (just as it is a challenge to represent a pinball's life in sign language); and yet, if this were the sole motivation, Stallard could have pursued this technical challenge with the child riding the dragon as the focal point. And yet, far from doing this, Stallard somehow regiments the child to the blurred background as well, against which the dragon appears.

What explains the photo's overarching composition is a logic whereby a "deaf life" emerges only in relation to an alternate encompassing scheme of value, a value scheme which, to most, makes the life trapped within it invisible. *To most,* the carousel dragon's plight is invisible—"but not to this photographer." (The photographer is an ideal "deaf audience" to the world of value.) Through the deaf photographer's lens, we see that what might have first appeared to us as a menacing and fearsome expres-sion-and might still appear to us this way if we do not "see" clearly—has somehow transformed itself into a fearful one, a kind of inarticulable cry—a cry that would occur if the dragon only knew this were possible.

In contemplating the compositional logic of the photo, we might ask: "What if the child riding the dragon is deaf?" The answer, I suggest, is that this does not matter. Even if the child is "actually deaf," there is still only one deaf character in the photo: the dragon. Against the photo's protagonist, everything else becomes "non-deaf," even a deaf signer. As a "deaf life," the dragon is defined against the value system that would make anyone-hearing or deaf-want to ride it. Interestingly, even if the viewer recognizes and "identifies with" the plight of the carousel dragon (just as the storyteller quite literally "identifies with" the pinball), this identification does not mean that the viewer of the photograph (or even Stallard herself) is actually against carousel rides.

The dragon is oppressed, but it is oppressed by a way of valuing the world that audience members affirm. This is fundamental to personifica-tion stories. To understand the plight of the deaf, this genre asserts, is to understand what it would be like for a carousel dragon to try to convince us all to shut down the circus.[2]

Protagonists of deaf narratives as a whole, I am arguing, emerge via a deaf "worldview," a distinct way of intuiting the composition of the world. This worldview is fundamental, and, as such, underlies other forms of deaf representation, such as Stallard's photo. It functions to define deaf protagonists relationally. The logic of relation is not only between the deaf life and what encompasses it, but fundamentally includes the *question* of whether that life is "seen."

Thus, what makes the carousel dragon "deaf" is not the fact that it is a carousel dragon. Carousel dragons, themselves, are not "deaf." Rather, what makes the dragon deaf is that it can be understood—and indeed "seen"—in a particular way. When "seen" by the deaf audience as an invisible protagonist, hidden by, or emerging only through, a value scheme which is not its own, it is then that the dragon becomes "deaf," i.e., it becomes "deaf" by the very nature of this construal. Thus, similarly, in the deaf cultural world, what makes a person deaf is not merely that he or she is deaf. And yet, neither is it necessarily that he or she signs, or values the deaf community. Rather, it is that he or she can be understood in the same way that the dragon and ABC storyteller can be understood. This is why hearing people, for example, no matter how deep their commitment to the deaf community, are never understood as "deaf." They may be said to "sign deaf," or even to "think deaf," but this is not the same thing.

FIVE GENRES WITH REAL-WORLD DEAF PROTAGONISTS

The stylistic reckoning of ABC and personification stories follows from their intrinsic stylistic character—it is this which stands out about them for their practitioners—and, more generally, from the central importance of signing skill within the deaf community. From the standpoint of scholarly treatment, this importance is privileged in the overarching reckoning of "sign language literature," i.e., a framing of the object of analysis which, in its nature, trains our eye on aspects of signing per se, rightly to be distinguished from the formal aspects of, say, English literature. In terms of this approach, it makes sense that "Deafsong" would receive its own category, since "song" and "narrative" are divergent in stylistic character. Similarly, it makes sense that "narratives of personal experience"—comprising the vast majority of deaf stories—would receive little formal attention. Such narratives do not aspire to high literary form—by definition, anyone can do them—and their stylistic character can be so negligible (at least in principle) that it is easy to imagine them being conveyed in writing rather than in sign language. It is impossible to imagine this for ABC or personification stories, or for "cinematographic" stories, or ASL poetry, or high achievements in ASL storytelling usually categorized as "original works." Style is also negligible in most narratives considered "folklore," which also receive their own separate category in contemporary analyses.

Above, I have tried to show that two very different stylistic narrative forms are systematically related to one another ("exact opposites") when the abstract properties of their protagonists is considered. This analysis argues against the position that the content of sign language storytelling is unimportant, doing so in part by defining "content" at a higher level of compositional structure. I have further tried to show that this compositional analysis, wherein an audience member's ability to "see" a protagonist is central, also accounts for other forms of deaf representation in systematic fashion, which, substantively, bear nothing in common with these narrative forms. The meaning of "deaf" that seems to emerge from all three representations, when considered in this way, bears no necessary relation to signing or to other familiar attributes of real-world deaf lives. Indeed, their narrative subject matter usually concerns elements from what might be considered the "non-deaf" world, figuring the meaning of "deaf" in relation to this. Although it is not possible to consider all genres of deaf narrative within the space of this essay, in what follows I will try to show that this compositional approach allows us to integrate key forms of deaf narrative which involve real-world deaf characters.

The pinball is "trapped," but resilient, never fully "penetrated" by the logic of the game. These two principles, I suggest, define two key genres of deaf narrative having real-world deaf protagonists, which can be illustrated with two stories signed by Lynn Jacobowitz on the ASL *Storytime* series (1991), "My First Day in Italy" and "At the Airport." The first of these is an archetype "deaf travel story." Of course, you don't have to be deaf to tell a story about a trip you've taken, but deaf travel stories are structured in a particular way. Most importantly, protagonists are always with a *deaf signing companion*. Thus, the genre contrasts in two key ways with the personification genre.

In the first instance, the protagonist is not "trapped within a game," but rather is "traveling." But, secondly, we see that the deaf traveler does not choose to travel the world *alone*. The first thing that a pinball does when it escapes its trappings, we might say, is find a deaf signing companion; this is fundamental to its successful engagement with the world, at least as modeled in this form. Jacobowitz represents herself in the story always with her traveling companion—when exchanging money, interacting with the cab-driver, walking the city, or looking for more Deaf signers—in each instance "touching base" with the deaf companion. Interestingly, provided that the protagonist is teamed up with a deaf companion, we find that she immediately proceeds, like the ABC storyteller, to enter into "games," or systemic spaces of relative confinement, wherein the integrity of her boundaries is at issue.

The brief money-exchange episode is a simple instance of this, but, more impressively, Jacobowitz narrates her decision to investigate an unknown public facility, which turns out to be a bathroom—a "water closet," or w-c. Inside the WC, the protagonist investigates an unknown system—a "bidet"—which specifically requires that her boundaries be compromised. That she is splashed with water when she least expects it (at least, this is how the story is told) is essentially a humorous episode, from which the deaf protagonist comes away happy and back to her deaf companion. She has been "exposed," but not for anyone to see. And she has in fact chosen this, being the "player" in this game.

A second deaf travel story on the *ASL Storytime* series, Mike Kemp's "See Now, Never See Again," similarly follows the protagonist's successful navigation through a foreign town with his deaf companion, ultimately leading them both to a willing deaf tour guide and, through him, to the local deaf club, where they meet scores upon scores of deaf people, thus emphasizing this underlying structural principle to the genre.

The centrality of deaf companionship to the travel story is best evidenced by considering the other Jacobowitz narrative. At the Paris airport, Jacobowitz makes it all the way to the check-in counter with her deaf companion, but, at this point, rather than signing, the deaf companion (this time a French friend) must speak orally to the attendant. Jacobowitz goes to where the attendant directs her, and despite her friend's best efforts in oral voice back at the desk, she finds herself isolated in an inspection room. The story proceeds to account for how the protagonist ("trapped" in this room "alone") must open her bags for these non-deaf officials, presenting her dirty laundry piece by piece for their scrutiny. After being made to expose her "insides" in this way several times, and a final inspection in which a metal detector is represented to have been thrust around her, and under her nose, and even into her mouth, the result is that the protagonist misses her flight. As she witnesses the plane taking off through the window, a tear emerges from her eye, but, in a willed reversal of this internal boundary transgression, Jacobowitz represents herself as "pulling her emotion back downwards, inside," with a sign iconically representing this. This latter sign is important, I suggest, as it figures the maintenance of the protagonist's internal "integrity" (meant in the physical sense of that term). Like the pinball, she is somehow still resilient—maintaining her "deaf spirit" against the relative boundary penetrations perpetrated on her, and the "entrapments" that have subverted her "travel."

Jacobowitz's airport story, at least the aspect of it that I have described here, falls within a category I call the "disgust story," named in this way because of the sign DISGUST that often marks it at the beginning or at the end. (Jacobowitz does not use this sign, and, indeed, the full extent of the story cannot be summed up by this label.) Disgust stories figure deaf domains being penetrated by non-deaf forces. The domain may be the protagonist's body, or mind, or a space which stands as a boundary for the protagonist, such as an elevator which opens in the back when the protagonist is clawing at the front, or a hotel room which a hotel manager barges into, or a larger forum containing many deaf people which, in some sense, a non-deaf entity is thought to violate.

Disgust stories tend to involve the protagonist unwittingly "revealing its raw insides," as when the deaf character in the famous elevator story, just noted, screams in terror in the elevator and claws frantically at the door, only later to realize that this event of personal "disintegration" has probably been witnessed from behind by hearing people in the library. The uncontrolled breaking forth of the protagonist's insides mirrors the logic of penetration from the outside: boundaries are transgressed inwardly, or outwardly, or both. As with the pinball and ABC genres, an under-lying principle of the disgust genre thus lies in the question of being seen—in this case, being seen in a state of "disintegration." This is why, in Jacobowitz's story, the protagonist "pulls her emotions back down" before returning from the window.

With penetration advanced as a key principle, the well-known deaf honeymoon story now appears in an interesting light. Bienvenu (1989) paraphrases the story as follows:

> A Deaf couple arrives at a motel for their honeymoon. After unpacking, the nervous husband goes out to get a drink. When he returns to the motel, he realizes that he has forgotten the room number. It is dark outside and all the rooms look identical. He walks to his car, and leans on the horn. He then waits for the lights to come on in the rooms of the waking angry hearing guests. All the rooms are lit up except his, where his Deaf wife is waiting for him!

While disgust stories narrate deaf protagonists being penetrated by hear-ing forces, the opposite takes place in the honeymoon story: it is now hearing characters that are penetrated by the deaf protagonist. The deaf husband finds his deaf wife by penetrating the boundaries of hearing characters—penetrating their rooms and their ears, ultimately control-ling their movement so that he may witness it. And, interestingly, this results in the deaf protagonist penetrating the room of his deaf spouse for none other than their honeymoon night. The honeymoon story is a combination of two distinct deaf narrative genres: the "zap" story (to borrow Bienvenu's term) and what I call "deaf intimacy" stories. Deaf penetrates hearing, and then deaf penetrates deaf.

Bienvenu uses the "zap" label to refer to the tale of a deaf signer who signs a conversation into a regular payphone at a restaurant. "When the deaf group left the restaurant," Bienvenu paraphrases, "they were amused to see the hearing people run over to inspect the phone." It is not simply that the hearing people were fooled (and, in this sense, "penetrated"), but, as with the hearing people in the motel, their movements are actually controlled by the deaf. Moreover, the raw insides of these antagonists (who had been mocking the deaf group earlier) are exposed: they are seen "running over" to the phone. The fact that the deaf protagonist is in a group is fundamental: zap stories are possible when deaf characters are together (as in the logic of travel stories), but disgust stories happen when the deaf protagonist is alone.

A more impressive example of the zap genre is Bill Ennis's "Mississippi Squirrel Revival" (1992) a narrative performed with a song-like cadence and verse structure, and thus suggesting itself as a form of "Deafsong." Yet reckoned in terms of its protagonist, it is an instance of the "travel" form culminating in an extravaganza of "zap" episodes.

It is an interesting travel story because, here, the traveling companion of the deaf protagonist (supposedly, Ennis as a young boy visiting his grandmother's house) turns out to be a squirrel. That is, Ennis, as narrator, constructs the squirrel as if it were a deaf companion, referring to it even as "my best friend." (There is deep irony here, no doubt.) Carrying the squirrel with him to the stuffy church on Sunday, the protagonist releases it from its box, and the squirrel rushes to the stage and proceeds to scurry up the pantlegs and skirts of various hearing church-members in the choir, unseen by them. In each case, they dance, spin, and sing out wildly, believing themselves to have been penetrated by the holy spirit, and openly confess their sins. Calling out their infidelities, this leads scores of others in the pews to stream forward and beg forgiveness and pledge themselves to missionary work in the deepest reaches of Africa. The logic of penetration yields a mirror logic of internal "disintegration," revealing what turn out to be the extensive iniquities of seemingly upstanding hearing people.

The "deaf intimacy" motif (deaf penetrates deaf) is best illustrated not by the honeymoon story, which depicts a universally approved form of intimacy, but rather by narratives where this motif might be negatively viewed. That is, when deaf domains are penetrated by hearing forces, the audience does not laugh, but rather sympathizes. When hearing domains are penetrated by the deaf, audiences chuckle—a deep justice has been done. But what about when domains of deaf protagonists are abruptly transgressed by deaf forces? As it turns out, even when the deaf protagonist is specifically trying to avoid this, it doesn't matter—deaf audiences read the event as funny, indeed as quite wonderful.

In Sam Supalla's "The Hand is Quicker than the Ear" (Rose 1992; cf. Kelleher 1986), deaf kids stay up late in their dormitory past their appointed bedtime, always having a special lookout system whereby they can run back and jump into their beds if the supervisor is seen coming. When the supervisor is deaf, they are sure they'll be fine since he can't even hear them running around. But it turns out they're wrong. The deaf supervisor strides over to the protagonist's bed, abruptly pulls off the blanket and thrusts his hand under the protagonist's shirt, placing his hand on the young protagonist's heart—i.e., the very core of him—to feel it beating hard from having just been playing. The story closes with this motif, and the forceful violation of the protagonist's space is not reacted to with disgust. Rather, it is a glorious event and the audience laughs with a kind of joy.

Disgust, zap, and intimacy stories form a subsystem of genres all based on penetration:

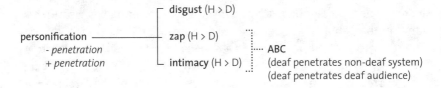

Methodologically, this logic was specified for these genres before it was considered in the personification and ABC forms. Starting from scratch, stories marked by the DISGUST sign were first grouped and compared, and this led to specifying boundary-penetration as central to them. In turn, this led to putting more stories into the group which were not marked by this sign but which manifested similar logics of penetration while also having the same type of audience reaction.

For example, once after viewing two improvised stories recorded at Gallaudet's Center for ASL Literacy a year before my research, the storyteller saw me the next day and asked which was my favorite. When I specified the one in which his grade school interpreter had habitually intervened upon his ability to interact with other students on his own, he simply nodded and signed DISGUST. He had not used this sign, however, in the telling. With this motif in mind, the observation of D > H forms (the opposite motif) and D > D forms became possible, and the relevance of this logic to other forms became investigable. Personification stories, for example, are typically "comedies." But in examining a personification narrative where a flower is cut and put into a vase, it became clear that this was not a comedy. This led to the observation that the typical personification protagonist is not penetrated. The ABC storyteller, meanwhile, penetrates a non-deaf system (the alphabet), and penetrates a relative number of audience members by signing and narrating with such mastery that his or her constraints are not seen.

Interestingly, there is a kind of "pinball story" where the protagonist is not penetrated, but which is not a comedy. The protagonist is a real-world deaf person "trapped within a game." An example is a deaf employee at the Post Office who has worked there for many years, but has never been promoted, even after approaching the management and the union. In this case, unlike the pinball, the protagonist understands the situation and "has arms and legs" and can move. But, unlike the ABC storyteller, the protagonist plays by the rules of the system. I.e., it is as if the protagonist tries to tell an ABC story by fingerspelling words. Speaking in the "alphabet" of the game in which he or she is trapped, the protagonist gets nowhere. This, of course, is not the employee's fault, and that is the point of the genre. The structure of the genre—the one-by-one listing of all the appropriate steps that the deaf protagonist goes through—might be said to articulate the view that deaf voice cannot be achieved in the world "as is."

I was introduced to this genre when pursuing stories about "deaf people overcoming obstacles." I had read this phrase in the literature, and so I asked about it in formal interviews. One of the first people I asked, a Gallaudet student from a deaf family, readily replied, "Well, actually, more than overcoming the obstacles, it's about failing to overcome them" (GO-OVER and FAIL were juxtaposed in a single diagrammatic construct). This response came much to my surprise, and I asked for clarification, which resulted in a long discussion with several examples. I asked for a name for the genre, and the student thought and replied, "....HATE STORIES." I have kept this label, as it seems to capture an interactive component of the form. When viewing a hate story, audience members are required, more or less, to subtly interject "how awful!" (AWFUL!) at certain points. The phonological, semantic, and pragmatic affinity between the signs glossed as HATE and AWFUL seems to make this label for the genre particularly appropriate.

Mandatory audience interjections in this conversational form give expression to the logic specified for personification and ABC stories, i.e., a differential logic of audience apperception, which also implies a logic of storyteller apperception. The material forms of these genres, in other words, cannot be specified in terms of the textual substance of the story itself, but rather must be specified over the entire storytelling forum, the social-interactive structure that unites storyteller, tale, and audience. Bahan (2001) foregrounds this as central to deaf narrative, and it is definitional of a Bakhtinian "dialogic" approach to literary texts (1981). Hate stories include this differential logic in their form ("does the audience member see the relevant thing or not?"), but additionally include the actual production of text on the part of the audience.

The storytelling forum of hate stories is usually a private conversation (archetypically not including hearing people), and the narrative breaks down without audience input since the narrative is structured to elicit recognition at specific moments. These moments can be characterized as points in the narrative where the protagonist's deaf life is "not seen" by non-deaf agents controlling its fate. Of course, the protagonist is seen as a physical person, but not, as it were, as a deaf protagonist. The inherent biases of the system which make the protagonist's plight impossible are not seen, or are even explicitly relied upon as legitimate means for denying the protagonist's desired movement. When the audience member perceives any aspect of this logic, and the necessary effects it will have, it is his or her role to make an unobtrusive remark of recognition. This essentially indicates to the teller that all people in the storytelling forum are "seeing" the logic of deaf life, as situated in the real world, in the same way.

Hate stories are thus more sophisticated than disgust stories in that it is not "penetration" (a relatively clear motif) that dictates audience response, but logics of entrapment. To perceive, these require a greater degree of deaf knowledge of the world. As with a pinball story, it is the full extent of this entrapment, its piece-by-piece itemization, that is key to the plot of a hate story. Just as episodes of a personification story may be discerned by attending to audience members' expressions of recognition (recognizing this or that additional aspect of the pinball game, for example), so too are episodes of hate stories divided by audience interjections.

CONCLUSION: DEAF NARRATIVE, DEAF VALUES,
AND DEAF STUDIES

A diagrammatic summary of the basic genres discussed thus far (a treatment of complex forms is beyond the scope of this paper) might look like this, with the personification genre appearing as an anchor point. In such a view, oppositions such as "folklore" versus "personal narrative," or

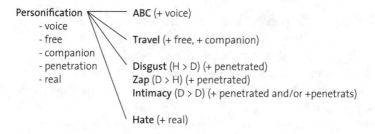

Personification
- voice
- free
- companion
- penetration
- real

ABC (+ voice)

Travel (+ free, + companion)

Disgust (H > D) (+ penetrated)
Zap (D > H) (+ penetrated)
Intimacy (D > D) (+ penetrated and/or +penetrats)

Hate (+ real)

"true story" versus "tall tale," or "literary" versus "conversational," to a large degree, fall out of the picture. It is not that these distinctions are unimportant; but, as starting points, they mask correspondences between forms that may help in our general conceptualization of deaf narrative.

Still, the opposition between personification stories and hate stories must be very important, or else one wouldn't be comic while the other is tragic. Similarly, it is notable that "disgust stories" are generally true stories, as are deaf intimacy stories, while the truth of "zap" stories is usually less certain. The latter are often "tall tales" (as with the Mississippi squirrel revival). Indeed, even if it were true that a whole group of hearing people ran over to inspect the payphone in the restaurant, it seems plausible that part of that narrative's underlying point is to highlight the overarching disparity in the potentials of hearing versus deaf voice "in the world as we know it" (no videophones there; probably no public TTYs in the restaurant at that time either).

While deaf penetrates hearing here, the system of deaf disenfranchisement is left untransformed. Similarly, even if the honeymoon story were true, it seems quite fortunate that the protagonist's ingenious idea does not meet with any trouble. The following diagram introduces these concerns, and highlights mastery of constraints as primary:

				- transforms non-deaf world	+ transforms
			- free, - companion	+ free, + companion	
		- resilient	+ resilient agains non-deaf forces		
	- real		Personification		
+ true	+ real	Disgust	Hate	Travel, Intimacy		ABC
- true				Zap	
		- penetrates non-deaf		+ penetrates non-deaf	

At the beginning of this paper, I suggested that Keith Gamache's lecture at the Deaf Studies _Today!_ conference could be understood as a type of "ABC story." By saying this, I have in mind that the ABC storyteller not only penetrates a non-deaf domain, as does the protagonist of a zap story, but, indeed, transforms or reconstitutes the logic of that domain. This is an achievement of deaf voice by definition, as the storyteller's performance manifests a central value of the deaf signing community (fluent iconic signing, specifically as contrasted with a non-iconic mode of language) on center stage such that its specific nature (not simply its name) is celebrated by all, including non-deaf people in the audience. The zap story, in contrast, does not depict a "public" celebration of the protagonist's achievement, with deaf and non-deaf applauding together.

To the contrary, the two groups are quite separate: the deaf husband slips into his deaf wife's room before anyone realizes the trick; the chaos with the squirrel happens with the deaf protagonist in the back of the church; and only as the deaf friends at the restaurant are leaving are they able to have their laugh at the hearing people running to the payphone. In each case, the ingenuity of the deaf is not represented as an achievement of public voice, happening on center-stage, but rather is "stealthy" and requires a great deal of luck, so much so that it seems questionable whether it could even have happened. Underlyingly, this may be part of the genre's message.

Gamache's lecture was overflowing with both deaf and hearing people, including the president of the university, and not only did he lecture about a deaf subject, but indeed the most important deaf subject: sign language. And not only was the lecture delivered in clear and impeccable sign, but, in fact, Gamache specifically referred to his "favorite" aspect of sign language etymology, which he called "mutation," a term traditionally referring to small processes of sound fusion or sound alteration across morpheme boundaries. (He did this only after a broad review of—an engagement with—etymological phenomena in both spoken and signed languages.)

One of Gamache's examples of sign mutation begins with a sign conveying the idea of an argument's points going by one's eyes so quickly that they are not understood—one doesn't "grasp" them. The creative mutation of this sign cited by Gamache involves the signer reaching out and grasping the point as it streams by, arresting its motion, looking at it from all angles, and then, humorously, releasing it so that it may resume its course, sailing by as it seemingly intended to do in the first place. There could be no audience member in the room—even those which did not speak sign language (but were relying on interpreters)—who could not have seen, quite clearly, what is so radically distinctive about sign language in comparison to spoken language, and indeed what is specifically celebrated about it by deaf signers. On analogy with the ABC genre, one might say that Gamache's "constraints" were the discourses of linguistic theory, one of which is "etymology." Gamache engaged the legitimate "alphabet" of scholarly discourse, but did so in a way that "transformed" it, allowing a rich process of sign language that has hitherto had no place in linguistics to be featured center-stage, referenced by one of its terms, but clearly extending the meaning of that term. Words in spoken language do not afford the kind of total diagrammatic reanalysis that Gamache refers to because, by and large, words in spoken language are not diagrammatic in nature.[3]

By making this comparison, I wish to suggest the degree to which Gamache's project, and the project of Deaf Studies in general, can be understood as emanating from the values of deaf culture as an "outward oriented" system of deaf companionship intrinsically tied to deaf engagement with the world, as schematized in all of the genres treated in this essay. Gamache's innovative engagement with linguistics, whereby he could foreground and celebrate a largely unstudied area of ASL, came, after all, in the context of a major conference already projecting a collaborative deaf presence into a traditionally "non-deaf" domain. The following diagram essentially condenses the organizing logic of the above diagram, but also extends it:

"The Pinball"   "ABC Storyteller" │ Deaf Studies

It is not simply that the personification genre features an "unrecognized" protagonist, but, rather, it features a protagonist that has absolutely no means of understanding itself or of articulating any possible understanding of itself in a way that would make sense in the world. The ABC genre, via its opposition to personification and hate stories, suggests an implicit native theory of voice: for a disenfranchised subject to achieve public voice, it is necessary to change the public terms of discourse which seem to make that disenfranchisement legitimate.

In this regard, Laura Mauldin's presentation at the conference, a film about the scarcity of Deaf Studies books at the Gallaudet library, might be mentioned in closing. As Mauldin suggests, libraries can be considered cites of political contestation in the pursuit of public voice. And yet, I would emphasize that the kind of voice most celebrated in the deaf signing world is not the written word, but rather the diagrammatic signing that Gamache forthrightly placed at center stage in his lecture—doing so both in his own signing and in the kind of signing he was analyzing. For this kind of voice to be represented in libraries requires more than books, since books, in fact, are simply unable to represent it. The "terms of discourse" of scholarship—here, the very technologies of discursive circulation—need to be transformed for deaf voice to be realized through Deaf Studies.

While the Deaf Studies *Today!* conference and the present collection of written essays are fundamental contributions to the growth of Deaf Studies, perhaps more fundamental yet would be collected volumes of polished "ASL essays" being made available in libraries—e.g., a rigorously composed signed essay for every presentation made at this conference. (Being in the audience of Andrew Byrne's lecture, it was veritably painful to know that his masterful presentation—an example of pure diagrammatic signing in an academic register—was going by unrecorded. How lucky sign language students would be to have such ASL essays assigned to them!) While compiling and editing such volumes may require special funding (though high-quality videorecording is pedestrian nowadays, and could readily be requested of presenters), such funding seems quite possible, perhaps especially if pursued in collaboration with select libraries. Indeed, the logic of such a transformative pursuit is so transparently sensible that it is easy to imagine it being applauded by all.

ENDNOTES

1.   The general argument is that a "systemic" approach to deaf narrative elucidates the character of each form better than its isolated treatment can. This approach is in harmony with classic anthropological approaches to sociocultural symbols. In Victor Turner's classic study of Ndembu ritual, for example, he writes that the anthropologist "must examine symbols not only in the context of each specific kind of ritual, but in the context of the total system" (1967:43). Similarly, in the Bakhtinian tradition of literary analysis (Bakhtin 1981, Voloshinov 1973; cf. Seitel 1999:85), it is argued that, to understand a particular character type within a literary formation, it is not enough to examine the appearance of that character type there, but rather one must survey its resonances in the entire range of discursive genres in a given society. My own study of deaf narrative seeks an understanding of any particular narrative always with respect to a proposed system of narratives. The study has been informed not only by a corpus of narratives performed on stage, but also by attention to conversational narratives, signed poetry, written poetry, written narratives, editorials in deaf news forums, visual art exhibits, plays, films, lectures, political speeches, the dynamics of classroom discussions, the dynamics of deaf gatherings, participation in sign language classes, and a range of other data including formal interviews in which specific stories, and sign language storytelling in general, were discussed. Early stages of the analysis were also periodically presented to deaf audiences for feedback.

2.   The dragon might be said to capture what Albert Ballin called "the quietude of the victim...who is usually unable to present his grievances convincingly" (1999[1932]:2).

3.   "Folk etymology," a process by which the meaning of a word or phrase is reinterpreted because of similarity in form to other morphemes or words in a language, if applied here, would also have to have its meaning extended, since the diagrammatic analysis on the part of a signer in this case is not a "mistaken" imposition on the language, but rather a correct analysis of the form's basic composition.

REFERENCES

Bakhtin, Mikhail. 1981. Discourse and the novel. *The dialogic imagination.* (Ed.) Michael Holquist. (Trans.) Caryl Emerson and Michael Holquist. Austin: University of Texas.

Bahan, Ben. 2001 (manuscript). Face-to-face tradition in the American Deaf community: dynamics of the teller, the tale and the audience. (To appear) *The poetics of vision, performance and the body: exploring American Sign Language literature, a multimedia anthology.* (Eds.) D. Bauman, J. Nelson, H. Rose. Berkeley: University of California.

Ballin, Albert. 1999 [1930]. *The deaf mute howls.* Washington, DC: Gallaudet.

Bechter, Frank. forthcoming. The deaf convert culture, and its lessons for Deaf Theory. *Sightings: explorations in Deaf Studies.* (Eds.) Benjamin Bahan and Dirksen Bauman. Minneapolis: University of Minnesota.

Bienvenu, MJ. 1989. Reflections of American Deaf culture in Deaf humor. *TBC news* 17 (September).

Cook, Peter. 1998. *From a gator ride to the dentist office* (VHS). Chicago: P.C. Productions.

Ennis, Bill. 1992. *Bill Ennis, Live at SMI* (VHS). Burtonsville, Maryland: Sign Media.

Jacobowitz, Lynn. 1991. "At the Airport" and "My first day in Italy." *ASL Storytime,* volumes 3 and 4 (VHS). Washington, DC: Gallaudet University ASL and Deaf Studies Dept.

Kelleher, Jane Frances. 1986. *Literature by Deaf Iowans: linguistic form and social function.* Unpublished dissertation (Comparative Literature). Iowa City: University of Iowa.

Rose, Heidi M. 1992. *A critical methodology for analyzing American Sign Language literature.* Unpublished dissertation (Communication). Tempe: Arizona State.

Seitel, Peter. 1999. *The powers of genre: interpreting Haya oral literature.* New York City: Oxford.

Turner, Victor. 1967. *The forest of symbols: aspects of Ndembu ritual.* Ithaca: Cornell.

Voloshinov, V.N. 1973 [1929]. *Marxism and the philosophy of language.* (Trans.) Ladislav Matejka and I. R. Titunik. Cambridge: Harvard.

ABOUT THE AUTHOR

Frank Bechter is a Ph.D. candidate in sociocultural and linguistic anthropology at the University of Chicago. Frank's research was greatly facilitated by professors and students in Gallaudet's ASL and Deaf Studies Department, and by Gallaudet's Center for ASL Literacy. Frank was one of 20 scholars contributing to the Deaf Studies Think Tank held at Gallaudet University in July of 2002, and his chapter, "The Deaf Convert Culture, And Its Lessons For Deaf Theory," will appear in the upcoming volume Sightings: Explorations in Deaf Studies, *edited by Ben Bahan and Dirksen Bauman. Frank began signing in 1993 in New York City, having no previous knowledge of the Deaf signing community. His ASL courses, all taught by Deaf instructors, led him directly to his interest in the signing mastery of ASL storytelling, and his decision to pursue graduate study.*

"Nearer My God To Thee, Michigan School For The Deaf," May 1906

Courtesy Gallaudet University Archives

Cultural Resistance: ASL Poetry

ANDREW BYRNE

Andrew Byrne is a PH.D. *candidate in Education at York University in Toronto, Ontario, specializing in ASL literature. He is also an adjunct professor to graduate students of Deaf Education.*

AMERICAN SIGN LANGUAGE (ASL), THE legitimate and natural language used by culturally Deaf people in North America for more than 175 years, has its own distinct linguistic structure, which is comprised of precise handshapes and movements. It is as precise, versatile, and subtle as any spoken language. It differs from spoken language in that it is visual rather than auditory. It must be mastered in the same way as the grammar of any other language in the world.

Unfortunately, ASL has been facing every form of prejudice and oppression from the majority culture since the infamous Milan Congress in 1880. The Congress was successful in passing a resolution declaring the "incontestable superiority of speech over signs for restoring the deafmute to society" (Lane, 1992, 119). In spite of an avalanche of evidence that ASL is a natural language with its own grammatical rules and syntax, the majority culture nevertheless views ASL as inferior and incomplete. They strongly feel that ASL is a crutch and hinders the development of the language of English. Many well-meaning but misguided educators believe that the only way for Deaf students to fit into the majority culture is through speech and lip reading. Therefore, they discourage and/or forbid its use in the classroom of Deaf students (Lane, 1992).

Deaf people have their own literary tradition and highly value it. ASL literature is a body of stories, poetry, humor, and other genres, which are passed on by the use of ASL from one generation to another by culturally Deaf people (Byrne, 1996). Because of the historical oppression of ASL, there exists only a small body of literary work (Kuntze, 1993). At the same time, ASL literature has been facing unwanted assimilation caused by influences of the majority culture. While some ASL poems and stories remain intact, others are so influenced by the majority world that they do not entirely belong to Deaf people. However, there are several genres of ASL literature where Deaf people have created examples of cultural resistance.

This paper will focus on one genre of ASL literature: poetry. I will present theories of cultural resistance and four examples of poems to indicate their resistance to the majority influences.

LITERATURE REVIEW

Duncombe (2002) explains that cultural resistance is "...culture that is used, consciously or unconsciously, effectively or not, to resist and/or change the dominant political, economic and/or social structure" (5). He also adds,

> ...cultural resistance can provide a sort of 'free space' for developing ideas and practices. Freed from the limits and constraints of the dominant culture, you can experiment with new ways of seeing and being and develop tools and resources for resistance. And as culture is usually something shared, it becomes a focal point around which to build a community (5–6).

Giroux (1983, 2001) states about a theory of resistance: "...in the behavior of subordinate groups there are moments of cultural and creative expression that are informed by a different logic, whether it be existential, religious, or otherwise. It is in these modes of behavior as well as in creative arts of resistance that the fleeting images of freedom are to be found. Finally, inherent in a radical notion of resistance is an expressed hope, an element of transcendence..." (p. 108). He also explains that "elements of resistance...become the focal point for the construction of different sets of lived experiences, experiences in which students can find a voice and maintain and extend the positive dimensions of their own cultures and histories" (111). Mitchell and Feagin (1995) stress that "...members of oppressed subordinate groups are not powerless pawns that merely react to circumstances beyond their control, but rather are reflective, creative agents that construct a separate reality in which to survive" (69).

The Applied History Research Group at the University of Calgary (2000) explains that "the act of resistance [represents] an attempt to establish and define cultural boundaries and to limit incursion by foreign cultural traditions" (3).

Collins (1991) points out that "...cultures of resistance or oppositional cultures arise to resist the matrix of domination by drawing on
cultural resources" (cited in Martinez, 1999, 34). She expands by stating
that one of the cultural resources is storytelling, including poetry.

According to Lane, Hoffmeister, and Bahan (1996), the English-
speaking majority has surrounded ASL users in school, at home, and
in the workplace, for many years. As a result, their ASL has a degree of
"contamination" by English: "Deaf people with Deaf parents and early
learners of ASL tend to use a grammar different from that used by hearing people, Deaf people with hearing parents, and other late learners
whose grammar is more closely related to English grammar" (p. 64).

There are several forms showing the influence of English on ASL.
When giving a presentation to a hearing audience with a limited knowledge of ASL, a Deaf presenter may utter several English words while he
uses ASL. He may also change the word order of his ASL sentences to be
more English-like. Another form is that a Deaf speaker utters ASL signs
and mouths their English glosses. Lastly, in a classroom with ASL-using
Deaf children, several teachers may use one of the artificial sign systems
and sign for each English word in an English sentence. Soon afterwards,
the children may pick up and use some English-influenced signs. With
no or limited knowledge in the areas of the hearing world's oppression
on Deaf people, the history of Deaf people in the United States and
Canada, bilingual philosophy of ASL and printed English, and ASL linguistics, a Deaf individual's ASL is more likely to be "contaminated" by
English-influenced pieces compared to a Deaf individual with extensive
knowledge in all of the areas.

DATA SOURCE

Using poetry in ASL as data, the four poems are as follows:

"Black Hole: Color ASL" by Debbie Rennie
"Cave" by Clayton Valli
"Deaf World" by Jed Galimore (rendition of Clayton Valli's poem)
"Liberation" by Patrick Graybill

RESEARCH METHODOLOGY

Content analysis has been utilized in analyzing each poem for evidence
of resistance. According to the Cambridge Institute for Research, Educa-

tion, and Management, content analysis is "a method of analysis used in qualitative research in which text (notes) are systematically examined by identifying and grouping themes and coding, classifying and developing categories" *(http://www.cirem.co.uk/definitions.html)*. One advantage of content analysis is that it "provides insight into complex models of human thoughtandlanguageuse" *(http://writing.colostate.edu/references/research/content/com2d2.cfm)*. It is important to be aware that ASL poetry loses a great deal of dynamic quality when transcribed and that it is naturally best to view it in its original form.

Name of Poem	Quality of ASL	Individual Dexterity in Execution or Performance in ASL	Evidence of Cultural Resistance?	Individual Consciousness or Unconsciousness of Resistance
"Black Hole: Color ASL"	Superior	Superior	Yes	Consciousness
"Cave"	Superior	Superior	Yes	Consciousness
"Deaf World"	Superior	Superior	Yes	Consciousness
"Liberation"	Superior	Superior	Yes	Consciousness

In addition to the table of the data analysis above, Martinez (1999) states, "The poet, the singer, is infusing her/his words with lived expression, with words that come from everyday lived experience. These words can tell of nature and work and joy. They can also tell of suffering and abuse. The truth of the song or the poetry is the truth of the writer's life" (48). Also, [s]tories are a language of resistance that serves to document the experience of oppression [and] voice a conscious opposition to that oppression. [They] are a conscious form of oppositional culture in prose and poetry" (50). There is prominent evidence that the Deaf poets attempt to use their poems to share their lived experience of being oppressed and to "voice a conscious opposition to that oppression."

FINDINGS

Based upon the content analysis of the poems, the finding is that even though the content of each is different from one another, all of the poems have one powerful similarity: *resistance*. Since ASL and its literature is the *single* commonality within the Deaf community and is the lasting proof fully representing who Deaf people truly are, the preservation of ASL and its literature is *crucial*. In this light, cultural preservation of ASL literature in its most proper form is *resistance*. ASL used in all of the poems appears to be in its most proper form as there is no evidence of English-influenced pieces within them.

Each of the poems will be discussed to indicate their resistance to the majority culture. The first poem is "Black Hole: Color ASL" by Rennie.

> Ladder, rungs, ladder upright
> I walk, come to ladder, climb up
> See pots of red paint, yellow, blue, green
> Blue skies, dip into paint, splatter paint
> Ladder shakes, people shake, I totter
> Paint spills, the ladder shaken to dislodge, paint spills
> Black hole looms, and I am endangered, paint spills
> I flail and stagger, black paint spreads, I flail
> Ladder is pulled down, I stagger and flail, struggle
> Black looms, black looms, black looms
> I fly and soar, colors all over, I fly
> Colors all over, I fly, I soar
> *(Peters, 2000, 167)*

In this poem, we see a basic narrative framework: a person makes the climb out of the hearing world and discovers ASL. Ecstatic, she (or he; the poem is translated using first person for convenience) is in her element; but the ladder is soon shaken, for people in the hearing world desire her return. Struggling to remain on the ladder, she feels at risk not just of falling but of being pulled into an immense, looming black hole. The deaf person perseveres, and even as the ladder is pulled down she takes off into the ASL world of "color," experiencing the freedom to express herself" (Peters, 2000, p. 167). Deaf people who have had the experience of being controlled by the hearing world and successfully breaking the chain with it would connect to Rennie's poem.

The next poem is "Cave" by Valli:

Two people are walking [each hand in the 1 handshape, moving forward side by side] and then split up. One goes off alone, while the other continues on his or her way and comes upon a cave. The poet enacts this person, possibly a young man, who steps into the cave, descends rough nature-hewed steps, and sets foot upon the uneven floor. Inside the cave are stalactites dripping from the ceiling and stalagmites rising from the floor; one has an especially large treelike and bulbous column. The young man makes his way through the tunnels and eventually reaches the back of the cave. The poet then enacts one or more workers who cut the steps into geometric rectangles, smooth out the rock formations from the ceiling, and add lights to illuminate the room. Other formations from the floor are completely removed so that the surface can be made even and level. Fans are installed to halt the condensation dripping from the ceiling. Guardrails are added at the entrance and a big chandelier emitting yellow, orange, and green flashes of light is hung within. A blue carpet is laid, and red and white seats are placed in rows. When all is ready, people line up and enter for a lecture; and the lecturer goes on and on about the great work that has been done (the "improvements" inside the cave). The poem culminates when Valli signs CAVE BLACK on his forehead and then turns in profile and positions his hands (in the shape for CAVE) over his right ear. (*Peters, 2000, 163–164*)

Valli's poem is strongly symbolic and has a hidden message. The journey into the cave is representative of a Deaf individual who selects to have a cochlear implant and of the lecturer who is a supporter of cochlear implants trying to impress hearing parents of Deaf children. In other words, Deaf identity is not valued. The majority culture views a Deaf individual who cannot hear as incomplete and lost. Thus, they feel the duty and necessity to restore the Deaf individual to the hearing world by fixing his broken ears with a cochlear implant. For the Deaf individual, if something is not broken, do not fix it. For the hearing person, it is quite the opposite.

"Deaf World" is the name of the third poem, which is expressed by Galimore:

> I was born in the world of sounds
> Put on hearing aids
> Hearing sounds (looking confused)
> Seeing people enjoying hearing music
> Hearing music (looking confused)
> Seeing people in a movie talking to each other
> Hearing sounds (looking confused)
> Hearing sounds and sounds (looking more confused)
> Seeing Deaf rocks
> Seeing Deaf water
> Seeing Deaf trees
> Seeing Deaf mountains
> Seeing Deaf clouds
> Deaf world
> Deaf world and I are the same
> Hearing world and I are not the same
> Hearing world is not mine!
> Deaf world is mine!
> (*Translated by Andrew Byrne, 2004*)

This poem focuses on a story about a Deaf person who feels no connection with the hearing world and discovers his place in the Deaf world.

Wearing a hearing aid and hearing unfamiliar sounds make no sense to the Deaf person. Seeing everything that is visual in the Deaf world makes a strong connection with him.

One of Graybill's widely known poems is entitled "Liberation" which is very simple but artful and powerful.

> English English
> Prodding, prodding
> Hand pushing down head
> Signing, signing
> Later chained, chained
> Anger, anger
> Comes to a head
> Free at last!
> Signing, signing
> Confrontation, you and me
> Resolved, let us bow
> Clasp hands
> Peace at last
> Wonderful
> Mine and yours
> Let us bow
> Equal in all.
> (*Peters, 2000, 160*)

"Liberation" is the representation of the poet's feeling of liberation from the bondage of the majority culture and of his joy to be able to use ASL in his everyday life. This poem reflects the experience of many Deaf people who were forbidden to use ASL when they were in a school, staffed with mostly non-deaf educators and administrators, who believed in restoring them to the hearing society.

IMPLICATIONS

ASL and its literature are the *single* commonality within the Deaf community and are the lasting proof fully representing who Deaf people truly are. The preservation of ASL and its literature is *crucial*. In this light, cultural preservation of ASL literature in its most proper form is *resistance*. With no or limited knowledge in the areas of the hearing world's oppression on Deaf people, the history of Deaf people in the United States and Canada, bilingual philosophy of ASL and printed English, and ASL linguistics, a Deaf individual's ASL is more likely to be "contaminated" by English-influenced pieces. With extensive and updated knowledge in all areas, the individual would make the effort to resist the influences from the majority culture and thus keep his ASL "uncontaminated" as much as possible.

These poems are a perfect but powerful example of resistance to the majority influences because there is no evidence of any kind of English-influenced pieces within them. According to the Applied History Research Group at the University of Calgary, "the act of resistance [attempts] to establish and define cultural boundaries and to limit incursion by foreign cultural traditions" (p. 3). I strongly believe that the four poems have been successful in establishing strong Deaf cultural boundaries and blocking (not limiting) influences by the English-speaking majority.

Studying ASL storytelling as a form of cultural resistance should be the priority in order to examine the body of ASL literature for the English-influenced pieces and find what is distinctively ASL and distinctly Deaf. In addition, other cultures re-inhabit sacred land or preserve sacred time. For the preservation of Deaf culture, the concept of creating and restoring sacred space in ASL literature should be central. Creating sacred space in the air through the expression of ASL literature passed from one Deaf person to another is a powerful concept. The recovery of ASL fluency preserved in the literature is imperative. This has enormous implications for the education of Deaf children and appreciation of hearing children in a multicultural education system.

REFERENCES

Byrne, A. (1996). ASL storytelling to deaf children: "More! more! more!" *Teacher Research in a Bilingual/Bicultural School for Deaf Students: Bilingual Bicultural Education for Deaf Students Monograph Series* (Serial No. 1).

Cambridge Institute for Research, Education and Management (2002). *Definitions.* Retrieved December 17, 2003, from http://www.cirem.co.uk/definitions.html

Collins, P. H. (1991). *Black feminist thought: Knowledge, consciousness, and the politics of empowerment.* New York, New York: Routledge.

Duncombe, S. (2002). *Cultural resistance reader.* New York, New York: Verso.

Giroux, H. A. (2001). *Theory and resistance in education: Towards a pedagogy for the opposition.* Westport, Connecticut: Bergin and Garvey.

Kuntze, M. (1993, October 20–22). Developing students' literary skills in ASL. In B. D. Snider (Ed.), *Post Milan ASL and English literacy: Issues, trends, and research* (pp. 267–281). Washington, DC: College for Continuing Education, Gallaudet University.

Lane, H. (1992). *The mask of benevolence: Disabling the deaf community.* New York, New York: Alfred A. Knopf.

Lane, H., Hoffmeister, R., & Bahan, B. (1996). *A journey into the DEAF-WORLD*. San Diego, California: DawnSignPress.

Martinez, T. A. (1999). *Storytelling as oppositional culture: Race, class, and gender in the borderlands*. Race, Gender and Class, 6(3), 33–51.

Mitchell, B. L., & Feagin, J. R. (1995). America's racial-ethnic cultures: Opposition within a mythical melting pot. In B. Bowser, T. Jones, & G. Young (Eds.), T*oward the multicultural university* (pp. 65–86). Westport, Connecticut: Praeger.

Peters, C. L. (2000). *Deaf American literature: From carnival to the canon*. Washington, DC: Gallaudet University Press.

The Applied History Research Group, The University of Calgary (2000). *Old world contacts: Cultural conversion*. Retrieved December 16, 2003, from http://www.ucalgary.ca/applied_history/tutor/oldwrld/contacttheory.html

Valli, C. (1995). *ASL poetry: Selected works of Clayton Valli* [VHS]. San Diego, California: DawnSignPress.

Writing Center, Colorado State University Department of English (1997–2001). *Advantages of content analysis*. Retrieved December 17, 2003, from http://writing.colostate.edu/references/research/content/com2d2.cfm

---

ABOUT THE AUTHOR

Born Deaf to Deaf parents in Perth, Ontario, Andrew Byrne graduated from the Ontario School for the Deaf in 1985, and Gallaudet University in 1989. Currently, he is working at York University as a seconded member of the Faculty of Education teaching to undergraduate and teacher preparation program students. In addition, he received a M.S. degree from McDaniel College (formerly Western Maryland College) and is an adjunct professor to graduate students of Deaf Education. He is also a Ph.D. candidate in Education at York University specializing in ASL literature. Andrew is also an accomplished storyteller, poet, and actor.

Utah School for the Deaf, date unknown

Courtesy Callahan Museum of the American Printing House for the Blind

How Utah's Deaf Community Got a Community Center of Their Own

MARILYN CALL
ROBERT G. SANDERSON, ED.D.

Marilyn Call is the Director of the Division of Services of the Deaf and Hard of Hearing in for the State of Utah. Robert G. Sanderson is a past president of the National Association of the Deaf.

WHEN DEAF PEOPLE COME FROM out of state to visit friends in Utah, they often come for a tour of the Sanderson Community Center in Salt Lake City. People are amazed that a little state like Utah has such a wonderful state-funded building which has become a second home of Deaf Utahns who live on the Wasatch Front. Since many have asked us how they could get a similar building in their state, this workshop was held to explain how Utah's Deaf community accomplished this.

It must be emphasized that there are many ways to go about getting a community center. We decided that state funding would be sought for this endeavor. Without hard money (as opposed to soft grant money) it would be next to impossible to pay for continuous upkeep of a community center and provide ongoing programs. There are certain principles that were followed that apply to any advocacy effort. The three biggest tips to remem-ber are get organized, do your homework, and be persistent!

GET ORGANIZED!

Start with a small steering committee. Develop goals and objectives with timelines. On this committee make sure you have gathered some worker bees. Find people who want the Center bad enough to commit the time. Make sure you have some committee members who can take time to talk to key decision makers during daytime hours. Identify core leaders from local Deaf and hard-of-hearing organizations and get everyone's buy in. Network with other grassroots disability advocacy organizations.

　　　　　　　　　　　　　　　Deaf Studies *Today!* · Volume 1 · 2004

EXPLORE ALL FUNDING OPTIONS

Will you go after county, city or state funds? Where does your Deaf and hard-of-hearing commission get its funding? Find out who has connections in high places. What about the DSDHH employees, are they on board? Can they open doors for your group?

DO YOUR HOMEWORK

Document needs and facts and pull this information to gather in a formal report. How many Deaf and hard-of-hearing individuals live in your area? Where is the critical mass? Do you have names and addresses? Identify the unmet needs of Deaf and hard-of-hearing people. A few of the unmet needs we started with included adult education classes, counseling, case management, independent living skills, senior citizen activities, teen groups, technology demonstration and repair, hard of hearing adjustment training, and social and recreational opportunities to reduce isolation. Sell the importance of having a service center for Vocational Rehabilitation counselors, DSDHH workers, etc. Find out what other states have community centers. Share this information as part of your report.

IDENTIFY THE DECISION-MAKERS WITHIN THE FUNDING SOURCE YOU DECIDE TO PURSUE

Identify which agency will support your dream and convince them to put it in their funding request to the state legislature. For Utah, Vocational Rehabilitation was the only agency providing services to the adult Deaf population. Vocational Rehabilitation is housed under the Utah State Board of Education. The first people we lobbied were the agency heads of the Department of Education, Rehabilitation and the members of the State Board of Education. Only after getting their support was it time to start lobbying the appropriate legislative committees. Always pay attention to timelines. If you start lobbying when the legislative session begins you will be about nine months too late.

SELL THE NEED FOR A BUILDING OF YOUR OWN

Sell the importance of one place to go where there are no communication barriers. Visit all of the other community centers in your areas. Survey the facilities to find out what hours deaf groups could use the building. Is there space for offices available? How is the lighting and the set up of the meeting rooms? Is assistive technology available? Put together a report to document the availability or lack of availability. Legislators like facts; it is better to argue with facts instead of just giving emotional pleas.

LEARN THE BEST WAYS TO LOBBY AND WHO TO LOBBY

Teach the community workshops on how to lobby by contacting their personal senator or representative. Personal face-to-face visits are always best for a first contact to sell your cause. Make an appointment and bring your own interpreter for a first visit. Make sure you have an interpreter who has a voice as persuasive as your signs. Know both your friends and who may speak against you. Make sure a powerful decision-maker never gets a sense of power struggles with in your group.

TARGET A CONSTITUENT

Include a constituent when you visit legislators (a hearing or deaf person) who is supportive of your cause. A constituent is someone who lives in the senator's or representative's district. Elected officials respond and usually support ideas brought to them by people who voted them into office or have the power and numbers to vote someone out of office.

BE PERSISTENT

Never, never, never give up. Rome wasn't built in a day. It may take several years to get all of the right elements together to make your dream of a community center a reality. Margaret Meade once said, "Never doubt that a small group of thoughtful committed citizens can change the world. Indeed it is the only thing that ever has."

ABOUT THE AUTHORS

Marilyn Call is Director of the Division of Services of the Deaf and Hard of Hearing in Utah. Previously, she was the executive director of the Legislative Coalition for People with Disabilities and has 20 years of experience lobbying for people who are Deaf/hard of hearing or disabled. She can be contacted at mcall@utah.gov.

Robert G. Sanderson received his Ed.D. from Brigham Young University. He was the president of the National Association of the Deaf from 1964 to 1968. Recently the Utah Community Center for the Deaf was renamed the Robert G. Sanderson Community Center for the Deaf in his honor.

DAVID G. SEIXAS,
First Principal of the Institution.

David G. Seixas, First Principal of the Pennsylvania School for the Deaf, Philadelphia, 1821

Courtesy Pennsylvania School for the Deaf and the Disability Historical Museum (*disabilitymuseum.org*)

Happy Hands: The Effect of ASL on Hearing Children's Literacy

MARILYN DANIELS, PH.D.

Marilyn Daniels is a professor of Communication Arts and Sciences at Penn State University, State College, Pennsylvania.

THIS STUDY CONCERNS ITSELF WITH the effect of sign language on typical hearing children's kindergarten education. The concept is not a new one and in fact can be traced to the seventeenth-century French philosopher Etienne Condillac who suggested that sign is an effective agent for hearing children's instruction. Two centuries later, Thomas Hopkins Gallaudet, founder of the American School for the Deaf and the pioneer of Deaf education in the United States, advocated sign language instruction for the hearing siblings of his Deaf students. He believed this would serve two purposes: 1) the Deaf child in the family would have easy access to other children with whom they could communicate in sign language and 2) the hearing children would increase their vocabulary and language proficiency.

In an 1853 issue of the *American Annals of the Deaf and Dumb,* Bartlett, recounting Gallaudet's earlier assertion, describes the principles on which he postulates Gallaudet based his convictions: "The more varied the form under which language is presented to the mind through the various senses, the more perfect will be the knowledge of it acquired, and the more permanently will it be retained." (33).

REVIEW OF LITERATURE

Sign language came into its own in the twentieth century with the publication of William Stokoe's *Sign Language Structure* (1960) indicating that American Sign Language (ASL) is a true natural language with rules for generating grammatically sound phonological, morphological, and syntactical structures. By the mid-1980s, with its status as a legitimate language firmly established, ASL was fulfilling foreign or modern language requirements in many high schools and colleges. As the twenty-first century begins, ASL has become the third most commonly used language in the United States.

Concurrent with the recognition of signs' linguistic attributes, it began to crop up in a variety of incarnations in elementary school programs. It was reported as a benefit for word recognition and spelling by Bowen, Mattheiss, and Wilson (1993); Daniels (1993, 1994a, 1994b, 1996a, 1996b, 1997, 2001a) has conducted many studies demonstrating signs advantages for vocabulary growth and retention; while Crawford (2001), Cooper (2002), Hafer and Wilson (1996), and Daniels (2002, 2003) noted signs' enhancement of reading ability. In the mid-1990s the International Reading Association began to recommend sign as a reading aid and a number of their conferences featured lectures with a view to promoting its benefits. Each of these research endeavors showed the positive effect the inclusion of sign had on typical hearing children's literacy in normal classroom settings in public schools.

There have also been some situations in the United States and the United Kingdom where sign has been used in an inclusive classroom with hearing and Deaf children. In Louisiana, a two-year study was conducted on the Tulane University campus replicating Daniels' (1994a) research design, which measured students' receptive English vocabulary growth. Heller, Manning, Pavur, and Wagner (1998) found "children who had been taught signing had significantly higher receptive English vocabulary scores on the PPVT (Peabody Picture Vocabulary Test) than did children who had not been taught signing." (52).

In "Sign in Education," an eighteen-month-long pilot program in the UK, both Deaf and hearing children were taught by a Deaf teacher using only British Sign Language (BSL) in a "voice off" mode for one afternoon a week. Robinson (1997) found all children scored higher on national curriculum tests which measured reading and spelling. An assessment based on collated academic evidence showed that instruction in BSL provided hearing children access to the curriculum, as well as offering additional benefits. Specifically, sign language increased students' enjoyment and motivation and helped them listen, look, and concentrate. This new aptitude to attend was credited with expediting concept development (1).

The assessment procedures in the UK program differed in one substantial way from the US programs. They were the first group of hearing students to have their sign language ability evaluated. The results indicated that the hearing children exposed to a half day of classroom instruction delivered in BSL achieved a level of BSL ability equal to that of their Deaf peers. Without direct tuition in BSL they had a basic sign vocabulary, were using grammatical features, displaying an appropriate use of space, placement, and location, and were beginning to use correct BSL syntax (the topic followed by the comment).

The following study strives to adapt the UK approach in a US kindergarten. Because of teacher licensing and certification requirements in the US, the teacher is not Deaf and speaks English. However, she is proficient in ASL and has been signing for over fifteen years. Also, there are no Deaf children in the classroom. But as Robinson (1997) points out when reviewing the UK project: "Children's motivation for acquiring basic signing skills does not appear to stem from interaction with Deaf children and adults so much as the language itself." (42). The purpose of the research endeavor was to assess the effect of sign language instruction in four critical aspects relating to typical hearing students' language development: (1) receptive English vocabulary, (2) expressive English vocabulary, (3) ASL ability, and (4) reading-readiness level.

METHOD

Participants. The study participants in the treatment class were 21 kindergarten pupils from a 300-student public elementary school in rural Vermont. There were seven boys and 14 girls in the class. The students were heterogeneous from a socioeconomic point of view and homogeneous in respect to ethnicity. English was their first language.

The research design consisted of a control class for aspects 1, 2, and 4. Although efforts were made to secure permission to use the schools other kindergarten class as a control class, the administration refused. They feared the teacher of the proposed control class would be upset if her students did poorly, inducing a morale issue. However, the administration was willing to provide the results of the non-treatment classes first grade placement tests. As these assessments are routinely conducted at the end of the academic year, this created no untoward attention. This measure would permit the reading readiness level of the treatment class and non-treatment classes to be compared. Therefore, the non-treatment class serves as a control class for only the fourth aspect (reading-readiness level) of this study.

Students were placed in the two kindergarten classes in the school in a random fashion. Both kindergarten teachers have been teaching for fifteen years and are considered (based on classroom observation and student' outcomes in previous years) to possess equal teaching ability. There were 20 students (8 boys and 12 girls) in the control class for the fourth aspect (reading-readiness).

Treatment Procedure. The teacher used sign language from the first day of school. At the onset, key ASL words were signed concurrently with spoken English. Gradually the English was eliminated and the ASL phrases remained. The teacher strived to use ASL syntax whenever possible. For instance, the question "Did you go to the store?" would be signed STORE GO YOU? in ASL. As the school year progressed an increasing amount of sign was incorporated. Eventually ASL was used for all classroom management with no voicing.

The students learned the signs easily and responded to the teacher with signs. They began with YES, NO, PLEASE, BYE, SEE YOU LATER, TOMORROW, and gradually acquired a larger sign vocabulary. Pertinent signs were taught for the stories shared at circle time and the teacher asked many questions which could be answered by signing YES and NO. This query response technique became an efficient assessment tool. Sign words were sent home in a weekly newsletter and the students showed parents and care-givers how to form the signs so they were able to learn this new language together.

The teacher used the manual alphabet and fingerspelling to teach the phonemic awareness that is considered crucial to the school's guided reading program based on New Zealand educator Marie M. Clay's procedures. She formed letters with the manual alphabet to help students distinguish between letter names and letter sounds, necessary for early reading success and strategic breakdown of unknown words. A manual letter was displayed at chest level, in the normal signing space, for the letter name, and placed near the ear for the letter sound. (To clarify for readers not familiar with this technique, the letter sound for the manual letter B is *bah* as in 'bat'; for the manual letter C, it is *cah* as in 'cat'; and so forth. The manual alphabet is simply a way of writing letters in space.)

For consonant sound awareness, the manual letter was formed and placed near the ear; for vowel sound awareness, the manual letter was formed with both hands and simultaneously placed next to each ear. Silent letters were signified by making the letter in the normal signing space and then covering the letter with the other hand. These procedures were effective for visual as well as auditory memory recall.

When the teacher taught reading, she spoke English and she used the ASL signs in English word order. For reading instruction all vocabulary words were introduced with their accompanying ASL sign. For each word, the children were shown the ASL sign, the English text for the word (displayed on a card in large print), and the target word was voiced by the teacher. The children repeated the process, signing the word and reading the word aloud from printed text. The teacher taught reading to groups of three or four children while they sat around a circular table.

ASSESSMENT PROCEDURES

(1) Receptive English Vocabulary. The receptive English vocabulary of the kindergarten students in the treatment class was evaluated with the Peabody Picture Vocabulary Test Third Edition (PPVT–III). The PPVT–III provides two different test plate books and forms for this instrument enabling researchers to assess vocabulary in a valid pre-post test design. Form A was used in September and Form B in June.

Like the original 1959 edition, and the 1981 revision, this 1997 third edition of the PPVT is an individually administered, untimed, norm-referenced, wide-ranged achievement test of the level of a person's vocabulary. The test is appropriate for persons 2 1/2 through 90 plus years of age. It was standardized in the US on a stratified sample of 2,725 persons: 2,000 children and adolescents and 725 persons over age 19. The sample was stratified to match the most recent U.S. Census data on gender, race/ethnicity, region, and education level. Raw scores are converted to age-referenced norms called standard scores with a mean of 100 (sd: 15). These standard scores take into account typical age-referenced vocabulary growth or maturation. A child of 6 years 1 month of age is expected to have a larger vocabulary than a child of 5 years 1 month. Therefore a standard score of 100 at any age connotes the anticipated typical vocabulary for that age.

(2) Expressive English Vocabulary. The expressive vocabulary of the kindergarten students in the treatment class was evaluated in May with American Guidance Service's Expressive Vocabulary Test (EVT). This assessment was conducted to insure that the students maintained their ability to express themselves in English while they were learning to express themselves in ASL. The EVT has only one test plate and form. It is impossible to implement a valid pre-post test design with this single form instrument. The EVT, a partner for the PPVT–III, is an individually administered, norm-referenced assessment of expressive vocabulary and word retrieval for children and adults 2 1/2 through 90 years of age. The EVT measures expressive vocabulary knowledge by labeling and synonym. The EVT and the PPVT–III were normed on the same nationwide standardization sample of 2,725 examinees. The EVT results are reported as standard scores with a mean of 100 (sd: 15). The conforming of EVT and PPVT–III allows direct comparison of the receptive and expressive vocabulary scores.

(3) Sign Language Evaluation. The sign language ability of the kindergarten students in the treatment class was evaluated following the UK Sign in Education model. The UK project used the Standardized Assessment of British Sign Language (SABSL) developed at the University of London in 1997. The SABSL is a production test designed to assess selected aspects of sign language phonology, morphology and syntax based on a videotaped picture description task.

In May, each child in the treatment class was asked by a person other than the teacher (in spoken English) to describe a picture using ASL with no voicing. They had not seen the picture before but had been exposed to the sign vocabulary represented in the picture. Their signed responses were videotaped. The videotapes of the picture description task were assessed by the State Director of Vermont ASL Programs. She is Deaf and ASL is her native language.

The ASL properties evaluated were phonology, morphology, and syntax. ASL phonology concerns handshape, location, movement, palm orientation and non-manual signals. ASL morphology incorporates pronominalization, pluralization, verb agreement, classifiers, temporal aspect, perspective variations, noun/verb pairs, multi-meaning, pronominal reference, spatial agreement, verb of motion and location, and noun modification. ASL syntax includes topicalization, questions, relative clause, negation and affirmation. Some of the properties of ASL were not necessary to perform the task. For example, negation or questions were not needed to describe the picture.

(4) Reading-Readiness Level. The reading-readiness level of the kindergarten students in the treatment class and in the control class was assessed in the schools usual manner by administering the Marie M. Clay Reading Recovery Observation Study (RROS) in June. The three specific aspects considered in this assessment are letter identification, word test, and concepts about print. The RROS is given to all kindergartners to determine their reading level for first grade placement. The treatment classes' RROS results were compared with the results from the schools other typical kindergarten class. This other typical class had not received the sign treatment and functioned as a control class for the reading-readiness aspect of this research study.

Difficulties can sometimes arise when interpreting results data form two pre-existing classes, but in this instance sufficient exit data exists, over an appropriate duration (five years), to clearly demonstrate the parity between the two classes. Although in human research it is virtually impossible to eliminate all confounders, no known disparity existed between the treatment class and the control class prior to the sign language intervention. The two kindergarten classes were considered analogous in respect to student ability and socioeconomic attributes. When students register for school they are placed in the two kindergarten classes in random order. At the end of the school year the students in each class are assessed with the RROS, and are placed in first grade classes according to their RROS results. Prior to this study the two kindergarten teachers had taught kindergarten in the school for five years and were considered to possess equal teaching ability as demonstrated by the fact that in every one of the previous five years the two kindergarten teachers' students' outcomes on the RROS had been comparable. (R. Rosane, principal, personal communication, September 7, 2003).

RESULTS

(1) **Receptive English Vocabulary.** The students earned the mean pretest standard score of 101.9 (sd: 4.47) on the PPVT–III (Form A) receptive vocabulary test and the mean posttest standard score of 115.9 (sd: 11.62) on the PPVT–III (Form B) receptive vocabulary test. A directional-paired t-test showed a significant increase between the pretest and posttest standard scores (t, df 20 = 8.46: p<.001).

The students earned the mean pretest age equivalent score of 68.0 months (5 years, 8 months) (sd: 8.13) on the PPVT–III (Form A) and the mean posttest age equivalent score of 93.8 months (7 years, 8 months) (sd: 19.14) on the PPVT–III (Form B). A directional-paired t-test showed a significant increase between the pretest and posttest age equivalent scores (t, df 20 = 8.35: p<.001).

(2) **Expressive English Vocabulary.** The students earned a mean score of 104.08 (sd: 10.72) on the AGS Expressive Vocabulary Test. A direct comparison of the students' EVT and PPVT–III (Form B) standard scores showed there was no significant or unusual difference between their expressive and receptive vocabulary at the conclusion of the treatment.

(3) **Sign Language Evaluation.** The students demonstrated an average rating on their ASL ability based on their age and the videotaped task. The

phonology assessment showed handshape, location, movement, and palm orientation for 90% of the signs used was correct. None of the students used any nonmanual signals. Students produced fewer morphology aspects. They accurately signed verbs of motion and location and 95% used a pronominal reference along with the verb. Number incorporation was an aspect they all used correctly. Students produced no properties of ASL syntax.

The ASL evaluator commented that she believed many of the children on the tape seemed fearful or intimidated. She felt the students needed to be more prepared for the videotaping experience. She was concerned that the evaluation was not representative of the students' actual ability.

(4) Reading-Readiness Level. On the Marie M. Clay Reading Recovery Observation Survey (RROS) Letter Identification aspect the treatment class earned a mean score of 50.6 (sd: 2.29) and the non-treatment control class earned a mean score of 33.2 (sd: 15.4). A directional t-test for independent groups showed a significantly higher score for the treatment class (t, df16 = 3.55: p<.001).

On the RROS Word Test aspect the treatment class earned a mean score of 3.6 (sd: 2.65) and the nontreatment control class earned a mean score of 1.2 (sd: 2.47). A directional t-test for independent groups showed a significantly higher score for the treatment group (t, df 16 = 1.89: p<.05).

On the RROS Concepts About Print aspect, the treatment class earned a mean score of 12.4 (sd: 2.505) and the nontreatment control class earned a mean score of 10.44 (sd: 3.68). A directional t-test for independent groups showed no significant difference between the groups (t, df 16 = 1.32: p>.05).

DISCUSSION

The students' receptive English vocabulary increased by 14 points. This represents a robust vocabulary gain. The age equivalent measure of the children's receptive English vocabulary escalated from 5 years, 8 months to 7 years, 8 months. The students attained a full two years of vocabulary growth during the nine month program. The age-referenced aspect of the PPVT–III prevents the conclusion that students' vocabulary growth was due to simple maturation.

Their substantial vocabulary increase should engender future academic advantages for these students. Because oral comprehension and reading ability is dependent on vocabulary knowledge (Dunn and Dunn,

1981, and Hirsch, 1998), educators claim students' vocabularies are keys to their academic success. In addition, the expanded vocabulary advantage will most likely be retained, as Daniels (1996b) found that students sustained the vocabulary gains, acquired during a similar sign language intervention, over a three-year period, even when no additional sign language support was provided.

The results of the expressive vocabulary test showed no significant difference between student's receptive and expressive vocabulary ability. It can therefore be assumed that although they were expressing themselves in ASL as well as English there was no diminution of their expressive English ability. This is an important finding as there was some concern that the focus on ASL expression might limit students' expressive English vocabulary.

The sign language evaluation showed the students acquired an appreciable amount of ASL. They learned the phonology first and best, which is the expected acquisition sequence in any new language. The finding that they displayed no nonmanual signals may relate to the fact that they were not taught ASL by a native signer. The nonmanual features of ASL primarily refer to facial grimaces which native signers use naturally. *Accent* in a spoken foreign language is an apt comparison to the nonmanual features of ASL. Their teacher undoubtedly did not emphasize or use this paralanguage because children of their age would normally reproduce these facial attributes easily.

Although the students did less well with ASL morphology, they did use appropriate numbers and in most instances signed the correct verb form. This seemed important. The disappointing finding was the lack of ASL syntax. No student used it. In the UK model all of the students used BSL syntax. There are several plausible explanations for this difference. First, the UK program was 18 months long. This is twice as long as the nine-month US program. Second, the UK program used a native signer while the US program did not. Third, there was concern that the videotaped assessment did not represent the students' true ASL ability.

The RROS reading-readiness results demonstrated a significant difference between the treatment class and the control class in the letter identification aspect of the survey. This is a notable factor because there is a body of literature that indicates a child's familiarity with the letters of the alphabet and speech sounds or phonemes is a strong predictor of the child's future reading capacity (Daniels, 2001b, 26).

Receptive English vocabulary, expressive English vocabulary, ASL ability, and English reading-readiness level were the four critical aspects relating to typical hearing students' language development evaluated in this research study. The outcome of assessments for each of these aspects indicated ASL instruction provided a literacy advantage for these students. Some evidence exists which suggests why this benefit occurred.

Studies conducted by Hoemann and Koenig (1990) established that hearing English speaking students learning ASL employ a separate memory store for each language even in the initial stages of language acquisition. One individual memory store houses the manual alphabet and ASL and another houses the English alphabet characters and English. A possible reason sign language helps hearing English speaking children to recognize letters and increase their English vocabulary may be that they a re now learning a new language, albeit at an early stage, and they have acquired two distinct memory stores to access for search and recall.

Sign training and use rely heavily on sight which is directly related to a child's physiological development. In fact, even though articulated language production and internal processing are developing in young children, they take most of their cues from what they see, not from what they hear. During the first six years of life the eyes are the most acute receptors of knowledge. Over half of the brain is devoted to visual processing and vision itself promotes a measurable impact on the visual cortex. Research findings by Goleman (1995) show that seeing stimulates the formation of increasingly complex neural circuitry in the brain.

This finding corroborates extensive studies by Bonvillian and Floven (1993) who found that both motor ability and visual perception account for the ease and speed of sign language acquisition in young children. At birth, the level of maturation of the motor centers is ahead of that of the speech centers. The developmental advantage presented by the motor centers is maintained during early development and continues in childhood. Basic motor control of the hands occurs before control of the voice and speech, and the visual cortex matures before the auditory cortex. These factors led Bellugi, et. al. (1994) to conclude that linguistic functioning in a visual-gestural language both requires and results in greater visual-spatial processing abilities thus demonstrating a physiological bias for using sign language with young children.

Research endeavors by Capirci, Cattani, Rossini, and Volterra (1998) and Parnis, Samar, Bettger, and Sathe (1996) provide additional support for the position of Bellugi, et. al. that a visual-gestural language is responsible for enhanced visual-spatial competence. The results of the educational experiences reported in Capirci et. al. (1998) demonstrate that hearing children who learn sign as a second language in the early school years improve more rapidly on tests of visual-spatial cognition than their schoolmates not receiving sign language instruction.

The foregoing evidence suggests a number of reasons why ASL provided a literacy advantage for these kindergarten students. However, this research did not seek to provide a reason. It could be one factor or a combination of them or something unsuspected. What the investigation does show is that hearing kindergarten students receiving ASL instruction made a statistically significant gain in receptive English vocabulary, maintained an appropriate amount of expressive English vocabulary while acquiring an average ASL ability, and tested higher than similar students on reading placement measures.

IMPLICATIONS AND CONCLUSIONS

In this study, ASL has been shown to provide academic advantages in a number of realms for hearing students' literacy:

- Although the study size was relatively small, the positive results indicate the ASL treatment should be replicated.
- Future studies ought to have a control class with pre and post-test data for all aspects of the research.
- Students would have a better chance of acquiring ASL syntax if the treatment procedure were extended over a longer period of time.
- By using a pre-kindergarten and a kindergarten class, over a two-year period, a researcher could more closely replicate the 18 month duration of the UK program.
- There are obstacles in acquiring a teacher who is a native signer, but doing so would undoubtedly be a boon for students' ASL ability.
- Furthermore, students should have more experience with videotaping before the videotaped ASL assess-ment is made. This would ensure that the picture test data would accurately represent the students' ASL ability.

For the present, this study's findings confirm those of previous studies that show enriching hearing children's kindergarten instruction with sign language increases their receptive English vocabulary to a statistically significant degree. It extends earlier research, by demonstrating kindergartners acquired a sufficient level of ASL phonology and morphology to understand and use the new language for communication, while simultaneously maintaining their expressive English vocabulary. And finally from the RROS results, this investigation provides some initial evidence that ASL raises the students' reading-readiness level.

REFERENCES

Bartlett, D. E. (1853). Family education for young deaf-mute children. *American Annals of the Deaf and Dumb*, 5, 32–35.

Bellugi, U., O'Grady, L., Lillo-Martin, D. , O'Grady Hynes, M., van Hoek, K.,. & Corina D., (1994). Enhancement of spatial cognition in deaf children. In V. Volterra & C. J. Erting (Eds.), *From gesture to language in hearing and deaf children* (pp. 278–298). Washington, DC : Gallaudet University Press.

Bonvillian, J. D., & Floven, R. J. (1993). Sign language acquisition: Developmental aspects. In M. Marshark & M. D. Clark (Eds.). *Psychological perspectives on deafness.* (pp. 229–265). Hillside, New Jersey : Lawrence Erlbaum Associates.

Bowen, C., Mattheiss, J. H. , & Wilson, R.M. (1993). The signing for reading success study group: An approach to staff development. *Literacy: Issues and Practices*, 10, 48–52.

Capirci, O., Cattani, A., Rossini, P., & Volterra, V. (1998). Teaching sign language to hearing children as a possible factor in cognitive enhancement. *Journal of Deaf Studies and Deaf Education* 3, (2), 135–142.

Cooper, B. (2002). The use of sign language to teach reading to kindergartners. *The Reading Teacher*, 56, (2), 116–119.

Crawford, W. (2001). Say it with sign language. *Principal*, 80, (5), 30–32.

Daniels, M. (1993). ASL as a factor in acquiring English. *Sign Language Studies*, 78, 23–29.

Daniels, M. (1994a). The effect of sign language on hearing children's language development. *Communication Education*, 43, 291–298.

Daniels, M. (1994b). Words more powerful than sound. *Sign Language Studies*, 83, 155–166.

Daniels, M. (1996a). Bilingual, bimodal education for hearing kindergarten students. *Sign Language Studies*, 90, 25–37.

Daniels, M. (1996b). Seeing language: The effect over time of sign language on vocabulary development in early childhood education. *Child Study Journal*, 26 (3), 193–208.

Daniels, M. (1997). Teacher enrichment of prekindergarten curriculum with sign language. *Journal of Research in Childhood Education*, 12 (1), 27–33.

Daniels, M. (2001a). Sign education: A communication tool for young learners. *The Pennsylvania Speech Communication Annual*, LVII, 77–95.

Daniels, M. (2001b). Dancing with words: *Signing for hearing children's literacy.* Westport, Connecticut: Bergin & Garvey.

Daniels, M. (2002). Reading signs: A way to promote early childhood literacy. *Communication Teacher*, 16 (2), 13–15.

Daniels, M. (2003). Using a signed language as a second language for kindergarten students. *Child Study Journal*, 33 (1), 53–70.

Dunn, L. & Dunn, L. (1981). *Peabody picture vocabulary test-r manual.* Circle Pines, MN: American Guidance Service.

Goleman, D. (1995). *Emotional intelligence.* New York: Bantam Books.

Hafer, J. C., & Wilson, R. M. (1996). *Come sign with us.* Washington, DC: Gallaudet University Press.

Heller, I., Manning, D., Pauvr, D., & Wagner, K. (1998). Let's all sign: Enhancing language development in an inclusive preschool. *Teaching Exceptional Children*, Jan/Feb, 50–53.

Hirsch, E. Jr. (1988). The theory behind the dictionary: Cultural literacy and education. In E. Hirsch, Jr, J. Kett, & J. Trefil (Eds.), *The dictionary of cultural literacy* (pp. xi–xv). Boston: Houghton Mifflin.

Hoemann, H., & Koenig, T. (1990). Categorical coding of manual and English alphabet characters by beginning students of American Sign Language. *Sign Language Studies, 67,* 175–181.

Parasnis, I., Samar, V., Bettger, J. G., & Sathe, K. (1996). Does deafness lead to enhancement of visual spatial cognition in children? Negative evidence from deaf nonsigners. *Journal of Deaf Studies and Deaf Education, 1,* (2), 145–152.

Robinson, K., (1997). Sign in education: *The teaching of hearing children British Sign Language in school.* Birmingham, England: Teesside Tec Press.

Stokoe, W. C. (1960). *Sign language structures.* Silver Springs, Maryland: Linstok Press.

ABOUT THE AUTHOR

Marilyn Daniels is a Professor of Communication Arts and Sciences at Penn State University. She authored Benedictine Roots in the Development of Deaf Education: Listening with the Heart, *and, most recently,* Dancing with Words: Signing for Hearing Children's Literacy.

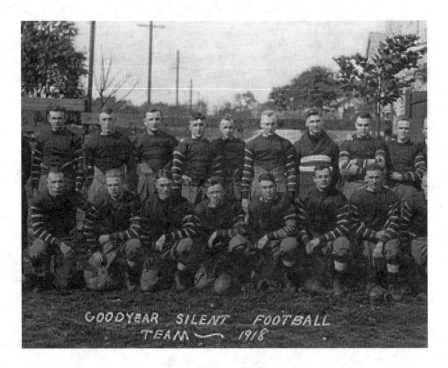

Goodyear Silent Football Team, 1918

Courtesy Gallaudet University Archives

The Role of Discourse in the Assertion of DEAF-WORLD Identities

BRYAN K. ELDREDGE, PH.D.

Bryan Eldredge is the coordinator of the ASL and Deaf Studies Program at Utah Valley State College. He is also a co-founder and co-chair of Deaf Studies Today!

THIS PAPER DESCRIBES THE WAYS deaf people in Utah Valley, Utah (see figure 1) create Deaf identities for themselves and how they bolster or challenge the assertions of others.

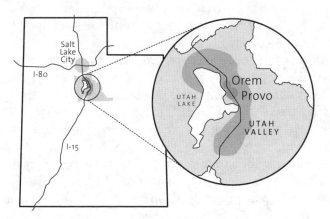

Figure 1: Map of Utah showing the location of Utah Valley (in gray).

It focuses on ways that individuals use discourse to create *personal identities*. Personal identities associate an individual with a group of other individuals who share similar beliefs, values, practices, norms, etc. commonly called "culture." Personal identities mark individuals as a certain *kind of people*. In contrast, *positional identities* designate an individual's position within groups; they mark individuals as certain *kinds of members*.

Deaf people present and interpret four types of performance to determine membership (insider status) or non-membership (outsider status)
in the DEAF-WORLD. Individuals interpret elements of performance either
positively or negatively with respect to membership in the DEAF-WORLD.
In this paper, I describe how some deaf people adroitly display such signs
to assert favorable identities. I explain how, in such cases, the signs serve
to unify interactants, perpetuating personal identities as Deaf for those
involved. In contrast, I describe how, at other times, performances are
interpreted negatively, thereby marking the performers as outsiders.
Finally, I delineate some of the effects these negative interpretations may
have, including marginalization of performers. I present six specific marginalizing practices Deaf people in Utah Valley employ to make clear the
distinctions they detect between themselves and those who present signs
(i.e., performative acts) that are not associated with the DEAF-WORLD.

Before moving on, it is important to note that observers often think
of identities as natural, as an inherent part of an individual's being.
Anthropologists disagree. They contend that individuals construct identities and that identities are malleable and multifaceted. Linguistic anthropologists demonstrate that language is one—if not *the*—primary tool
people employ to both create and project identities. I suggest that this is
the case in the DEAF-WORLD. Deaf people purposively produce forms of
talk that are associated with a specific community of users to negotiate
DEAF-WORLD membership.

The discourse-centered approach to language and culture (Sherzer
1987; Urban 1991) offers ways to investigate these issues. This approach
situates culture in the discourse of a given community, in the actually-
occurring utterances exchanged in the course of everyday life that are
"in themselves, forms of social action" (Graham 1995:6)[2]. Utterances are
not significant simply because they carry referential messages; they gain
at least equal significance because they are "material segments of reality"
which function as "ideological signs" (Voloßinov 1973 [1929]:11). In this
sense, "talk is practice" (Schieffelin 1990:16), and individual speakers
purposely use the linguistic resources to achieve particular social goals
(Bauman 1983; Duranti 1994; Graham 1995; Kulick 1992; Schieffelin
1990; Urban 1991, 1996a, 1996b).

Following Hymes (1972), linguistic anthropologists refer to the
appropriate use of discursive forms within a community as "communicative competence." Hymes recast Chomsky's use of *competence* away
from cognitive constructs (which were rooted in structuralism) and into
the realm of practice. Duranti explains that "[t]o be a competent member
of a given speech community means to be an active consumer and pro-

ducer of texts that exploit heteroglossia³ and at the same time reproduce at least the appearance of an overall encompassing system" (Duranti 1994:6). This is reminiscent of Sapir, who writes, "'He talks like us' is equivalent to saying 'He is one of us'" (1996[1933]:51).

My study reveals that most Deaf people in Utah Valley employ two major processes in these discursive negotiations. I call these two broad processes (1) *unification*, and, (2) *marginalization*. These processes take different shapes and each is semiotically complex. Unification is the unmarked process; it is characterized by "smooth" interactions, interactions that proceed as participants expect. After exploring unification, we will examine the marked process of marginalization.

LANGUAGE AND IDENTITY

Within linguistic anthropology a significant body of literature deals with the relationships between language and identity. Different authors view the nature of that relationship in different ways. One perspective holds that "identity is dependent on specific relationships and sociocultural contexts" and, as a result, speech styles (or language choices) "reflect" the speakers' understandings of themselves (Okamoto 1995:312). This means that a number of simultaneous social factors, such as gender, age, social class, or ethnicity directly influence a person's linguistic behavior (Velásquez 1995) and that differences in people's speech "reflect the social distinctions deemed important by the community of speakers" (Gal 1984 [1978]:292). In this way, individuals signal their identity (and/or their identity is inferred by others) by their speech. As Kroskrity notes, "one's speech is a linguistic biography" (1998:112). And at least one analyst, Mary Bucholtz (1995), argues that a person's linguistic skills alone are enough to allow the individual to "pass" as a member of a given group. Insufficient skill level often results in an "outsider" identity.

The actual signaling and interpreting of an individual's identity(s) occurs through semiotic processes. The use of a discursive feature, such as a particular language or speech style, functions as a *sign vehicle* or, more simply, a *sign*. Peirce defines signs as something that stands for something to somebody "in some respect or capacity" (1985:5). Peirce's semiotic framework has been used to "explain the processes by which instances of discourse operate as complex, multifunctional signs, [because it] offers a more analytically specific paradigm than do other interpretive approaches" (Graham 1995:7). This framework recognizes three different kinds of sign-object relationships. Peirce calls the connections between signs and objects *interpretants* and explains that there are various types of *interpre-*

tants. For example, when a sign's connection to its object comes by virtue of similarity between the sign and object the relationship is iconic and the sign is said to be an *icon.* An indexical relationship exists when signs called *indexes* acquire their meaning from a spatial or temporal co-occurrence with their objects. Finally, *symbols* are connected to their objects by conventional rule or law. Symbols are essentially the "arbitrary" relationships emphasized by Saussure (1966)—their relationships to their objects are unmotivated and are rule governed.

These processes interact one with another. For example, in the case of codeswitching, those present recognize the language a speaker[4] uses as having similarities to other instances of that language being used. Therefore, an iconic connection exists between the present speech act and previous instances. In turn, this similarity acts as an index linking the speaker to a specific speech community because the speech form and the community have shared a contiguous relationship over time (Silverstein 1976).

CONSTRUCTING IDENTITY

Speech can *reflect* a person's identity, but, as Susan Gal explains, there is an even stronger relationship between language and identity: "Categories of women's speech, men's speech, and prestigious or powerful speech are not just indexically derived from identities of speakers. Indeed, sometimes a speaker's utterances *create* her or his identity" (1995:171). The difference here is significant. The act of speaking serves not simply as a mirror through which identity is reflected; rather, speaking plays a crucial role in actually constructing identities (Bauman and Briggs 1990:69; Duranti 1992; Gal 1989; Lindstrom 1992; Livia 1995; Mills 1995; Silverstein 1979:206–207). An individual's choices to use one language over another to assert a more situationally favorable identity exemplifies how participants use discursive forms to negotiate identity (Kroskrity 1993, 1998; Kulick 1992) or, for example, to associate themselves with a more upwardly mobile status (see Gal, 1984 [1978]). Within a single language, the use of "respectful words," such as honorifics, function "not only as labels for an already existing reality but also as ideologically loaded tools for defining the situations in which speakers *qua* social actors co-construct their context" including their individual identities (Duranti 1992:89; see also Gumperz 1972:12; Friedrich 1966). Researchers have identified ways in which children, cross-culturally, are socialized in the process of constructing identities through discourse practices (Cook-Gumperz 1995; Kulick 1992; Schieffelin 1990).

Hill and Zepeda note that people tend to negotiate for themselves a favorable presentation of "self" (1992:197) or "best identity" (1992:204). Goffman (1967) calls this "face." Hill and Zepeda (1992:204) argue that some identities are "problematic—even stigmatized." Speakers walk a fine line as they attempt to construct both personal and positional positive identities for themselves. There are serious consequences when the code chosen (or not chosen) is "seen as expressing social distance and 'outsiderness' to his [community]" (Hill 1995{1985}:408). The distinctions indexed by discursive acts "are not trivial" and they become very significant "when people end up in the 'wrong place,' as outsiders in a community" (Hill and Zepeda 1992:206).

Identity formation can be particularly difficult terrain to navigate through discourse because some discursive practices are valued differently within a speech community. Factors such as the interlocutors' socioeconomic class or gender make a difference (Smith-Hefner 1988; Trudgill 1972) because "different ideologies recognize or highlight different units of language as salient and as indicative of speakers' identities" (Gal 1998:326). To further complicate matters, the way a given form is interpreted is culturally specific, making cross-cultural interpretations very complex (Basso 1979; Cook-Gumperz 1995; Gal 1995; Hill and Zepeda 1992; Kroskrity 1993; Silverstein 1976).

THE SIGNS OF MEMBERSHIP: UNIFICATION

In negotiations over identities, Deaf people mutually assert personal identities as Deaf people. This is *unification*; it occurs when people highlight similarities among themselves. Unification results from interactions in which participants present performative acts that index relationships to the DEAF-WORLD. When an individual sees another's discursive performance as similar to his or her own, he grants status equal to his own. He or she is interpreted as being Deaf. Similarities between the performances mutually reinforce each participant's claims to a Deaf identity. In essence, through this process individuals say, "I am Deaf, and since we are alike, you are Deaf, too."

Unification comes about when individuals present signs that others interpret. These signs come in a variety of forms. Before I describe these forms, however, I must point out again that, in negotiations of this sort, individuals interpret a variety of different parts of the interactions, and different people often interpret the same thing differently. Expectations about the propriety of various behaviors in given contexts always mediate these interpretations. Matching behavioral patterns to expectations lies at the heart of culture. Urban (1989) explains,

> The behavioral, including discourse, patterns of others may be assumed
> without the behavior or discourse simultaneously representing them
> referentially as assumed. This kind of assumption or imitation I will call
> 'iconic otherness' of the self. This is the basic stuff of culture—the par-
> ticipation of individuals in socially transmitted patterns of action and
> representations of the world, which are adopted 'unconsciously' and with-
> out reflection.
>
> At the same time, the adoption of such a pattern is a sign, in particular,
> an icon of the adopted pattern. Insofar as the imitation is faithful, the behav-
> ior, including speech, of the imitating actor is a sign vehicle capable of
> being read by others. (1989:46)

The behavioral patterns of actors are not the only sign vehicles. When
the expectations for behavior (which invariably index ideologies) become
apparent to others, they will themselves become the subjects of interpretation. Goffman describes this process, saying that in interactions each
person

> tends to act out what is sometimes called a *line*—that is, a pattern of
> verbal and nonverbal acts by which he expresses his view of the situation
> and through his evaluation of the participants, especially himself. . . . [I]f
> he is to deal with their response to him he must take into consideration
> the impression they have possibly formed of him.
>
> The term *face* may be defined as the positive social value a person effec-
> tively claims for himself by the line others assume he has taken during
> a particular contact. (1967:5)

Individuals assume "lines" that they believe will present a positive face,
based on their beliefs about how others will interpret them.

Deaf people assume lines by presenting four different elements of
discourse. These elements serve as sign types that indicate DEAF-WORLD
membership and form the basis for unification. They are as follows:

1) The Referential Content Of Talk[5]
2) The Linguistic Form
3) Discursive Form
4) Nonlinguistic Behaviors

THE REFERENTIAL CONTENT OF TALK

It is widely recognized that the referential content of talk, which is the
propositional message, is important for establishing connections to the
DEAF-WORLD. Analysts have long recognized that referential content of
introduction exchanges is important to issues of DEAF-WORLD identity.

Introductions are significant because here individuals make multiple evaluations about who their interlocutors are and how they relate one to another, and because first impressions go a long way. In essence, the referential content of introductions is largely about identity.

Deaf people undertake fairly extensive interactional routines when meeting or being introduced to someone new. Introduction exchanges are fairly uniform among Deaf people around the United States[6] and they are salient enough that curricula for teaching ASL include examples and exegesis of prototypical introduction routines (Lentz, et al. 1988). The specific signal forms vary by context (such as who is being introduced to whom, and when), but each of these signal forms addresses the need to establish connections between interlocutors. Typically, a person introducing an acquaintance to another will give the acquaintance's name. First the introducer then gives other information relevant to Deaf identity, such as mutual acquaintances, onset of deafness, deaf family members (and whether they sign) or, in the case of those whose introduction to signing is fairly recent, when and where the person learned to sign. Introductions, including self-introductions, often also include people's places of origin, which is frequently stated in terms of the residential school they attended.

The sign of membership for which I use the term "referential content" is actually quite narrow. Rather than the meanings of any and all utterances, I here use "referential content" to describe information explicitly about individuals' backgrounds and about their experiences in and with the DEAF-WORLD. For example, in 1999, when the staff members at a camp for Deaf children met for the first time, they took turns introducing themselves before beginning their training. The camp director instructed the staff to give their name, where they were from, and the position they would hold while working at the camp. Many of the individuals, like Danny[7], gave only this information:

> Translation:
> Danny: Hi. My name is Danny. I'm from Orem, Utah. I will work as the [staff position].

However, more than three years later, while reviewing the videotape I took of this meeting, I noticed that those who attended residential schools out of state, like Garret, gave a subtly different introduction.

> Translation:
> Garret: Hi. My name is Garret. I moved to Utah from [state]. I will [duties of staff position].

Garret and the others who followed this pattern had all lived in Utah for ten years or so. Still they were not content to say, "I'm from [city], Utah." Rather, they said, "I moved to Utah from [name of state where attended residential school]." These individuals displayed the kind of felt-connection to their residential school that Deaf people often cite to be a consequence of the school's role in opening the doors to communication and socialization.

Exchanges of such information serve a number of purposes. First, they do simply what they purport to do: they tell something about each person. The door to conversation is then opened and, once the interlocutors discover common ground, they have something to talk about. This in itself can serve to unify relations. The information that is given is equally important to making judgments about identities. It is not just information for information's sake. The significant point here is that interactional routines allow culturally Deaf people to present ties to the DEAF-WORLD— *in the form of referential content*—and to judge the ties of those they meet to the DEAF-WORLD. Residential school experience, deaf family members, acquaintances with other Deaf people, and other such information suggest levels of DEAF-WORLD affiliation. Presumably, the speaker will share at least some of these facts with other people who are involved. The potential result is unification and bonds between the interactants and the DEAF-WORLD.

Negotiations about identity are never just about the identity of one person. The connection between interactants in unifying processes works to simultaneously assert Deaf identities for at least two people.

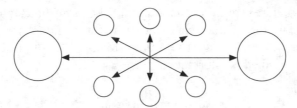

Figure 2: Shared traits link various members (circles represent people and arrows represent shared traits).

By implication, it asserts similar identities for anyone else who shares the trait being discussed. Similarities between people who share identities other than "Deaf" can be subject to the same principles. For example, deaf people who share oralist backgrounds may take comfort in their shared identities. My focus has been on Deaf identities because this identity is positively valued in the DEAF-WORLD, not because the unification processes are significantly different in other situations.

Finally, with regard to the importance of referential content of talk, what is not said is just as significant. Judgments about DEAF-WORLD membership are often tied to behaviors that are considered either hearing- or Deaf-like (i.e., they are indexically linked to either hearing or Deaf people). The use of the telephone is one behavior that is negatively valued in the DEAF-WORLD. Despite the fact that several Deaf people in the area can use the telephone fairly well, I have only rarely seen first meetings between people who consider themselves Deaf in which one of them said something to the effect of, "I can speak and can even use a telephone." The reason for this is clear. To volunteer information about speech abilities and telephone skills is to link oneself to an outsider identity. In fact, I have only seen these proclamations made by deaf people who had only recently begun any real contact with the DEAF-WORLD. In these cases, the individuals said something like, "Well, I'm mostly deaf, but I can hear some..." suggesting that for them *deafness* is still largely about hearing ability rather than social relations.

Admissions to hearing-like abilities or behaviors can limit a person's chances for DEAF-WORLD acceptance. On the other hand, presenting ties to the DEAF-WORLD, such as attendance at residential schools, bolster the chances of acceptance.

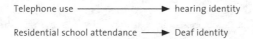

Telephone use ⟶ hearing identity

Residential school attendance ⟶ Deaf identity

Figure 3: Personal traits index (represented by ⟶) various identities Within DEAF-WORLD ideology.

Further complicating this process is the fact that judgments are not only based on the content of such statements, but on the appropriateness of their being made in the first place and the form(s) they take when they are made, as we will examine below. Referential content is important, but it is not the only or perhaps even the most important part of an exchange. Many introductions and first meetings do not follow this script for referential exchange. But even in those cases, identity negotiations are of great significance. Numerous aspects of all interactions are judged for what they say about the speaker. Not least among these is linguistic form, the second of our four signs.

LINGUISTIC FORM

In addition to *what* people say, the linguistic forms they use also serve as signs that are subject to interpretation, and the interpretations affect understandings of membership status. Generally, "linguistic form" refers to a specific language (such as English, Spanish, or ASL) although I will demonstrate below that this is an oversimplification.

Linguistic form refers to a speaker's ability to use a particular language and a speaker's choice to use it rather than other languages. Linguistic form centers on interlingual choices. Speakers have many options when multiple languages are available, and the choices they make are sign vehicles that index identity. For example, the referential content of what deaf people say about themselves during introductions is important. However, Deaf people judge introductions in large part on the forms in which they are presented. Individuals might present identical referential content about themselves through two different kinds of signing, such as ASL and something else. Judgments about these individuals will differ despite the similarity of the content of their messages. Simply put, the form of signing a person uses may have more semiotic weight than what he or she says.

Graham (2002) notes a similar phenomenon in the language choices among Amazonian Indian spokespersons. She writes,

> Facing national and international audiences, indigenous spokespersons invoke language, among other expressive forms such as bodily adornments, to 'perform' or instantiate identity. Conscious of the 'pragmatic salience' (Errington 1985: 294–295) their languages hold for members of the dominant society, Indians strategically deploy linguistic practice to legitimate their 'otherness.'

> Western ideologies of identity posit essential ties between language and culture and impose external definitions of what counts as legitimate in Indians' discursive practice. (2002:188–189)

Individuals take advantage of the conceptualized ties between language and culture in DEAF-WORLD interactions when they choose to use one language (or one signed representation of a spoken language) over another. Deaf people employ ASL and particular *styles* of ASL (a subject that space does not allow me to pursue in this paper) to 'perform' elite identities. The failure to employ valorized identities through effective language performance has the opposite effect. Individuals are attributed lower statuses.

Several deaf people in Utah Valley can give all the "right answers" about their backgrounds to indicate a Deaf identity, yet because of the way they sign, they struggle against alternative interpretations of their identities.[8] The way they sign—interpreted as English-based signing, which I describe below as "poor" ASL—does not agree with what they say. In these instances, the language in which they communicate overwhelms the referential content of what they say, and they are repeatedly judged as something other than culturally Deaf.

Deaf people associate certain "clusters of formal characteristics" (Urban 1985:313) as being "signed English" or "not ASL." The formal characteristics that typify signed English include MCE affixes, initialized signs, heavily linear constructions, signed English idioms, exaggerated over-mouthing, and lack of grammatical non-manual signals. While signed English is not ASL, it is a form of signing and it serves as a sign vehicle. Its use highlights the contexts in which its use would be appropriate (e.g., by orally-raised deaf people, in schools run by hearing people where ASL is frowned upon, or by speech pathologists). It also indexes topics of discussions that deal with perceived deficiencies in deaf people and the efforts to enlighten them in the ways of the hearing world. Specifically, manual codes for English index the hearing-controlled deaf education establishment. The result is that Deaf people associate this style with outsiderness.

While most Deaf people consider contact signing as something other than ASL, it is important in the DEAF-WORLD. As a marked form of signing, its use highlights contexts associated with outsiders. Contact signing is more generally accepted than MCEs. However, Deaf individuals gauge its appropriateness in the perceived identity of the individual's interlocutor as well as the interlocutor's signing abilities. Contact signing may be appropriate for Deaf people when they are interacting with hearing signers or with other outsiders who communicate more easily in contact signing than in ASL, but it is generally inappropriate for use between culturally Deaf persons.

Judgments about the appropriateness of linguistic forms in ASL are similar to those based on language standards more generally, wherein the use of standardized forms becomes the emblem of membership (Silverstein 2000). The language(s) not used are just as important as the language used. Keep in mind that the language used is not really what individuals judge; rather, it is the *choice* to use that language from among other possible alternatives that is significant. ASL fills this role as an emblem of membership in the DEAF-WORLD. However, membership is not simply indexed by the production of grammatical ASL sentences in conjunction with referential content. The process is much more complex. Among other things, it includes internal variations within ASL, which I will describe below.

At the beginning of this section I stated that to define a linguistic form as a particular language is an oversimplification. This is true because no speaker presents a whole language in his or her speech. Rather, individuals present words, phrases, or sentences which listeners interpret to be tokens of a particular language. On the surface this distinction may appear to add unnecessary complexity to the matter; however, in the case where two languages are closely related, or when two languages are in intense contact with each another, an individual's utterances may not always clearly be part of one language or another.

This is the case in the DEAF-WORLD where artificial sign systems representing English have borrowed ASL words as their core vocabulary. This ambiguity is exacerbated by the presence of "contact signing," resulting in a continuum between ASL and English signing. In this case, certain lexical items (for example, to take one level of analysis) are regularly associated with one form or another while ASL and MCEs may share other lexemes. The result is a semiotically complex situation in which individuals take certain signs and sign formations to index a particular language (or, in the case of MCEs, to index a code for language). The language, in turn, indexes certain identities.

DISCURSIVE FORM

The third category of interpretable signs of identity is discursive form. Discursive forms are those elements of discourse that fall outside of referential content and linguistic form. These sign vehicles deal primarily with the organization of certain features of talk. They primarily come in two varieties: *style* and *discursive organization*.

Style. The term "style" refers to formal intralingual choices among a range of potential varieties of talk. Style contrasts with linguistic form. Both terms refer to linguistic choices, but style refers to choices between speech varieties within a single language rather than to choices among different languages that, in the present discussion, are related to "form." To speak of *styles* (plural) is to acknowledge formal differences among various ways of speaking. Examples of styles that English speakers recognize are particular kinds of talk that are characteristic of political speeches, comedic monologues, pep talks, and many others. Because stylistic variations are intralingual, a speaker's use of the various available styles has more to do with positional identity than it does with personal identity. At this point, the significance of styles lies in they ways they contrast with discursive organization.

Discursive Organization.[9] Discursive organization is the way discourse unfolds; members of the DEAF-WORLD make judgments about this as they about content and style. In every human interaction, participants bring expectations about how discourse should proceed (Schlegoff 1972; Schlegoff 2000; Schlegoff, Jefferson, and Sacks 1977). These expectations take many forms. Some of these expectations deal with matters of style as I have explained. Discursive organization extends beyond style to encompass other aspects of the organizational structure of discursive interactions. It includes a fairly wide range of phenomena, many of which involve politeness.

Four types of organizational elements are the most common and most influential in the DEAF-WORLD:

1) The appropriate use of interactional devices such as turn-taking and turn-giving, attention getting, topic introduction, and leave taking.
2) The (in)appropriateness of various topics for discussion, including taboo subjects such as bodily functions, sex, or physical appearance.
3) The organization of information within narratives, such as a chronological presentation of events.[10]
4) The performance of ritualized interactional routines, such as greetings or collaborative joke making.

Significantly, these elements operate below the level of conscious awareness; Deaf people do not generally consciously track their progression. These elements usually become apparent only when they go awry. When interactions unfold in a straightforward manner, the door to unification is opened. The ease with which an exchange takes place highlights shared knowledge and expectations among participants. The uninterrupted flow of interaction is born of common expectations, which come from past discursive experience that is linked to the DEAF-WORLD.

NONLINGUISTIC BEHAVIORS

I use the term nonlinguistic behaviors for the fourth kind of signaling behavior that plays into unifying processes. With this phrase, I refer to a broad range of behaviors that include, but are not limited to, gestures and the etiquette of nonlinguistic behaviors such as whether to talk with your mouth full or empty.[11] These behaviors also encompass nonlinguistic actions that are judged for appropriateness and are closely tied to notions of etiquette.

Nonlinguistic behaviors come in two main varieties: ritualized and nonritualized. Most members of a group will interpret ritualized behaviors in the same way; they are conventional. A bow or curtsy, military salutes, and arm signals used by traffic cops all fall into this category. Nonritualized behaviors are interpreted but unlike ritualized behaviors they are much less likely to be interpreted the same way by different people in the same context. Things like swinging a foot, placing a napkin on one's lap, and avoiding eye contact in elevators fall into this category. These can be interpreted with respect to identity because members of certain communities may demonstrate certain regularities in their use. However, the behaviors themselves do not have generally-agreed-upon interpretations.

Saying that these behaviors are nonlinguistic does not suggest that they are entirely removed from language; they are not. In fact, many nonlinguistic behaviors are related to language in one way or another. Many of them are timed to talk. For example, a wave of the hand may emphasize a point simultaneously being made with speech. Other nonlinguistic behaviors are triggered by talk. Many gestures, particularly obscene ones, can be provoked by talk.

Nonlinguistic behaviors are important in several ways. First, they are part of the communication context. They help determine how the discourse will flow, guiding it from one potential turn to another. Second, these behaviors act as signs that index identity. Virtually all behaviors are meaningful in some way—people look for and see meaning in them. The key here is that people base their interpretations of nonlinguistic behaviors on their expectations for how one ought to behave. When a person's behaviors match the expectations others have for members—for example, for Deaf people—there is potential for a unifying process.

This unifying process occurs in two different, but related, ways. First, when behaviors match expectations—when turn-taking proceeds without incident, people feel comfortable that they are positioned at a comfortable distance, and so on—communication moves smoothly. In short, people feel comfortable because they have categorized, perhaps subconsciously, their interlocutor(s) as "normal." When there is nothing particularly unusual about the way the other person acts, when nothing that would overtly mark the person as being unfamiliar with the ways of the group, members are at ease.

The second way these behaviors act as signs is through their association with specific groups of people (and are frequently subject to stereotyping). For instance, bowing slightly with one's eyes cast downward and holding one's hands closely to the side indexes Asian cultures. Salutes are associated with the military or other highly structured, discipline-based organizations such as the Boy Scouts of America. We have already discussed some examples of behaviors that are linked to either Deaf or hearing identities, including the use of the telephone, the use of ASL, speaking in Deaf gatherings, and so on.

Similarly, the failure of addressees to maintain eye contact with a signer almost always indicates nonmember status to Deaf people. Signers can look away from addressees, but the opposite action creates a break in communication. Those experienced in the DEAF-WORLD almost never take their eyes off a signer without first asking for a pause. However, oral training for deaf people teaches deaf children to do just that. Because the aim of oralism is to restore deaf people to hearing society, oral deaf people are taught to break eye contact at regular intervals, even as they are trying to lipread. Throughout an oral deaf child's early years, parents and teachers emphasize that they must not stare at a speaker, both because it is rude and because it will give away their deafness. The irony, of course, is that in DEAF-WORLD settings, looking away is the rude behavior. The person who breaks eye contact is associated with hearing people and hearing ways. The nonlinguistic behavior is indexically linked to hearing people and those who perform it are associated with that group as well. This same process occurs with a wide variety of nonlinguistic behaviors.

SUMMARIZING UNIFICATION

Deaf people regularly present and interpret the four kinds of sign vehicles I have discussed here in their identity negotiations. These interpretations are potentially unifying in that individuals create Deaf identities for themselves by tying them to the identities of their interlocutors and vice versa. They accomplish this through skillfully displaying interpretable identity indicators. However, another layer of complexity is important to these negotiations. Thus far I have only implied it: individuals never engage in these negotiations in a vacuum. Contextual factors play an important role in determining how interlocutors interpret the sign vehicles that are present.

CONTEXT

Context is not a sign vehicle that indexes individuals' identities. It does, however, affect the indexical relationships associated with the referential content, the linguistic form, the discursive form, and nonlinguistic behaviors. To understand how these interpretations take place, we must consider the role of context in interpersonal exchanges.

Context is generally understood as the situation in which an event occurs. This includes details such as location, time, and the people who are present. However, to say that discourse takes place "within a given context" is to overlook the role that discourse itself plays in the creation of context.

Duranti (1992) argues that there is a reflexive relationship between language and context and that the use of language itself helps to define just what the context is. Lindstrom explains,

> Context is a field of power relations. It is not, however, a frozen field. Context rolls as people talk. Preexisting discourses and discursive conditions do set limits on talk, but they are never totally determinant. People can occasionally say the unsayable. They can contest the context, by evoking available alternative or competing discourses. There is an interrelation between talk and context. (1992:102–103)

Lindstrom rightly argues that contexts are contestable, and that they are contested through language (Woolard 1992). Context is not a linguistic form, nor a discursive form, per se, but interlingual and intralingual choices derive their meanings principally from their association with and relation to context. Simultaneously, language choices create context. As I use it here, context is constantly under construction during all interactions. It is not a static environment in which people find themselves. Context is a dynamic creation that owes its existence, in large part, to acts, discursive and otherwise. Each act affects context, either by maintaining it or by changing it. Significantly, context itself is constituted by fixed particulars of the environment *and* utterances and other acts by those present. Hanks argues that the context is an ideological construction, saying,

> native speakers *typify their own language and speech*. This means in turn that the semantics and context of speaking are partly defined by the ideas of native speakers, however distorted these may appear from an analytical perspective. (1996:170; emphasis in original)

To summarize, linguistic forms act as signs that are interpreted as being linked to the group. But to simply use ASL is not enough. One must make stylistic choices within ASL and the forms chosen must be appropriate to the context. One must give the right answers (i.e., referential content), in the right language (i.e., linguistic form), and in the right way (i.e., discursive form). In all of these cases, what is "right" depends largely on context, even as context depends on the interaction itself. To successfully manage these different aspects of an interaction is to display a degree of communicative competence. When interactants share this communicative competence, it invokes unification that mutually supports the claims of each person to DEAF-WORLD membership. In other words, it creates an inclusive "us."

In describing the process of unification, I said that individuals present sign vehicles of various types through discourse and that others alternatively see these as indexing identities similar to or different from their own. I also said that judgments of similarity lead to unification. On the surface at least, unification appears to be mutually beneficial to those involved; it supports claims to Deaf identities and it asserts a similar personal identity for others. This can be the case, particularly in interactions involving only two people.

However, in more complex contexts, unifying processes can be used to discredit or limit some claims to Deaf identities. This is possible because not all interactants in a given setting will share the highlighted "Deaf qualities." In fact, the similarities among some participants are highlighted precisely for the purpose of exposing their absence in others. The result is marginalization. *Marginalization* highlights differences, not similarities.

MARGINALIZING PRACTICES

In the previous section I presented four different parts of interactions that are judged for evidence of identity. Positive interpretations allow the interaction to proceed "normally," resulting in unification with favorable identities being asserted and accepted. Not surprisingly, negative interpretations have significant influence on judgments of identity as well; foremost among them is the process of marginalization. However, unlike unification, which flows from uninterrupted exchange, marginalization is a process that individuals *invoke* through certain practices. I call these *marginalizing practices*. They highlight *differences* or point out inequalities in status among the participants. These practices distance Deaf people from those they perceive as outsiders;[12] they simultaneously reinforce insider status and identity boundaries. As with unification, in marginalization we see that negotiations about identity are never about a single person or even a single group of people. When invoked, marginalizing practices mark individuals as *relatively* more or less Deaf. When one is marginalized, others are *centralized*.[13]

Marginalizing practices come into play in three contexts: 1) when one or more of the interpretable signs presented during discursive acts does not meet expectations for culturally Deaf people; 2) when these signs trigger association with some entity other than the DEAF-WORLD; or, quite often, 3) both of the above. These practices result from negative interpretations of the four types of signs discussed in the previous section.

In this section I present six different practices that Deaf people use to marginalize others. It is likely that there are other practices common to other local communities and perhaps even in use within Utah Valley, but these six practices are both common and effective within this community. They are:

1) Refusal to Engage
2) Direct Criticism
3) Intentional Linguistic Opaqueness
4) Foreigner Talk
5) Affected Incomprehension
6) Mocking

REFUSAL TO ENGAGE

The first marginalizing practice is a *refusal to engage*. Two forms of refusals are widely used in Utah Valley: The *short-term refusal* and the *long-term refusal*. With short-term refusals, Deaf people who are making new acquaintances will make quick judgments about those they meet. When the referential content of a person's signing, their language or discursive forms, or nonlinguistic behaviors indicate a significant difference from the Deaf person (or at least his or her ideas about what constitutes Deaf identity), the Deaf person breaks off the interaction after a very short time. To do so they will sometimes contrive excuses for why they cannot stay and talk thereby demonstrating signs of politeness (see Brown and Levinson 1999 for a discussion of how politeness may be a universal of language use).

Long-term refusals occur when individuals continually avoid engaging in conversations with those whom they judge as lacking a Deaf identity. This does not mean that Deaf people will never interact with these people. They will when necessary, but they actively avoid unnecessary interaction. For example, when I asked one Deaf woman, Shannon, how she would describe bad signing, she said it is "expressionless, linear" signing that resembles English. Tellingly, she then added, "I don't associate with those people."

This avoidance does not go unnoticed. In the interviews I conducted, some people expressed frustration at being left out and others told me that the people they tend to avoid sometimes accuse them of ignoring them. The interviewees said that they usually explain that they are not trying to avoid anyone but they just find that they do not have much to talk about with some people. In a few extreme cases, long-term refusers excused their avoidance of people who use something other than ASL on the basis that communication is just too slow and tedious.

In interviews, some Deaf people acknowledge that they do practice refusals as I witnessed. These admissions are interesting because long-term refusals are paradoxical. They appear to contradict an ideology Deaf people explained again and again, that it is important to try to interact with deaf people whose signing and experiences are different from their own. My experience confirms that Deaf people generally are open to potential new DEAF-WORLD members. In such cases, it is important to give the deaf or hard-of-hearing person a chance to become Deaf. Deaf people who themselves have only recently gone through this acculturation process often mention that some Deaf people are more patient than others. One woman told me,

> It depends on the individual. Some are opposed to SEE and will resist people who use it. They might even be rude to them directly. Others are more patient and will try to teach them, saying, 'Do you know that sign?' and try to change them and give them time to change. You can't change instantly. That's impossible. It takes time. I've been learning ASL for three years now.

Even those who are willing to help in most instances do not always do so. The dividing line rests on judgments of what a person's abilities and experiences are. It also has to do with personal history and a person's attitudes towards changing his or herself. As Shannon, introduced above, told me, "If the person is willing to change, people will support that and ....they will be excited. But if she won't change, they just leave her alone and don't say anything." Those who are willing to respond and who demonstrate a desire to become "more Deaf" are given more leeway. In these cases, it is not so much their current skill level but where they appear to be headed that makes the difference. The consequences can be quite severe for those who are not willing to change. I asked a Deaf friend of mine what happens to those who do not conform. He told me,

> They are limited socially. They might not go as regularly to socialize with people who are good signers, like at the Deaf center a few people will show up....They won't participate as much. They might sit by themselves and watch volleyball tournaments or basketball tournaments. Then they might see someone [they do associate with] and they will get all excited and wave. They have the same group of people they interact with. They become, well they don't really get involved with us; they have their own group of people who are on the same level communication wise and they will all sit together.

DIRECT CRITICISM

The second marginalizing process is *direct criticism*. This express form of marginalization exposes shortcomings in abilities. More importantly, it

highlights differences in ideological positions. Direct criticism says something about the identities of both parties and it accentuates distance. Deaf
people often aim direct criticisms at "bad signing," although they address
other behaviors as well, and these are sometimes sharp. One informant
with an oral background told me that she often sees people criticize others by saying, "You are wrong!" This informant objected to such direct
criticism, contending that encouragement would help individuals more.
Significantly, she associated criticism of this sort with ASL users. She
said direct criticism serves no purpose. In fact, her observation may illuminate just how purposive and effective it can be. Directness indexes those
who do it to the DEAF-WORLD even as it marginalizes its targets. It may
have a similar effect on those who object to its use.

Direct criticism, however, need not be serious to be effective. At times
it appears as attempts to belittle or mock another's, but it can also be
offered kindly in the form of a suggestion and still be a form of marginalization. Direct criticism signals a failure to meet the expectations of
the critic. And although it potentially results in marginalization of the
person who was criticized, it does not necessarily preclude him or her
from claiming a Deaf identity. In fact, criticism of this sort is an attempt
at acculturation. Criticizing individuals shows them the things that mark
them as outsiders. Pointing out weaknesses does more than explain why
people do not belong. It illuminates the road to belonging. The ideology
holds that pointing out shortcomings is helpful because it opens the way
to eliminating them.

INTENTIONAL LINGUISTIC OPAQUENESS

The third marginalizing response, *intentional linguistic opaqueness,* is
related to refusals to engage. I fell victim to it several times early in my
introduction to the DEAF-WORLD. In practice, intentional linguistic opaqueness occurs when Deaf people knowingly use language forms that are
difficult or impossible for a would-be interactant to understand. Deaf
people will engage the interactants, but along the way they deliberately
attempt to make communication fail, placing the blame for the failure
on the other person's lack of competence. More precisely, the communication does not fail; the exchange clearly communicates a message, but
the message is something other than what they talk about.

The message is simply that the signer and his or her interlocutor do
not share the same skills and experiences. That differential puts the interlocutor in a very powerless situation. Because the talk is incomprehensible, it shifts attention away from the referential content of talk and places

it squarely in matters of identity. This practice is relatively rare. In fact, I was not able to capture the practice on video during my fieldwork, although I saw it performed on several occasions during that time and over the years prior to it. I have also discussed the practice with informants, all of whom admitted not only to having seen it, but to having done it themselves.

Deaf people use this tactic when an individual with limited ASL comprehension skills pretends to understand what the Deaf person says.[14] This pretending is a common defense mechanism among hearing ASL students who find humiliation in admitting their failure to understand.[15] When Deaf people recognize that an individual is just nodding his head without really understanding, they sometimes turn the discussion in ways that will expose the pretense and further embarrass the outsider.

This practice calls direct attention to the marginalized person's linguistic deficiencies; by highlighting them, the person is picked on. There are two parts to this act. The first is to ensure that the victim's comprehension is not complete. The second part is to turn the topic in such a way that the victim head nods agreement to something that proves he or she does not understand.

To do this, the signer will generally ask a question like, "So do you make out with your brother all the time?" To further ensure that the content of the question is not understood, signers turn to even more "pure" forms of ASL (those unlike English in various respects). They avoid iconic signs in forming such questions and they eliminate mouthing.

Signers also use relatively obscure signs as well as classifiers and role shifting (which allows the omission of some pronominal references and makes those that remain harder to follow). They may also speed up the signing and add more fingerspelling. What is made clear is the nonmanual marker for a yes/no question, which most novice signers readily recognize. When victims are presented with what they see is clearly a question although she does not understand the content, she is left with only two courses of action. The individual can either admit not understanding—and thereby demonstrate a gap in her linguistic ability, or she can continue to feign understanding, such as nodding in agreement and pretending to understand. The latter choice invariably results in even more extreme attention to the linguistic differences, because when the opaqueness is intentional, the signer who is trying not to be understood will be able to see when the other person is lost. Yet either response highlights a difference between the signer and the victim, thereby marginalizing the victim.

Deaf people view intentional linguistic opaqueness as a kind of joke. It is, however, an unkind joke, making an interlocutor look bad by exposing important weaknesses. When individuals choose to be intentionally opaque, it is usually because they are frustrated by having to interact with someone whose communication abilities are clearly unDeaf. He or she is usually annoyed with the person being marginalized. In this case, the attempt to marginalize is intentional.

What the victim is made to agree with depends on the degree to which the signer wishes to humiliate him or her. A mild humiliation might consist of getting the victim to agree he or she is Deaf when everyone knows this is false. A more vicious attack would have the victim unwittingly agreeing to having committed some kind of crime or an inappropriate sex act. This practice commonly takes place in the presence of another person who can be in on the trick. The third person may or may not actively participate, but his or her presence serves to solidify the contrast between the person being tricked and the one doing the tricking, thereby marking the distinction between the Deaf people's "us" and the outsider's "you." In this sense, intentional opaqueness can be simultaneously marginalizing and unifying.

FOREIGNER TALK

Of course, Deaf people do not always obscure what they say from those who are not proficient in ASL. Certainly, there are many times when Deaf people adjust their signing to be more readily understood by an outsider. This phenomenon of linguistic accommodation, commonly known as foreigner talk, is found in various cultures around the world (Crystal 1987). Some aspects of *foreigner talk* appear to be universal while others are culturally specific (Anonymous 1991). In the DEAF-WORLD, foreigner talk consists of form simplification. Signers slow down, use English syntactic structures, and mouth English words.[16] Utterances in foreigner talk are often short and function words are omitted. Foreigner talk is also characterized by a great deal of repetition and circumlocution to work around gaps in the outsider's knowledge.

Significantly, foreigner talk is a particular speech style that Deaf people employ to accommodate others. Ostensibly, it facilitates communication among people whose native languages differ. Its use in the DEAF-WORLD is normally an honest attempt at helping someone with minimal ASL skills understand what's being communicated. It is used in a wide breadth of diverse contexts, from business transactions to flirting. One result of using foreigner talk is the marginalization of the Deaf person's interlocutor. This marginalization differs from some other forms in that it is not mean-spirited.[17]

Foreigner talk results from an attempt to communicate. The need for it in an exchange makes clear the discrepancy in language skills between Deaf and nonDeaf peoples, but it does so in an attempt to cross those differences. As we saw in the exchange between Nancy and Maryann, foreigner talk unites interlocutors in a shared endeavor: discourse. But this style also highlights the differences between them. The switch to foreigner talk asserts opposite identities for the interlocutors, foregrounding linguistic power differentials. In other words, foreigner talk marginalizes.

AFFECTED INCOMPREHENSION

The fifth marginalizing practice is almost the opposite of intentional linguistic opaqueness. *Affected incomprehension* occurs when Deaf people pretend not to understand a person who uses SEE or who signs poorly in some other respect.[8] This is particularly effective when the addressee, who feigns an inability to understand, has a well-established identity as a culturally Deaf person. The effect is to exclude the signer from access to communication within the group. In effect, it says, "You sign, but you don't speak our language."

In practice, Deaf people feign not understanding by repeatedly saying, "What?" or simply staring at the signer with a perplexed look and perhaps a shrug of the shoulders. Often the person being marginalized does not immediately recognize what is happening. After several repetitions, the person feigning incomprehension begins to laugh or otherwise makes it obvious that he or she is giving the outsider a hard time. With the person's admission of understanding, the outsider's signing style is highlighted as being significantly different from that of Deaf individuals. It says, in essence, "Even though I really understand you, the way you sign gives me reason not to." Accenting this important difference results in distancing between the signer and the addressee.

Feigned incomprehension is also a relatively rare phenomenon, rare enough that I could not find an example of it in my video recordings although I have witnessed it several times. It is usually seen as a kind of joke, although it is still important. Victims of affected incomprehension usually get the message. When possible, they often adjust their signing away from the "incomprehensible" or negatively valued form. In cases where this is not possible, the outsider is rendered powerless and they may feel that any communication that takes place from that time forward is by the grace of the Deaf person who puts up with an inappropriate communication system.

MOCKING

Mocking is simply the belittling of another's acts. Both linguistic and non-linguistic acts are subject to this practice. Sometimes Deaf people mock a person's actions directly, in that person's presence. This can take two different forms that I call *friendly* and *serious*.

Friendly Mocking. Friendly mocking is presented as teasing. A Deaf person may sarcastically repeat something someone says or does. If it is friendly mocking, the repetition is done with a smile or at least with some kind of "repair work" to frame it as helpful guidance.[19] This friendly teasing allows the participant an "offering," the opportunity to correct for the offense, thereby "saving face" (Goffman 1967). This differs from direct criticism, which is done in the form of sarcastic imitation and is usually accompanied by plenty of chuckling, if not laughter.

Friendly mocking is marginalizing because it calls attention to a perceived inadequacy in a person, creating a difference between the mocker and the target. Significantly, the difference ostensibly exists between the target and DEAF-WORLD members. Framing the mocking as "friendly" usually diffuses the tension that normally results from mocking, but does not erase the inadequacy it highlights.[20] For the most part, friendly mocking has more to do with excusing the mocker for a mistake or lack of skill than it does with preserving a bond between the mocker and the victim.

The very act of pointing out the inappropriateness of the victim's signing (or any other action) distances the mocker from the target. It does so in two ways. First, it highlights the inadequacy of the "victim's" signing. Second, it highlights the competence of the person doing the deriding. Friendly mocking places the target in a powerless position. If mocking is presented as teasing, the target is the butt of the joke and his or her inadequacies are the punch line. Even when the mocker colors the mocking as guidance, the target's need for guidance is highlighted, and the person deriding him or her is set up as one capable of providing guidance.

It is important to note that very often this kind of mocking is directed not at hearing people, but at deaf people who are being enculturated. A Deaf woman, Shannon, described this to me during an interview. She said:

Shannon: Sometimes they [SEE signers] get teased or mocked.

BKE: Really? Like what?

Shannon: Like *(As another person using SEE.)* I HAVE... *(As ASL user.)* [They will] jostle other person and say sarcastically, "HAVE?!" Get out!

> BKE: Do you tell them straight to their face like that, or do you just keep quiet and walk away and then talk about them to other people?

> Shannon: Both. Both. Both. (As ASL user.) "That's SEE!" *(As SEE user.)* "Oh. I didn't know HA*VE*, HA*S*, HA*D* were SEE. Really?" He/she is ignorant but the Deaf community will mock him or her, plus *(As another Deaf person.)* They will bump each other with their elbows and say, "Did you see her using SEE. She doesn't belong." (As herself.) It's not fair. She doesn't know, just like me in junior high. I went in and didn't know that was SEE. It was just signing and that was great. I was surprised later to realize the specifics.

Shannon's account describes how Deaf people repeat offending elements of others' signing. It also highlights some forms of signing that are considered characteristic features of the SEE sign, specifically initialized signs and English grammatical function words. The kind of mocking Shannon describes clearly marginalizes those who use SEE. However, it is aimed at standardizing signing in the DEAF-WORLD in more highly valued forms and at discouraging the use of forms that belong to the hearing. Not all mocking is intended to be so helpful.

Serious Mocking. Serious mocking is unapologetic. It is usually done in such a way that hearing people find offensive,[21] particularly when they are its targets. Deaf people, however, with their more accepting views towards direct speech, may recognize it as painful but will not characterize it as rude or uncalled for. It is not unusual for serious mocking to have attached a comment to it regarding what the usage indicates about the victim. For example, the mocker may also label the victim as hard-of-hearing or THINK-HEARING.

Serious mocking can be done either in the presence of the target, or later, away from the target. In either case, it is potentially damaging to the mocked person's identity as a DEAF-WORLD member. When engaged in serious mocking, the mocker imitates individuals (or groups of individuals), taking on characteristics of the individuals' signing. At times what the mocker says may reflect the talk of the victim(s), but often it does not. The form of the signing is the important part. In performing their imitations, mockers often refuse to identify the individual(s) they imitate, although the imitations usually make the target quite clear. However, by not explicitly stating the target's name, the mocker maintains his or her innocence against resulting accusations of impugning or backstabbing.

Regardless of whether the victim's identity remains anonymous, serious mocking marginalizes anyone whose signing resembles the behavior that is mocked. It both establishes and maintains lines separating "us" from "them." Deaf people (as well as interpreters and other hearing people who are closely allied with them) very often carry on short interactions in exaggerated "unDeaf" forms of signing. These exchanges typically include exaggerated over mouthing of English words and/or the use of MCE signs or constructions. Mocking of this sort is more than mere repetition of mistakes; it is a playful and skillful display of the interplay between ASL and various forms of English. Mocking is a display of meta-linguistic awareness and significance.

In this respect, the mocking (when performed properly) serves a purpose beyond marginalization and beyond being a good sport; it is also a unifying practice. It says, in essence, "This is not who we are" or "That kind of language use is not ours, and it is laughable. We can share our disdain for it." By extension it points to essential differences between Deaf people and those whose signing or other acts are alien. As with affected incomprehension, the same practice that marginalizes two or more people can simultaneously unify others. Mockers not only point out failings in others, but they also demonstrate their own knowledge and abilities. Bystanders to the mocking may participate through expressions of support for the mocker or simply by laughing at the mocking. This is yet another example of unification.

Finally, the similarity of a given instance of mocking to previous mockings creates iconic and indexical links to the past. But more important than the links to the past are the links to other Deaf people who executed those past acts. The links tie the mocker to a diachronic set of social networks, the DEAF-WORLD, and distances the target from it. In all of these cases, the actions of Deaf people call attention to the indexical relationships between the signs and those who use them.

FUNCTIONS OF MARGINALIZATION PRACTICES

It is tempting to assume that marginalizing practices are the product of petty self-interest, constituting little more than a form of discrimination. But marginalization, like unification, serves some specific social functions that aid in the perpetuation of the DEAF-WORLD itself. Marginalizing certain people serves to protect the DEAF-WORLD from outside influence. This insulates the DEAF-WORLD from those (deaf or hearing) people who have political ideas and allegiances that are out of line with Deaf-centered views. Significantly, the absence of these marginalizing practices can be just as significant as their presence. That is, the absence of marginalizing processes can in itself function as a sign of acceptance and can serve to validate and perpetuate Deaf identities.

IDEOLOGY AS MEDIATOR

In this paper I have shown that linguistic forms often indicate identities and relations to communities. These forms are sometimes interlingual, valorizing one language over another, wherein speakers take advantage of paradigmatic relationships among languages through the intentional use of code switching and similar resources.

Even within a single language, however, certain forms are favored over others. For example, in the American media we find very few examples of national broadcast journalists who speak with southern "drawls" or Boston accents. Those who normally have such accents are coached toward more standard forms of pronunciation.

These intralingual distinctions, including the preference for particular sounds, words, phrases, and other structures, imply something about speakers. The forms speakers use suggest something about where the speakers' place of origin, among other things including their intelligence, education, mood, social class, ethnic group, and attitudes. Speakers often choose between forms to achieve particular ends.

Most people are aware that we make judgments about each other's speech. It is vital to remember, however, Woolard's admonition (1998) that ideological interpretations always mediate the forms' *effects* that are created by language use—be they either inter- or intralingual. The meanings associated with specific language forms gain their significance from culturally constructed language ideologies. They evolve out of interactions over time. Among other things, this implies that both the forms and their *interpretations* are susceptible to change through continued use. The form of a given utterance always differs in at least some small respect from every other instance. Eventually, these differences can have a cumulative effect, and the form itself is consistently different from its previous shape.

In the case of ASL, their similarity to past performances, their salience as tokens of a DEAF-WORLD type, perpetuates a sense that it is "the same" community. In much the same way, an individual is identified as being Deaf because he or she is "the same as" other Deaf people. The point is that specific linguistic forms trigger judgments, but it would be a mistake to say that the forms are at the heart of what is being judged. In reality, the forms' significance lies in the language ideologies individuals see them as representing. In essence, language use is the window through which observations and subsequent judgments about ideology are made.

IMPLICATIONS

The foregrounding of discourse practices in identity formation as well as its role in the perpetuation of the DEAF-WORLD carries numerous implications. Perhaps most obvious and most important is the need for deaf children to have contact with Deaf ASL users early and often. Educational tracking of deaf children very often aims to put as much emphasis as possible on the acquisition of speech, and all too often, exposure to signing is regarded as a detriment to their learning. The research presented here is directly relevant to this topic because it suggests that not only does a late introduction to both ASL and to Deaf adults limit children linguistically, but it therefore significantly limits them socially as well.

Those without early access to a signed language will probably be marginalized when they try to enter the DEAF-WORLD. The contribution of this work is a clarification as to why this happens and of the processes by which it takes place. Those with early access to Deaf ways have a better chance of achieving a sufficient degree of communicative competence to establish themselves as members of the DEAF-WORLD. By the same token, those like the deaf children of Deaf adults who are most likely to be enculturated early and to be placed in educational programs which value and use ASL (regardless of whether or not speech is also taught).

CONCLUSION

This paper has focused on the processes involved in the assertion of personal identities in the DEAF-WORLD. I have explained how deaf people establish themselves and each other as certain kinds of people through their display of signs that index them as members of the DEAF-WORLD. Judgments based on these signs can result in a process of unification, or the judgments lead to various marginalizing practices. Discourse reflects people's ideas about themselves; it highlights the social distinctions that the community of users deem important. Day-to-day interaction among deaf people both exposes and reweaves the social fabric of the DEAF-WORLD. These practices simultaneously mark individuals and their addressees as certain kinds of people.

A culture's discourse practices rely on the ability of individuals to replicate and recontextualize value-laden language forms. Choices to use given forms are based not simply on the need to convey the referential content or message; they are also based on judgments about the appropriateness of the particular form in a given situation. Because ideologies about what constitutes appropriate language use are not evenly distributed, one-to-one uncontested relationships with social or linguistic groups do not exist. In this way, ideology mediates interpretations of discursive acts. These ideologies are pejorative (in a Silversteinian sense) in that they serve to perpetuate imbalances between insiders and outsiders.

Finally, the practices of unification and marginalization described here operate in opposition to one another. However there are some similarities between unification and marginalization. First, as the names suggest, unifying processes highlight the *similarities* that bring people together and marginalizing practices highlight the *differences* separating them.

Second, the same discursive forms can accomplish either of these disparate ends. As we have seen, the use of more "pure" forms of ASL can serve either end (unifying the link between individuals who easily use and understand these forms, even as they magnify differences between those who do and do not use them easily), suggesting that the forms themselves are not endowed with this power. It is their skillful use in certain contexts and the ability of their users to invoke appropriate interpretive frameworks that imbues them with meaning. The third way that unifying and marginalizing practices are similar is that they serve the same ends. Each serves to establish and maintain individuals' identities. And, on a level that transcends one-to-one relationships is the shared aim, or in Peircean terms, *final cause*, of defining and maintaining both individual relations to the DEAF-WORLD and the DEAF-WORLD itself.

Finally, these findings suggest that educational planning for deaf children should take into account the social consequences associated with various approaches. Students who are denied access to DEAF-WORLD discourse practices may find it difficult to acculturate later in life. Educational practices that deny deaf children access to traditional DEAF-WORLD discourse practices condemn many individuals to a life between two worlds, the DEAF-WORLD to which they do not belong, and the hearing one, in which they never can. Ultimately, this threatens the very nature of the DEAF-WORLD.

ENDNOTES

1.   Many writers have adopted the practice of using the capitalized form, "*Deaf*," to indicate cultural affiliation while reserving the lowercase, "*deaf*," in reference to those who are audiologically deaf but who are culturally hearing. I find this distinction is a useful way of marking a meaningful cultural distinction in my research, without causing problems (see Baynton 1996 and especially Wrigley 1996), so I adopt it herein.

2.   Austin first popularized the idea that speaking is a kind of social action (1962). Goodwin and Duranti (1992) trace this to Malinowski, who wrote in 1923 that language "must be conceptualized as a mode of practical action" (quoted in Goodwin & Duranti 1992:15). This idea is common to most work in contemporary linguistic anthropology (Duranti 1997).

3.   Heteroglossia, a term borrowed from Mikhail Bahktin, means "the simultaneous existence of multiple norms and forms" (Duranti 1994:6).

4.   I use the term "speaker" in reference to those who use signed as well as spoken language.

5.   Here again *talk* refers to verbal communication, either signed or spoken.

6.   These routines may be used in ASL-using communities beyond U.S. borders, and they almost certainly are in parts of Canada.

7.   "Danny" is a pseudonym, as are all other names of individuals from the community in which I worked.

8.   This is, of course, an oversimplification. Other factors affect these interpretations, including, at times, the ways they used to sign, their attitudes, and sometimes their education.

9.   "Referential content" and "discursive organization" are related but they differ in important ways. Recall that as I used "referential content" earlier in a limited way. As a sign of membership, I restricted "referential content" to the content of relatively direct claims about DEAF-WORLD membership, or at least to personal history and attitudes associated with them. "Discursive organization" deals with content of talk as well, but it centers on matters of etiquette and acceptable social behavior.

10.   In the DEAF-WORLD, narratives are almost always given chronologically, with a recounting of events that came first coming before those that followed. To proceed in any other order is to appear confused and disjointed.

11.   Talking with one's mouth full is rude in hearing company, but it is standard procedure in the DEAF-WORLD because when food is in your mouth, your hands are free to sign.

12.   Significantly, marginalization is the territory of those who assert Deaf identities for themselves. Those who do not are not at liberty to marginalize others from the DEAF-WORLD in this same respect. They may, however, employ similar practices to marginalize deaf people from more mainstream (i.e., hearing) identities.

13.   Individuals need not be clearly members, or core members. They just need to be more clearly members than the marginalized person(s).

14.   They do not always use this when someone pretends to understand, but that is generally the situation in which it is invoked.

15.   I fell victim to this practice several times when I was first learning ASL.

16.   The dividing line between foreigner talk and contact signing is an interesting matter. There appears to be some overlap in form, but I am not convinced that they are the same thing. This is an interesting topic for further research.

17.   Foreigner talk is sometimes used jokingly. On occasion, Deaf people misunderstand, or fail to understand, something someone says. An interlocutor may jokingly switch to foreigner talk as if he or she were an outsider. This kind of switch is generally good-natured.

18.   Sometimes deaf people pretend not to comprehend speech, but this is such a hit-and-miss proposition that invariably there is some incomprehension and/or misunderstanding. Still, in signing environments, Deaf people sometimes refuse to cooperate in spoken exchanges. The fact that a person is speaking in such an environment is already an overt marking of outsiderness, but the refusal to cooperate creates a power differential. The person unable to sign proficiently is left feeling powerless, a turnabout over usual relations between speaking and signing peoples.

19.   For discussions of repair work see Schlegoff, Jefferson and Sacks (1977), and Schlegoff (1997, 2000). See Dively (1998) for a discussion of conversational repairs in ASL.

20.   Interestingly enough, although Rodney has Deaf parents and has been deaf his whole life, this individual did use MCE extensively in his youth. His parents promoted that use at the insistence of educators at the boy's school who warned them that if they used ASL with him, his English would suffer. Late in adolescence he made a concerted effort to jettison MCE for ASL, but old habits die hard.

21.   Originally, I called serious mocking "malicious." However, I decided that "malicious" reflects a hearing-centered view. A Deaf-centered view might label it "protective" or some similar name. I decided upon "serious" here because this term incorporates aspects of both perspectives, although admittedly in somewhat different ways.

REFERENCES

Austin, John L. (1962) *How To Do Things With Words*. Oxford: Clarendon Press.

Basso, Keith (1979) *Portraits of 'The Whiteman': Linguistic Play and Cultural Symbols Among The Western Apache*. New York: Cambridge University Press.

Bauman, Richard (1983) *Let Your Words Be Few: Symbolism of Speaking and Silence Among the Seventeenth-Century Quakers*. Prospect Heights, Illinois: Waveland Press, Inc.

Bauman, Richard, and Charles Briggs (1990) Poetics and Performance as Critical Perspectives on Language and Social Life. *Annual Review of Anthropology* 19:59–88.

Baynton, Douglas C. (1996) *Forbidden Signs: American Culture and the Campaign Against Sign Language*. Chicago: University of Chicago Press.

Brown, Penelope, and Stephen C. Levinson (1999) Politeness: Some Universals in Language Usage. In *The Discourse Reader*. A. Jaworski and N. Coupland, eds. pp. 321–335. London: Routledge.

Bucholtz, Mary (1995) From Mulatta to Mestiza: Passing and the Linguistic Reshaping of Ethnic Identity. *In Gender Articulated: Language and the Socially Constructed Self*. M. Bucholtz, ed. pp. 351–374. New York: Routledge.

Cook-Gumperz, Jenny (1995) Reproducing the Discourse of Mothering: How Gendered Talk Makes Gendered Lives. In *Gender Articulated: Language and the Socially Constructed Self*. M. Bucholtz, ed. pp. 401–420. New York: Routledge.

Crystal, David (1987) *The Cambridge Encyclopedia of Language*. Cambridge: The Cambridge University Press.

Dively, Valerie L. (1998) *Conversational Repairs in ASL. In Pinky Extension and Eye Gaze: Language Use in Deaf Communities*. C. Lucas, ed. pp. 137–169. Washington, DC: Gallaudet University Press.

Duranti, Alessandro (1992) Language in Context and Language as Context: The Samoan Respect Vocabulary. In *Rethinking Context*. C. Goodwin, ed. pp. 77–99. Studies in the Social and Cultural Foundations of Language. Cambridge: Cambridge University Press.

— (1994) *From Grammar to Politics: Linguistic Anthropology in a Western Samoan Village*. Berkeley: University of California Press.

— (1997) *Linguistic Anthropology*. New York: Cambridge University Press.

Friedrich, Paul (1966) Structural Implications of Russian Pronominal Usage. In *Sociolinguistics*. W. Bright, ed. pp. 214–253. The Hague: Mouton and Co.

Gal, Susan (1984 [1978]) Peasant Men Can't Get Wives: Language Change And Sex Roles In A Bilingual Community. *Language in Society* 7:1–16.

— (1989) Language and Political Economy. *Annual Review of Anthropology* 18:345–367.

— (1995) Language, Gender, and Power: An Anthropological Review. In *Gender Articulated: Language and the Socially Constructed Self*. M. Bucholtz, ed. pp. 169–182. New York: Routledge.

— (1998) Mulitiplicity and Contention among Language Ideologies: A Commentary. In *Language Ideologies: Practice and Theory*. P.V. Kroskrity, ed. pp. 317–332. Oxford Studies in Anthropological Linguistics. New York: Oxford University Press.

Goffman, Erving (1967) The Nature of Deference and Demeanor. In *Interaction Ritual: Essays on Face-to-Face Behavior*. pp. 47–95. Garden City, New York: Anchor Books.

Goodwin, Charles, and Alessandro Duranti (1992) Rethinking Context: An Introduction.

In *Rethinking Context: Language As An Interactive Phenomenon*. A. Duranti and G. Charles, eds. pp. 1–42. New York: Cambridge University Press.

Graham, Laura (1995) *Performing Dreams: Discourses of Immortality Among the Xavante of Central Brazil*. Austin: University of Texas Press.

Gumperz, John J. (1972) Introduction. In *Directions in Sociolinguistics: The Ethnography of Communication*. J.J. Gumperz, ed. pp. 1–25. New York: Holt, Rinehart and Winston.

Hanks, William F. (1996) *Language and Communicative Practices*. Boulder, Colorado: Westview Press.

Hill, Jane H., and Ofelia Zepeda (1992) Mrs. Patrico's Trouble: The Distribution of Responsibility in an Account of Personal Experience. In *Responsibility and Evidence in Oral Discourse*. J.T. Irvine, ed. pp. 197–225. New York: Cambridge University Press.

Hymes, Dell (1972) On Communicative Competence. In *Sociolinguistics*. J. Holmes, ed. pp. 269–285. Harmondsworth, Middlesex: Penguin.

Kroskrity, Paul V. (1993) *Language, History, and Identity: Ethnolinguistic Studies of the Arizona Tewa*. Tucson, Arizona: University of Arizona Press.

— (1998) Arizona Kiva Speech as a Manifestation of a Dominant Language Ideology. In *Language Ideologies: Practice and Theory*. P.V. Kroskrity, ed. pp. 103–122. Oxford Studies in Anthropological Linguistics. New York: Oxford University Press.

Kulick, Don (1992) *Language Shift and Cultural Reproduction: Socialization, Self, and Synctretism in a Papua New Guinean Village*. New York: Cambridge University Press.

Lindstrom, Lamont (1992) Context Contests: Debatable Truth Statements on Tanna (Vanuata). In *Rethinking Context: Language as an Interactive Phenomenon*. C. Goodwin, ed. pp. 101–124. Studies in the Social and Cultural Foundations of Language No. 11. New York: Cambridge University Press.

Livia, Anna (1995) "I Ought to Throw A Buick at You": Fictional Representations of Butch/Femme Speech. In *Gender Articulated: Language and the Socially Constructed Self*. M. Bucholtz, ed. pp. 245–278. New York: Routledge.

Mills, Sara (1995) Feminist Stylistics. In *Analysis at the Level of Discourse*. pp. 159–197 (Chapter 6). New York: Routledge.

Okamoto, Shigeko (1995) "Tasteless" Japanese: Less "Feminine" Speech Among Young Japanese Women. In *Gender Articulated: Language and the Socially Constructed Self*. M. Bucholtz, ed. pp. 297–328. New York: Routledge.

Peirce, Charles Sanders (1985) Logic as Semiotic: The Theory of Signs. In *Semiotics: An Introductory Anthology*. R.E. Innis, ed. pp. 1–23. Bloomington: Indiana University Press.

Saussure, Ferdinand de (1966) *Course in General Linguistics*. New York: McGraw-Hill Book Company.

Schieffelin, Bambi B. (1990) *The Give And Take Of Everyday Life: Language Socialization Of Kaluli Children*. New York: Cambridge University Press.

Sherzer, Joel (1987) A Discourse-Centered Approach to Language and Culture. *American Anthropologist* 89:295–309.

Silverstein, Michael (1976) *Shifters, Linguistic Categories and Cultural Description. In Meaning in Anthropology*. H. Selby, ed. pp. 11–55. Albuquerque: University of New Mexico Press.

— (1979) Language Structure and Linguistic Ideology. In *The Elements: A Parasession on Linguistic Units and Levels*. C.L. Hofbaur, ed. pp. 193–247. Chicago: Chicago Linguistic Society.

Trudgill, Peter (1972) Sex, Covert Prestige, and Linguistic Change in The Urban British English of Norwich. *Language in Society* 1:179–195.

Urban, Greg 1989) The 'I' of Discourse. In *Semiotics, Self, and Society*. B. Lee and G. Urban, eds. New York: Mouton de Gruyter.

— (1991) *A Discourse-Centered Approach to Culture: Native American Myths and Rituals*. Austin: University of Texas Press.

— (1996a) *Metaphysical Community: The Interplay of the Senses and the Intellect*. Austin: University of Texas Press.

— (1996b) Entextualization, Replication, and Power. In Entextualization, Replication, and Power." In *Natural Histories of Discourse*. G. Urban, ed. pp. 21–44. Chicago: University of Chicago Press.

Velásquez, María Dolores Gonzales (1995) Sometimes Spanish, Sometimes English: Language Use Among Rural New Mexican Chicanas. In *Gender Articulated: Language and the Socially Constructed Self*. M. Bucholtz, ed. pp. 421–469. New York: Routledge.

Vološinov, V. N. (1973 [1929]) *Marxism and The Philosophy of Language*. I.R. Titunik, transl. Cambridge: Harvard University Press.

Woolard, Kathryn A. (1998) Introduction: Language Ideology as a Field of Inquiry. *In Language Ideologies: Practice and Theory*. P.V. Kroskrity, ed. pp. 3–47. Oxford Studies in Anthropological Linguistics. New York: Oxford University Press.

— (1992) Language Ideology: Issues and Approaches. *Pragmatics* 2(3):235–249.

Wrigley, Owen (1996) *The Politics of Deafness*. Washington, DC: Gallaudet University Press.

ABOUT THE AUTHOR

Bryan Eldredge is the coordinator of the rapidly expanding ASL and Deaf Studies Program at Utah Valley State College (UVSC). He is also a co-founder and co-chair of Deaf Studies Today! Bryan taught ASL and Deaf Studies at Brigham Young University and The University of Iowa before coming to UVSC. He holds a Ph.D in linguistic anthropology from The University of Iowa and earned a M.A. in linguistics from BYU. Bryan was awarded Professional certification from the American Sign Language Teachers Association in 1996. Bryan's research interests include the relationships between discourse and identity, the role of discourse in the perpetuation of the Deaf-World, language ideology, Peircean semiotics, language, and gender.

American School For The Deaf
(American Asylum, At Hartford, For The Education
And Instruction Of The Deaf And Dumb), 1817

Courtesy American School For The Deaf

Beyond the Classroom Walls: Community-Based Learning Opportunities

JUDY FREEDMAN FASK, M.ED., CI/CT

Judy Freedman Fask is the Director of the ASL/Deaf Studies program at the College of the Holy Cross in Worcester, Massachusetts.

MY GOAL AS AN INSTRUCTOR is to guide the students on a journey that challenges, supports, and empowers them to discover their purpose in life and to practice their values. It is my goal to offer them the looking glass, not to see just themselves, but to see in their reflection the vast community around them. For those students interested in learning American Sign Language (ASL), it is not enough to simply teach the language. With the learning of a new language (ASL) students should be introduced to the community who use the language, the cultural identity of the group and the conflicts that continue to exist regarding communication. It is therefore my responsibility to provide students with the foundations of the new language, an understanding of a new community and opportunities to create respectful partnerships. By having this approach, both the students and the community see the worth of collaborative efforts in our world for individuals and for the greater community.

Community-based learning (CBL) is an approach that can open the doors and lead to this type of community collaboration. Community-based learning (sometimes referred to as "service learning") is a fairly new term used in the higher educational setting, yet a concept and practice that have quickly been gaining attention from many colleges. Schools historically have established "volunteer" programs and are just now recognizing the distinct difference between CBL and volunteerism.

Community-based learning (CBL) can be defined as a pedagogy using courses that involve an experiential learning component and involve service to the community. It is a form of *experiential* education in which the students engage in activities that address *human* and *community* need together with structured opportunities that are intentionally designed to promote student learning and development. CBL is different from "volunteer work" because although it offers the individuals' services to members in the community, CBL has the additional distinction of also including reflection and reciprocity. CBL is the *intentional* integration of service and learning (Jacoby and Associates, 1996).

CBL utilizes various pedagogies that link the service within the community to the academic learning. The integration of this experience and theory is what brings the meaning of true learning and understanding to the students. Students realize that what happens in school involves not only their individual learning, but has broader connections to others.

Jacoby and Associates explain a four step cycle that CBL follows. It includes first the experience, then a reflection of that experience, a synthesis and abstract conceptualization followed last by the going back into the community and applying the new knowledge.

At Holy Cross, this approach was being followed within the ASL/ Deaf Studies classes without realizing the formal identity as Community Based Learning. It first happened innocently in response to a need that was expressed from within the Deaf community. A phone call came from a mother who was interested in a hockey program for her deaf son. This inquiry led to what is now known as the DEAFinitely hockey program in collaboration between the College of the Holy Cross Deaf Studies program and the Midstate Jr. IceCats youth hockey program. In 1994, this mother could not find a hockey program where her deaf son could learn the skills of skating in the language he would understand, ASL. I looked at this as an opportunity to create a CBL program that would benefit this young child, the Holy Cross ASL students, and the greater community.

We were made aware of a need in the community and creatively responded, utilizing the resources of students and the College. We established a program that is fully accessible to deaf children in terms of language (ASL) and the focus can then be on learning the skills of hockey, creating friendships with other players, and having fun. The current program also now includes both Deaf and hearing hockey coaches.

Since that first hockey program was created, we have established five ongoing community programs and created over 30 more collaborations and partnerships that benefit both Deaf community members and ASL students. At the time when this first happened, I didn't realize there was a name attached to this idea of linking the theory of classroom learning to the actual hands-on experience in the community. It all simply made great sense to me, and it still does. Looking back, the community programs that we first established might have been seen as more of "volunteer" opportunities, even by me. Both the experiential learning component and the service to the community were happening, but was there a formal reflection piece tied to what we were doing? The students and I would discuss the issues they saw, the skills they used, and the experiences they gained. This was done more informally during meetings outside of class, during office hours, or in class during discussions.

In 2001, the distinction between volunteerism and community-based learning became even clearer. The Donelan Office of Community-Based Learning was established at Holy Cross. I was eager to be a part of this and learn how this concept fit more formally into the liberal arts college curriculum and the Deaf Studies program. I saw how other instructors incorporated the service learning concept within their courses and how it has now become a philosophy used at Holy Cross to integrate the College mission of "service to others" into the academic curriculum at the College. It validated what the ASL/Deaf Studies program had been doing since 1994 and has given me an increased awareness and direction of how better to bring in the reflective piece of this service learning concept into the ASL/Deaf Studies curriculum.

Currently, students in the elementary ASL classes are required to take the language class plus an ASL lab practicum which is one additional hour per week. We keep the students informed and invite them to the many Deaf community programs offered at Holy Cross and in the Worcester area. The students take advantage of the opportunities and get involved on a "volunteer" basis, gaining exposure and familiarity with members of the Deaf community.

No formal reflection papers are required of students at this level. It is a way to get their feet wet. The intermediate ASL classes then offer the students a choice of the one hour ASL lab or one hour of a CBL option in addition to their regular ASL weekly classes.

Students choosing CBL in intermediate level ASL classes commit to be involved weekly for at least one hour per week for the duration of the semester at a specific site. It usually is more than the hour required. CBL programs for intermediate level ASL classes include:

- DEAFinitely Hockey: Holy Cross and Midstate Jr. IceCats Hockey league (started fall 1995)
- DEAFinitely Figure Skating: Holy Cross (started fall 2002)
- DEAFinitely Swim: Holy Cross (started spring 1999)
- Visiting elderly Deaf at a local nursing home (started fall 2003)
- Big Brother/Big Sister program with deaf "littles" (started fall 2003)

Considerations when setting up a CBL program include finding the appropriate sites, making appropriate matches between students and sites, funding travel to the sites, incorporating the reflection process, and because it is a college course, evaluating the students.

One of the biggest challenges has become finding the appropriate sites to accommodate the number of students interested. There are some local programs that offer linguistic and cultural immersion into the Deaf World, but many more are located well beyond the classroom walls and even beyond Worcester, Massachusetts. Setting up collaborations takes time, effort and patience. You are asking an agency person to participate in something that will add to their job duties and take additional time. It is important to consider and meet the goals of both the student and the site. Most people with whom I have worked have been especially generous with their time, guidance, and commitment to this program. They see the value of learning in their environment for the students and that the value and skills the student offers them.

Another consideration is the travel cost and time. If resources are not within the immediate area of your school, you will need to get creative and find ways to transport the students to sites located further away. For local sites we have been fortunate to utilize the CBL office at Holy Cross for travel vouchers for gas or cab fare. The travel cost can become a personal burden for the student if not subsidized.

Grants are another source of funding for student travel, but typically this is a one year option and grants are not renewed for the same purpose each year.

Reflection time and the approach to reflection are really the heart of this community-based learning approach. Keeping journals is one way for students to log their experiences. Students saw the use of the journal entries in two different ways. Some felt the entries were more reactive to the experience of the day and should not be graded. Others felt guidelines or specific issues could be tied to the journals so students could comment on their day but also connect it to a specific theme or reading.

It is important to bring the readings from class into the reflection process, both in journals and in classroom discussion.

The communication skills and attitude of the ASL students vary and it is important to consider both when placing a student at a specific site. Yes, the student is at the site to learn more sign and to better understand the Deaf community, but it is not fair to the site to place a student in a situation where he or she could not communicate with the people at the site. Note there may be an initial period of "culture shock" and lack of confidence in signing ability when entering a new site. This is to be expected when entering a new community and students are amazed at how much their skills do improve by the end of the semester. They also realize this improvement is due to their own increased use of the language, increased confidence, and increased willingness to "step outside the box" to learn. This immersion works similarly to a student learning a spoken language and doing a semester abroad in a foreign country. (I actually would suggest this CBL model for other foreign language programs.)

The formal reflective component with classroom discussion, journal writing, and student presentations enable the students to better synthesize their learning throughout the semester. Reciprocity between student and community members happens as teachers become students and students become teachers (even as young as age four).

One of the more challenging aspects of a CBL course is the valuation of students' progress. How do you evaluate this "learning process"? At Holy Cross, we use a CBL evaluation form for the students and for the sites. Some site supervisors are more accurate and realistic than others when grading students. I devised an additional evaluation form that allows site supervisors to separate the communication abilities of students from other critical factors such as attitude, willingness to work with others, motivation, punctuality, and consistency in attendance at the site.

One of the best evaluation tools that I have used is the formal presentation that the student makes to either a class of ASL students or to the community and site supervisors at an Academic Conference at the end of the semester. Students develop a poster and also a power point presentation that includes an overview of their site, a summary of their duties, a review of what they felt they learned, and, most importantly, how this experience really tied in to a more general learning experience that can be applied even further in their lives.

Because of the high demand of time, coordination, follow-up, and making theory connect to practice, some instructors are apt not to choose a CBL option. However, think twice about what it is you want your students to learn and how they can best do that. The community is an incredible resource to educators and students. Remember, too, that the students and resources of the College have much to offer the community. This is a way for colleges to make contributions directly to their community, then further to the national and global needs of the world as these young students leave the campus with more awareness, knowledge and tolerance of others.

In the more advanced course "Experience in the Deaf Community," students are required to attend a weekly seminar plus complete six hours of an internship experience fully immersed in the Deaf community and use ASL or the manual communication style of the site. This course does include the most formal reflective component with classroom discussion, journal writing and student presentations at an academic conference. Internship sites have included the following places:

- Quinsigamond Community College; Worcester, Massachusetts
- The Learning Center for Deaf Children; Framingham, Massachusetts
- A.L.L. School: classroom; Worcester
- Deaf Theater: ALL school; Worcester
- DEAF, Inc; Allston, Massachusetts
- The Deaf Blind Contact Center, DB Play; Allston
- Boston Children's Hospital, BCDC; Boston, Massachusetts
- R.I. School for the Deaf; Providence, Rhode Island
- Deaf Catholic Ministry; Brighton, Massachusetts
- Pasta Pals; SSDS and the Worcester Public Schools
- Reading to CODA; Millbury, Massachusetts
- Shrewsbury Public Schools, Home schooling project; Shrewsbury, Massachusetts
- Northeastern University, ASL program; Boston, Massachusetts
- American School for the Deaf; West Hartford, Connecticut
- Deaf Senior Center; Worcester
- DeafBlind Contact Center; Allston
- Video Documentary of the various Community Based learning sites
- Massachusetts Commission for the Deaf and Hard of Hearing; Worcester
- Massachusetts Commission for the Deaf and Hard of Hearing, legal department; Boston
- Employment Options; Marlboro, Massachusetts
- Horace Mann School for the Deaf; Allston
- UMMC Early Intervention; Worcester
- Major Edwards Elementary School; W. Boylston, Massachusetts
- Temple Emanuel Nursery School program; Worcester
- Center for Living and Working; Worcester
- Deaf Community Center; Framingham

From this last CBL internship experience, students definitely see the connection between what they learn in class and the theory taught from textbooks to the real world happenings. They not only become aware of the direct effect they have on an individual and a community, but they understand the greater moral and ethical implications for the general society.

From the hockey story where there was a of lack of access to a program for one deaf individual, students become aware of the reality and impact of a single experience and can then apply it to the larger community. This then leads students to be further aware and understand the issues of access, power, oppression, and equality for members within a society. It encourages students to not sit back idly, but to increase their understanding of issues underlying social and political injustices. It encourages students to have increased social responsibilities and make change when they can; to open up doors for access, communication, and opportunities. CBL heightens students' understanding of the human differences and most definitely encourages them to work collaboratively with others.

In their final reflection paper, students made the following comments about CBL:

"[it] increased my knowledge of cultures beyond my own and made me aware of and concerned with issues I never know existed before."—L.B.

"I was linking theory with practice every moment of my internship. This experience has helped me feel more comfortable in new and different situations and approaching people who have different languages and backgrounds than I have."—C.O.

"Through the CBL project, I have learned a great deal about myself, about Worcester, and about my future goals. I can apply many things I learned in this program to other parts of my life—especially the feeling I have now of being a real member of the Worcester community...I feel an increased responsibility to do my part and give back."—A.R.

"My perspective on community and culture has changed. I learned how to be accepting of other cultures even if they do not always make sense to me. I am more open-minded and eager to learn about different cultures-whereas before I was happy staying within my own box."—C.B.

"The mutual gift of friendship that I gained has inspired me to continue working with Deaf seniors in the future."

"I truly was able to understand how important it really was just to be able to be committed and consistently show up. The most important gift I can offer to others is my time."—T.M.

"By participating in the CBL program I was able to see firsthand how individuals can create change and the power one person can have. I realized that even a small task can make a difference, whether in one person's life or in an entire community."—K.S.

"My experience with Deaf theatre has not only helped me to improve my ASL, but it has helped me establish meaningful ties to the Deaf community. It has helped me tie the language together with a better understanding of Deaf culture as well. It is the best possible supplement to an ASL language class...This combination of skills and application is what leads to true knowledge."—E.S.

"Visiting A. and R. [and other Deaf seniors] every week [in the nursing home] I get a chance to learn new vocabulary, to use ASL in every day conversation, and to learn about the challenges facing them as members of the elder Deaf community. More importantly, I know that they look forward to our visits because we are sometimes the only people that know ASL that they come into contact with each week. We have become very close to A. and R. over the year and I hope that our visits are as meaningful to them as they are to me."—H.S.

Through community-based learning, students are intellectually and emotionally engaged, and thus they *learn*! As importantly, these students become genuine, caring human beings whose hands, heads, and hearts will create a world that is kinder, more loving, and more tolerant than ever imagined.

REFERENCES

Jacoby, B. and Associates. (1996) *Service-Learning in Higher Education.* San Francisco: Jossey-Bass .

Lane, H., Hoffmeister, R., and Bahan, B. (1996) *A Journey into the Deaf-World.* San Diego: DawnSign Press.

ABOUT THE AUTHOR

Judy Freedman Fask is the Director of the ASL/Deaf Studies program, which she began developing in 1994, at the College of the Holy Cross in Worcester, Massachusetts. Her focus has been on developing community relations, creating more complete access to programs for members of the Deaf community, and experiential learning opportunities for the Holy Cross ASL students. She holds a M.A. in Education of the Deaf from Smith College, a M.S. in Vocational Counseling from Springfield College, a B.A. degree with Cross Cultural Education certification from the University of Massachusetts, and is a nationally certified ASL/English interpreter. She lives in Worcester with her husband and five children.

Satisfaction and Negative Experiences of Deaf Leaders with Interpreters

LAWRENCE H. FORESTAL, PH.D.

Larry Forestal is an assistant professor of Teaching American Sign Language Emphasis toward a Bachelor's degree and state licensure at the University of Utah, Salt Lake City, Utah.

THIS STUDY WAS BASED ON American deaf leaders' cumulative response to a national attitude survey in 2000–2001. In addition, it was excerpted from Dr. Larry Forestal's dissertation entitled, "A Study of Deaf Leaders' Attitudes towards Sign Language Interpreters and Interpreting."

Age, education, and frequency of use of interpreters were personal characteristics of deaf leaders in relation to attitudes whereas satisfaction and negative experiences with interpreters were experiential characteristics based on their direct relation to the interpreting interaction.

The word "leader" refers to officers and board members of the National Association of the Deaf (NAD) and State Associations of the Deaf at some point between 1960 and 1999. A total of 502 leaders responded to the attitude survey in 2000. Only 394 leaders (217 male and 177 female) were qualified for this attitude study on the basis that they answered all attitude-scale questions in the third part of the survey.

The mean age of the leaders was 53.4. Younger leaders used interpreters more regularly than older leaders. Those leaders (265) with a college degree were inclined to use interpreters more regularly than those leaders (129) without a degree. Those leaders with a master's degree and those leaders who never attended college were statistically different. Thus, education was related to attitudes.

55% of the leaders confirmed having negative experiences with interpreters. Those leaders with negative experiences used interpreters more frequently than those leaders without negative experiences. Nearly 84% were satisfied with interpreters they had used within the past two years.

Speaking of the difference between older and younger leaders, older leaders were inclined to show gratitude and appreciation for interpreters, whereas younger leaders possessed a strong tendency to criticize or complain about interpreters. Why? Was interpreting a new profession? Was there a lack of knowledge about the interpreter's role? Was mainstream education a factor? Was a lack of sense of history about sign language interpreting another reason?

In this study gender, age, frequency of use of interpreters, education, negative experiences, and satisfaction with interpreters were attitude variables. In relation to the significance of each attitude variable, gender was not significant whereas all the other variables were significant. Age and frequency of use of interpreters accounted for 4.2% and 2.2% respectively of the variance in attitude scores.

Negative experiences and satisfaction with interpreters accounted for 6.5% and 9.1% respectively of the variance in attitude scores. On the whole, satisfaction and negative experiences together accounted for 15.6%; their combined influence on attitudes was approximately two and half times greater than age and frequency of use of interpreters, both of which accounted for 6.4% of the variance in attitude scores.

There are numerous examples of deaf leaders' statements about their negative experiences:

1. "An interpreter took over to say things which I should take care of."
2. "Once certified, interpreters think themselves as God's gifts to the deaf."
3. Paternalistic attitudes toward deaf consumers of interpreter services
4. "Interpreters go over boundaries."
5. No facial expression
6. Poor receptive skills
7. Bad personal habits and poor hygiene
8. Superior behavior, looking down on non-certified interpreters
9. CODAs have ego-control problems.
10. Exaggerated ASL and facial expression
11. Gossip
12. Interpreter's own opinion thrown in
13. SEE, not ASL
14. Too much make-up and jewelry
15. Violations of confidentiality and the Interpreter Code of Ethics
16. Not qualified to interpret in the court setting
17. "I saw an interpreter's misdeeds in the operating room but the supervisor defended him or her."

18. "An interpreter treated me as if I were an illiterate person."
19. Interpreters did not use updated technical sign vocabulary.
20. It took three weeks to get an interpreter.

A question of why interpreter competency is very important came up often in the study. In the process of analyzing survey data, interpreter competency was the only attitude domain with consistency. 68% of the leaders believed that CODAs (children of deaf adults) make better or more skilled interpreters than non-CODAs. 181 leaders (46%) cited poor sign-to-voice interpreting as the first reason for their negative experiences. There is no doubt that interpreter competency is the key to an interpreter's success in the profession.

In the area of interpreter education or training, both CODAs and non-CODAs should be trained and certified. The Section 504 regulations under the Vocational Rehabilitation Act of 1973 and Congressional Amendments mandate the continued development of competent interpreters. Advocates of the interpreting profession should be committed to pursuing additional and new funds for interpreter education.

How can interpreting improve for the benefit of deaf communities? First, interpreter education with an emphasis on the development of structured sign-to-voice interpreting skills should be a high priority at all levels of government and in public and private sectors. Second, mentor interpreters should be paired with student interpreters in the field of interpreter education. Third, the educational exposure of student interpreters to deaf adults should be maximized in the local and regional deaf communities.

ABOUT THE AUTHOR

Larry Forestal grew up in the summer resort of Asbury Park, New Jersey, with deaf parents and two deaf sisters. He attended Gallaudet University and obtained his doctorate at New York University. At the University of Utah, Larry is presently an assistant professor of Teaching American Sign Language Emphasis toward a Bachelor's degree and state licensure. During his 1984–86 presidency, the National Association of the Deaf recognized American Sign Language as a legitimate language in a position paper: American Sign Language and English, and Communication and Language Rights of Deaf People. He is a Board member of the Utah Association for the Deaf. He and his wife, Geraldine Francini, live in Salt Lake City and Surprise, Arizona.

"Preservation of the Sign Language," National Association of the Deaf, 1913.
George W. Veditz makes a plea for the preservation of "God's most noble gift to the deaf,"
the sign language.

Courtesy Gallaudet University Archives

The Role of Etymology and Evolution in the Study of American Sign Language

KEITH GAMACHE, jr., M.A.

Keith E. Gamache, Jr. is an adjunct instructor of ASL/Deaf Studies at Utah Valley State College and Brigham Young University, Provo, Utah.

STUDIES OF SIGNED LANGUAGES ADDRESS many different questions: Why do aged deaf persons sign differently as compared with young deaf persons? Why do signs differ in various cities and regions of the country? Why does American Sign Language (ASL) have a mixture of abstract, iconic, and fingerspelled loan signs (lexicalized fingerspelling)? Aren't there rules to distinguish their differences? How can we tell what is "right" or what is "wrong" with so many variations? This exploratory study aims to answer the question, "In what ways might a concerted effort to understand the origins of ASL signs inform the field of Deaf Studies?"

Historically speaking, there is a challenging dearth of records about signed language and even fewer studies of it before the 1960s (Bahan, Hoffmeister, and Lane 1996:63) as William Stokoe and his associates began to spearhead signed language research. Following in their footsteps, current research needs to continue to break new ground enabling us to better understand the origins of signed languages. In studying ASL etymology, we can come to understand three critical effects on ASL: how ASL originated, how those early beginnings led to present use, and how ASL might change—or be changed—in the future.

Admittedly, I became fascinated with ASL etymology thanks to my students, who constantly ask questions of me—sometimes to the point of annoyance—about where signs come from or how they have come to be. Over time, however, the topic began to intrigue me, and I have been studying it ever since.

As those familiar with the Deaf-World know, the ASL we know today has its beginnings at Hartford, Connecticut when Thomas H. Gallaudet, Laurent Clerc, and their first seven pupils came together in 1817 (Lane 1984:225–226). Gallaudet was a Protestant minister concerned for the welfare of the Deaf; Clerc was a deaf schoolteacher at the national school for the deaf, St. Jacques, in Paris. The *Langue des Signes Francaise* (LSF) Clerc brought with him to America eventually intermixed with the native signs the pupils already used. Some of those pupils came from Martha's Vineyard in Massachusetts, which was known for having a disproportionately high number of deaf inhabitants during colonial times (Baker-Shenk and Cokely 1980:51–53).

This integration of LSF and native home signs formed the foundations of modern ASL. The blending was so impactful, in fact, that during Clerc's later return to France, upon meeting Jean Massieu, one of his closest French friends, Massieu criticized Clerc for using signs that were vastly different from the French deaf community's sign language (Lane 1984:227). Massieu's criticism was not limited to Clerc's signing; Clerc and other Deaf Americans were heavily influenced by mainstream American culture, customs, traditions, and language. The resulting composition of his American students' native signs and Clerc's original LSF had probably evolved so dramatically that a French person visiting in 1830 would have likely required a great deal of work and concentration just to make sense of the signing.

Despite the rapid infiltration of Clerc's LSF with other forms of signing and the subsequent creation of "Early ASL" (Baker-Shenk and Cokely 1980 and Bahan, Hoffmeister, and Lane 1996) it is interesting to note that evidence of written French and LSF is still present in present-day ASL. For example, Table 1 illustrates that some present-day ASL signs retain handshapes that appear to be initializations of French words.

Obviously, the manual alphabet that French deaf people used was employed as a means of "initializing" signs with the first letter of the spelling of their spoken French counterparts, a process repeated in American English with ASL. The significant question here is at what point, and in what ways, did spoken/written French begin to influence LSF?

When the Abbe Charles de L'Epeé, the founder of the French national school, first began to teach Deaf students, he noted that they already had a language of signs which he learned from them in order to communicate with them (Moore and Levitan 1994;47–49). How did Deaf people communicate, then, in the first place? I maintain that signed languages arise, through a natural process of language creation and evolution, out of deaf people's need to communicate. Because Epeé was the first to establish the school for the deaf in Paris, it is clear that the deaf people who Epeé taught

Spoken French	Translation	ASL handshape
aider	to help	A
aimer	to love	A
chercher	to look for	C
voir	to see	V (Figure 1, 1a)
manger	to eat	M

Table 1: Evidence of the influence of written French on LSF and early/current ASL.

Figure 1: The ASL sign TO-SEE

Figure 1a: Detail of the V handshape in the ASL sign TO-SEE

did not have formal schooling. If they were illiterate, how could they have known the alphabet? Apparently Epeé introduced the alphabet in his "methodical signs" (a system of signing aimed at imitating the grammar of spoken French) employed at the school (Lane 1984:86).

But how did Epeé learn of a manual alphabet? One theory suggests that monks in the Spanish clergy used the same manual alphabet between the 16th and 18th centuries (Lane 1984; Van Cleve and Crouch 1989). Because many monks took vows of silence, they may have devised a manual alphabet in order to bypass the rules and communicate with each other. It is conceivable that, as some researchers have suggested, they may have passed it along to educators of the deaf and deaf pupils (Van Cleve and Crouch 1989:11–12).

Such is the case of Ponce de Leon and the Velasco brothers, Francisco and Pedro (Lane 1984:90–95). Epeé may have learned fingerspelling from teachers in other countries, such as Spain, where de Leon hailed from. French manuscripts, however, claimed that Epeé and others developed the alphabet on their own. For example, the letter 'D,' Epeé said, originated from the French word, *dieu*, or God. The handshape was made by pointing upwards to the heavens (Figure 2). Other documents explained that some handshapes represented the tongue and mouth movements of certain letters. However, the validity of this claim is difficult to judge.

The relationship between LSF and spoken/written French—and its subsequent carryover into ASL—is akin to the process of borrowing that

Figure 2: The FSL/ASL handshape 'D'

Figure 3: The ASL sign ON-THE-FENCE

takes place in virtually all languages that come into contact with others. Indeed, there are many examples in modern English.

One such example can be found in the names of the twelve months of the English calendar. Historically, Latin, (which would eventually give birth to modern romance [or romanic] languages such as French, Spanish, and Italian) was the *lingua franca* of the Roman Empire. English, however, had derived from older Germanic languages. When Caesar sacked Europe and Britain in the first century B.C., (both of which were under Germanic control at the time), the languages of these countries came under heavy influence of the Empire's language. A thousand years later, Normandy (or northern France) would control much of Britain and import romanic lan-

English word	Latin word	Additional Latin meaning and/or derivation
January	Janus	Roman god of sky
February	Februa	Roman festival of purification
March	Mars	Roman god of war
April	Aprilis	Venus (Roman goddess of beauty) or "fruitful"
May	Maia	Roman "Mother Earth"
June	Juno	Roman goddess/queen of heavens
July	Julius	Named for Roman dictator Julius Caesar
August	Augustus	Named for first Roman emperor Caesar Augustus
September	septem	Latin "seven"
October	octo	Latin "eight"
November	novem	Latin "nine"
December	decem	Latin "ten"

Table 2: The Latin origins of English month names. *Note: The Roman calendar originally had only ten months, and was used primarily for charting agricultural seasons. (The time periods of January and February never existed in the Roman calendar, because farming could not be done during this time. Later they were added later to round out the number of months to twelve.)*

guage to the Britons. The influence of the meshing and evolution of languages can be seen in the modern names of the twelve months (Table 2).

During the European Renaissance, the English language added several new words by borrowing from many different languages (Merriam-Webster 1991) as demonstrated in Table 3:

French: date, escape, infant	Arabic: hazard, magazine
India: bandanna	Italian: carnival, fiasco, pizza
Dutch: bikini, cliché, discotheque	Russia: robot, czar
Chinese: gung ho	Portuguese: cobra, molasses
German: delicatessen, pretzel, swindler	Spanish: sherry, mosquito
Japanese: tycoon	American Indians: moose, raccoon, skunk
Greek: comedy, thermos, autopsy	Norwegian: scatter, skin, law

Table 3: English words that have origins in other languages.

Cultures can also influence how peoples shape languages. Not all languages can be translated fully; people view life in a variety of ways and are exposed to new ideas and concepts through language use. Researchers continue to learn about language through these different perspectives.

Take the Spanish of the Americas, for example, which contains many classificatory terms for people of varying ethnic backgrounds (e.g. *español, mexicano, mestizo, mulatto,* etc.). These ethnic identities are an important part of the public consciousness because they carry with them privileges in education, employment, and social esteem.

The significant point here is that there are important relationships between a culture and the *form* of its language. Italians have many more names for pasta varieties that Americans would not be familiar with. The French are famous for their cheese, having varieties in the thousands. People who live in frigid areas would describe snow in several different ways as compared to those who live in warm places. It is understandable that cultures influence language use and their vocabularies.

The relationship between language and culture is just as important for Deaf people. ASL is a highly visual-gestural language, a primary source of frustration for students. ASL students generally struggle to transition from a primarily linear (auditory) language to a primarily spatial (visual) one. Instead of simply *saying* "a woman is beautiful," ASL gives *spatial descriptions* of various aspects of her beauty. Instead of *saying* "that food is delicious," ASL *shows* how the food is delicious. ASL's visual imagery is accomplished through classifiers and other spatially-agreeing forms that have no word-for-word equivalents in spoken languages.

For example, the concept of 'undecidedness' (glossed as ON-THE-FENCE, Figure 3) uses only one lexical item in ASL while conveying the equivalent concept in English requires several lexical items. Conversely,

ASL does not categorize objects or create noun categories with the same efficiency that English does. ASL does not have, for example, singular lexical choices for concepts such as 'weapons,' 'tools,' and 'utensils.' ASL simply conveys object groupings in a different way.

ASL also borrows vocabulary from many languages, chief among them English. My high school English teacher, who was a very proficient ASL user, admitted to me that he was only 75–80 percent fluent. I only understood this when I became a teacher myself. I realized that I too only maintain 75–80 percent ASL vocabulary/grammar usage, not 100 percent. I am constantly exposed to English every time I open a newspaper, watch a television program with captions, or use a TTY. If I find myself in a situation with little to no exposure to English for period of time, I notice that I am much more attuned to ASL than I might be during course of a routine day.

It is interesting to examine how influences from Deaf culture have affected changes in ASL lexical forms. It is well documented that Deaf people have long experienced the oppression of a majority culture, minimized because of their alleged inabilities to hear and communicate. There is, of late, a movement to eliminate or alter signs which can be traced to an alternative derivation or signing system (e.g. Signing Exact English, or SEE). SEE signs, based on the idea that English morphemes have unique signs, rely heavily on initialization and are perceived as "not ASL."

Figure 4: The ASL sign TO-DEVELOP   Figure 4a: The MCE sign TO-DEVELOP

What is the impetus behind this movement? Is it a way of venting frustration at the majority? For example, shortly after the American military action against Iraq in 2002, public sentiment among the French people was that of disdain and American "bullying." In response, Americans shot back with a linguistic "jab" of their own, renaming French fries as "Freedom fries." Is the inclusion of alternative signs a similar battle? Table 4 presents a number of ASL signs that have been initialized as parts of Manually Coded English (MCE) systems:

DEVELOPMENT (Figure 4, 4a)	UNIVERSITY	PLANT
PERSON	PARTY	VOLLEYBALL
GUILTY	ADULT	FREE
TRY	DOCTOR	GOVERNMENT

Table 4: ASL signs that have been initialized in MCEs.

Many initialized signs have found their way into common usage even among ASL users who eschew MCEs (see Table 5):

FRUITS	VEGETABLES	HURRY
FURNITURE	HONEST	TOILET
HISTORY	FAMILY	BEER
CHURCH	TOYS	IDEA

Table 5: Initialized ASL signs

I believe that Deaf people and ASL have benefited from MCEs. An interesting dilemma arises, however: initialized signs seem to be retained in the language yet native users "deny" their validity. Are Deaf people "less ASL" because they use initialized signs? Which is more important: to have a "SEE-less" lexicon and utilize more fingerspelling or to create absurd signs which the community hasn't yet accepted? I have seen many deaf people who decry SEE signs yet don't use correct ASL grammar. I believe one of the reasons this happens is because most Deaf people don't learn about ASL or take ASL classes in the same way hearing people learn about English and take English courses. As a result, many Deaf people do not have a high level of metalinguistic awareness regarding ASL. Formal instruction would help Deaf people better understand the linguistic properties of ASL. This in turn would have an affect on ideologies about ASL, making it more highly valued even within the Deaf-World.

With the advent of better visual recording technologies, scholars and researchers are better able to preserve sign language samples; products such as *Preservation of Sign Language* by Sign Media, Inc., *Signs Across America* by Edgar Schroyer, and *Charles Krauel: a Profile of a Deaf Filmmaker* by Dawn Sign Press are wonderful examples. We need more of them. We need to study further to see the evolution of sign language. Unfortunately, the earliest known video recording we have of signed language is of a young Deaf women signing "The Star Spangled Banner" in 1902 (Gallaudet University Library). Before that time, there are only glimpses here and there from writings and illustrations of Deaf and hearing people who employ sign language. We need to continue to collect videotapes from various people and to study them.

Today, some scholars are working to determine how signed languages have evolved through time. For the most part, signed languages began

Figure 5: The ASL sign VOTE   Figure 6: The ASL sign HOME

with iconic symbols that later evolved to more to arbitrary ones. Over the past century, *iconic* signs, or signs that derive their meaning because of a physical resemblance (similarity) between the words and their referents, have tended to become more arbitrary (Baker-Shenk and Cokely 1980:37–40). Iconic signs are still prevalent in ASL today:

SAD	TRAFFIC	TENT
JUDGE	CHOOSE	WEEK
ATTENTION	POSTPONE	GRAVY
VOTE (Figure 5)	WOOD	TICKET

Table 6: Highly iconic ASL signs

Still other ASL signs have evolved in form to become relatively more arbitrary:

HOME (Figure 6)	DEAF	TOMATO
BOY	ENVY	COMPUTER
WOMAN	STEAL	HELP
HORSE	INFORM	WILL

Table 7: ASL words that have become relatively more arbitrary over time

ASL is a living language and continues to change and adapt to handle the needs of Deaf people in a changing world. Over time, the meaning of a given word can be expanded as new meanings are attached to a word. The English words 'set' and 'run' have 410 and 185 distinct meanings, respectively. Table 8 demonstrates some ASL signs with multiple meanings:

PEPSI and ITALY	NEWSPAPER and PRINT	GLASS and DENTIST
SUNDAY and WONDERFUL	NEWS and INFORM	ESCAPE and ELOPE

Table 8: ASL "homonyms"

In order to incorporate new concepts into ASL, sometimes two or more ideas are combined to define a new one; Table 9 illustrates some ASL "compounds":

ASL compound	English translation
SICK + SPREAD (Figure 7)	epidemic
FACE + STRONG	resemblance
EAT + NOON	lunch
SLEEP + SUNRISE	oversleep
SLEEP + DRESS	pajamas
BLUE + SPOT	bruise
WRONG + HAPPEN	accident
TIME + SAME	simultaneously
THINK + ALIKE	agree
BODY + BURN	cremation

Table 9: ASL compounds

There are also signs that are modified in a certain way to give another shade of meaning. I call these signs "mutations" (see Table 10):

UNDERSTAND/MISUNDERSTAND	EXCITED/DEPRESSED
CLEAR/UNCLEAR	TEACH/NOT TEACHING
PROUD/UNPROUD	COMMUNICATE/MISCOMMUNICATE
ACCENT	SELFISH/UNSELFISH
CLEVER/NOT-SO-CLEVER	BUSY/NOT BUSY

Table 10: ASL "mutations"

Why such changes? Deaf people seek to simplify their communication in the best way possible from time to time. It is a natural tendency. Dialects provide a productive area to examine the connection between language and culture. Although dialects that differ from "standard" forms are often considered improper, these judgments are not based in linguistic reality. Dialectal differences are not a matter of "right" or "wrong"; rather, they are a matter of habit or preference. As of yet, there is no clear standard form of ASL. However, it is possible to recognize a signer's circle of friends, family, or place of origin based on his/her signing.

Figure 7: The ASL compound SICK + SPREAD   Figure 8: The North Carolina variant of TRUCK

Particular signing styles index signers as being from specific regions of the country. The sign for CHRISTMAS used by Deaf signers in Maine uses a 8 handshape that touches the signer's waist, representative of the stickiness of sap from pine trees. The sign for TRUCK used by Deaf signers in North Carolina looks very similar to the ASL sign GRASS; it is an iconic representation of the front grill of Mack trucks, which are popular in the area (Figure 8). The ASL sign EXCUSE-ME used by Deaf signers in Texas is visually identical to the sign for EMERGENCY used Deaf signers in California.

Interestingly, the divergence of various dialects in England has worried some enough that the government has taken steps to establish an official English dialect. Would Gallaudet University, which is considered by many to be the linguistic and cultural center of the American Deaf Community, ever consider doing something similar? While Gallaudet has no *official* power to mandate linguistic usage, it clearly already has effects on the use of ASL around the country. Students who return home after studying at Gallaudet often bring with them a particular style of signing that others recognize as being characteristic of the university. The fact that these individuals have a college education and are often active in local community politics and leadership gives credence to their signing as "proper."

From studying the content of old videos of ASL, we see Deaf people use relatively more fingerspelling than Deaf people use today. What is less clear is the reason behind the change. There are several possibilities: perhaps fingerspelling is used less because it is cumbersome or because hearing people struggle so much with fingerspelling that they create new signs. Similarly, Deaf signers today use more facial expressions, more mouth morphemes, and less body movements than did signers of the past. (There is also a tendency today for signers to tilt their bodies backwards— much to my chagrin.) Many older Deaf people have also expressed displeasure about the ever-changing rules of sign language brought upon by younger deaf generations.

Viewed from a global perspective, we would do well to consider how ASL has been influenced by other sign languages. Certainly Clerc was not the only Deaf immigrant to bring his sign language to America. The Deaf community in the United States found itself involved in the Deaf-World community because of the 1880 Milan Conference. That involvement continued with subsequent conferences on Deaf education. Over the years, the American Deaf community has become increasingly more present on the world scene through participation in the World Games of the Deaf and the World Federation of the Deaf (Bahan, Hoffmeister, and Lane 1996:132, 138). It seems likely that exposure to other signed languages has had an affect on ASL.

I attended the 2003 Deaf History International Conference in Paris and was captivated by certain signs from other countries. Interestingly, many of these signs are coming into widespread use among American Deaf people. This constitutes an interesting case of "language borrowing" in which signs for concepts indigenous to other countries are seen as being "correct." In many cases, ASL signs are discarded in favor of the "more authentic" borrowings.

Etymology is not an exact science. The study of word/sign origins should help us appreciate and to improve our language. For the most part, this presentation has been focused on vocabulary use. There is a lot of ground to cover in this field. I hope that more studies will be devoted to this type of research in the near future.

REFERENCES

Bahan, Ben, Robert Hoffmeister, and Harlan Lane (1996). *A Journey Into the Deaf-World.* San Diego: Dawn Sign Press.

Baker-Shenk, Charlotte, and Dennis Cokely (1980). *American Sign Language: A Teacher's Resource Text on Grammar and Culture.* Silver Spring, Maryland: T. J. Publishers.

Gallaudet University Library (n.d.) Retrieved September 21, 2004, from http://library.gallaudet.edu/dr/faq-oldest-deaf-films.html

Lane, Harlan (1984). *When The Mind Hears: A History of the Deaf.* New York: Vintage Books.

Merriam-Webster (1991) Introduction. *Merriam-Webster New Book of Word Histories.*

Moore, Matthew S., and Linda Levitan (1993) *For Hearing People Only.* Rochester, NY: Deaf Life Press.

Van Cleve, John Vickery, and Barry A. Crouch (1989). *A Place of Their Own: Creating the Deaf Community in America.* Washington, DC: Gallaudet University Press.

ABOUT THE AUTHOR

Keith E. Gamache, Jr., M.A., is an adjunct instructor of ASL/Deaf Studies at Utah Valley State College and Brigham Young University. Keith is a native Californian and is well traveled, having lived in Illinois, New York, Maryland, Texas, Oregon, and Washington. Keith got involved in this profession by accident some five years ago and has enjoyed it since that time. He grew up in a large Deaf family spanning three generations. Keith's interests include etymology, second language learning, creative signing, and anthropological studies.

Gallaudet University Student Protest, U.S. Capitol Building, Washington, D.C. March 1988

Courtesy Gallaudet University Archives

Dysconscious Audism: What Is It?

GENIE GERTZ, PH.D.

Genie Gertz is a full-time lecturer and an Assistant Professor in the Department of Deaf Studies at California State University, Northridge (CSUN).

"CONSCIOUSNESS" IS NECESSARY FOR ANYONE to become a full-fledged member and to participate in social change that benefits his/her own community. "Consciousness" means a set of attitudes and beliefs held by the group that includes recognition of a membership in and shared interests with a specific group. Consciousness is important in any culture, and even more so in any minority culture. Consciousness is also crucial for judging another culture in terms of one's values and for understanding one's community before one can contribute to social change.

In order to become a full-fledged Deaf member, he or she must go through the similar process for building up Deaf consciousness. Deaf people's recognition and respect for American Sign Language and Deaf Culture must take place before they can cultivate a Deaf consciousness to their fullest potential through their involvement in the Deaf community. Many Deaf people start learning about their distinct culture much later in their lives (Padden 1986).

For Deaf people, a cultural identity is critical. When Deaf people are together, they each contribute to group formation, maintenance, and social ties within the Deaf community, yet each Deaf person has his or her own individual personality. Deaf traditions, customs, values, and behaviors are significant factors for effective socialization within this group. Deaf people, like other minority groups, constitute a *cultural* group, a group in which many Deaf people see themselves as members. In this sense, Deaf people simply do not view themselves as disabled. As Padden and Humphries (1988:44) cogently point out: "'Disabled' is a label that historically has not belonged to Deaf people. The term suggests political self-representations and goals unfamiliar to the group. When Deaf people discuss their deafness, they use terms deeply related to their language, their past, and their community."

For many years most hearing people have constructed "deafness" through a disability model. The disability model promotes the pathological perspective of deafness in which the deaf person is considered disabled, helpless, and stigmatized (i.e. needs to be "fixed"). More often than not, the pathological perspective further perpetuates society's larger view of Deaf people as being inferior and subhuman. From this perspective, Deaf people are seen as needing "rehabilitation" to become pseudo hearing individuals for the sole purpose of assimilating into the mainstream American society.

The hearing majority continues to regulate the affairs and lives of Deaf people through public school education, legislation, and the media. They develop an agenda for Deaf people similar to the ones for all other people with disabilities. In this manner, the goals of hearing professionals in their work with Deaf people tend to address mainly preventive measures. They attempt to fix or solve hearing problems, provide new technologies in the hope that Deaf people will participate effectively in hearing society, and endorse "helping professions" for their work with Deaf people. They keep imagining the "best" solutions for Deaf people, by perpetuating and expanding their own activities based on the ability to hear. The disability model is strong, pervasive, and is controlled by the powerful hegemonic forces in which hearing people engineer the lives of Deaf individuals. It is so powerful that, even though raised in a Deaf culturally-rich setting, many Deaf people absorb some behaviors and beliefs indicating that they are fully responsible for their own failures.

The Deaf consciousness, however, is often weakened by the hegemonic forces of the dominant society of hearing people that decides what is best for Deaf people. Constant weakening of Deaf consciousness brings uncertainties and creates difficulties for Deaf people to map out a clear understanding of their Deaf experience. While hearing people have been seeking only a cure for deafness, Deaf people have increasingly experienced their own Deaf life as having many flaws. This distortion has consequences: Deaf people can't fully comprehend their actions and where they might stand in today's world.

Some Deaf people absorb such beliefs that they are at fault for these deficits. This kind of discourse alleging the inferiority of Deaf people has led to the blurring of a clear Deaf consciousness. As Deaf people grow up and believe what hearing people say about them, they internalize the "deficit thinking" practice, laden with audistic values which, in turn, breeds *dysconscious audism* within themselves. They do not even realize that they are actually perpetuating oppressive behavior.

With the term "dysconscious audism," I propose a new concept which would be defined as a form of audism that tacitly accepts dominant hearing norms and privileges. It is not the absence of consciousness but an impaired consciousness or distorted way of thinking about Deaf consciousness. Dysconscious audism would adhere to the ideology that hearing society is dominant and more appropriate than the Deaf society. Such deaf people can be characterized as not having fully developed Deaf consciousness, and they may still feel the need to assimilate into the mainstream culture.

Presently, there is still a sizable group of Deaf people who would be categorized "dysconscious audists" because they haven't developed their own Deaf consciousness to the fullest. Generally, their Deaf consciousness is distorted to varying degrees. Dysconscious audistic Deaf people unwittingly and unknowingly help to continue the kind of victimized thinking; they are responsible for their own failure. Such thinking enables hearing people to continue pathologizing Deaf people. The critical aspects of dysconscious audism are that it:

- Disempowers Deaf people from becoming liberated
- Disables Deaf people from expressing Deaf cultural pride
- Intimidates Deaf people and limits their promotion of the Deaf perspective
- Hinders Deaf people from attaining real education
- Denies Deaf people of full acceptance toward ASL
- Weakens Deaf people in the development of their Deaf identity

The weakening of Deaf experience is often contributed by the lack of Deaf consciousness within the present context and the impact of hegemonic forces. Hearing people's obsessions, as one example, over the cure of deafness contributes significantly to the weakening of Deaf people's identity. When the Deaf person's identity is distorted, they cannot fully understand their own behaviors. A large number of Deaf individuals are not even aware that they possess, to varying degrees, these kind of audistic behaviors and attitudes.

The recognition in the features of dysconscious audism can contribute not only to a better understanding of the Deaf community as a cultural entity but also add to the body of knowledge regarding the Deaf community and its people. In addition, the negative perception that has been perpetuated about the Deaf community for so long might be reduced by increasing an understanding of Deaf consciousness.

REFERENCES

Gertz, G. (2003). *Dysconscious audism and critical deaf studies: Deaf crit's analysis of unconscious internalization of hegemony within the deaf community.* Unpublished doctoral dissertation, University of California, Los Angeles, California.

Padden, C. and Humphries, T. (1988). *Deaf in America: Voices from a culture.* Cambridge, MA: Harvard University Press.

Padden, C. (1996). From the cultural to the bicultural: The modern deaf community. In Parasnis, I. (Ed.) *Cultural and language diversity and the deaf experience* (pp. 79–98). Cambridge: Cambridge University Press.

ABOUT THE AUTHOR

Genie Gertz has been affiliated with the Department of Deaf Studies at California State University, Northridge (CSUN) since 1995 as a full-time lecturer and, most recently, as an Assistant Professor. Genie obtained a doctorate from UCLA in Social Sciences and Comparative Education with a concentration in Racial and Ethnic Studies. She earned a B.A. degree and a M.A. degree from Gallaudet University and New York University, respectively. Born deaf, Genie came to America from St. Petersburg, Russia and settled in New York City when she was eight years old. Genie not only was on the national board of Deaf Women United from 1995–1999, but also developed a course on Deaf Women at CSUN.

The Nature of Sexual Abuse Reported By Deaf Adults

LYNNETTE JOHNSON, M.S.W.
KRISTYLYNNE BRADY, L.C.S.W
LARRY L. SMITH, D.S.W.

Lynnette Johnson is a therapist in private practice. Kristylynne Brady is in private practice and is the State of Utah Assistant Relay Administrator. Larry L. Smith is a Professor at the Graduate School of Social Work, University of Utah.

INTRODUCTION

SEXUAL ABUSE IS A PERVASIVE problem that crosses cultural, socioeconomic, and ethnic populations and boundaries. While there has been much research in the area of sexual abuse in the general population, there has been little research on sexual abuse in the Deaf population. General hearing population statistics indicate that 38 percent of girls and 16 percent of boys are sexually abused before the age of 18 (*Center Against Sexual Abuse,* 1998). The congressionally-mandated *Third National Incidence Study of Child Abuse and Neglect* reports that girls are sexually abused three times more often than boys in the general or hearing population (*Child Abuse Statistics,* 1998).

Studies on the sexual abuse of Deaf individuals reveal that 50 percent of Deaf people have been sexually abused (Sullivan, Vernon and Scanlon, 1987). More specifically, "54 percent of Deaf boys and 50 percent of Deaf girls" have experienced sexual abuse (Chenoweth, 1998, p. 2). Chenoweth added that these abuse figures do not include residential settings for disabled children. This finding raises grave concern because most Deaf children in the United States attend residential schools from pre-kindergarten through high school. Therefore, the actual number of Deaf children who are victims of sexual abuse could be much higher than 50 percent (or in other words half of the Deaf population) (see Appendix 1). Chenoweth also found that "some forms of abuse within institutions have traditionally been seen as acceptable and many workers in those institutions actually believe they are doing these things for the person's own good" (1995, p. 1)."

There were five studies found in an extensive review of the literature on the sexual abuse of Deaf individuals. Much of the research has focused on Deaf children within residential schools (Sullivan, et al., 1987; Mertens, 1996; Sullivan, Scanlon, and LaBarre, 1986). Mertens (1996) study, "Breaking the Silence About Sexual Abuse of Deaf Youth," hints at possible cultural attitudes that may be present in propagating sexual abuse. Some of the respondents in this study:

> noted that there were sanctions from the Deaf community if a Deaf person reported on another Deaf person for sexual abuse.

> I knew but I did not want to report. My name would be bad. The Deaf community would think my name is bad.

> People suspected but nobody would do anything. The Deaf community knew. That's pretty typical residential school stuff.

> Staff were afraid of speaking out against another Deaf person... (p. 356).

Another study conducted at Gallaudet University reported the "sexual knowledge, behavior, and sources of information among Deaf and hard of hearing college students" (Joseph, Sawyer, and Desmond, 1995). This study supported the earlier findings that sexual abuse is prevalent among Deaf children and also indicated that this may impact Deaf college students and the prevalence of sexual assault at this later age.

Although there have been studies focusing on the sexual abuse of Deaf youth, there are no extensive studies administered to Deaf adults regarding sexual abuse. Noting the high percentage of sexual abuse among Deaf children, sexual assault reported by Deaf college students, and the lack of sexual abuse information gathered from Deaf adults led the authors to conduct this study. It was hoped that further information could be found as suggested by the work of Joseph (1995) that would determine more of the nature of sexual abuse that occurs among the Deaf and hopefully lead to ideas to lessen its occurrence.

PURPOSE OF THE STUDY

The purpose of this study was to investigate the nature of sexual abuse among the Deaf population. This study focused on Deaf adults who had the maturity and vocabulary to describe sexual abuse that children can't always articulate. The purposes of this study included:

1. Describe the nature of sexual abuse as reported by Deaf adults.

2. Determine if there are cultural factors or beliefs that impact the perpetration of sexual abuse and/or the propagation of sexual abuse among the Deaf.

METHODOLOGY

The study was exploratory. Data were collected from a self-administered anonymous questionnaire consisting of three sections: Section I: The Abuse; Section II: After the Abuse; and Section III: Suggestions. All survey respondents were given the questionnaire individually.

The survey questionnaire included the following:

Section I: The Abuse, consisted of 14 fill-in-the-blank or check-off questions regarding demographics. The topics included if the participant was Deaf or hard of hearing, what type of school they attended (residential, mainstream program, other), age, who perpetrated the abuse, how many perpetrators there were, etc.

Section II: After the Abuse, included four open-ended questions focusing on how the abuse had affected the person's life and relationships.

Section III: Suggestions, included recommendations that the respondent may have for other Deaf and hard of hearing individuals who had experienced abuse, advice for counseling professionals who work with Deaf sexual abuse victims and perpetrators, and ideas for stopping sexual abuse among the Deaf and hard of hearing population.

The final part of the survey included a Likert-type scale that measured the respondent's beliefs about behaviors that may be considered sexual abuse. The purpose of these questions was to ascertain what factors, attitudes, or beliefs in Deaf culture may contribute to sexual abuse.

Each questionnaire was administered individually in American Sign Language (ASL). The questionnaire administrator signed a description of the instructions and questions in ASL. Participants also received the questionnaire in written format. Participants were informed through ASL and in the written format that if they did not understand certain questions that they could have the questions signed to them so that they could understand what was being asked. Participation in the survey was voluntary and no compensation was given for participation.

SAMPLE

There were approximately 200 participants at Utah's first Deaf Mental Health Conference. All 200 conference participants were invited to participate in the study. Utah Deaf Mental Health: Coordinated Community

Services also invited clients to participate in the study. There were 15 adult participants in the study ranging in age from 18 to over 50. Eleven participants were Deaf, three were hard of hearing, and one was a hearing grandchild of Deaf adults. Nine respondents attended a residential school for the Deaf, three attended school in a mainstream program, and two attended a regular public school. One respondent was enrolled in both a residential school and mainstream program, and another respondent attended both a regular public school and a residential school.

FINDINGS

The reported abuse ranged on a continuum from not having experienced sexual abuse but being aware of it, to witnessing sexual abuse, to having experienced violent rape. Nine participants were victims of sexual abuse while six had not experienced sexual abuse. Four of the six respondents who had not experienced sexual abuse reported they had either a Deaf friend or family member who had experienced sexual abuse. Nine reported incidents involved multiple perpetrators and two incidents involved one perpetrator. Fourteen perpetrators were Deaf and seven were hearing.

The four respondents who did not experience sexual abuse, but were aware of it happening to a Deaf family member, Deaf friend, or classmate reported the following responses. One respondent indicated, "a boy dorm counselor molested the boys when I was [at the residential school]; One girl had been molested by her father; one teacher molested five kids. That teacher got fired but they didn't put him in jail."

A parent of a Deaf, multiply-handicapped child reported that "because my daughter has multiple handicaps, she was unable to describe the abuse, but a bus driver heard some strange sounds and looked in the rearview mirror to investigate. The bus driver saw a Deaf boy with his hands up my daughter's blouse on her breasts. The bus driver said my daughter was obviously uncomfortable with this touch. The Deaf school reported the incident to the parents of the boy and they called the boy in to talk with him and that was the end of it. We didn't press charges and the law was not involved at all. Also, when my daughter attended the school, a teacher was fired for sexual abuse."

A respondent who is over age fifty reported "in my Deaf school one girl got pregnant from her Deaf father. They expelled that girl from school." These replies are from respondents who were not personally victims of sexual abuse, but were aware of abuse occurring.

As the range of abuse became more severe, the following information emerged. The victims reported that their abuse ranged from molestation to rape (see Table 1). Eight respondents indicated they were molested in a residential school setting, i.e. in the school, dorms, or bus. Ten reported molestation that occurred in a non-school setting. Three incidents involved digital penetration of the vagina, one victim experienced digital anal penetration, and four respondents were required to manually stimulate their male perpetrator's genitals.

Two incidents involved injury to the genitals of the victims that required medical attention. Three respondents indicated that they were required to perform oral sex on the perpetrator. Two victims experienced attempted rape, while three were raped by their perpetrators. One victim became pregnant from the sexual abuse (see Table 1).

Action	Number of Responses
Being aware of it happening, but not a victim	4
Picked on for sex	1
Molested in a school setting/bus	8
Molested in a non-school setting	10
Touched on the breasts	5
Touched on the vagina	6
Digital penetration of vagina	3
Digital penetration of the anus	1
Forced to manually stimulate perpetrator	4
Orally stimulate perpetrator	3
Perpetrator masturbated in front of victim	1
Injury to victims genitals	2
Attempted rape; perpetrator unable to penetrate vagina	2
Rape; intercourse involved	3
Pregnancy resulting from rape	1
Didn't specify	3

Table 1: Type of Sexual Abuse (N=15)

The following responses illustrate the nature of the abuse experienced by the victims of sexual abuse in this study. One respondent said, "An adult neighbor sexually abused me in his home." Another victim reported, "I was abused in my home by a relative," and another victim indicated, "I was molested on the bus by boys from school, touched on the vagina and breasts."

Violence also occurred which ranged from coercion, little violence, to extreme violence. Three respondents were forced into the abuse by the threat or use of guns. Two respondents indicated the perpetrators threatened them with a shovel. Ten respondents did not indicate the use of weapons in the abuse.

The following responses illustrate the violence of the abuse: "My perpetrator told me that he had a gun that he would use on me if I didn't comply." "My aunt threatened me with her gun if I told anyone what she had done to me." Two respondents said: "When he put his fingers inside of my vagina, he scraped my vagina. It hurt very much." In both instances where vaginal injury occurred, medical attention was required. Two respondents were threatened by their perpetrator when "he spread my legs open and he put the shovel by my vagina. He told me if I didn't have sex with him he would shove it up my vagina." Each perpetrator had their own methods of sexual abuse that appealed to him. Sexual abuse occurred as they forced the victims to do things they did not wish to do, and because he was in a position of power over the victim, the victim could not stop the abuse.

AFTER THE ABUSE

Effects of the sexual abuse were reflected in the section of the survey called "After the Abuse." In this section, victims expressed how the abuse had impacted their lives. The section on "After the Abuse" revealed that all nine victims of sexual abuse experienced difficulty dealing with life after the abuse. The effects of the abuse on the respondents was present regardless of the severity of the abuse or the violence used in perpetrating the abuse. The only common factor in the comments were that all respondents continued to deal with the effects of the abuse in their current lives. Each of the nine victims experienced different results from the abuse. Often the impact related to relationships with others.

The following are responses that show how abuse effected respondents. One respondent said that the abuse had left the victim with these effects: "angry, upset, nightmares, social anxiety, low self-esteem, depression, confusion, dissociation, and crave for attention." Another respondent said the impact of abuse was: "feeling crazy and weird. I always felt different from everyone else. I felt alone for a lot of years..." One respondent who had multiple perpetrators, said that she sexually abused her husband. Another talked about having a fear of intimacy, not trusting in relationships and not "knowing what to do."

Reflecting how the abuse had impacted the victim's life, one respondent said, "I slept around until I got married, I thought you had to have sex to have a boyfriend and I had to have a boyfriend because I didn't want to be alone. I am sometimes attracted to women because I think they won't be mean like men are mean." A victim said: "I wouldn't breastfeed my children because I thought I would be abusing them. I regret that sometimes now; that something that should be natural had to get all twisted." Another replied: "I am scared of marriage. I have to go through healing process so I could be a better person for future marriage and relationships with men/friends. Going through the healing process is kind of a waste of time, but it's worth it." One respondent who had not been sexually abused, but her spouse had been a victim of abuse responded that "Sexual abuse destroyed most of our marriage! Very difficult marriage relationship and family relations."

These responses are reflective of the ways that the abuse impacted the lives of victims of sexual abuse in this study. Regardless of the severity of abuse, all nine victims had dramatic impact from the abuse.

SUGGESTIONS

This section of the survey revealed why the respondents think that sexual abuse occurs with the Deaf and hard of hearing population and suggestions they may have to stop abuse. The respondents who experienced or were aware of abuse in the Deaf residential school setting expressed the idea that dorm supervisors don't watch the children under their supervision carefully enough and children learn sexual behaviors from other Deaf individuals (children and adults). It was felt that there were no family values in the dorm residence which may have contributed to the abuse that occurred in this setting.

Another theme emerged as well. In the instances where the sexual abuse occurred within families, the responses seemed to be either on the extreme of "I don't know what to do" or "tell someone no matter what." There didn't appear to be any middle ground or ideas in this area. These responses point to common themes that occur with hearing victims of sexual abuse within families. The idea that the victim is unaware of what to do is not surprising. Contrastingly, often when victims become adults and have either maturity or healing to recognize the abuse as such, the common idea that comes from this empowered state is, "tell someone, no matter what." These two types of answers were reflected by the respondents in this area of the survey. A final theme in the responses was for the victim of sexual abuse to go see a counselor.

ATTITUDES AND BELIEFS ABOUT SEXUAL ABUSE

This section indicated some possible beliefs about sexual abuse that may exist in the Deaf culture. Questions about sexual behaviors were given with the intent of finding out if there were common attitudes or beliefs about what constitutes abuse. There were four questions in this section of the survey that showed power imbalances that occur with sexual abuse. Two of the questions illustrated sexual abuse. One question showed curiosity which may be considered normal for the age group described and one question described normal behavior. The responses showed some interesting beliefs about what constitutes sexual abuse. A question used to demonstrate the power imbalance in sexual abuse was: "A six-year-old girl was touched by 15-year-old boy on the breasts." Thirteen respondents answered correctly that this was "abusive" behavior. Illustrating this idea further would mean that a freshman in high school touched a kindergartner, indicating an obvious power imbalance found with sexual abuse cases. Only one respondent rated this behavior in the normal range.

Another question illustrating the power imbalance involved with abuse was: "A 10-year-old girl touches a two-year-old's vagina and nipples." Nine responded correctly that this was abuse. Four respondents indicated that this behavior was in the normal range. A question reflecting what may be considered in the normal/curiosity range was: "A seven- and eight-year-old boy show each other their private parts." Six responses said that this behavior was normal. An equal amount of responses (six) said that this was abuse. One response indicated that they didn't know. The final question indicated: "A father bathes his two-year-old daughter." This question illustrated a normal behavior. The responses to this question showed that thirteen felt this was normal and one responded that this was abuse. One respondent did not complete this section (see Table 2).

It would appear from these responses that in two of the instances, respondents were very clear about what constituted abuse. It would also seem that in the instance involving same sex perpetrators, the respondents showed less surety about what constitutes abuse. Finally, the numbers were split exactly in half when responding to whether children of the same age showing each other their private parts was sexual abuse. These results show confusion among the Deaf community about what constitutes abuse. This confusion may be one of the reasons that sexual abuse is propagated among the Deaf population. This would be worth studying further.

Action	Normal/ Curiosity	Abuse	Don't know
A six-year-old girl touched by a 15-year-old boy on her breasts	1	13	-
A 10-year-old girl touches a two-year-old girl's vagina and nipples	4	9	1
A seven-year-old girl and eight-year-old boy sneak into a bedroomand show each other their private parts	6	6	2
A father bathes his two-year-old daughter	13	1	-

(One respondent did not complete this section.)

Table 2: Beliefs and Attitudes about Sexual Abuse (N=15)

DISCUSSION

This study found that most of the perpetrators were hearing impaired. There were half as many hearing perpetrators (seven) as there were Deaf perpetrators (fourteen). In the beginning of the study it was felt that most of the sexual abuse reported in the literature was being perpetrated by people who can hear who took advantage of a "silent" and oppressed population. Chenoweth (1998) showed that disabled populations are more likely to be sexually abused than non-disabled populations because they are less likely to tell what is happening to them. The hearing impaired are a group of people who cannot "talk," and the researchers of this study felt that perpetrators of sexual abuse on this population were people who can hear. This study found that to be true, but unexpectedly found that sexual abuse is perpetrated on Deaf victims twice as often by Deaf perpetrators as hearing perpetrators.

It seems that the Deaf community may not realize the impact that sexual abuse has on members of the community. It also seems that there is a great need to educate the whole Deaf community about the effects of sexual abuse. With the rate of sexual abuse and the number of hearing impaired individuals that perpetrate on each other, there would seem to be a feeling in the culture that what is happening is normal. This would leave room for further study to explore if the community understands how damaging and lasting the effects of abuse are.

Another result that emerged was where the abuse happened. The studies sited previously showed that abuse does occur in the residential school setting. No study has looked at sexual abuse that happens outside of residential schools. This study showed that the abuse happened at home as well as at school, and the abuse happened more often at home than at school. There were eight incidents reported at school or on a school bus. There were ten incidents of abuse that happened in a home setting. Therefore, there is a need for increased safety for children both in the schools and at home. It would seem that the abuse is happening in all aspects of the victims lives. There seems to be no "safe place" for the children victims of sexual abuse, and efforts need to be made to increase their safety.

The nature of abuse found in this study could have several reasons why it is occurring. It could be that parents of Deaf children do not understand sign language and therefore are unable to "hear" their children's cry for help, but this is only one aspect of the problem. The trend recently with hearing parents of Deaf children is that they are learning sign language to communicate with their children. With parents who can sign, language is not the barrier to communicating about abuse. The secrecy of sexual abuse is common whether the abuse happens with hearing or Deaf individuals. The problem of secrecy is not unique to Deafness, but the amount of abuse with this population is of great concern.

The respondents showed confusion about what constitutes sexual abuse. This may be getting to the core of the problem of abuse among the Deaf. The Deaf population are perpetrating against one another, and it may be because they do not know the difference between what is appropriate and inappropriate touch.

It may be that a lack of knowledge coupled with the confusion about individual rights explains the increased rate of Deaf people perpetrating against each other. A perpetrator may feel that he or she is only experimenting with sexual touching, and may not realize the violation of boundaries on his victim, which constitutes sexual abuse or sexual assault.

In the suggestion section, there was partiality given to the idea to go see a counselor if sexual abuse had occurred. This was the advice that respondents had to give to another Deaf community member who had experienced sexual abuse. This is significant to therapists and others who work with the Deaf population in these areas. It would almost seem that the Deaf see sexual abuse as something "too big" for them to help with by listening to a friend or through other means of support.

Being aware of this as counselors, and also being aware of the high incidence of sexual abuse among the Deaf population, it would seem that a required intake question in assessing the needs of Deaf consumers should be weather the client has been sexually abused. Understanding the confusion found in this study around what constitutes sexual abuse, the question may need to be along the lines of, "Has anyone ever touched you sexually in a way that you did not want to be touched?" or "Have you ever been forced to have sex?" Questions of this nature may access the information on sexual abuse that would be helpful for further diagnosis and treatment.

A final idea that may contribute to the high incidence of sexual abuse among the Deaf is that the Deaf consider themselves as family. In the core of the culture, Deaf individuals become a surrogate family to each other. The familial patterns that are common with sexual abuse and people who can hear could parallel the abuse that was expressed in this study. The secrecy surrounding abuse that keeps abuse within familial circles could also explain the secrecy and denial found in the Deaf community at large surrounding this sensitive issue. Further studies may be directed at this relationship in the Deaf community as it relates to sexual abuse.

Limitations to this study include the small sample size utilized. The findings could be generalized if the sample were larger. Ways to increase the sample size may include compensation for participation in the study. Another idea would be to administer the questionnaire via video to a larger group which would increase the sample size and decrease the time for administering the survey.

CONCLUSION

Results of this sexual abuse survey demonstrate the nature of sexual abuse reported by Deaf adults. The responses give insight to what happened to the victims, and beliefs and attitudes in Deaf culture which may promulgate sexual abuse.

As the survey showed the violent nature of the abuse that occurred, and beliefs that may impact sexual abuse in the Deaf culture, efforts may be directed toward using these ideas to help in several arenas to decrease sexual abuse. There may be educational efforts within the Deaf community to help. These efforts may occur within the Deaf schools, by therapists who work with this population, and also in the Deaf community.

Age appropriate prevention education for Deaf children, youth, and adults regarding rape and sexual abuse should occur. This education may help to reduce the occurrence of sexual abuse which was found in this study.

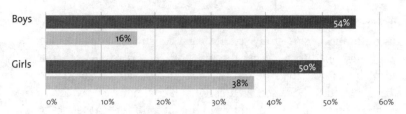

Appendix 1: Percentage of Sex Abuse Occurence Between Deaf and Hearing
Perpetrators on Boys and Girls (■ = Deaf; ▨ = Hearing)

REFERENCES

Center Against Sexual Abuse, (1998). Retrieved from http://www.syspac.com/~casa/stats.htm.

Child Abuse Statistics, (1998). Retrieved from http://www.nvc.org/edir/childabu.htm#csa.

Chenoweth, L. 1998. *Violence and disability.* Retrieved from http://www.geocities.com/HotSprings/2891/abuswom.html.

Joseph, J., Sawyer R., Desmond S. (1995). Sexual knowledge, behavior and sources of information among Deaf and hard of hearing college students. *American Annals of the Deaf.* 140(4), 338–345.

Klopping, H. (1985). The Deaf adolescent: abuse and abusers. In G.B. Anderson and D. Watson (Eds.), *Proceedings of the National Conference on the Habilitation and Rehabilitation of Deaf Adolescents.* Washington, DC; National Academy of Gallaudet University, 187–196.

Mertens, D.M. (1996). Breaking the silence about sexual abuse of Deaf youth. *American Annals of the Deaf.* 141(5), 352–358.

Sullivan, P.M., Scanlan, J.M., & LaBarre, A. (1986). *Characteristics and therapeutic issues with abused Deaf adolescents.* Presentation at Second National Conference on Habilitation and Rehabilitation of Deaf Adolescents, Afton, Oklahoma.

Sullivan, P.M., Vernon, M., & Scanlon, J.M. (1987). Sexual abuse of Deaf youth. *American Annals of the Deaf.* 132(4), 256–262.

ABOUT THE AUTHOR

Lynnette Johnson is a therapist who works with the Deaf population. Her work on Deaf sexual abuse is in publication process and will be available this year in the book, Deaf Way II: Selected Proceedings *from Gallaudet University Press. She has presented on deaf clinical issues at international conferences including Deaf Way II at Gallaudet University as well as many other venues on the state, regional, and national levels. Lynnette has a passion for using and developing best practices when working with the mental health issues of the Deaf community.*

Absence from Influence:
Perspectives of Administrators and Graduates on the Deaf Community's Exclusion from the Decision-making Process in Deaf Education

SHARLA JONES, PH.D.

Sharla Jones interprets for Deaf adults at a community college in Pasadena, California. She is currently writing a chapter for Gender in Education.

I WANT TO THANK THE people at UVSC for hosting a "Deaf/hearing friendly" conference—they are far and few between and we need more of these kinds of venues to share information between hearing and Deaf scholars, to share research and bolster the production of Deaf studies. Everyone here probably holds vehement, intense, and passionate feelings on the subject of Deaf education. It is an emotionally charged issue; it is political and personal in nature. It is an area worthy of study, research, and most of all *action*.

I want to explain about myself and a bit about my background. In 1986, I was introduced into the Deaf community through the Bob Rumball Center for the Deaf in Toronto, Ontario. I socialized with Deaf senior citizens while learning the intricacies of ASL, joined in with my new Deaf teachers and younger friends as we marched in protest in 1988 following the DPN revolution of Gallaudet for our own "Deaf Ontario Now" to improve education for Deaf children; it was then I truly learned of an inequality existing in Deaf education, a "colonization," to use Lane's analogy from *Mask of Benevolence*, and a discrimination of human rights.

From 1989 to 1991 I lived in California as a missionary, and volunteered often at the Fremont and Riverside Schools for the Deaf. This gave me an inside look at large residential schools in practice and was a great learning opportunity for me. In 1991 I returned to Canada to formally begin my profession. I began interpreting for mainstreamed high school students and for the administrators at the Jericho Hill School for the Deaf, in Vancouver, British Columbia. What truly got my wheels turning on the ineffectiveness of Deaf education was the fact that I was interpreting staff meetings for the principal and vice principal of a large provincial Deaf school and voice interpreting for the Deaf teachers so that their colleagues would understand them. I would often think to myself, "Isn't there something wrong with this picture? Don't they all teach Deaf children? Why can't they understand each other?"

I realized that in my limited capacities, I needed to become more educated, so I embarked on my own journey through higher education, attending Utah Valley State College and Brigham Young University.

I studied. I interpreted. I tutored Deaf college students and I taught sign language to other hearing people. I studied psychology and eventually taught two behavioral science courses to Deaf students at Utah Valley State College. In this context, I was exposed to students' inner feelings about college, the challenges it posed, their backgrounds of struggle through secondary school, and the doubts of ever graduating. Remedial English and math seemed their "lot in life" many times. As a teacher and friend, my views of the situation grew more salient and I knew I wanted to delve into solutions for finding more equality within Deaf education.

What I came away with in the five years of being here in Utah were close relationships with people who had many opinions about Deaf education, how it could improve, and how drastically difficult it was for many Deaf adults to be heard—whether trying to impact the system through the new generation of their own Deaf children, or climbing the ladder of academic success themselves to be able to work in positions of influence.

In 1997 I moved to Los Angeles, and in 1998, enrolled in graduate school at the University of California, Los Angeles (UCLA). I continued to interpret, mostly sticking to education where I felt—and still feel—the most useful. Hopefully, you can see where my journey has led me and perhaps some of you can identify with what I went through.

THE JOURNEY BEGINS

In June 2003 I completed my dissertation, which originally focused on how hearing administrators who run Deaf educational programs in Los Angeles justify the results of test scores of Deaf children in comparison to hearing children's scores. But, as I will explain, my question dug much further than statistics or simple reasoning.

I was trying to show a larger picture of the situation in Deaf education to my UCLA professors and this was challenging. They weren't convinced my whole premise was as obvious as I was stating in initial reporting. I had to approach several professors at UCLA who were in involved slightly with special education, and they showed ambivalence towards my notion that Deaf adults should be considered and included in the decision-making process. One professor, who had quite a clinical approach, was in fact quite rude about the idea I was presenting and said to me while I was interviewing him, "What makes you think Deaf people have anything to say that would help the situation in Deaf education? How can they administrate to a younger generation?"

I was instantly spurred on by other like comments, like one from another prominent professor: "Sharla, I'm going deaf too and I don't know the first thing about Deaf education; my hearing loss doesn't make me an expert! At least the people in special education have the credentials." To explain the inadequacy of some special education credentials and Deaf education preparation to this person, I could clearly see I was barking up the wrong tree in finding in him a supporter.

Then the whole idea of bilingual education presented itself; professors that preached its efficacy and supported this notion for Spanish speakers in California seemed to embrace my ideas more wholeheartedly and they became the feasible allies for my study. I know to this audience, bilingual/bicultural education is not a new idea, yet at UCLA—a medical research university—this view wasn't commonplace, although a few seeds had been planted.

I am deeply grateful to the Deaf scholars who were literally pioneers coming before me, introducing the concept of Deaf Community and Deaf Culture to this large and famous institution.

The study then developed further. I had to include the Deaf perspective and, to show how drastic the difference was, document the distinct disparity with the hearing administrators involved. My initial pilot studies centered on general ideas, on people's personal stories about their education. I filmed storytelling by Deaf adults for two hours at a time and documented narratives that included confusing and emotional journeys, stories of inconsistency during K-12 years in school. A common phrase found through these encounters was, "I felt like we were guinea pigs."

> I'm a little bit disgruntled when parents or teachers, who know that their student will be soon graduating from high school, don't reveal to the child what reality they will face or prepare the child to enter the real world. They don't prepare them for college, where they will encounter different expectations. No one really prepared us—nothing—and so now we have no hope? It's like we were a big experiment. Like they were just experimenting on us the whole time to see what we could do with what they gave us. The lack of information, what we would handle and what we would glean from it. That really ticks me off. I hated feeling like a Guinea pig.

This kind of leads me to my fixation to always prove to other people that
I am capable and that I can do things on my own. —Deaf graduate

Many Deaf adults discussed their experiences as educational "experiments." Their schooling options and systems were tremendously varied:
mainstreaming with hearing children (being alone in the class with or without an interpreter), oral public school, oral private school, state residential
Deaf school, enclosed classroom within a hearing school, and TRIPOD
(a Los Angeles area-based educational program).

Some of the subjects in my study group had even endured a mishmash
or some combination of these options and systems. That detail was a bit
frightening as you can wonder 1) how a small child is supposed to cope
with the rapid transition of different kinds of programs in a short period
of time and 2) what this will do to him or her psychologically. This happens at important developmental stages in a child's life—never mind the
methodological changes—and the differing environments themselves
could be detrimental in its impact. This is all done in the spirit of experimentation, like reinventing the wheel to satisfy parents or fitting with the
familial expectations, the medical community, the latest research, etc.

Interviewing these Deaf adults brought other issues as well which
I'll discuss later on. But the initial results—their advice and knowledge
of what worked and what didn't work in Deaf education—was invaluable
in forming the comparison with the hearing administrators. It became
almost problematic because of the division, the gulf between my two
study groups. A middle group was in need of exploration as well.

With the encouragement of my reading committee (as well as members of the Deaf community since they were always referring me to
experts who were Deaf themselves), I included my third and very helpful
test group, Deaf administrators. Those were the people who had personally experienced a myriad of methodologies in Deaf education, who
navigated through bureaucracy to succeed academically to the point of
becoming educational administrators and educators themselves.

I was looking for a bridge to make sense of the two sides of the story
I had documented thus far and interviewing the Deaf administrators
proved to be the most enlightening. Their enthusiasm was infectious; they
had invested their professional lives in a way that I could see most of the
hearing administrators had detached themselves from, the Deaf children
they served. Often I saw the phrase repeated, "I look at them and see
myself and my struggles as a child." One Deaf administrator explained:

A Deaf teacher, teaching the Deaf? That did not sit well with everyone. And
because I spoke and signed simultaneously, they didn't like that. Well,
you know I was oral growing up, but there I was using sign as well. To

make matters worse, they refused to give me a contract. Based solely on the fact that I was Deaf. No contract. It was eight years before they would give me a contract for teaching. So they got me a lot cheaper too, that's the price we pay for being pioneers in our lives. I did not go through the proper process because I was not hired directly through the district, and plus I was so naïve about the way things worked. I fell in love with the school. I could see myself in those kids. Game over! I had to stay here for them. Oddly enough, I felt bad for my principal. She fought hard for me. Really. I mean she—I am so grateful—she wrote wonderful reports about my teaching performance to the city. Those reports were not accepted. She finally persuaded them to send five people to come and watch me teach, observe my class for one full week. After that they were finally convinced. Again see, I was very naïve, innocent. I didn't realize I was breaking barriers. I didn't realize. I mean I was so young so I didn't challenge them very hard; I thought it was going to be a constant fight throughout my career.

I noted a reparation process, a literally redeeming quality to their work, where conversely, the hearing administrator was again in foreign territory, not having the connection to the Deaf community once the workday was over and done with, and only having Special education background experience in a general sense.

The Deaf administrator also had different so-called "survival strategies." Often the hearing administrator was so bogged down by the sheer immensity of the paperwork, the IEPs, and demands from the school district, and state red tape that it became difficult to even accomplish the running of the program. Budgetary concerns were huge; administrators seemed very overwhelmed by the physical aspect of running the program. Most alarming, the Deaf children themselves were not often the focus of their conversations, or the forefront of their activities.

Deaf administrators were very conscious of the individual: story after story of individual students made up a large percentage of interview time. They did have their frustrations with the bureaucratic aspect of their jobs, but their central focus rarely wavered from the students.

MATERIALS FROM MY STUDY

I collected nineteen interviews, lasting about two hours each. After the interviews were conducted, the audiotapes from the hearing participants, and the videotapes from the Deaf participants (which had to be translated from ASL into written English; I used a voice recognition software program in my laptop with a microphone to help with this process) had to be heavily edited. It was a lengthy process.

What's more, I had fieldnotes from classroom observations of over three years time in various settings and notes taken from various Deaf events (Deaf coffee nights to Deaf Expos to DeafWay II where spontane-ous conversations arose concerning education) to compile. I had taken photos of Deaf murals I found in high school-enclosed classrooms, Deaf poetry performances, Deaf artwork, literature reviews of hundreds of resources (the books I separated into two categories: hearing-supportive vs. Deaf-supportive), journal articles, dissertations from other universi-ties, and the three pilot research projects I had conducted previously.

There were many different mediums I included in my materials, including critiques of movies and documentaries (my advisor wanted me to include an element of media representation because that is what the general public is usually educated on) such as *Children of a Lesser God* and *Sound and Fury*. I watched any Deaf movie that had education as a theme or a topic that would impact education. The Internet was also an important part of my research: I subscribed to all listservs that catered to Deaf educators, sign language users, or parents of Deaf children and fol-lowed the threads that were directly helpful to my study. Ultimately, the volume of information was enormous and it took a full year to compile my literature review, transcribe the raw data I myself had gathered and try to focus on my immediate and most pressing research questions.

Not to be self-deprecating, but by no means did I feel I became some sort of expert in the larger scope of Deaf education; I was even more acutely aware of what I didn't know and the holes that were apparent in research already available. Finding the common threads from interview-ing guided my writing. The main issue was the Deaf community having a voice in the decision-making process and impacting the system. I used also another research technique called "participatory research" where my research subjects could read and respond to their interviews afterwards; I was constantly revising and they helped hone in on what they really meant after reading their own transcripts.

I also attempted to share the information I had gathered in a multi-cultural approach, meaning that I conscientiously included people in the study who, by their definitions, were members of various minority groups. Although the hearing administrators were mostly female, I did my best to include different ethnicities and a person with Deaf parents (CODA). In all groups, both genders, differing sexual orientations, ethnicities, immi-grant status, income levels, religious affiliations, and of course, hearing status were all represented; all these identities were factored into who was selected for research participation.

For the graduate group and the Deaf administrators group, although Deafness was the common thread, their individual backgrounds and identifications varied greatly: deaf, culturally Deaf, hard of hearing, and cochlear implanted. In retrospect, it is surprising that I even found any common threads of agreeance on any issue among the research subjects.

As a researcher, I couldn't exactly scold the hearing administrators or even admonish them to do better, although I think my presence and interest in the subject sparked deeper thoughts on their part on where their programs were headed, especially when the issue of higher education was proposed. When we discussed, for example, how many students might be going on to college, we had to admit that even on a community college level, the numbers were dismal.

I was also interested in conducting this research as a hearing person with knowledge of ASL. For research purposes, I didn't devulge my background or experience as an interpreter or my personal or political views; I wanted their stories and comments straight and unadulterated. I think if I had been a Deaf individual with an interpreter, the hearing administrators may have balked and not offered their views in such an honest light. Yet on the other hand, all the Deaf individuals knew I was hearing and may have also slanted their comments because of who I was. I was clear to point out these possibilities of bias in my research.

As a side note, the role change of researcher instead of an interpreter brought great catharsis to me. To actually document and report on details in Deaf education that, for so long I had been privy to, yet could not devulge, was a liberating experience.

SOME CONCLUSIONS FROM THE RESEARCH

> It is a lamentable fact that in matters relating to the deaf, their education and well-being, few if any take the trouble to get the opinion of the very people most concerned—the deaf themselves. —John H. Keiser, Gallaudet College, Class of 1905[1]

Hearing Administrators. Hearing administrators were overwhelmed with the many aspects involved in Deaf education. The time constraints, the writing of IEPs, the pressure to improve Deaf students academic levels in the scheme of providing an equal education, the parents who either demanded too much or too little from the school, budgetary concerns, unqualified teachers and interpreters; the list goes on and on. There was a certain degree of *deficit thinking* displayed while the hearing administrators considered why Deaf education was so deplorable. From R. Valencia's *The Evolution of Deficit Thinking*:

> The deficit-thinking model, at its core is an endogenous theory—positing

that the student who fails in school does so because of internal deficits or deficiencies. Such deficits manifest, it is alleged, in limited intellectual abilities, linguistic shortcomings, lack of motivation to learn and immoral behavior...advocates of the model have failed to look for external attributions of school failure. How schools are organized to prevent learning, inequalities in the political economy of education, and oppressive macropolicies and practices in education are all held exculpatory in understanding school failure.[2]

In short: it is the *student's* fault and not the school's. The deficit thinking the administrators showed may have stemmed from working for lengthy amounts of time in a system where students who perform poorly in academics are the norm and not the exception (their reasoning, not mine). These administrators seemed tired of the constant battle they were fighting with the school district or state board of education, which left little time to concentrate on the important issues of positively improving student achievement levels. They all agreed reading was a key skill that Deaf students have to master but, in reality, they personally knew very few avid readers who were Deaf.

Hearing administrators tended to view Deaf students as unequal to hearing students basically because of inadequate educational foundations, late starts, confusion over educational methodology, constant catch-up, and lack of critical thinking skills. One hearing administrator who was a CODA (child of a Deaf adult) was the only hearing person interviewed in the study to suggest that Deaf adults needed to become involved in Deaf education and that the system should reflect a more bilingual education.

This administrator also had more innovative ideas on changes in Deaf education that the other more hearing-supportive administrators did. She suggested that for every Deaf child in public education, a Deaf adult should be a representative for him or her on the administrative side when decisions are being made concerning the child's education. She also suggested a mandatory preparation time for students in mainstream situations with their interpreters, so that the student could take responsibility for gleaning as much information from mainstream classroom time as possible.

Conversely, two of the hearing administrators interviewed omitted the word "Deaf" from their vocabulary completely. They believed the harder a person worked, the easier time he or she would have in passing in the hearing world, with proper amplification and enough speech therapy. Their programs had no Deaf adult involvement whatsoever, thus by this absence, the conversations were easily focused on the children's deficits only, in the here and now. The world they worked in revolved around speech, lip-reading, and getting a jump ahead on materials that the hearing children were exposed to. This is still very much reality in 2004.

Another hearing mainstream administrator commented that she was overwhelmed by budgetary restraints and the scarcity of available and qualified interpreters. She was adamant that tutoring and mentoring was impossible. She was also overworked, responsible for all special education services rendered to all children at the school. She estimated that she personally was in charge of getting appropriate special services for about 300 students.

Deaf Graduates. Many of the subjects felt unchallenged in school and felt that the material that was offered in Deaf education was watered down. Most graduates felt disappointed by the inequality in comparing their education to a hearing person's. One subject expressed the sentiment quite succinctly, understanding that many Deaf people are not prepared to go on to higher education, and only fit in academically for menial labor or receiving SSI (Social Security supplemented income):

> From my perspective and from what I experienced, my education was pretty worthless. *Maybe* it was okay for preparing a person for perhaps community college level, but worthless for a person entering competitive higher education. I notice that many Deaf coming from various Deaf programs must enroll in remedial courses in college to play catch up even before their college level classes can begin. That's like repeating high school all over. Then they are shocked, trying to get any higher education! Deaf education cheats a Deaf person! —Deaf graduate

In an optimistic turn, many research subjects felt that having a Deaf teacher was important and that the most essential skill for a teacher to have was excellent signing ability. Many graduates believed that teachers who had high expectations of their students produced higher levels of achievement. A few research subjects revealed that teachers who secretly signed, when the administration had forbidden it, won their students' hearts and minds and gave them a better education.

One research subject was insightful as she explained that Deaf education would not improve for the better until there were more Deaf doctors, Deaf lawyers, and Deaf politicians in the world, then the top-down effect would occur and Deaf education would be positively impacted:

> I'm not sure Deaf education would improve if there were more Deaf administrators. I will tell you my reasoning, because if there were more Deaf adults within the political structure or medical community then yes there would be improvement in Deaf education. Because as Deaf people become teachers, principals and such; that's good, yes, and positive, but

the real power is in that political arena and in the medical community. If those Deaf professionals are not part of the process that make the decisions in general for education, then Deaf education will never improve. Gallaudet, for example, is ruled by money; that college is ruled by Congress and we have to fight Congress first before we can carry on with Deaf education. I can see Deaf education improving if there is Deaf representation within our political system and more Deaf doctors, lawyers, and such. It is all a political fight. —Deaf graduate

The Deaf graduates related stories that were often disheartening. One subject admitted to cheating regularly to pass classes. A common element was physical abuse in their educational experiences, either from speech teachers or impatient classroom teachers who were at their wits end trying to communicate in an ineffective fashion. The physical power demonstrated over the graduates was commonplace, mostly due to rules restricting signing and attention-getting methods for oral training.

A couple of graduates reported that they were self-educated, since their own situations failed to provide literacy and scholarship. They took matters into their own hands, excelling in reading basically out of sheer boredom or desperation when teachers would not give them the information they required.

A couple of graduates commented on how teachers would use them to help tutor the rest of the class to learn the material since the teacher could not effectively communicate, thus holding that bright student back from progressing. One research subject expressed the feelings of bitterness, about the atrophy in her enthusiasm for learning, her lost years being illiterate, and overwhelming confusion due to an ineffective education. She was extremely grateful for a short period of time she spent at a Deaf school where she felt awakened by other Deaf people, discovered herself in her true identity and learned many survival techniques to navigate in a hearing world. From another Deaf graduate:

> I suggest that hearing administrators really listen to Deaf people and to what they say they need. Deaf people tend to explain the situation only to have the administration shun them, shrug them off, keep them at arms length, so most Deaf people feel they do not get heard; their suggestions hit a wall that is impenetrable. We feel that the administrators only work for the money. They like the glory of a position, they get paid for and they can feel important. Any suggestion made by a Deaf person doesn't seem to be taken seriously. It's been a problem in Deaf education anywhere you go. The administrators really have closed minds. They need to have an open mind and listen to the Deaf community. Quit treating Deaf children like Guinea pigs. It's as though the administrators just stand by and watch and wait for us to come of age and leave the school and they can chalk another one up for getting someone out the door. —Deaf graduate

A few Deaf graduates were involved in education as adults; some Deaf adults were working with Deaf children as teacher aides and in their realm of authority they were implementing elements of bilingual-bicultural education where they could. They were sharing what they knew with hearing parents and trying to influence the Deaf children whom they came into contact with for the better.

Deaf Administrators. Deaf administrators agreed about one thing: Deaf education can and should be improved, and several of them had ideas on how to start the process. Several subjects urged for more research to be done in the field, especially more Deaf-supportive scholarship, researching how bilingual/bicultural education can improve scholastic ability among Deaf children. A few subjects mentioned the need for appropriate assessment tools, fitted for Deaf children instead of for hearing children. A few subjects also saw the need for a better-suited curriculum and a more Deaf-centered approach to Deaf education, all more in line with bilingual/bicultural education methodology.

All of the administrators wanted the hearing adults involved in Deaf education to end their paternalistic attitude and mentality of oppression as these hearing people heavily influence the lives of Deaf children. They agreed that everyone should have a higher expectation level instated which would filter down to the students as they perform the tasks they are expected and taught to perform.

All of the research subjects in this category expressed a desire for more parental involvement, for more family members signing to each other and for a support group to band together in this effort. One subject in particular noticed other factors that compounded the language issues in the home such as poverty, non-English speaking parents, and options like cochlear implants without ASL for children.

Each of the Deaf administrators faced discrimination in their lives and realized what the students needed to combat the inequalities in the world. The students needed confidence in themselves, strong literacy skills, and a steadfast identity and purpose as contributing members of society.

Five out of six Deaf administrators were adamant about Deaf residential schools being the best option still for Deaf children, under the condition that the schools should improve to be on par academically with hearing schools. The one administrator that did not feel the same was pushing for day school programs, still educating Deaf children together, but making sure that they went home at night to be with their families and contributing to the family community as well and encouraging better communication lines between family members.

All of the administrators were in favor of a bilingual approach, using ASL and written English. The discrimination for supporting this kind of education for Deaf children was felt among some of these research subjects in a very tangible way. Three research subjects had been fired from positions in education where they had been promulgating these concepts.

> I think attitudes need to change and hopefully they will, so that only bilingual/bicultural philosophy will be used within the teachers' training programs—because they need it. They don't need to mess around with all the different options, it's so confusing to the general public. Luckily, bilingual/bicultural education is starting to expand and grow. In the future, with more research to back up our findings, it will solidify as a valid educational philosophy for the Deaf. I am very hopeful that residential schools all over the United States will eventually adopt this philosophy and keep it. It is the perfect place for bilingual/bicultural to be used, and I am hopeful for the future in this endeavor. —Deaf administrator

The administrators still adhered to the theory that bilingual/bicultural education could improve the quality of the Deaf children's lives, appreciating the culture of their legacy, considering their difference in physicality as their strength and being Deaf as a resource to draw from. Because of the bureaucracy surrounding how Deaf education is conducted, they saw hope in the smaller-scaled charter school for the Deaf and supported this kind of program.

SOLUTIONS FROM THE DEAF COMMUNITY

There were several ways the Deaf community was generating information, taking action, and making strides in bettering the situation for the next generation of Deaf people. From my involvement with a particular research subject, an invitation was issued to me to become part of a political coalition. This group of people was formed to write a specific assembly bill to the state legislature in hopes of passing a law requiring better education for Deaf children who attend state-run special schools and for language proficiency testing among the educators.

Through association with this political coalition, I witnessed how a group of concerned Deaf-supportive people took action and made small steps towards improving education. The coalition was also offering parents a forum where they could vent their frustrations in a safe place. Having this outlet and resource in each other made a positive impact on many people who formerly had no recourse when confronted with bureaucracy at the Deaf school. Bell Hooks, an African American feminist educator, has encouraged:

[w]e must have more written work and oral testimony documenting ways barriers are broken down, coalitions formed, and solidarity shared. It is this evidence that will renew our hope and provide strategies and direction for future feminist [and Deaf] movement.[3]

In an effort to bridge the obvious gap represented by hearing administrators and Deaf adults, organiz ations such as California's IMPACT hold conferences yearly for parents, teachers, paraprofessionals, and members of the Deaf community, to discuss ways to improve Deaf education. Started in 1986 by twelve parents of Deaf children, IMPACT's membership has grown to over four hundred, providing a mechanism whereby parents can impact local, state, and national legislative processes. At the 2002 conference held in San Diego, keynote speakers addressed ongoing research on how culturally Deaf people are setting trends in the educational field.

Deaf Way II, an international conference held in Washington, D.C. during July 2002 was an excellent example of what the Deaf community was doing to improve the quality of life for Deaf people everywhere, filtering down to Deaf education as well. Dr. Laurene Gallimore, a plenary speaker during the conference posed the question, "Deaf education: whose way is it?" She explained how accessibility in Deaf education is a civil right we all need to protect. She warned parents that the principals at the mainstreaming schools do not know what the situation is. "We have to fight for resources and the hearing parents need access to the right information. The system is Goliath and we are David, yet can we fight the system? As Fredrick Douglas said, 'Fire and thunder is needed!' Rebuke it! Fight for civil rights!"

She related a story of Frankie, an 18-year-old African-American from Alabama whose parents finally won a court case in 1998 for the provision of an equal education. A personal tutor was hired to assist Frankie, as he had previously spent his entire education in a hearing school, sitting day after day coloring pictures. That is all his educators had deemed him capable of doing. In two years of intensive tutoring, Frankie's language competency was improving. One day his tutor was unable to come to school. The next day, incensed with her, he bawled her out, telling her "I can't afford to miss a day! I've missed far too much already and you must never do that to me again!" The question was left to the audience to ponder, "How many more 'Frankies' are out there?" Dr. Gallimore called for the Deaf community to produce collaborative efforts and to hold more "Deaf/hearing-friendly conferences."[4]

In a presentation at Deaf Way II, the idea was proposed for a "heritage school" to be organized. This concept was modeled after other language-specific schools: a German school in Chicago, a Chinese school in Boston, and a Japanese school in Long Beach all gave children an opportunity to learn about their heritage and language on Saturdays. While many Deaf children are within mainstream situations, they could learn about Deaf culture and ASL through attending a heritage school on the weekends to fill in the gaps in their education.

The idea was proposed to include Deaf children, hearing siblings, parents, and the Deaf community at large so that greater understanding could be fostered between the groups. Deaf adults could offer creative curriculum including storytelling, poetry appreciation and cultural information. Families who live in remote areas could make a weekly commute. The researchers who were presenting this idea stressed the importance of having Deaf adults on the board of directors and having a parent-coordinator, reaffirming the partnership between Deaf and hearing people.

We can see that when the conviction is to better the Deaf education system, using the Deaf community as its guide, using children's strengths, then perhaps the cyclical hopelessness will be replaced with progress in a very tangible and obvious way.

NEED FOR FURTHER RESEARCH

There is a great need for more research to be done in the area of Deaf education. As one administrator in my study pointed out, there are many opinions floating around and little substantiated fact to qualify as actual research. Bilingual/bicultural schools have been mentioned several times throughout this dissertation, thus investigating the philosophy and practice adopted by the few cites currently engaged in bilingual/bicultural education would be beneficial to study. Understanding exactly how the children are affected and producing better scholarship through bilingual/bicultural education would be valuable research.

Out of basic necessity in a quantitative study, an actual accounting of how many Deaf adults in the United States and Canada use ASL on a daily basis as their primary language would be beneficial information for educators. To understand the "Ph.D. pipeline," interviewing Deaf adults who have obtained doctoral degrees and how they navigated the systems in place would also be helpful.

There is a need for more research on the assessment tools for Deaf children that are appropriate for the ways in which Deaf people learn to read and process information. Tools are also needed to assess Deaf children's ASL comprehension and expression. There is a need to investigate better tracking devices for following through with a Deaf student after graduation, thus ensuring a better transition into higher education or employment. There is a need to search out different Deaf alumni organizations, to see if certain groups of alumni have had more success as adults and why.

As the critical incident technique revealed, there is also a great need for research on cochlear implants and their long-term effects on people. There is also need for research delving into the medical profession and its attitudes on the Deaf, and the education medical doctors receive about the Deaf community. In Los Angeles, I met a unique doctor: an ear, nose, and throat specialist who required all of his interns to read materials on Deaf culture and the Deaf community to make more informed decisions regarding Deaf people. Admittedly, he knew he was a rarity, being hard of hearing himself, and encouraged those around him to educate themselves on this linguistic minority and to become more sensitive. Cochlear implant companies need to be researched, and information on the success rates, failures rates, long-term usage, complications from surgery, and any allegations of health problems due to the surgery need to be documented carefully.

There is a need to research the different state schools' hiring policies, and qualifications for employment to teach and administer Deaf education and any state laws enacted for language proficiency. Research on teacher training programs would also be helpful, to understand the mindset formed and the information received while training to become a teacher for the Deaf. It would be interesting to see if the programs for teacher training included many members of the Deaf community for their contributions and guidance.

TURNING THEORY INTO PRACTICE

The research presented here has touched on a large issue of the Deaf community's involvement in Deaf education and the differences found between administrators and graduates. The narratives presented offered a concise picture of the division (Deaf-supportive versus hearing-supportive) by directly quoting various people involved in Deaf education. The recommendations given by these people are valuable for others to consider when making decisions that impact Deaf programs, both as parents of Deaf children, and hearing administrators who may be open to the ideas presented, that Deaf adults have the experience, the hindsight and the passion to improve a difficult situation.

The theory behind my work was of marginality and from the standpoint of the oppressed minority to reform education, thus the selections of the most convincing comments from the interviews were conscientiously decided upon. Peter McLaren and Henry Giroux have written:

> Educational researchers who are able to name social injustice often extend their role of researchers to that of social activist. But if the concepts of domination and oppression are not part of a researcher's vocabulary, then it often follows that the researcher's analysis will likely remain disinterested, neutral, and devoid of social criticism.[5]

In that vein, this research was pointedly interested in campaigning for more Deaf representation in the administration of Deaf education, an idea that has escaped the consciousness of many hearing administrators, which act constitutes discrimination and a violation of civil rights. George Veditz, a former president of the National Association of the Deaf, said in 1910:

> A new race of pharaohs that knew not Joseph is taking over the land and many of our American schools. They do not understand signs, for they cannot sign. They proclaim that signs are worthless and of no help to the Deaf. Enemies of the sign language, they are enemies of the true welfare of the Deaf.[6]

Sadly, the situation in Deaf education has not changed much, as demonstrated by the information delineated in this composition. Even recently, in 2003, a Deaf teacher in my study, young and hopeful to teach using a bilingual/bicultural curriculum, must answer to the principal who was educated in audiology, the pathology of deafness, and who does not know how to sign.

Hearing people who were crusading for "normalcy" have historically defined our understanding of what it means to be Deaf. Leonard Davis, a CODA, writing about this ideology of normalcy and the way this plays a part in the exclusion of Deaf people remarked:

> The hegemony of normalcy is, like other hegemonic practices, so effective because of its invisibility. Normalcy is the degree zero of modern existence. Only when the veil is torn from the bland face of the average, only when the hidden political and social injuries are revealed behind the mask of benevolence, only when the hazardous environment designed to be the comfort zone of the normal is shown with all its pitfalls and traps that create disability—only then will we begin to face and feel each other in all the rich variety and difference of our bodies, our minds, and our outlooks.[7]

To view Deaf education as something beyond special education for disabled children, to consider the adult community of Deaf people as *the* resource to tap into and utilize and include in the decision-making process and to consider the Deaf as a linguistic minority would be a radical departure from the current established system of education. Bilingual/bicultural education in its definition would honor both worlds inhabited by Deaf children. The need for change is apparent, and if this change does not occur, what will happen to the next generation of Deaf children?

> The myriad options that confront parents almost from the moment when hearing loss is diagnosed, the variety of placements, the confusion over making predictions based on hearing level, the inability of the professionals to bring parents together with members of the Deaf-World (professional and non-professional), and the attitudes that prevent Deaf professionals from joining in policy decisions—counseling parents and becoming teachers and administrators—all serve to maintain the failure of education for the average Deaf child...In this new era of information technology, the price Deaf students are paying for the rejection of the language and culture of the DEAF-WORLD in Deaf education gets higher every day. Either Deaf education must be reconceptualized and restructured to match the education of other language minorities, or the field of special education must prove adaptive enough to accommodate the needs of this distinct cultural group."[8]

The counsel from Deaf adults in my study strongly urges administrators who govern Deaf education to consider carefully what they as members of the Deaf community have to offer, and to recognize bilingual/bicultural education as a solution to the problems encountered and as a viable approach to a more equitable education system for Deaf children. Why is this important?

> Our decision-making apparatus must be altered to allow for a system based on multiple, rather than majority rule. Does this lead to chaos and tyranny? Of course, there are great risks, but new promises.[9]

ENDNOTES

1.   *American history through Deaf eyes.* May–June 2002. [Museum exhibit]. Washington, DC: Smithsonian Institute.

2.   Valencia, R.R. (1997). Conceptualizing the notion of deficit thinking. In R.R. Valencia (Ed.), *The evolution of deficit thinking: Educational thought and practice.* London: Falmer, p. 2.

3.   Hooks, B. (1994). *Teaching to transgress: Education as the practice of freedom.* New York: Routledge, p. 110.

4.   Gallimore, L. (Plenary speaker). (2002, July 12). *Deaf education: Whose way is it?* Washington, DC: Deaf Way II.

5.   McLaren, P. (1997). *Revolutionary Multiculturalism: Pedagogies of dissent for the new millennium.* Boulder: Westview Press, pp. 26–27.

6.   Padden, C. & Humphries, T. (1988). *Deaf in America: Voices from a culture.* Cambridge: Harvard University Press, p. 36.

7.   Davis, L. (1995). *Enforcing normalcy: Disability, deafness, and the body*. London: Verso, pp. 170–171.

8.   Lane, H., Hoffmeister, R. & Bahan, B. (1996). *A journey into the DEAF-WORLD*. San Diego: DawnSignPress, p. 313

9.   Rust, V. (1991). "Postmodernism and its comparative education implications." *Comparative education review*. 35:4, p. 618.

ABOUT THE AUTHOR

*Sharla Jones has been involved with the Deaf Community since 1986, gegin
ing her interpreting career in Canada where she was born and raised. After
attending Utah Valley Community College (now UVSC), Brigham Young
University, and UCLA for various degrees in psychology and education, she
is back to her passion—interpreting for Deaf adults at the community
college level in Pasadena, California. Presently she is writing a chapter for*
Gender in Education, *written with a group of UCLA women.*

History of the American Indian Deaf

WALTER P. KELLEY, PH.D.

Water P. Kelley, one of the two founders of the Intertribal Deaf Council (IDC), is on the organization's Council of Elders. He is an author and consultant in Arizona leading a task force on American Indian Deaf issues.

AS THE AMERICAN INDIAN PEOPLE have gone through drastic changes throughout American history, those tribal members who were deaf and hard of hearing were also affected. From the 1800s to the present, many Deaf individuals had not been treated well by their tribal communities. In addition, many of them had been forced to assimilate into the White culture. As a result, these people had to decide a life between the dominant American culture and the Deaf World. However, some did retain their traditional American Indian culture.

AMERICAN INDIAN SIGN LANGUAGES

In the late 1500s, Europeans who explored the Great Plains and the Great Southwest reported signs being used among the American Indians. The Spaniards documented that signs were used among the tribes living in what is now New Mexico and Arizona. Some linguists and historians believe that priests traveling with the Spaniards learned the signs in order to communicate with the Indian people they met along the way. A few of them returned to Spain and introduced the signs to other priests who decided to use them as a means of communication inside the monasteries since no spoken words were allowed. A few years later, one Spaniard learned the signs and used them as a way to teach the Deaf. His school was reported to be the first school for the deaf.

The French had also been thought to learn signs from the Cree and other tribes living in the Great Plains. Some Cree individuals were taken to France where the signs were later picked up by street people living in Paris. Years later, one clergyman saw the signs used between two deaf girls and decided to use them as a way to teach Deaf children.

Many American Indian signs exist today but are slowly disappearing. One sign language, the Plains Indian Sign Language (PISL), can still be seen. PISL was primarily developed as a facilitator for intertribal contact between the different American Indian tribes in the Plains region. The Plains extended from what is now the state of Texas northward to Canada; and, at its widest point, stretched from what is now western Arizona through Oklahoma (Taylor, 1978). The Plains Indian tribes had spoken languages different from one another to where PISL was developed to ease intertribal communication. The signs were used during hunting and trading among the different tribes and it was also used for storytelling and for a variety of ceremonies. Tribes residing in the Plains region known to use signed language were the Cheyenne, the Comanche, the Kiowa, and the Sioux.

With the arrival of the United States military in the Plains region in the late 1800s, formal studies were conducted on the signed language used among various Indian tribes on the Plains (Clark 1885, 1982; Dodge, 1882; 1978; Seton, 1918). According to accounts of Plains Indians, the main function of their use of signed language was intertribal communication. In the late 1900s, Cody (1970) and Tomkins (1969) among others developed a comprehensive dictionary of the signs. Within the past ten years, a couple of studies (Farnell, 1995; McKay-Cody, 1998) explored what is left of PISL.

Not only in the Plains area were signed languages used, they were also found as a means of communication among tribes living outside the area (Johnson, 1994; Scott, 1931; West, 1960). Two such sign languages known today are the Keresan Pueblo Indian Sign Language (KPISL) and the Diné (Navajo) Sign Language (DSL). KPISL is believed to have developed at one New Mexican pueblo by family members in order to communicate with their offspring, siblings, and relatives who were deaf (Kelley, 2003; Kelley and McGregor, 2003). KPISL had passed from one family's eldest brothers and sisters to hearing and deaf siblings, nephews, and nieces. KPISL is also used among non-family members living on the pueblo. It has been found to function in two significant ways: (a) as an alternative to spoken language for hearing tribal members and (b) as a primary, or first, language, for deaf tribal members.

Diné Sign Language (DSL) was developed perhaps by family members for the same reasons as for KPISL. Davis and Supulla (1995) reported that a signed language was used within a large Northeast Arizona Diné family consisting of a high genetic incidence of deafness. Six out of 11 family members were found to have hearing loss and had used the signs, mostly a more complex home-sign system that developed over several decades among a community of signers. Many of the hearing members in the family used the signs with the deaf relatives. Davis and Supulla found that the signs were not based on ASL grammatical features. DSL was found among other families living in the same area but very little information on the signs was obtained (McGregor, 2002). Further study is suggested to document other Diné families that have Deaf family members in order to determine whether these families demonstrate a similar linguistic development as the first family that was studied.

A SIGNIFICANT HISTORICAL EVENT

At Wounded Knee Creek in December 1890, Sioux Indians under the leadership of Big Foot were informed that they would be disarmed and moved to Pine Ridge, South Dakota. The Sioux stacked their guns in the center, but the soldiers were not satisfied. The soldiers went through the tents, bringing out bundles and tearing them open, throwing knives, axes, and tent stakes into the pile. Then they ordered searches of the individual warriors. The search found only two rifles, one brand new, belonging to a young man named Black Coyote. Black Coyote raised his gun over his head and cried out that he had spent much money for the rifle and that it belonged to him. Black Coyote was deaf and therefore did not respond promptly to the demands of the soldiers. He would have been convinced to put it down by the Sioux, but it was not apparently possible. He was grabbed by the soldiers and spun around. Immediately, a shot was heard; its source is not clear but it began the killing. The only arms the Sioux had were what they could grab from the pile. The Sioux tried to run but all were gunned down "like buffalo." Only four men and 47 women and children survived and were taken to an Episcopal mission after a long wait outside in the bitter cold.

THE INTERTRIBAL DEAF COUNCIL

The Intertribal Deaf Council is the only North American non-profit organization for Deaf, deaf-blind, and hard of hearing American Indian, Alaska Native, and First Nations individuals and their families. IDC began in the summer of 1994 as the National Association of the Native American Deaf (NANAD). (In the following year, NANAD's name was changed to IDC.) IDC was set up to allow Native Deaf individuals to have a place to

meet and share their dreams, ideas, and concerns. This year's conference will be the tenth. Last summer, IDC had its first spiritual gathering
at the Mohawk Nation in New York. Here, participants gathered to meet
in harmony and no political issues were discussed.

RESEARCH AND PUBLICATIONS ON
THE AMERICAN INDIAN DEAF

Prior to IDC's founding, published information on the American Indian
Deaf was sparse. The first piece of literature on the Deaf was the book
Queer Person (Doubleday/Duran), written by R. Hubbard in 1930, that
told the story of a young Indian Deaf individual facing obstacles while
growing up but had became a famous chief. The next publication on the
Indian Deaf was not written until 53 years later. In 1983, Robin Massey
wrote the article "An interview with Michael Bird" that was published in
The BiCultural Center News.

In 1992, the article, "Where do my kindred dwell? Using art and storytelling to understand the transition of young Indian men who are deaf,"
written by N. Eldridge with J. Carrigan, was published in *Arts in Psycho-
therapy.* In the following year, another publication written by Eldredge,
"Culturally affirmative counseling with American Indians who are Deaf,"
was published in the *Journals of the American Deafness and Rehabilitation Association.* Hammond and Meiners, 1993, wrote two articles, "The
Well-Hidden People in Deaf and Native Communities" in *The Deaf American Monograph Series* and "American Indian Deaf Children and Youth"
for *Multicultural issues in Deafness,* edited by Christensen and Delgado.

After the founding of IDC, an abundance of dissertations, research
papers, articles, and books on the American Indian Deaf began to be published. Sharon Baker's dissertation, "The Native American Deaf Experience: Cultural, Linguistic, and Educational Perspectives" (1997), investi-
gated the diversity of the American Indian Deaf experience among eight
deaf respondents from the Cherokee, Creek, and Chickasaw tribes living
in Oklahoma. Another dissertation, "Pueblo Individuals who are D/deaf:
Acceptance in the Home Community, the Dominant Society, and the
Deaf Community" (2001), written by Walter Kelley, explored difficulties
Pueblo Deaf face in today's mainstream society.

The research supported the idea that there was some kind of collaboration or network system needed to help resolve many of those problems.
In the following year (2002), Tony "Mac" McGregor in his dissertation
"Life History Of Coyote Eyes," a Diné deaf rug weaver found that Diné art
such as weaving is best taught at home, and not at the school for the deaf.

In addition, a few articles on the Native Deaf were published. They include "Vocational Rehabilitation of the Hearing Impaired Native American" in *Journal of Rehabilitation of the Deaf* (Massey, 1992); "Pueblo Indian Children who are Deaf" in *Deaf Studies VI: Making the Connection* (Kelley, 1999); "The 'Well-Hidden' People in Deaf and Native Communities" in *The Deaf American Monograph Series* (McKay-Cody, 1999), and "Contemporary Native Deaf Experience" (Dively, 2001) for the reader and sourcebook *Deaf World*.

Two books, *Silent One: The Adventure of A Hearing Impaired Herione* (1998) written by Teresa Battisti-Cole; and *Step in the Circle* (2003), edited by Damara Paris and Sharon Wood are also found on the market. Recently, the movie *Hidalgo* (Touchstone, 2003) depicted the story of what had happened during the Wounded Knee tragedy.

PROJECT STUDIES ON THE NATIVE DEAF

Within the last few years, several project studies were conducted. One was the National Multicultural Interpreter Project developed at El Paso Community College in 2000. The Project recruited individuals to become interpreters in the multicultural community. It also developed interpreting training workshops.

In 2003, another project, *Circle of Unity: Pathways To Improving Outreach to American Indians and Alaska Natives who are Deaf, Deaf-Blind, and Hard of Hearing* was conducted by the Rehabilitation Research and Training Center for Persons who are Deaf or Hard of Hearing at the University of Arkansas. The study gathered information from different sources in order to develop a publication for distribution to community, state, and tribal rehabilitation counselors,

Presently, the Arizona Commission for the Deaf and the Hard of Hearing (ACDHH) is conducting a study entitled "Hearing Loss among Native American Tribes in Arizona." First, town meetings were conducted throughout Eastern Arizona to gather information on available and needed services to the Native Deaf. Afterwards, a task force will be created to determine what would be the best method to enable American Indian Deaf individuals living in Arizona to receive the same services as those the mainstream Deaf community.

AMERICAN INDIAN ARTS

Outstanding artworks produced by Deaf individuals can be found among the different Native groups. Four well-known artists have had their names and works published in art and/or history books. One, Blackfoot wood-carver John Louis Clark, created pieces that were treasured by collectors.

Clara Montoya of San Ildefonso Pueblo and Claudio Naranjo of Santa Clara Pueblo worked with hearing sisters who created beautiful pottery. Clara was a master in polishing black-on-black pottery made by her well-known sister, Maria Martinez, whose works are highly sought by collectors all over the world. And, Claudio's sister was the famous potter Teresita Naranjo.

Carved *kachinas* (wood-painted dolls) made by one other Pueblo artist, Shelton Talas (Hopi), can found in many museums and homes of art collectors. Joselita Galvan of Zia Pueblo, has shown her weavings at the world renown Indian Market in Santa Fe. At presently, she is the only deaf person at the market that has over 500 artists selling art. Two other Pueblo Deaf individuals, Eileen Shije, Zia, has produced a few clay pottery pieces and Lionel Cruz (Ysleta) is known for his skill in sewing beautiful moccasins.

Some Diné Deaf individuals have created beautiful rugs, watercolors, and leatherwork. One such artist is Dennison Long of Arizona who weaves beautiful Yei and sand painting rugs. One of his weavings was displayed at Gallaudet during Deaf Way II.

In museums all over the world, portraits of Deaf American Indians painted by the Anglo deaf artist Joseph Sharp of New Mexico/Montana can be seen. Some of the individuals Sharp painted were somewhat involved in the Battle of Big Horn and other battles against the U.S. Army.

CONCLUSION

The intent of this presentation is to give individuals an understanding of the American Indian Deaf. Not all publications regarding the American Indian Deaf are mentioned. After the founding of IDC, numerous articles and books were produced, and not all could be mentioned. Further information on the listed publications can be easily found on the Internet.

ABOUT THE AUTHOR

Elder Walter Paul Kelley received his doctorate at the University of Texas at Austin, his M.A. at Gallaudet University, and his B.A. at Baylor University. Dr. Kelley, one of the two founders of the Intertribal Deaf Council (IDC), is on the organization's Council of Elders. He has spoken on the American Indian Deaf and hard of hearing and their culture and languages at different national conferences/conventions such as the National Indian Education Association (NIEA) Convention, Deaf Way II, and Deaf Studies VI and VII, and many others. Presently, Dr. Kelley is a consultant in Arizona leading a task force on American Indian Deaf issues; in 2001 he completed one study on the Pueblo Deaf living in New Mexico. Dr. Kelley is also a writer of stories on Deaf and disability culture and history primarily geared for young children. He has published several books for children.

Students at the Alabama School for the Deaf signing "Alabama," c. 1920

Courtesy Gallaudet University Archives

The Cochlear Implantation of Deaf Children: Unasked and Unanswered Questions

J. FREEMAN KING, ED.D.

J. Freeman King is the director of Deaf Education at Utah State University, Logan, Utah.

> I am aware that many object to the severity of my language; but is there not cause for severity? I will be as harsh as truth, and as uncompromising as justice. On this subject I do not wish to think, or speak, or write with moderation...I am in earnest, I will not equivocate, I will not excuse, I will not retreat a single inch, and I will be heard. —William Lloyd Garrison, abolitionist

THE IMPETUS FOR WRITING THIS essay is not an attempt to debunk the positive benefits that have been evident in a few cochlear implanted children. Rather, the intent is to foster evaluation and critical thinking as to why the medical profession, society, parents of deaf children, and education has stampeded so rapidly into this "new frontier."

Initially, it is important to understand there is a vast difference between *acquiring* a first language and *learning* a language. Hearing individuals have been blessed with the luxury of having had the opportunity to acquire a language literally from the "womb to the tomb," based on the simple fact they are able to hear. Hearing infants are immersed in language from the moment they are born until the day they die. The infant who is deaf does not have this luxury, and therefore, for this child, a spoken language is one that must be laboriously learned in order to be mastered. Because of the unique differences between acquiring (an effortless, intrinsic occurrence) and learning (a process that in no way can be termed effortless and intrinsic), the deaf infant is penalized immediately when it comes to English or any auditory-based language.

The cochlear implant, touted as a miracle cure for nerve deafness and the magical antidote which leads to hearing and speech and therefore access to the English language, can be successful for some late-deafened adults. Of course, due to his status, the case most readily pointed out is that of conservative talk show personality Rush Limbaugh, who, because of being able to once hear, already had a full, complete language intact and had *acquired* English in its spoken form before becoming deaf. Notice the crucial terms: "able to once hear," "language intact," and "*acquired* English in its spoken form."

At best, the implant creates a sensation of sound through direct stimulation of the auditory nerve. Jean Andrews, the director of Deaf Education at Lamar University states, "unlike Limbaugh, who already spoke and had acquired language, deaf children must go through years of arduous speech training to learn how to translate these sensations, and even then there are no guarantees that the cochlear implant will foster language development." (Andrews, 2002). It is clear that cochlear implants do not correct hearing in the sense that eyeglasses correct vision to 20/20. Making this analogy is totally unfounded when trying to ascertain exactly what cochlear implants can or cannot do. Nancy Niedzielski, a linguist at Rice University goes on to say:

> It is true that these implants have been invaluable tools for post-lingually deafened adults such as Limbaugh, who had already learned to talk before he became deaf and thus already had auditory pathways; and while there are some benefits, too, for children who have some residual hearing, there is absolutely no evidence that profoundly deaf infants will receive such benefits.

> Make no mistake: this cochlear implantation procedure is brain surgery, and destroys the child's cochlea in the process. Teaching children to interpret the input takes years, and outcomes are extremely varied. Some children never acquire the ability to make sense of this information (the "sensation of sound"). Meanwhile, they have lost precious time that could have been spent learning to speak, read, and write using American Sign Language [as the first language of communication and instruction].

> Parents desperately want to do the right thing when they learn about their infant's hearing loss, but misrepresenting the benefits of cochlear implants without honestly addressing the dangers [and misconceptions] is cruel (Niedzielski, 2002).

The American media machine, as well as vested interest entities—organizations which promote speech and hearing, the medical profession, and often, educators—are guilty of promoting the exception as the rule. Resultantly, the populace and parents of deaf children often naively accept the uncensored, unedited, and unexplained word as fact: the cochlear implant is able to give all deaf children speech and hearing.

Headlines proclaiming, "Sweet Music for the Deaf" (*Newsweek*); "With Implant and Hard Work, Deaf People Can Hear, Speak" (*L.A. Life*); and, "New Hope for Deaf Children: Implant Gives Them Hearing and Speech" (*American Health*) along with numerous other misleading articles in the American media and television programming promote a distorted, if not unfounded, belief regarding the effectiveness and purpose of the cochlear implant.

Certainly, the overriding goal of childhood cochlear implantation is to enable deaf children to communicate orally. Even though the cochlear implant is touted as doing exactly this, the scientific research to assess whether this goal is achieved is extremely limited (Dubow, Geer, and Strauss, 1992). Most of the studies have serious methodological limitations, such as pooling results from distinct groups, selective reporting, neglecting statistical tests of the reliability of findings, and following procedures that allow experimenter bias to influence results (Lane, Hoffmeister, and Bahan, 1996).

The benefits of the cochlear implant have been generalized to include all deaf children who have been implanted or might be implanted. In general, the less demanding the definition of "benefit," the greater the percent of implanted children who receive that benefit. Thus, nearly all implanted children can detect environmental sound; a large number can identify many of those sounds (Lane, Hoffmeister, and Bahan, 1996). However, detection and identification of isolated environmental sounds should not be construed to mean detection and identification of any or all speech sounds.

Some children achieve higher lip-reading scores with an implant than without one, and a few can understand spoken language (these tend to be late-deafened who had already acquired English as their first language). However, some experts in the field of audiology are of the opinion that ninety percent of early-deafened children benefit as much from a tactile aid as from an implant (Oliver, 1991), thus eliminating the need for invasive surgery.

Even if the benefits of the cochlear implant outweighed the risk/benefit ratio, because of the cultural values in conflict, the surrogate decision making in the process—and heaven forbid, the ethnocide that might eventually happen—the best that can be hoped for is a child who is still deaf. The best that the implant can do even with the exception that is called the rule is to approximate a moderate to severe hearing loss. After implantation, there remains a child whose primary language input is still of a visual nature; a child who will benefit from having a language that is visu-ally accessible; a child who has a right to a cultural affiliation that is easily accessible; and a child who has a right to an education that will ensure literacy. Literacy must be the primary objective of education, not a pipe dream of being able to "hear" that will supposedly lead to speech. The equation of speech/hearing equaling intelligence and literacy is totally unfounded and unfair.

There are pertinent questions that must be asked that have, as of yet, not been satisfactorily answered by the numerous entities advocating the cochlear implantation of deaf children. The American Society for Deaf Children (a national organization of families and professionals commit-ted to educating, empowering and supporting parents and families to cre-ate opportunities for their children who are deaf and hard of hearing in gaining meaningful and full communication access, particularly through the competent use of sign language, in their homes, schools, and com-munities) poses the following questions:

1) **Has the deaf child had a meaningful trial with hearing aids?** It is often quite difficult to fully ascertain how much benefit a young child is receiving from the use of a hearing aid simply because young children do not have the ability to describe the sounds they are hearing or to be aware of sounds they are not hearing. It should also be noted that high technology aids might not be available to a child due to the fact that many insurance plans exclude coverage of hearing aids. Therefore, until this question can be answered, should the course of blindly implanting a deaf child, and hoping for positive results, be followed?

2) **How much time can be devoted to therapy?** Neither the problem-atic success of a cochlear implant nor the ability to interpret the sounds coming through an implant happens automatically. A significant time commitment to therapy with trained specialists, as well as arduous work at home by family members is necessary for even minimal success.

3) **What, in fact, is the definition of "success" for the implant; and what do the parents do if their version of "success" is not achieved?** With cochlear implants, parents' dreams of speech comparable to that of a hearing child are usually not realized, regardless of the propaganda and hype from the medical and educational establishments. Once the cochlear implant is in place, the cochlea is destroyed, and the option of returning to hearing aids is totally lost.

4) **What is the perspective of the cochlear implant in relation to the overall needs of the deaf child?** The cochlear implant must be viewed as a tool that can provide sound awareness (much like a high tech hearing aid) with the hope of having the child achieve spoken language use with years

of training. However, superseding the hope of spoken language, must be the goals of developing overall language ability which leads to literacy, social emotional development, and general academic progress during the time while spoken language skills might or might not be developing.

5) How much exposure should the deaf child have to the Deaf Community? Members of the Deaf Community are found in all levels of education and employment, and they experience the full range of personal reward and challenge, regardless of their use of technology. Many parents of newly identified deaf children are not aware of the potential and the achievements of deaf children and adults.

6) Is it possible for the deaf child to use American Sign Language, maintain his/her Deaf identity, and use the cochlear implant? Even though some medical and educational professionals discourage families from using sign language with their implanted child; many families value the continued role of sign language for their children. Additionally, more professionals are beginning to see the benefits of using sign language and participation in the Deaf Community for implanted children. Remembering that the implanted child is still a deaf child, regardless of what auditory benefit might be gained from the implant, the question must be posed as to whether or not the child is still primarily a visual learner. If so, then it is only common sense that the communication mode, which offers the most efficient entry into deep and meaningful language, should be maintained.

7) How much of an influence do portrayals of implant "miracles" and pressure from medical and educational practitioners have? It must be understood that implanted children vary widely, and the decision whether to implant a child is a serious and individual one. This decision should be made only after careful consideration of the facts (Position Paper of the American Society for Deaf Children, 2002). These facts are often not transmitted to the parents, and if they are transmitted, are often veiled in half-truths and hollow promises.

The American Society for Deaf Children, in its effort to provide families with straight talk and unbiased information regarding cochlear implants, has also developed a definitive position paper setting out principles which it believes apply universally to deaf children, their families, and the professionals who serve them. These principles apply regardless of whether the family chooses a cochlear implant for their child, hearing aids, other hearing technology, or no hearing technology at all:

Parents

- Parents have the right to make informed decisions on behalf of their children. (The word, "informed," is vitally important. Too often *coersion* is misinterpreted as *information*.)
- Parents benefit from meeting other parents of deaf children from a variety of backgrounds, experiences, and philosophies.
- Parents benefit from meeting successful deaf children and members of the Deaf Community from a variety of backgrounds, experiences, and philosophies.

Deaf Children

- Deaf children have the right to be valued and respected as whole children capable of high achievement, regardless of their degree of technology use (hearing/assistive technology). The moment American education of deaf children makes the paradigm shift from trying to clone little deaf children into becoming little hearing children is the moment when education of the deaf will make a quantum leap into providing what is educationally, emotionally, and socially appropriate for deaf children.
- Deaf children have the right to meet and socialize and be educated with other deaf children.
- Deaf children have the right to achieve fluency reading and writing English, and to the extent of their ability, speaking English. American education, in general, and American deaf education, in particular, is guilty of educational elitism. There is much that can be learned from successes in other countries. For example, the Scandinavian countries of Sweden and Denmark have initiated bilingual programs in which competencies in both the native sign language and the written form of the spoken language are the goals. Resultantly, Sweden and Denmark have seen marked success with the fostering of literacy in deaf children. Yet, in the United States, we continue to graduate deaf students who are reading on the average at the third or fourth grade level! Without a doubt, we are trying to be all things to al people, and as a result pleasing none. It is past time that Deaf education as we know it in the United States be buried, and a phoenix be given the opportunity to rise from the ashes. Systemic change must occur and new paradigms must be established.

Professionals

Medical, hearing health, and educational professionals serving deaf children and their families have a responsibility to:

- Be informed about the successes of deaf persons from all walks of life, including those who use American Sign Language as their primary language and those who do and do not use cochlear implants.
- Recognize the benefits of early language-including sign language-and work to ensure that deaf children's language development-whether signed, spoken, or both-progresses at a rate equivalent to that of their hearing peers.
- Refer parents to a wide range of information sources, including deaf individuals, families with deaf children, schools for the deaf and local, state, and national parent and deaf adult organizations (Position Paper of the American Society for Deaf Children, 2002).

Scholars on both sides of the debate (pro- and anti-implantation) have suggested that it is time to stop looking solely at speech and language results, or at cost-effectiveness numbers, and to start looking also at important psychosocial issues such as:

- Are implanted children making friends?
- Are implanted children communicating in comfortable ways with the world around them?
- How do implanted children explain the implant to themselves and to others?
- Are implanted children truly participating in classroom situations, whether in the mainstream or in specialized schools?
- Are the ostracized or accepted as children or teenagers who happen to use an implant?
- When they grow up, with whom do they socialize?
- Do they cherish both deaf and hearing friends?
- Whom do they choose as life partners?
- What kind of jobs do they get?
- Do they continue to use the implant on a consistent basis?

(Christiansen and Leigh, 2002)

The answers to these questions will ultimately be necessary to determine the effectiveness or lack of effectiveness of the cochlear implant because answers will transcend speech effectiveness, language effectiveness, and even literacy. After the implant, who will the deaf child be? Will the child lose his/her identity as a person, and assume another identity based solely on the expectations of parents and professionals?

REFERENCES

American Society for Deaf Children Position Paper on Cochlear Implants (2002). *The Endeavor,* Spring, 2002, 8–9.

Andrews, J.F. (2002). "What works for Limbaugh fails many deaf kids." *Houston Chronicle,* June 3, 2002.

Christiansen, J.B. and Leigh, I.W. (2002) *Cochlear Implants in Children: Ethics and Choices.* Washington, DC: Gallaudet University Press.

Lane, H., Hoffmeister, R., and Bahan, B. (1996) *A Journey Into the DEAF-WORLD.* San Diego, California: DawnSign Press.

Niedzielski, N. (2002). "Implants for deaf questioned." *Houston Chronicle,* May 14, 2002.

Oliver, M. (1991). "Multispecialist and multidisciplinary—a recipe for confusion?" *Disability, Handicap, and Society,* 6, 65–68.

ABOUT THE AUTHOR

Dr. J. Freeman King is presently the director of Deaf Education at Utah State University. He has directed teacher training programs in Deaf Education at the University of Southern Mississippi and Lamar University. Dr. King has worked as a classroom teacher, coach, Dean of Students and supervising teacher at New Mexico School for the Deaf and Louisiana School for the Deaf. Dr. King has published numerous articles for professional journals and is the author of two books related to Deaf education, Basic American Sign Language Principles for Hearing Parents of Deaf Children *and* Introductions To Deaf Education: A Deaf Perspective. *He has been involved internationally with teaching and research, having prepared teachers of the deaf and researched sign languages in China, Mexico, El Salvador, and Honduras.*

Creating and Using an American Sign Language Laboratory

ERIC R. LYNN

Eric Lynn is an adjunct ASL instructor and the ASL Lab Coordinator at Salt Lake Community College, Taylorsville, Utah.

(Included here is a portion of Mr. Lynn's presentation, focusing on sample activities that can be implemented in a college-level ASL langauge lab and photographs of the premises.—Editor)

HOW BEGINNING/CONTINUING ASL STUDENTS
BENEFIT FROM THE ASL LAB

Using Deaf facilitators, the ASL lab is designed to give students practice in American Sign Language in four different of skill levels. Each lab session is focuses on different topics that will help improve student's expressive and reception skills. The lab is limited to eight students and introduces different topics each week. The ASL lab is for all students studying in levels one to four. This lab is offered on a credit basis only and contains video recording, videotapes, one-on-one individual, and numerous instructional videos. This lab also provides the same curriculum used in the classroom with the related visual and media materials. The ASL lab is intended to be an immersion experience. No English is spoken.

DEMONSTRATION (ASL I/IOIO LAB)

"Where's Bob?"
Materials needed: Stuffed animals or dolls, and items which are examples of various forms of transportation (a car, a bus, a train, a bike, etc.)

Figures 1–8. Images of the ASL Lab at Salt Lake Community College

Objectives:

- Student will practice producing and understanding fingerspelled three-letter names.
- Student will practice real world orientation indexing and spatial referencing.
- Student will practice non-manual markers for "very close" and "far away."

- Student will practice negation and affirmation.
- Student will practice using WH-Q questions (WHERE, HOW)

The dialogue format below should be written on the board:

Interaction:
1. Split the students into two groups of eight people. Decide upon finger spelled names for each stuffed animal or doll. Use fingerspelled names with which students are already familiar (Ann, Eve, Liz, Pat, Sam, Jim, Joe, Bob). Since there will be two groups, two animals/dolls can have the same name. Tell the students the name of each stuffed animal and divide them between the two groups.
2. Pair up students in each group, and give one stuffed animal/doll to one person in each pair.
3. Tell the students with the stuffed animals/dolls to leave the room and hide the animals/dolls somewhere within the building, then return.
4. When the student returns, the pairs should follow the dialogue format outlined on the board:

Signer A: Ask where your stuffed animal/doll is by fingerspelling its name and asking where it its.

Signer B: Tell where it is.

Signer A: Ask how you should go to get the animal/doll.

Signer B: Tell Signer A which form of transportation to use (BUS, TRAIN, CAR, BICYCLE, WALK, etc.)

Signer A: Pick up the item indicating that form of transportation and go find the animal/doll.

5. When students return with their animal/doll, tell the students to switch places. If time permits, tell students to switch partners and animals/dolls.

Be sure students use correct non-manual question markers (NMM) when asking WH-Q and YES/NO questions, distance markers "eeee" (very close), "ahhh" (far away), and markers which indicate negation (headshake side to side) and affirmation (head nod).

Help students with unfamiliar transportation vocabulary.

ABOUT THE AUTHOR

 *Eric R. Lynn was born deaf and raised in Dublin, Ireland, and came to the United States in 1982. Eric received his Associate of Art degree from Ohlone College in Fremont, California. He has also conducted numerous profes- sional presentations both locally and nationally. Eric is a member of the National Association of the Deaf, American Sign Language Teacher Associa- tion, Conference of Interpreter Trainers, and Utah Association of the Deaf. He is working towards a B.A. with an emphasis in teaching ASL. Eric is cur- rently employed at Salt Lake Community college as the ASL Lab Coordinator and an adjunct ASL instructor.*

Cancer Education in ASL: A Visual Education Medium for your Community

SHANE MARSH
PATRICIA BRANZ

Shane Marsh is a community health educator at Deaf Community Services of San Diego, Inc.; Patricia Branz is the Deaf Community Health Representative in the Cancer Education Program at the Rebecca and John Moores UCSD Cancer Center in San Diego, California.

(While Mr. Marsh and Ms. Branz presented this paper at the Deaf Studies Today! conference, Georgia Robins Sadler, Michael Bovee, Barbara Brauer, and Raymond Trybus also contributed to this project. Their respective credits are listed at the end of the article.—Editor)

OVERVIEW

THE DEAF COMMUNITY AND THE medical professions have always had an uneasy relationship. Communication barriers make it difficult for physicians to establish rapport with their deaf patients. Specialized medical vocabulary makes communication difficult for all individuals who speak English as a second language. An even bigger problem is that the Deaf and hard-of-hearing community have barriers to accessing basic health promotion information that people who hear can routinely use to create a growing foundation of health knowledge. Studies of baseline health knowledge confirm this impression.

Research studies showed there was a huge need for accessible cancer education programs for the Deaf and hard of hearing community (DHHC). A series of research studies showed that videotapes in American Sign Language (ASL) with native signers as hosts, plus voice-overs and open captioning and many graphics, could help get life-saving information to the DHHC. The creation of these videos evolved over a series of four separate research studies to find the most effective way to get health information to the DHHC. Now, there are ASL videotapes available on various types of cancers. The DHHC nationwide can access them through the Internet, Captioned Media Program, and participating American Cancer

Society offices, and deaf-friendly ministries. Research studies prove the videos can help the DHHC gain increased health knowledge.

This paper will describe the steps taken to: 1) recognize and measure the health information and care needs of the DHHC; 2) develop and test new educational programs; 3) collect the statistical data needed to show the effectiveness of the ASL videotapes; and 4) involve the DHHC in the process from start to finish. This paper will also demonstrate that when the DHHC gets involved with research, they can improve the health information and care that is available to the community.

A PARTNERSHIP IS FORMED

Leaders from Deaf Community Services of San Diego, Inc. (DCS) and the Rebecca and John Moores UCSD Cancer Center met to discuss whether the DHHC had adequate access to cancer information and care. Concurring that serious problems existed, the two organizations agreed to create a partnership to define the strengths and weaknesses of the current situation. They also sought additional partners to help them as the partnership's understanding of the problem became more clearly defined. Leaders within the UCSD Department of Communication (Dr. Carol Padden) and Gallaudet University (Dr. Barbara Brauer) quickly agreed to bring their personal and organizational expertise to the partnership. Bovee Productions (Michael and Barbara Bovee) subsequently agreed to lend its expertise to the partnership when the decision was made to capture the cancer education program permanently on videotape to permit more widespread distribution of the information.

THE FIRST STUDY: A FEASIBILITY STUDY

The partnership first conducted a feasibility study with a $7,000 grant from the UCSD Academic Senate. It evaluated the barriers deaf women face in obtaining information about breast cancer and care. It also tested a breast cancer education program adapted for the DHHC to determine how the adapted education program could be improved for the community. Working in small groups of about five women each, a total of 26 Southern Californian women participated in the study. First, they filled out a survey that measured their basic knowledge of breast cancer. Then they took part in a breast cancer education program presented by a culturally sensitive hearing female doctor using ASL interpreters. A follow-up survey measured how much they learned from the presentation. The women also reported their problems accessing health information and care. Then they took part in a group discussion about the various health-related issues that they considered to be important. The results of the first study showed that there were definite problems accessing health information for the deaf women. The problems listed included: 1) lack of interpreters; 2) the loss of privacy when using interpreters; 3) minimal gestures or patience from health providers in dealing with communication needs of the DHHC; 4) a lack of health education workshops for the DHHC; 5) the technical medical terms that women couldn't comprehend; and 6) a lack of closed captioned videos or programs on TV about health topics.

THE SECOND STUDY: A DEMONSTRATION PROJECT

The second study was a demonstration project funded by the Susan G. Komen Breast Cancer Foundation with a $25,000 grant. This grant enabled the partnership to develop a breast cancer education program that would be done entirely in ASL by a deaf native signer along with many graphics shown with an overhead projector. Three hypotheses were tested for this study:

- Hypothesis 1: Deaf women would show low level of cancer awareness and few sources of information.
- Hypothesis 2: Deaf women would show low adherence to breast cancer screening guidelines.
- Hypothesis 3: The deaf community would reject the modified cancer education program.

Deaf and hard of hearing women (N=123) between the ages of 19 and 88 participated in this study, in small groups of five to 12 women per training session. They completed a baseline survey to test basic knowledge of cancer and breast cancer guidelines before the presentation, and a follow-up survey to test the effectiveness of the modified cancer education program. After the data collection was completed, the native signer ran a focus group to gather participants' opinions about the training program and to solicit suggestions and concerns among the participants. The participants came from Los Angeles, Orange, and San Diego Counties.

RESULTS

The first two hypotheses were proven true while the third hypothesis was proven false. Collected data examples to test these hypotheses include:

Hypothesis 1: "Deaf women would show low levels of cancer awareness and few sources of information."

True. Only 16.2% of the subjects felt well informed about cancer. Further, 10% of the women reported no knowledge of breast cancer and 52% of the women reported no knowledge of colorectal cancer. Lack of knowledge of other cancers fell between these two extremes. These were all cancers that can be cured with early detection and prompt treatment

Hypothesis 2: Deaf women would show low adherence to breast cancer screening guidelines.

True. Less than 20% of the women reported doing monthly breast self-examinations, yet when offered a breast model, none of the women could demonstrate how to do a proper exam. This is in spite of the fact that 53% of the women reported that a health care provider had taught them how to do such an exam.

Of the 44 women age 40 and older, only five reported have had a clinical breast examination by their health care provider in the past year and only five reported having had a mammogram in the past year.

Hypothesis 3: The deaf community would reject the modified cancer education program.

False. The women were unanimous in their enthusiasm for the program and their willingness to provide suggestions that would improve the program. They suggested doubling the number of slides and visual aids to keep the content of the educational program the same as would be delivered to a hearing audience. They also suggested efforts to build the audience's medical vocabulary through handouts. They suggested committing the content to videotape so that the information could be distributed to the community through a train-the-trainers program. Finally, they urged the program coordinators to create comparable educational programs for men from the DHHC.

THE THIRD STUDY: A MULTIFACETED APPROACH TO PROBLEM SOLVING

First Component: Creating and testing a breast cancer education video. The Alliance Healthcare Foundation funded the partnership with $118,000 to create the third study. The partnership's first task was to create and test a breast cancer educational video in ASL with voice overlay and open captioning: "Every Woman Counts." To test the usefulness of the video, 123 women signed informed consent documents giving their permissions to serve as study participants. They then completed baseline surveys of their knowledge, participated in the video-based breast cancer training program, and then completed a follow-up questionnaire and participated in a focus group to discuss the program. Two months later the women completed another survey to see how much knowledge they had retained. The format of the video is a casual presentation, filmed in a casual home setting with a "host" who uses simple English to talk with a small group of women about breast cancer in ASL.

The presentation of the information follows this general order: A general explanation of cancer itself, the importance of early detection of cancer as opposed to late detection, the survival rates of people from both the late-detection group and the early detection group, risk factors, metastasis, and a description of three medical procedures to test for breast cancer. Extensive use of graphics and live footage of mammograms, clinical breast exams (CBE), and breast self exams (BSE) to show exactly what each procedure entails and how each procedure is accomplished provide visual aids to the video.

Treatment options, such as lumpectomies and mastectomies are also described in ASL and slides are shown to give further depth of details; additional treatment options such as radiation therapy, chemotherapy, and hormone therapy were listed. These therapies are also explained in detail using both ASL and visual slides. The video also included an explanation of clinical trials and what they may involve, as well as contact information for the National Cancer Institute, the American Cancer Society, and the National Institutes of Health. This Breast Cancer educational video is the first of its kind and confirmed that it is possible to resolve many of the communication barriers that the DHHC faces in dealing with the medical profession. The project's secondary objectives were:

1. To raise greater community awareness of cancer.
2. To raise the medical literacy of the DHHC.
3. To raise health professionals' awareness of the DHHC and its health needs
4. To raise nationwide awareness within the DHHC about its health information and care needs.

The results of this study were reported at national and international meetings and in the *Journal of Cancer Education*, helping to raise health professionals' awareness of the unmet health needs of the DHHC.

Second Component: Creating and testing a prostate cancer education program for the DHHC. The grant also allowed the partnership to create a prostate cancer education program prototype using overhead transparencies. A train-the-trainers model was again used, with all the trainers being native signers.

Third Component: Develop dissemination strategies for the videotapes. Education programs are only of value if the community can access them. Thus a major focus was to develop strategies to disseminate the videos locally and nationally, to the degree possible. Deaf Community Services of San Diego helped to distribute the videos locally. The State of California's Breast Cancer Early Detection Partnership Program helped to disseminate the tapes statewide. The Captioned Media Program evaluated the video and enthusiastically accepted the breast cancer education video for on-going distribution.

THE FOURTH STUDY: CREATE AND DISSEMINATE A
SERIES OF CANCER EDUCATION VIDEOS

A $754,000 grant from the California Endowment Fund enabled the partnership to use its acquired knowledge to create a series of cancer education videos.

Creating the Scripts. The ultimate goal of the script is to provide accurate and up-to-date information on the prevention, diagnosis, and treatment of cancers in a manner that is accessible to all members of the DHHC. The educational script is created by a health professional using the most up-to-date, comprehensive information. The script is then submitted to the Medical Advisory Committee for review. The committee members assure that all information is accurate and clearly presented.

The Deaf Community Advisory Committee members next review the script to assure that the information will be delivered in the most "deaf-friendly" way possible. This includes assuring that vocabulary is clear, concepts are well explained, and that the video will include graphics that are easy to understand and visually appealing. Since the graphics are so critical to the accurate delivery of the information, only colors that are accessible to those who are color-blind are used.

Finally, an ASL specialist converts the English script into ASL gloss, in order for the actors to be able to process the information in ASL grammatical order.

Creating the Videos. Volunteers who are native signers audition to serve as the videos' hosts and educators. A panel of ASL experts and the production team videotapes each actor/actress's screen test to determine the most qualified person for each role. Members of the DHHC are then recruited for the "audience" and for "Deaf Life" scenes. Prior to the video shoot, an ASL specialist coaches all the actors on their performance. During the shoot, the ASL specialist is on-stage to assure that the actors and audience participants continue to deliver their information with clarity. Once the various segments of the script are put together, the Deaf Community Advisory committee reviews the rough cut of the video for quality and accuracy of the information portrayed throughout the video screen and determines where additional graphics or summaries would increase comprehension of the complex information being conveyed.

The information conveyed in these videos is complex. Most members of the DHHC have only had limited access to health information. Hence, having a visually appealing video is critical because it will encourage the members of the DHHC to view the video more than once. Once the Deaf Community Advisory committee gives its approval, the video's ASL is translated back into English so that the open captioning and voice overlay tracks can be added so that the greatest number of people can access this important information. After a final verification by two interpreters that these two tracks have been placed consistent with the ASL being presented, the master copy of the video is sent off for duplication.

Finally, the efficacy of the video is tested. Participants again take a pre-test, view the video, and engage in discussion about the video. They then complete a post-test questionnaire immediately after the discussion and again two months later to see if viewing the video helped to make a long term increase in participants' knowledge, attitudes, and health promoting behaviors.

DISSEMINATING THE VIDEOS: A FIVE-PART STRATEGY

One: Word-of-mouth. The partnership is testing several ways to help the DHHC become aware of the videos. It works with the seven agencies that serve the deaf and hard of hearing in major cities throughout California, including Los Angeles, Fresno, Sacramento, the Bay Area, and Riverside. Each Deaf Community Services is encouraged to use these cancer education videos in one of the educational seminars they host. They are also encouraged to invite a representative from the American Cancer Society, the National Cancer Institute's Cancer Information Service, or a local hospital to attend the meeting to answer questions that audience members may have.

Members of the DHHC who attend the seminars receive videos to bring home and share with their friends and family. Thus the partnership relies heavily on the "word-of-mouth" spread of information that is a major strength within the DHHC.

Two: The National Clearinghouse of Captioned Media. The National Association of the Deaf (NAD) provides the Captioned Media Program, a national clearinghouse and lending library of videos and films with captions for the DHHC. The partnership provides copies of its cancer education to NAD for on-going distribution. People may request these videos for viewing, free-of-charge.

Three: Deaf ministries programs. To ensure that the cancer education program reaches even small communities across the country, the partnership found 400 churches, synagogues, temples, and places of worship with deaf congregations. Multiple invitations to join the free cancer education partnership were sent to each organization and 141 ministries joined the partnership. They have each received copies of the videotape and guidelines about inviting representative from the American Cancer Society, the National Cancer Institute's Cancer Information Service, or a local hospital to attend the meeting to answer questions that arise from audience members. Using mapping software, it is possible to visually see the full extent and potential health impact of the partnership's participating deaf ministries.

Four: A Web-based cancer education program. The DHHC needs to be able to access to this information whenever questions or concerns arise, day or night. Therefore, the video was created so that it could be posted on the Internet. The script uses a series of questions and answers between the host and the audience members throughout the entire video. As a result, each of the small question and answer segments of the video can be placed on the Internet as streaming videos: *www.cancer.ucsd. edu/deafinfo.* When viewers enter the Web site, they are encouraged to sign on so they can be notified of future additions to the site. Software that measures use of the site allows the partnership to monitor the number of time the site is accessed, how long it is used, what question and answer segments are used most often, and whether the visitors to the site are accessing the ASL or print version of the information presented.

Five: National conferences. The Community Health Educators employed on this grant also go to national conventions and conferences to share the information about the cancer education program and videos. The partnership's participation in Deaf Studies *Today!* is one such example. The other members of the partnership also attend national conferences for their own disciplines with the goal of raising awareness of the health needs of the DHHC and encouraging their colleagues to work collaboratively to help address the needs of the members of the DHHC.

THE FIFTH STUDY: CREATING CULTURALLY-SENSITIVE HEALTH CARE PROVIDERS

The partnership's newest undertaking, funded by a five-year, $1.5 million grant from the National Cancer Institute, is to train a group of UCSD medical students about Deaf Culture and ASL within the context of cancer control information. Medical students who complete this training program (including a summer immersion program at Gallaudet University) will be prepared to serve as clinical leaders who are ready to help the leaders of the deaf and hard of hearing to improve the community's access to health information and care. This project was reported separately at Deaf Studies *Today!* (see pages 255–265).

CONCLUSION

This program offers a model of how Deaf Community Service organizations can find other civic-minded organizations to help advance the health and well being of the DHHC. It shows that each member of the partnership can have different, somewhat overlapping, but equally important roles. Together, the partnership's contribution to the DHHC can be greater than simply the sum of the individual member's contributions.

REFERENCES

Bowe, F., Watson, D., and Anderson, G. Delivery of Community Services to Deaf Persons. *Journal of Rehabilitation of the Deaf.* 1973

Moores, Donald. F. *Educating the Deaf: Psychology, Principles, and Practices.* Illinois: Houghton Mifflin Company, 1996.

Padden, C. and T. Humphries, *Deaf in America: Voices from a Culture.* Cambridge: Harvard University Press, 1988.

Rosenstein, J., and Lerman, A. *Vocational Status and Adjustment of Deaf Women.* New York: Lexington School for the Deaf, 1969.

Sadler, G.R., Clark, D., Huang, J., Padden, C., Galey, T., Elion, L., Brauer, B., Ko, C.M. Bringing Breast Cancer Education to Deaf Women. *Journal of Cancer Education.* 16, 225–228, 2001.

Sadler, G.R., Huang, J., Padden, C., Elion, L., Galey, T., Gunsauls, D.C., Brauer, B. Bringing *Health Care Information to the Deaf Community. Journal of Cancer Education,* 16, 105–8, 2001.

Sadler, G.R., Galey, T., Bovee, M. Reducing Disparities in the Ceaf and Hard of Hearing Community's Access to Health Care and Social Services. *Partnership Perspectives,* 3(1)41–50, 2003.

Schein, J.D. *The Deaf Community: Studies in the Social Psychology of Deafness.* Washington, DC: Gallaudet College Press, 1968

Supalla, S. *Equal Educational Opportunity: The Deaf Version.* T.J. Publishers, 1992.

ACKNOWLEDGEMENTS

This project was underwritten with grants from the California Endowment, National Cancer Institute (R25 CA101317 and R25 CA65745), Alliance Healthcare Foundation, San Diego Affiliate of the Susan G. Komen Breast Cancer Foundation, and the UCSD Academic Senate. The contents of this article are the sole responsibility of the authors and do not necessarily represent the official beliefs of the funding agencies. The American Cancer Society generously provided educational materials for the project. The partnership also wishes to acknowledge the supportive guidance given by: Dr. Carol Padden, UCSD Professor of Communication; Leslie Elion, JD, community advocate; Thomas Galey, MS, Executive Director of Deaf Community Services of San Diego, Inc. (1998–2003); Maria Savoia, MD, Vice Dean for Medical Education, UCSD School of Medicine; and David Rappaport, Ph.D., Dean of Admissions, UCSD School of Medicine. The authors also thank Edward W. Holmes, MD, Vice Chancellor for Health Sciences, Dean, UCSD School of Medicine, and I. King Jordan, Ph.D., President, Gallaudet University, for their enthusiastic supportive leadership since the inception of this program.

ABOUT THE AUTHORS

Shane Marsh works with Deaf Community Services of San Diego as a Community Health Educator. He received his B.A. in Sociology from San Diego State University, and is in the process of obtaining CDI certification. Shane has taught ASL classes for the past seven years and provides day workshops for ASL students several times throughout the year. Meanwhile, Shane educates the deaf community about cancer on a state-wide and national basis. Patricia Branz received her B.A. from Gallaudet University and currently works for the UCSD Cancer Center in San Diego as the Deaf Community Health Representative in the Cancer Education Program. She has over thirteen years of diverse teaching experience in universities, elementary, and middle school institutions.

CONTRIBUTING AUTHORS

Georgia Robins Sadler, MBA, Ph.D.
Associate Director, Rebecca and John Moores UCSD Cancer Center and Clinical Professor of Surgery, UCSD School of Medicine

Michael Bovee, M.A.
Bovee Productions, San Diego, CA

Barbara Brauer, Ph.D.
Professor Emeritus, Gallaudet University

Raymond Trybus, Ph.D.
Executive Director, Deaf Community Services of San Diego, Inc.

overdue: A Paradigm Change for the Gallaudet University Library

LAURA K. MAULDIN

Laura Mauldin is currently an M.A. *candidate in Deaf Studies, with a concentration in Cultural Studies, at Gallaudet University.*

THIS PAPER ACCOMPANIED THE SCREENING of an original short film titled *overdue*. This film was birthed out of the writer/director's experiences with literary resources while doing research at Gallaudet. It is a reflection of both the discovery of disparities and a call for change. As a student in the Deaf Studies department, I wanted to create a film that would examine the frustration with the currently available texts and elicit discussion of how to change the quality and quantity of resources. Finally, this film is a call for reclaiming the public space of libraries by actively participating in altering the current geography of library and literary collections.

FILM SYNOPSIS

In *overdue*, a woman enters the library looking for specific titles which discuss the notion of deafness as a cultural/political identity from a cultural studies perspective. She discovers that a specific book has had the status of "lost" for the past three years. She then ventures to the designated area for texts on deafness and finds that the shelves are filled, one after another, with rows and rows of audiological texts. At the end of the film, her frustrations become apparent as she cannot penetrate the plethora of medicalized representations.

The film ends with her response of angrily throwing the books from the shelves. Throughout the film, the use of intense color and line seeks to present this as a visually glaring issue, to bring the misrepresentations out of the dark, murky silence traditionally associated with libraries. *over-*

due also uses point-of-view shots to enhance the participation of the audience in hopes of capturing the subjective experiences of the viewers.

ANALYSIS

As Gallaudet negotiates its role in both the academic world and as the center of Deaf culture, the library becomes a space which personifies the inequitable distribution of power based on assumptions about language modes. Library collections are traditionally understood to be comprised of written texts, texts which are based on spoken languages. Gallaudet offers a unique environment to explore these assumptions and offer challenges to them. It is within this context that one must recognize Gallaudet's library as a site of struggle. Gallaudet University's powerful position as the liberal arts university for Deaf students provides it with the unique opportunity to redefine the notion of "text," integrate other notions of literacy, and reflect and inform a distinctly Deaf cultural agenda.

The library, and its collection, is the heart of an academic institution. The role of the library is informed by the established goals of the university. Through the dissemination of information, the library acts as a conduit of the values of the university. The university library then becomes the center of knowledge and a space of inquiry. The library's collection determines the presentation and exchange of information, and is therefore an active participant in the architecture of student knowledge. The nature of the texts available plays a powerful role in determining the cultural representations deafness or lack thereof. The collection also determines the scope of knowledge about these subjects. The number of copies of each work and accessibility to them are also indicative of the value placed upon them. The nature of the collection not only determines the information available, but also shapes the relationship that the students have with the library.

Gallaudet is renowned for housing the greatest collection of historical texts and literature on deafness in the world. While this is certainly a great achievement, the collection is far from being finished and we must take care not to accept its existence without challenge. There is an overwhelming variety of audiological texts, but a relatively slim selection of current texts offering cultural representations of deafness challenging the medicalized view. For a myriad of reasons, texts offering politicized views of deafness have a limited existence. Given the relatively recent emergence of Deaf culture, it is not surprising that the number of texts in alignment with a Deaf cultural identity remains relatively low. A recent examination of the collection reveals that some Deaf cultural texts had simply not been acquired, had been lost and not replaced, or were not available to check out. Rather, they could be viewed in a room for a specific period of time, but not taken outside of the library. Additionally, texts in general cultural studies were also not readily available. Creating an academic cohesion with other cultural studies fields—African-American Studies, Women's Studies, Gay/Lesbian Studies—provides access to theoretical frameworks adopted by other cultural groups, acts of cultural resistance and individual/collective narratives of difference. Such an approach solidifies the validity of Deaf culture and Deaf studies.

When asked, both graduate and undergraduate students, as well as faculty, often categorized Gallaudet's library as a "hearing library." This is a clear assertion of a Deaf identity in distinct opposition to hearing people, but it is also clear assertion that Deaf literature and discourse is at odds with the current library collection at Gallaudet. This misalignment is expressed though the development of a Deaf "oppositional identity." In Bell Hooks' work, she describes the formation of an oppositional identity as fundamental in the process of liberation. (1990:15) An oppositional identity characterizes the representations of deafness found in the library as incongruous with a Deaf identity and Deaf cultural values. It also labels the library as a place which reflects a hearing consciousness, rather than a Deaf consciousness.

This opposition serves to not only markedly reject an ownership of the information within the library, but also influences the relationship with the medium in which it is presented. The Gallaudet library houses texts which predominately occur in written English and while this form of text is valuable, the underrepresentation of cultural deafness in these texts incites a fragmentation of literacies on multiple levels. That is, students not only feel at odds with the many of the representations of deafness in content, but also in form.

As a university, Gallaudet is operating within the greater scope of academic culture in the "hearing world." This is particularly important for understanding the complexity of the Deaf university's relationship with academic culture at large and in understanding deaf students' relationship with their university library. The nature of inquiry and the production of knowledge in academic culture are understood and valued within a framework of literacy in a spoken and/or written form of language. These values have long been apparent in academia. Anthropologists of the nineteenth century categorized societies as either primitive or civilized. In the twentieth century, this paradigm shifted into defining populations as either oral or literate. These latter categories, however, often reflect the same negative and positive connotations as the preceding divisions.[1]

The possibility of inverting this paradigm is one that is uniquely possible at Gallaudet. The elements needed to redefine text and literacies with an integrative, novel approach exist nowhere but at Gallaudet University. This would not only be beneficial to the university as a whole, but could incite a dramatic change in students' relationships to the library, and hence to inquiry and the pursuit of knowledge.

While the construction of a Deaf oppositional identity acknowledges that these representations are rejected, it does not actively seek to change the information available. However, Hooks goes on to write of "self-actualization" and states that, "Opposition is not enough. In that vacant space after one has resisted there is still the necessity to become...one develops critical thinking and critical consciousness, as one invents new, alternative habits of being" (1990:15).

Self-actualization identifies the need to actively participate in the creation of knowledge. Perhaps Gallaudet's greatest asset is its capability to encourage and facilitate the production of new Deaf cultural texts which not only occur in written form, but in a visual medium as well. Films and videos in ASL have long been in production. However, these texts are not seen nor advertised in such a way that reflects a true integration of literacies within the space of the university's library. Integrating visual media into the library's design itself, as well as making the availability of visual media apparent, would illicit encourage students to engage in academic pursuits. This would serve to acknowledge the value and validity of ASL media and thus ASL texts. This would also be a reflection of the university's greater mission. Certainly, the acquisition of as many written texts corresponding to a Deaf cultural identity is imperative. This will require that the library obtains other cultural studies texts in an effort to forge interdisciplinary connections with other schools of thought as well.

Taking the position of acknowledging and integrating a new definition of literacy, and therefore *text*, the library can become a space which values and preserves the medium of American Sign Language (ASL), as well as other sign languages from all over the world. Encouraging production of and facilitating access to an abundance of Deaf cultural texts is vital to obtaining power over representations of deafness. In the struggle for a Deaf visibility that is in alignment with a Deaf consciousness, it is imperative that the representations of deafness are not only diverse and politicized, but also visible and accessible. This demands that both English and ASL literacies be placed side by side, on an equal footing, and easily found in the university's library.

This will not only alter the geography of the library's collections, but will also alter the relationship that students have with the library and their quest for knowledge. In the article, "From Teaching to Learning: A New Paradigm for Undergraduate Education," Barr and Tagg begin their discussion of a new paradigm for learning with this:

> In its briefest form, the paradigm that has governed our colleges is this: A college is an institution that exists to provide instruction. Subtly but profoundly we are shifting to a new paradigm: A college is an institution that exists to produce learning. This shift changes everything. (1995)

By integrating the literacies that deaf students possess and the values of a Deaf cultural identity into the quest for knowledge that the library represents, a powerful partnership could be forged. This space could become the center of knowledge for those who come to Gallaudet and could redefine the university's library as a Deaf place of learning. As Friedland states, "Place is the fusion of space and experience, a space filled with meaning, a source of identity" (1992).

ENDNOTES

1.   See *Literacy with an Attitude,* p. 121, by Patrick Finn for further discussion of this. He briefly discusses the implications of Havelock's research attributing the emergence of certain societies from a primitive, oral society into a civilized state after the introduction and mastery of reading and writing.

REFERENCES

Barr, Robert B. and Tagg, John. 1995. "From Teaching to Learning: A New Paradigm for Undergraduate Education." In *ChangeMagazine.* November/December 1995.

Finn, Patrick. 1999. *Literacy with an Attitude: Educating Working-Class Children in Their Own Self-Interest.* New York: State University of New York Press.

Friedland, Roger. 1992. "Space, Place and Modernity." In *A Journal of Reviews: Contemporoary Sociology.* Volume 21, Number 1.

Hooks, Bell. 1990. *Yearning: Race, Gender, and Cultural Politics.* Boston: South End Press.

ABOUT THE AUTHOR

Laura Mauldin is currently an M.A. candidate in Deaf Studies, with a concentration in Cultural Studies, at Gallaudet University. She graduated from the University of Texas at Austin with a Bachelor's degree in Linguistics in 2001. Laura is hearing and has maintained strong ties to the Deaf community since attending a public school which had a number of deaf students. She is currently working on research related to the overlapping themes in Deaf Studies and Queer Studies. She hopes to produce work which will bring Deaf Studies to discussions in the broader scope of Cultural Studies.

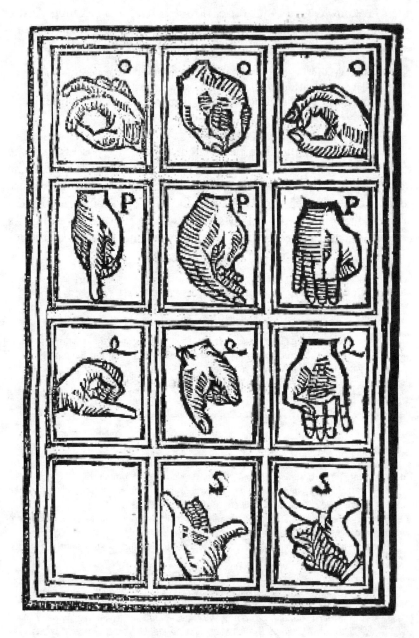

Woodcut containing an early representation of a digital sign language; *Thesavrvs Artificiosae Memoriae*, Cosmas Rossellius (d. 1578); Venice, Antonio Padovani, 1579.

Deaf Artists in America: Colonial To Contemporary

DEBORAH MERANSKI SONNENSTRAHL, PH.D.

Deborah Meranski Sonnenstrahl taught art history and museum studies at Gallaudet University for 32 years. She is a professor emeritus at Galludet.

SOMETHING IS MISSING IN THE development of disciplines of study related to Deaf Studies. Much emphasis (and rightfully so) has been made on the study of American Sign Language (ASL) and Deaf Education. Historical aspects of language and education are widely documented.

Any student in ASL is familiar with the infamous resolution passed at the 1880 Milan Conference that prohibited the use of ASL in classrooms. Also well documented is the 1960s research of Dr. William Stokoe that recognized ASL as a legitimate and structured language. This knowledge spearheaded various formal studies in the areas of Deaf Culture, Deaf History, Deaf Leaders, and even Deaf Theater.

Yet despite all the advanced in the general field of Deaf Studies, Deaf art as a formal study remained neglected until 1989 when a small group of Deaf Artists held a workshop prior to the first Deaf Way Conference and Festival. This small band of artists devised a manifesto that announced a new art movement, De'VIA (an acronym for Deaf Visual Image Art) where artists incorporated Deaf experiences and themes in their work. While this effort may have raised the awareness of some, Deaf artists continue to receive scant attention—articles on them appear on the scene occasionally and randomly.

The lack of focus on the study of Deaf art as a part of Deaf cultural studies is an ironic phenomenon; of all the disciplines, art is the most visual. This would seem a perfect match for a Deaf person who depends on vision for communication. Despite the obvious cultural significance of the artwork, the study of Deaf art is one of the last (if not the last) topics to appear in a formal format or incorporated in the Deaf Studies curriculum.

Since Deaf Way I, Deaf artists have held several workshops, discussions, and meetings across the country. It was not until the beginning of the 21st century, however, when we finally saw a formal and structured study of American Deaf artists in the form of my book, *Deaf Artists in America*. In other words, Deaf artists' significant contributions needed to be documented, which would deepen the understanding of and enhance the credibility of Deaf Studies. How did these Deaf artists see their world? How did they see themselves as an artist, a Deaf person, or a Deaf artist? How did they participate or behave in their world? These artists give us the answers through their works.

Deaf artists like their hearing contemporaries utilized what they knew. Deaf artists like their hearing peers went through changes. Deaf artists were influenced by the current events of the day. Deaf artists—like all artists—painted, sculpted, and photographed what they were experiencing. William Mercer (1765–1839), the first known Deaf artist in America painted scenes from the Revolutionary War. He knew and understood the nuances of the war (his father was killed at the Battle of Princeton, a pivotal point of the War) and was a personal friend of George Washington.

Augustus Fuller (1812–1873) became one of the earliest documented cases of discrimination against Deaf people. When he was thrown into a jail for disrupting the peace in a tavern he wrote to his brother pleading for him to come and interpret for him. Due to communication barriers the officials ignored his version of events, and the police would not give him the time of the day. Fuller also gave us the first known portraits of a prosperous Deaf couple who were his classmates at the American School for the Deaf. Both husband and wife are shown holding pens in their right hands, a nod to their educational stature that also subtly demonstrates their preferred communication mode when conversing with hearing people.

We are in debt to those artists who shared the Deaf World with others. A shining example would be Theophilus Hope D'Estrella (1851–1929) whose incredible black and white photographs give us insight into life at an American residential school for Deaf students in the 1800s. He used his art training to give his photographs a professional and creative quality. There was also Redmond Granville (1871–1935) who was called the American Impressionist painter of the West (he came from California) where he showed us how the California poppies and landscapes bathed in sunlight could be a serious study of the changing effects of light. He also influenced early films when he taught the silent film star Charlie

Chaplin the importance of body language and sign language as a means of communication.

Today's Deaf artists continue the tradition of teaching us to see the world with both old and new eyes. Betty Miller (1934), who is often called the mother of De'VIA, shows us in *Deaf Dancers* how the painting's subjects "hear" the music, represented by small squares in front of their eyes to show the vibrations created by music. Chuck Baird (1947) cleverly uses an ASL sign to shape one human hand as a bottle pouring syrup on a stack of pancakes in *All American Breakfast.*

Alex Wilhite (1960) broke the traditional mold by using abstract elements with a De'VIA sensibility. What Wilhite did in *Blue Raindrops,* was to visually capture "sounds" he heard after receiving his cochlear implant. We get the gist of how raindrops sounded to the artist, giving us an opportunity to expand our horizons.

There is no end to the list of Deaf artists who play an important role in increasing our understanding and awareness of Deaf-related issues.

Fortunately there are a few institutions of higher education for Deaf students who are beginning to integrate Deaf Art into their curriculum. Numbers are beginning to grow, but too slowly for anyone's benefit. Deaf art is done by Deaf artists using visual means. The rich cultural lessons of this work should be included in every Deaf Studies curriculum and done quickly.

ABOUT THE AUTHOR

Deborah B. Meranski (formerly Sonnenstrahl) earned a B.A. degree from Gallaudet University, a M.A. degree from Catholic University of America, and a doctorate from New York University. She taught art history and museum studies at Gallaudet for 32 years and was named professor emeritus upon her retirement in 1996. Dr. Meranski is a long time advocate of Deaf artists and has been showcasing their works for forty years. She is the author of Deaf Artists in America: Colonial to Contemporary, *which captured the coveted Benjamin Franklin Award in the academic/education/ teaching category in 2003.*

Gallaudet College faculty members, 1867

Courtesy Gallaudet University Archives

Training Medical Students In Deaf Culture, American Sign Language, and Cancer Control

MELANIE C. NAKAJI, M.A., M.S.

Melanie Nakaji is a project manager and ASL instructor at the Rebecca and John Moores UCSD Cancer Center in San Diego, California.

(While Ms. Nakaji presented this paper at the Deaf Studies Today! conference, Georgia Robins Sadle, Sherry He, Debbie Lok, Deborah Jenkins, Bonnie Sherwood, Barbara Brauer, and Raymond Trybus also contributed to this project. Their respective credits are listed at the end of the article.—Editor)

GOALS OF THE PROGRAM

THE NATIONAL CANCER INSTITUTE FUNDED the Rebecca and John Moores UCSD Cancer Center (UCSD) to develop and evaluate an American Sign Language, Deaf culture, and cancer control program for medical students.

The program will produce physicians who 1) are well informed about cancer prevention and control; 2) respect the Deaf and hard of hearing community's (DHHC) cultural beliefs, values, and traditions; 3) are comfortable working with the DHHC through the use of sign language interpreters; 4) have a solid working proficiency in American Sign Language (ASL); 5) have the ability to integrate all these bodies of knowledge to improve the DHHC's access to health information and care; and 6) will serve as clinical leaders and role models in advancing the health of the DHHC.

BACKGROUND

This optional program is the result of a partnership that includes: Deaf Community Services of San Diego, Inc.; Gallaudet University; the University of California San Diego's School of Medicine; and the Moores UCSD Cancer Center. Through this partnership, members of San Diego's DHHC meet health professionals who have a genuine interest in developing the skills needed to provide health care for the DHHC. The DHHC helps train the medical students by participating in student-led health seminars, attending clinics staffed by students, serving as patient simulators for the medical students, and integrating the students into the social fabric of the community.

As a result of the deepening working relationships with UCSD's participating medical students, the members of San Diego's DHHC are becoming more sophisticated consumers of health care and more proactive in the two-way communications process required to get their health care needs met.

RECRUITMENT OF STUDENTS TO THE TRAINING PROGRAM

While all incoming, first year medical students are eligible for the program, preference is given to students who 1) anticipate pursuing careers in primary care medicine, 2) are high academic performers, 3) can demonstrate proficiency in a second language other than English so that their acquired cancer control knowledge can benefit other cultural groups as well, and 4) can demonstrate a commitment to serving disadvantaged communities.

The school's Office of Admissions informs all applicants of this supplemental training program and invites them to indicate if they would like to receive a training program application packet in the event that they are accepted to the UCSD School of Medicine. A second invitation is sent with the students' acceptance letter. Students entering the program sign an IRB-approved informed consent document confirming their intent to stay in the program throughout their medical school training and give the project director permission to use all their performance data to help evaluate, and promote replication of, the training program.

INCENTIVES TO PARTICIPATE IN THE TRAINING PROGRAM

Five qualified applicants are selected to receive an $8,000 annual fellowship that is paid monthly, contingent upon their good academic standing in the program. Other students may participate, but without the stipend.

All participating students are offered one-on-one guidance in the development of their Independent Study Project if they agree to work on a project that is related to the DHHC. Stipend-funded students are also guaranteed funding to attend the ASL and Deaf Culture residential immersion program at Gallaudet University during the summer between their first and second years of medical school. Significant efforts are made to secure funding to enable non-stipend funded students to attend the Gallaudet program. Once students are enrolled in the program, strong supportive bonds develop among the students that are reinforced by the students' ability to communicate in a language that no one else in their school can understand.

TRAINING ACTIVITIES IN THE PROGRAM

Enroll in Cancer Control and Elective ASL Courses. Medical students enroll in six consecutive elective classes of ASL, Deaf culture, and cancer control during their first and second years of medical school. This series of ASL and deaf culture class builds students' basic ASL proficiency while teaching medical terminology in ASL with a special focus on 1) care for patients who are deaf or severely hard of hearing, 2) cancer related issues, and 3) research with the DHHC. Time is also devoted to teaching the medical students about issues unique to the hard-of-hearing and late-deafened patients they will also encounter. A majority of these patients use English as their primary language, making it easier to prepare the students to care for these patients optimally. The course provides an intensive team-based learning environment where the goal is the most rapid progress in the shortest time.

The instructor uses an interactive teaching method, the Michaelsen Method, that is optimally suited to promoting, as well as assessing, language acquisition and knowledge of core concepts in cancer control and Deaf culture. This method dramatically differs from the didactic traditional teaching approach. With the Michaelsen Method, students independently prepare for classroom assignments and then work in groups to apply to the classroom activities the core concepts they have learned in their homework assignments. They complete the required reading assignments and learn new morphology, phonology, fingerspelling, facial expressions, and cancer control information from textbooks, articles, sign language videotapes, and their assigned ASL mentor interpreter. Students are then tested on their knowledge and language acquisition through a multi-pronged testing approach (See "Assessing Students' Progress" later in this article).

Meetings with an ASL Mentor Interpreter. Each quarter, students are paired with a new ASL mentor interpreter. Students engage in 12 hours of mentorship activities during their eight-week elective curriculum. The student and interpreter discuss 1) deaf culture; 2) ethical issues that can occur between their Deaf patients and doctors; and 3) interpreters' roles, strengths, and limitations. Aside from elaborating on DHHC's cultural issues, the mentors act as "tutors" and practice with their student by assisting with the translation of English sentences into ASL. Most importantly, however, is the feedback and constructive criticism the mentor interpreter provides to the student. These sessions are periodically videotaped to enrich the tutors' and trainer's feedback.

Co-lead the Health Seminar Series for the DHHC. During the medical students' first and second years in the program, they each create a student-led health seminar for the DHHC with the assistance of the project trainer and coordinator. They select a topic, recruit a speaker who is an authority on the topic, and then assist with the mechanics of producing the seminar. They also present part of each seminar using their expanding ASL skills. The seminars are done in collaboration with the project's subcontractor, Deaf Community Services of San Diego, Inc. (DCS) and the Pre-Health Professional for the Deaf Club (description follows). ASL interpreters translate the English portion of the health seminar series.

The health seminars focus primarily on nutrition, physical fitness, cancer prevention, and early detection topics. At one seminar, for example, a registered dietician gave a presentation on the importance of eating a high-fiber, low-fat diet. To gain experience speaking in ASL before an audience, medical students showed examples of similar foods with widely different fiber levels and how to read the nutrient labels on each product. The popularity of these free dinner seminars is increased by the limited seating capacity (50 to 65), the deaf-friendly social setting, and the participants' desire to help create physicians who are competent serving the DHHC.

At the beginning of the health seminar, a short, simple questionnaire is distributed to get the audience thinking about the topic. Students help their assigned small group translate the survey into ASL. Immediately following the survey, the presenter's discussion addresses content covered in the survey. An easy-to-understand, visually appealing slide presentation accompanies each presentation. Throughout the seminar, medical students practice their signing skills by interacting informally with their assigned small group and answering specific questions. Interpreters roam the room to help the speaker and students answer individual participant's questions. The interaction lays the foundation for the DHHC to develop a personal relationship with future physicians and gain greater trust with the medical community.

By the time the students graduate from medical school, each student will have at least a dozen health promotion seminars they are prepared to offer to the DHHC organizations located in the cities where they will do their residencies and set up their clinical practices. DCS of San Diego will contact the local DCS agencies in those communities to introduce the physicians and explain their desire to help advance the health of the local DHHC and the training they have been given to do so.

Co-lead the Pre-Health Professional for the Deaf Club with Undergraduate Partners. Sustainability is a concern for all new programmatic initiatives. To help address this issue, the medical students help coordinate a pre-health professionals ASL and Deaf culture club for undergraduates. The club encourages students who are already learning ASL to consider careers in the health and science professions and encourages students who are in pre-health professional disciplines to take ASL classes. This club gives medical students the opportunity to serve as mentors and role models to undergraduates who are interested in serving the DHHC, as well as to practice their signing skills.

Club members learn about volunteer and interaction opportunities with the DHHC from guest speakers, flyers, and handouts. They are also encouraged to help the medical students and the training program staff run the Health Seminars for the DHHC, thereby learning about cancer control simultaneously with the DHHC participants. Through this mechanism, the program hopes to generate a steady stream of applicants to health professional schools who already have at least a moderate level of proficiency in ASL and deaf culture.

Attend the Gallaudet University Summer Immersion Program. Between the students' first and second years of medical school, they attend a four-week summer immersion program at Gallaudet University in Washington, D.C., a cultural and educational center for Deaf people around the world. The students live in the dorms with deaf students, eat their meals with the students, and to the degree that they are invited, they will socialize with the deaf students. There is a welcoming party to help introduce the students to local DHHC leaders and a visit to the National Institute on Deafness and Other Communication Disorders (NIDCD) to explore the research activities underway throughout the nation, as well as the extramural funding opportunities that will be available to these students after they finish medical school.

The Fourth Year Elective. While at Gallaudet, students are also encouraged to explore where clinical opportunities exist that serve a large deaf and hard of hearing clientele. Students can seek preceptorships at their settings to fulfill their fourth year electives. They can work with doctors/nurses at camps for deaf children, work with doctors who care for DHHC patients, or work in audiology clinics.

Conduct Independent Study Projects Related to the DHHC. All

UCSD medical students must complete an Independent Study Project (ISP) as a graduation requirement. The medical students involved in the DHHC training program are encouraged to conduct their ISP on a project with the DHHC. One student, for example, is conducting a comparative analysis on undergraduate males' baseline knowledge of testicular cancer information at UCSD and Gallaudet University; another student is norming the multidimensional Health Locus of Control Instrument for use with the DHHC. These research opportunities help expand the body of knowledge about where health disparities exist within the DHHC and how the health and well being of the Deaf community could be advanced. Presentations and publications of the data gathered through these ISPs serve as vehicles for disseminating the information to national audiences and showcasing the training program itself.

ASSESSING STUDENT PROGRESS WITH MULTIPLE MEASURES

This program has multiple outcome measures. Simple measures, for example, are how many students are retained in the program each year, how many students become members of the Pre-Health Professionals for the Deaf Club, how many members of the DHHC attend the Health Seminar Series, and how many attend multiple seminars.

Measuring students' growing knowledge of clinical content related to cancer control can be accomplished with a simple paper and pencil test. The evaluation methods implemented for assessing how well students can integrate and apply their ASL proficiency, Deaf culture knowledge, and the application of cancer control knowledge is achieved through three assessments: 1) individual and group Readiness Assessment Tests (RAT), 2) videotaped simulations with deaf patients, and 3) videotaped self-exercises. Through these assessment measures, the program coordinators seek to address each of the learning goals of the program in a holistic manner while using assessments for which inter-rater reliability can be determined, thereby assuring evaluators' consistent objectivity.

The Readiness Assessment Test (RAT): The Michaelsen Method. Once each quarter, the Michaelsen RAT is administered (Michaelsen, Knight, and Fink, 2004). Students take an individual test and then a group test in order to assess their comprehension of sign language in the context of cancer control. Prior to administering the individual and group test, the instructor delivers a short story in ASL that integrates Deaf culture and cancer control information. The story is slowly delivered twice. Students are encouraged to write notes in English on the information conveyed during the story, but may not ask for sections to be repeated.

After the story is told, students independently complete a fifteen-question objective test and submit the written test for scoring. While some test questions have clear right and wrong answers, other questions are intentionally designed to be controversial. Some questions have ethical and/or cultural issues embedded in the clinical question. For other questions, the instructor has intentionally omitted a key piece of information from the story that is needed to reach a conclusive answer. The questions effectively test the students' receptive skills, clinical knowledge, and ability to address culturally sensitive situations appropriately, and their grasp of clinical content.

Once the individual tests are collected, students then work in small teams to translate the written test questions from English into ASL. Where students lack the necessary vocabulary, the instructor teaches it and then students practice delivering the same test questions in ASL. Once they are comfortable with the test questions, the students then compare each of their individual answers to each question and work collaboratively to reach a consensus about the correct answer to the test question and how it should be answered it in ASL. If the group cannot reach a consensus, they submit their weighted answers for the group. The entire small group discussion is done using only their ASL skills.

Each group's answer sheets are immediately scored by the instructor and returned to the students, along with their individual test scores and an explanation of why the instructor selected a particular answer. The groups reconvene to develop an appeal for why the answers they selected were better than the answer the instructor selected. Through the appeal process, they can raise their score. The appeals process presents another opportunity for students to engage in an interactive dialogue in ASL. The instructor reviews all appeals and gives feedback to the students in ASL. Any appeals granted result in additional points being added to both the individual and group scores. The friendly competition that ensues throughout this quarterly testing keeps the classroom lively and the students stimulated and fully engaged in the learning process.

Assessment of Expressive and Receptive Skills: Patient Simulations. The medical students engage in two videotaped patient simulations each quarter. Members of the DHHC serve as the patient simulators. The simulators learn a vignette from the curriculum developed by Catchum Project at the University of Texas Medical Branch at Galveston ("The Catchum Project," 2004). Prior to interviewing the patient, the medical student receives a written statement of the patient's reason for scheduling the office visit. The student then interviews the patient to collect a medical history, addresses the patient's concerns, educates on cancer related issues, and strives to establish a level of trust that will motivate the patient to return for his next visit.

With one vignette, for example, a 15-year-old adolescent male seeks an appointment with the doctor to obtain a sports physical and to inquire about testicular self-exams. The student is only told that the patient is an adolescent male who needs a physical in order to be on the baseball team. After building rapport with the patient, the student should have elicited further information about the reasons for the visit including the testicular cancer concern. Thus, this vignette also incorporates cancer control knowledge that the student must impart to the patient, as well as Deaf culture sensitivity demonstrated by rapport building with the patient and the use of ASL skills necessary to communicate with the patient. While the students are rapidly gaining ASL skills, the training program emphasizes that student's ASL skills are primarily for rapport building with their patients. Their skills will not reach a level where they will be able to eliminate the need for interpretive services in the health care setting.

All patient simulations are videotaped and independently scored by trained evaluators using an established numeric rubric to assess students' skills. Prior to using the UCSD Patient Simulation Assessment Instrument, the evaluators' inter-rater reliability rate is established. Since this instrument measures student's skills with communicating in ASL and interpreting the information in ASL, it measures both receptive and expressive skills. Fifty percent of the students' score is derived from expressive skills, such as the ability to produce accurate signs, appropriate knowledge and use of signs, signing concepts accurately, and effective use of non-manual markers. The remaining fifty percent is derived from the students' receptive skills: ability to understand fingerspelling and numbers, appropriate turn-taking within the interaction, appropriate use of cultural behaviors such as eye contact and use of gestures, and appropriate responses to the deaf patient.

Students are also scored on their mastery of the cancer knowledge related to the vignette and their ability to apply their cancer knowledge in the medical setting. The objective assessment tests from the Catchum Project are used to measure this outcome The Catchum Instrument also helps evaluators to assess the students' ASL receptive skills. Scores from the quiz are used independently and also incorporated into the "receptive categories" on the scoring rubric. Finally, the patient simulator provides feedback on each student's receptivity, rapport building, eye contact, and ability to express ideas and gain the patient's trust. This holistic approach to student evaluations allows for a more accurate assessment of the degree to which program goals are being achieved.

Assessment of Expressive Skills: Videotaped Self-Exercise. During each academic quarter, students receive a list of commonly occurring questions about a particular cancer topic that relates to the patient simulation. They are to master asking these questions in ASL and given the resources to develop comprehensive answers to them. Students learn about risk factors, early detection options, and ways to reduce health risks. After practicing in the classroom and with their interpreter mentors, students are videotaped while they sign their questions and the answers they would give to the patient.

Trained evaluators then independently score the students' performance on the videotape using the Self Exercise Assessment Numeric Rubric. The inter-rater reliability rate is established for this instrument prior to using it to score the students' self exercises. Using a scale of one to five, with five representing "exceptional skills" and one representing "serious work is needed," evaluators assess students' expressive skills: fingerspelling, signing skills, and use of face grammar. The first category, fingerspelling, assesses the accuracy, clarity, and rate and speed of fingerspelling. The second category, signing skills, measures the production of signs and to what degree they are accurate, the appropriate use of classifiers, and their ability to sign ASL grammatically correct. Lastly, face grammar assesses not only use of facial expressions, but also eye gaze, role shifting, use of signing space, and cultural behaviors such as turn-taking, nodding, and signing OH-I-SEE. The instructor reviews the scores from the evaluators and provides a composite numeric and written summary of each student's assessments. These are shared with the students and the interpreter mentors and they are encouraged to view the videotaped self-exercise for additional feedback. Thus, the videotaped self-exercise allows evaluation of the students' proficiency in ASL and their ability to apply their cancer control knowledge in a clinical setting.

SUMMARY

While this program to train medical students in ASL, Deaf culture, and cancer control will be evaluated over five years, the results from the first year of the program are very promising. Finding a way to create a stream of health care providers who are keenly sensitive to the needs of the Deaf and hard of hearing community will be an important step in reducing the barriers this community faces to accessing health information and health care. The multi-pronged program has helped students to acquire skills faster than in a standard classroom setting. When this program format is combined with the high intelligence of the medical students, the supportive and reinforcing learning environment, their proficiency in at least two other languages, and their desire to serve the DHHC, the final outcome is a group of students who are gaining mastery in about half the time that would normally be anticipated.

ACKNOWLEDGEMENTS

This project was underwritten with grants R25 CA101317 and R25 CA65745 from the National Cancer Institute, the Alliance Healthcare Foundation, the California Endowment, the San Diego Affiliate of the Susan G. Komen Breast Cancer Foundation, and the UCSD Academic Senate. The contents of this article are the sole responsibility of the authors and do not necessarily represent the official beliefs of the funding agencies. The American Cancer Society generously provided educational materials for the project. The partnership also wishes to acknowledge the supportive guidance given by: Dr. Carol Padden, UCSD Professor of Communication; Leslie Elion, JD, community advocate; Thomas Galey, MS, Executive Director of Deaf Community Services of San Diego, Inc. (1998–2003); Maria Savoia, MD, Vice Dean for Medical Education, UCSD School of Medicine; and David Rappaport, Ph.D., Dean of Admissions, UCSD School of Medicine. The authors also thank Edward W. Holmes, MD, Vice Chancellor for Health Sciences, Dean, UCSD School of Medicine, and I. King Jordan, Ph.D., President, Gallaudet University, for their enthusiastic supportive leadership since the inception of this program.

REFERENCES

The Catchum Project (2002). Retrieved May 15, 2002, from http://www.catchum.utmb.edu/resources/resources-osc.htm

Michaelsen, L. K.. Knight, A. B., & Fink, L. D. (Ed.). (2004). *Team-based learning: A transformative use of small groups in college teaching*. Herndon, Virginia: Stylus Publishing.

ABOUT THE AUTHORS

Melanie C. Nakaji earned her B.A. from the University of North Carolina at Greensboro and both her M.A. in communication and M.S. in rehabilitation counseling for the Deaf from San Diego State University. As an advocate for the Deaf's right to accessible information via the media or through sign language interpreters, she conducts research related to the quality of closed captioning on news and educational programming and on effective communication in the health care setting.

CONTRIBUTING AUTHORS

Georgia Robins Sadler, MBA, Ph.D.
Associate Director, Rebecca and John Moores UCSD Cancer Center and Clinical Professor of
Surgery, UCSD School of Medicine

Sherry He, Medical Student I
UCSD Cancer Center

Debbie Lok, UCSD Academic Intern
Rebecca and John Moores UCSD Cancer Center

Deborah Jenkins, Resource Associate,
Deaf Community Services of San Diego, Inc.

Bonnie Sherwood, Interpreter
Deaf Community Services of San Diego, Inc; Registry of Interpreters for the Deaf

Barbara Brauer, Ph.D.
Professor Emeritus, Gallaudet University

Raymond Trybus, Ph.D.
Executive Director, Deaf Community Services of San Diego, Inc.

Gallaudet University student protesters march in Washington, D.C., March 1988

Courtesy Gallaudet University Archives

Why Use *Triumph of the Spirit: The DPN Chronicle (TOTS)* in *your* Program?

ANGEL M. RAMOS, PH.D.

Angel Ramos was a Fulbright Scholar and is the first Deaf person of Hispanic descent to receive a doctorate degree from Gallaudet University.

AS YOUR STUDENTS ENTER THE field of Deaf education, interpreting, or other related profession, it is critical that students leave your program as members of a group that is accepted and respected by the Deaf community. Hearing people can be categorized into three groups (Table 1):

Type	Description
Partners	Hearing people who believe that Deaf people are their equal, who believe that "Deaf people can do anything hearing people can do, except hear."
Ignorants	Hearing people who look down at Deaf people and believe Deaf people "are not ready to function in a hearing world." Their belief is due to ignorance.
Plantationists	Hearing people who look down at Deaf people and believe Deaf people "are not ready to function in a hearing world." Their belief is not due to ignorance but rather a 'plantation mentality' in which they truly believe that Deaf people are not capable people. They are often in positions of power and control over Deaf individuals—power and control they do not want to give up.

Table 1: Types of Hearing People

Let me elaborate. *Partners* are hearing people who have a very positive attitude about Deaf people, who treat Deaf people as their equal, and who believe that "Deaf people can do anything hearing people can do, except hear." Partners have the same expectations of Deaf people as they do of hearing people. For example, I consider Dr. Tony Martin, Dr. Jean Andrews, Dr. Zanthia Smith (my former colleagues at Lamar University) as Partners because they treated me just like they did other hearing colleagues— no more, no less. They also had the same expectations of me as they had of other hearing members in our department. Their expectations of Deaf students in the bachelor's and master's degree program in Deaf education were also the same as those for hearing students. There are many examples of Partners in *Triumph of the Spirit (TOTS)*—Reverend Jesse Jackson and former U.S. Vice-President George Bush are just a few:

> The problem is not that the students do not hear. The problem is that the hearing world does not listen. —Reverend Jesse Jackson, 1988

> The Congress, the Courts, and the Administration have strongly supported the right of people with disabilities to hold positions of trust and leadership...Gallaudet has a responsibility to set an example and thus appoint a president who is not only highly qualified but who is also deaf. —Vice-President George H. W. Bush, 1988

The second group of hearing people, *Ignorants,* are hearing people who have a poor attitude toward Deaf people, and who feel Deaf people are not as capable as hearing people. I experienced an excellent example of this when I graduated from college. During my junior and senior year of college, I worked during the summer in New York City as a counselor at a group home for hearing children. My hearing loss was not a problem since I could lipread and speak very well. The children enjoyed having me around as did the staff.

Upon graduation from college, a full-time position became available at the group home which I applied for. The staff interviewed me and made me their top candidate for the position. I was then interviewed by the human resource director at the hospital that operated the group home, whom I shall call Mary. The interview was proceeding beautifully until Mary read on my application that I was Deaf. All of a sudden the tone of the interview changed. Here is what happened:

Mary:	Are you Deaf?
Angel:	Yes.
Mary:	I am sorry. I cannot give you the job.
Angel:	Why?
Mary:	Because you are Deaf.
Angel:	So?
Mary:	How can you hear someone knocking on the door?
Angel:	That isn't a problem. People can ring a bell that will make the lights flash in the group home. I will know if someone is at the door.

Mary: But what if the telephone rings?

Angel: Not a problem either. There is a device we can put on the phone so that when it rings the lights will flash also. The flashes for the door and the phone will be different so I will know which is which.

Mary: But you can't talk on the phone.

Angel: True. But there are always other hearing people working in the group home who can answer the phone.

Mary: But what if there is a fire?

Angel: Mary, you don't hear a fire, you smell a fire.

Mary: I just don't feel comfortable letting you supervise the children.

Angel: Are you saying Deaf people do not make good parents?

Mary: No, I am not saying that. It is just that I would not feel comfortable having you supervise my own children.

Mary is a classic example of an Ignorant. She did not feel comfortable having a Deaf person supervise her children and could not give any logical explanation. I left her office and filed a Section 504 complaint against the hospital with the Department of Justice (DOJ). A year later the DOJ lawyer finally addressed my case. The DOJ lawyer asked Mary if I was the top candidate for the position, and she responded "Yes." Then the DOJ lawyer asked if the only reason I was denied the job was because I was Deaf. She responded "Yes." That was all the DOJ lawyer needed to hear. The hospital agreed to offer me the position, to have all their hiring practices reviewed for a full year, and to refrain from future discriminatory acts. By that time I already had another job so I didn't accept the offer.

I will never forget the train ride back home and my encounter with Mary who was on the same train car with me. She apologized again and again and asked me repeatedly to accept their job offer. She realized that Deaf people could do the job. Although I didn't accept the job offer, today that hospital has hired Deaf people and has offered services to many Deaf children. From an Ignorant, Mary became a Partner. Through this whole process she learned that Deaf people are as capable as hearing people, and from then on she treated them as equals. This is what we need to do with Ignorants—educate them so that they become Partners.

Then, there are the *Plantationists,* hearing people who have low expectations of Deaf people, who feel they are superior, who try to keep Deaf people beneath them to maintain their power, their economic wealth, feelings of superiority, or for other reasons. We've all met them. Fortunately, Plantationists are few. Unfortunately, Plantationists tend to be in positions of authority, and make the lives of Deaf people miserable.

The question is, what type of student will graduate from your program—Partners, Ignorants, or Plantationists? Obviously we want them to be Partners. This is why your students need to read *TOTS*. It teaches hearing people that Deaf people *are* ready to function in a hearing world; that Deaf people *can* do anything hearing people can do, except hear; that Deaf people share the same emotions, dreams and struggles as hearing people; that the majority of hearing people are Partners; that, in the words of Rev. Jesse Jackson, "The problem is not that the students do not hear. The problem is that the hearing world does not listen." *TOTS* is an attitude adjustment book—it will help your students become Partners.

Not only will *TOTS* help your students to become Partners, it will also help them better understand the Code of Ethics which interpreters are bound by. The story of how Spilman, Chairperson of the Gallaudet Board of Trustees, blamed her interpreter for the quote "Deaf people are not ready to function in a hearing world" is one that will have a lasting impact on your students. Your students will learn that if they ever use an interpreter they can be confident that the subject discussed will remain confidential. With 70 to 80 percent of beginning ASL students not continuing past ASL 2 courses, this might be the only opportunity to teach your students the need for them to become "Partners" and the role of an interpreter. That is why I strongly recommend that *TOTS* be used in ASL 1 and ASL 2 classes.

Throughout the years, I have found that the best teachers, the best interpreters, the best professionals who work with Deaf people, are those who are also members of the Deaf community. What does the Deaf community look like? How can your students enter and become accepted members of the Deaf community?

I have developed a model, called the "Circles of Membership in the Deaf Community," to help hearing people visualize what the Deaf community looks like:

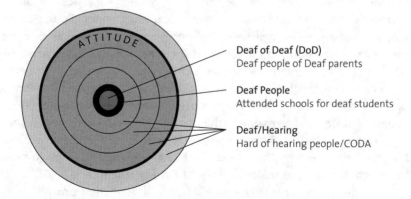

Figure 1: Circles of Membership in the Deaf Community

As this model indicates, there are various circles of membership in the Deaf community, with the core membership (inner circle) consisting of those Deaf individuals of Deaf parents, otherwise known as "Deaf of Deaf" (DoD). Hearing people can never be members of the core group. Late deafened adults, such as myself, can never be members of the core group. Deaf people with hearing parents can never be part of this core group either. They can, however, get closest to the core group.

For example, those Deaf people who attended residential schools for the deaf are the closest (indicated by the thick black circle around the inner circle). Even children of Deaf adults (CODAs) can never be part of the core group.

Some individuals are very close to the center, some are at various distances, and some are members of the Deaf community but not accepted by many Deaf people (outer circle). The reason some people are members but not accepted is because of their *attitide*. People with the right attitude, who are Partners, will be accepted while those individuals who have a poor attitude, the Ignorants and the Plantationists will not. Another model has been developed to show students how they can enter the Deaf community, called "Requirements to Enter the Deaf Community":

This model can be used when a person wants to enter *any* new culture; to enter a new culture, a person must learn the culture, must learn the lan-

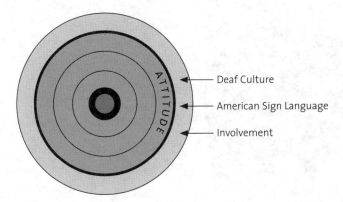

Figure 2: Requirements to Enter the Deaf Community

guage, and must get involved in the community. Hearing students who want to join the Deaf community must do the same thing—they need to learn about Deaf culture, learn the language (ASL) and be involved in the community. To be an accepted member, however, a person must also have the right attitide; he or she must be a Partner:

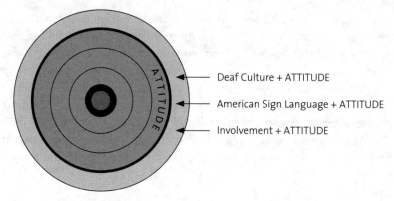

Figure 3: Accepted Members of the Deaf Community

Accepted members of the Deaf community do not necessarily have to be fluent in ASL. An excellent example is Harlan Lane. He is an accepted member of the Deaf community even though he is not a fluent signer. The reason he is an accepted member is because he has knows the culture, has been involved in many Deaf events, and is a valued Partner of the Deaf community. Obviously, those individuals who have greater knowledge of Deaf Culture, who have mastered the language, who are more involved in the Deaf community, and have a great attitude will be closer to the inner circle:

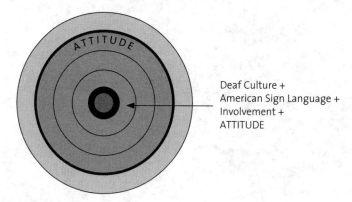

Figure 4: Moving Closer to the Center of the Deaf Community

This is not a novel concept nor is it something unique to the Deaf community. For example, I am a member of the Puerto Rican community. White people who learn Spanish and Puerto Rican culture will be accepted by the Puerto Rican community as a member of their community. However, they will never be part of the core group—those individuals born in Puerto Rico of Puerto Rican parents. Although I am a member of the Puerto

Rican community since my parents are Puerto Rican, I speak the language fluently, and I have lived the culture from birth, I will never be a member of the core group of the Puerto Rican community. Why? I was not born in Puerto Rico. I am not a native Puerto Rican and native Puerto Ricans will not accept me within their core group. It's not just Puerto Ricans born in the mainland, this also applies to Italians, Russians and other ethnic groups born in the United States. That is just the way it is.

So, hearing people can enter the Deaf community but will be at different levels of membership within the Deaf community and proximity to the core group. Obviously, one should strive to get as close to the center as possible. Use these models to teach your students how important it is to learn everything they can about Deaf culture, the importance of being fluent in ASL, the importance of attending Deaf community event and being involved in the community, and especially to have the right attitude. Use these models to teach them that the more the more knowledge they have of Deaf culture the closer they can get to the inner circle. This means learning about the language, history, values, politics, folklore, religion, customs, and other traits of a culture. This is where *TOTS* becomes valuable for beginning ASL students. It gives students an excellent introduction into Deaf culture—its history, politics, social issues, and other areas that will wet the students appetite and motivate them to learn more and more about Deaf culture.

Please keep in mind that not everything discussed in *TOTS* is suitable for beginning ASL students. Besides the historical events of DPN (Deaf President Now), there are some topics in *TOTS* that should be discussed in Deaf culture classes or advanced classes as they require greater knowledge of the Deaf community. Following are just three examples of topics that should be taught in advanced classes:

Why did Dr. Jordan initially not support the students [during the Deaf President Now protest in 1988]? It was not just Dr. Jordan who did not initially support the students: most of the Deaf faculty at Gallaudet also did not initially support the students. The Deaf employees at Gallaudet supported the students behind closed doors but were too afraid to make their support known publicly. Why? Fear of losing their jobs, fear of losing future promotions, putting their personal needs before those of the Deaf community. This has not only happened at Gallaudet University, it has happened at the Southwest Collegiate Institute for the Deaf, at the Idaho School for the Deaf and the Blind, and other places.

There are Deaf individuals who will put the Deaf community first, and others who will put their jobs and careers first. It is a dilemma faced by Deaf people all over the country. They may have families, a mortgage, car payments, a career that could be put at risk if they confront the majority culture. Should they risk it? Each Deaf person has to answer that for themselves.

Who is the beacon of light of the Deaf community? Many people believe that Gallaudet is the beacon of light for the Deaf community, however, this is not true. First, Gallaudet has always been slow to accept change and has often been behind the times. It took years before women were accepted into the college; years before Black students were accepted into the college; years before Deaf students were accepted into the Gallaudet Graduate teacher training program; years before a Deaf person was accepted as president of the university. Indeed, change occurs very slowly at Gallaudet.

Second, Gallaudet is first and foremost an *educational* institution. Gallaudet might testify to Congress, give us Deaf Way, Deaf Studies, regional centers—these are all educational activities. Gallaudet is not in the business of fighting for the rights of Deaf people. The Deaf President Now protest made that very clear. It was not the board of trustees or the Gallaudet administration that fought for a Deaf president; it was the Deaf students, the Deaf community, and their Partners who fought for their rights and "educated" Gallaudet.

Was there a "Gallaudet" protest? It was not a Gallaudet protest; it was a Deaf community protest. So many people refuse to celebrate Deaf President Now (DPN) because they believe it was a "Gallaudet thing." Nothing could be further from the truth. Yes, it happened at Gallaudet and it was the Gallaudet students who staged the protest, but it was the Deaf community and Partners from all over the world who helped the students succeed. It was the Deaf community and Partners who donated over $40,000 in cash and supplies in just one week. Without the Deaf community, without the Partners, would the students have succeeded?

There are many more topics that should be left for advanced classes. As teachers, you can start the attitude adjustment in ASL 1 classes with *TOTS*, help guide them into becoming Partners, and continue helping them enter the Deaf community with more in-depth discussions in subsequent classes. The Teacher's Guide that accompanies *TOTS* includes a list of objectives for beginning, intermediate and advance classes that will help you guide your students into becoming full, accepted members of the Deaf community.

I hope you find *TOTS* to be an excellent addition to your program, whether you teach ASL, Deaf Culture, Introduction to the Deaf Community, or other Deaf-related courses. I wish you the best in your endeavor in having your students graduate as Partners and full members of the

Deaf community. For more information on TOTS, log onto our Web site, *triumphofthespirit.com.* If would like to receive a complimentary copy of the book or the Teacher's Guide, send an email to *rrpublishers@aol.com.*

ABOUT THE AUTHOR

Dr. Angel Ramos is the first Deaf person of Hispanic descent to receive a doctorate degree from Gallaudet University and one of the first Deaf people to be a Fulbright Scholar. Dr. Ramos has been very active in the educational, social, and political arena of the Deaf community. During the DPN protest, he was Chairperson of the DPN Fund and experienced firsthand the students' struggles and march to victory.

Virginia School for the Deaf, Staunton, 1872

Courtesy Callahan Museum of the American Printing House for the Blind

Where Have We Been, Where Are We Now, and Where Are We Going?

J. MATT SEARLS, PH.D.

J. Matt Searls is a faculty member at the National Technical Institute of the Deaf/Rochester Institute of Technology in Rochester, New York.

CRITICAL EVENTS AND SOCIAL CHANGES have marked different periods in the history of deaf people and shaped their future. While we have made significant progress in the last 30 years, some issues facing deaf people have persisted and remain unresolved today. The fundamental question we must address is, how much progress have we really made? How do we compare to other social (e.g. racial and ethnic) groups in terms of progress? Why is it not possible to resolve issues, such as access to education, work and communication, and personal, social, and cultural identity in light of cochlear implants and other technology?

In reviewing the history of the education of the deaf, one will find that our deaf ancestors shared and debated many of the same concerns. Topics discussed over the years have included communication, identity, accessibility, rights, literacy skills and education. In light of our long history and the present circumstances, what will our future be like? I will highlight periods of enlightenment and decades of struggles and challenges in the history of deaf people. Towards the end of this paper, my discussion will revolve around four areas I believe could shape our future.

EDUCATION: THE ENLIGHTENMENT AND THE EMERGENCE OF COLONIZATION

Baynton (1996) reported that all histories of the deaf emphasize two turning points for the education of American deaf people in the nineteenth century. One was the establishment of the first school for the deaf in Hartford and the second turning point was the attempt to replace the use of sign language in the classroom with the exclusive use of lip-reading and speech.

The year 1817 marks one of the most important events in deaf history when Thomas H. Gallaudet and Laurent Clerc, a deaf person, established the first permanent school for the deaf in Hartford, Connecticut, on April 15. Their efforts were noteworthy because several attempts, by individuals who were not deaf themselves, to establish a first school for the deaf in North America had failed. The success of this effort indicated true partnership between two men from very different backgrounds, but with a unifying vision to provide deaf people with an education. Evidently, both of these men were able to overcome obstacles related to language and communication (i.e. English vs. French, and spoken vs. signed language) and cultural differences. Clerc was one of the key figures in persuading the privileged members of the United States Congress of the need for funding in order to promote and expand educational opportunities for the deaf. Through his teaching, he also made it possible for deaf graduates from the Hartford school to establish more than 20 other schools for the deaf in this country. The success of these efforts demonstrates an amazing ability to obtain support from legislators in various states.

After the establishment of the Hartford school, attempts to educate deaf children gained momentum. During the colonial period, education was a privilege for the wealthy and economics made it necessary for other children to leave school early to help at home. The Hartford school represented one of the first attempts to break down the educational divide between the upper and lower classes. The school was also the forerunner in providing public education to deaf students, regardless of socioeconomic status. Vocational education began at schools for the deaf before it became part of the mainstream public school system. The "Age of Enlightenment" created many opportunities for deaf children. For instance, Groce's (1984) study of Martha's Vineyard reported that deaf Vineyarders who received tuition assistance from the State of Massachusetts were at times able to stay at school several years longer than their hearing siblings and friends.

Because of this, deaf people were among the more well-educated individuals who could read, write, and do all that was necessary to fish, farm and support a family, function in town offices, and act as responsible citizens. Groce gave an ultimate example of mainstreaming, where the hearing community never thought of deaf islanders as "deaf" or as a unified "deaf community" because deafness was not a stigma. Social change within the deaf community resulted from the education provided by the schools for the deaf and the unique deaf community on the island of Martha's Vineyard. Things were progressing well for deaf people in the 19th century but the struggle for self-preservation began when the oralist campaign against sign language emerged.

History indicates that the oral-manual controversy shaped the life of the deaf community in a variety of ways. In the early years, sign language was taught in many schools for the deaf and, in 1858, approximately 41 percent of deaf adults were teachers. A resolution to ban sign language in the classroom received a majority vote at the 1880 Milan Conference. The resolution discouraged schools from retaining and hiring teachers who were deaf. Ladd (2003) discusses the emergence of oralism as a form of colonization of language and culture. *Colonization* is a systematic development in which there are social constructions that identify one group as an object of manipulation. Thus, colonization constructs a minority group, and that is exactly what the hearing culture did to the Deaf culture. Colonization of the Deaf occurred once oralism and the speech method was introduced; the idea was to make the Deaf appear as similar to the hearing as possible knowing that this will perpetuate their separate and unequal status. This often gives rise to internalized oppression in order to "fit in" with the oppressor better and gain benefits from the powerful. Eventually, educational philosophy shifted to the combined system.

Baynton (1996) wrote that the combined system meant supplementing speech with fingerspelling but forbidding sign language. In other approaches, speech alone was used in the classroom, with sign language permitted outside. Sign language was only permitted for use with "oral failures." Henri Gaillard, a deaf Frenchman, observed the use of the combined system at the New York School for the Deaf, known as Fanwood. In this system, students used the combined method with classes taught either in sign language or in spoken language and continued to use sign language outside of class (Buchanan, 2002). Language(s) tend to reflect culture and society. The inequality characterizing the colonization of the deaf community is therefore reflected in the relative status of ASL related to English. Woodward and Markowicz (1980) have used the concept of diglossia to describe the marginal status of ASL in the hearing community, reflecting to the relationship between ASL and English as "diglossia with bilingualism" (Bochner and Albertini, 1988). ASL has been marginalized as a language in much the same way as deaf people have been marginalized in the hearing world.

Education for the deaf has gone through many changes over the years. Classes taught in the combined system method have evolved to simultaneous communication (SimCom). SimCom does not meet the linguistic requirements to be a language. It is a mixture of ASL vocabulary, invented signs, and English word order. Today, many teachers of the deaf use SimCom in classrooms. We are short-changing our deaf students if we do not use a natural language (such as ASL) that is fully accessible to them. Marschark (1997) reported that teachers of deaf children who use SimCom may leave 20 to 50 percent of what they say out of their signing, without realizing how much information is lost. There is no evidence to support simultaneous communication as an effective approach to teaching and learning. Furthermore, only about 30 percent of all spoken English words are lip readable. At present, few schools use the bilingual/ bicultural approach where ASL and English are taught in classrooms with some success. One wonders why promoting access to language and information in the most effective manner is not taking place.

Edwards (1997) has reported that deaf adults were relatively more literate during the 1800s. She studied writing samples from deaf people in publications and suggested that writing skills among these deaf people were higher than one would generally find in our students today. If that is the case, then why do half of deaf high school graduates continue to read at or below the 4th grade level after over 200 years of experience in teaching deaf students?

While there is not a simple answer, we acknowledge that lack of literacy skills, low expectations of students, poor communication skills among teachers, ineffective communication policies, ambiguous mission statements, and poor management skills all add to the obstacles we face today. Teaching deaf students presents additional challenges for educators. Especially today, teachers are finding that paperwork, accountability, and teaching-to-the-test cloud the art and enjoyment of teaching.

Residential schools, the hub and bedrock of our culture, face declining enrollment and restrained budget. Such schools have a completely different student profile today than compared to the early 1970s. Presently, many students enrolled in these schools have other physical challenges as well. Additionally, with the implementation of PL 94-142 (the Individuals with Disabilities Education Act), other educational options exist. These options shifted the resources away from residential schools for the deaf. Demographic studies conducted by Gallaudet Research Institute (2000–01) indicated that more than 80 percent of deaf children are currently in mainstream programs. Quality interpreters are few and far between in many public schools. Unlike students in residential schools, these students experience social and communication barriers. In some cases, their isolation leads to difficulties engaging in social activities with their hearing peers. Their identity as deaf or hard of hearing individuals is marginalized due to limited socialization with their peers and growing up in families with minimal communication. Students from residential schools share a similar social experience to that of hearing students. A study conducted by Holcomb (1990) concluded that social assimilation experience among deaf students from mainstream programs indicated developmental gaps.

TECHNOLOGY: PAST AND PRESENT

For years, technology has been both a friend and foe for deaf people. Vocational education made it possible for deaf graduates to obtain jobs in skilled trades, especially printing. Before talking movies, silent movies were accessible to the public including the deaf community. Deaf actors, such as Granville Redmond, regularly appeared in silent films. After the introduction of talking movies, deaf people did not have access to films, nor were they offered roles in films. The introduction of closed and open captioned films has made it possible to attend movies. However, choices are obviously limited only to captioned films. Fortunately, deaf actors are slowly breaking through the glass ceiling once again.

Hearing aids, which are used by many deaf people, have been available since the 1930s. Cochlear implants, available since the 1970s, are modern technology used among the younger generation of deaf children. Other than helping the recipients to hear sounds for communicating in spoken English, it is not clear how these devices enhance the learning experiences of deaf children.

Cochlear implants among young children are growing at an alarming rate regardless of long-term risks or benefits. The risk of developing bacterial meningitis is high compared to children in the general population (Reefhuis, et al., 2003). Children with cochlear implants spend many hours receiving speech and auditory services instead of improving their literacy skills. Unfortunately, limited communication, a limited fund of knowledge, minimal socialization, ongoing isolation, and low expectations are some of the ongoing challenges that may impede healthy psychosocial development in deaf children, including those with cochlear implants.

Newborn hearing screening programs are currently available for early identification of deafness in children. The earlier we identify hearing loss in newborn infants, the better prepared we can be in assisting the family to deal with the discovery of deafness. Since medical and audiological professionals are usually the ones parents meet first, there is a strong possibility that the deaf community will not be part of the early intervention team. However, the deaf community should be part of the team in the parent-infant program.

The information age has significantly enhanced modern technology. Information is at the tip of our fingers. Voice-activated computers may be the next advancement in technology. Literacy, logic, and problem solving are critical skills in remaining competitive. TTYs, pagers, and other means of electronic communication are widely available to deaf people. However, one also wonders if all the advancements in mass media, electronic technology, hearing aids, and cochlear implants have resulted in significant progress in the literacy and educational achievement of deaf high school graduates.

ADVANCEMENT: THE SHIFT

The shift from a pathological to a cultural model began 30 years ago after Stokoe claimed ASL had similar grammatical rules and features to those found in spoken languages. Deaf culture and a new sense of pride emerged. Deaf people saw themselves from a new angle. The 1988 Deaf President Now movement further promoted the civil rights of deaf people. The Americans with Disabilities Act was enacted into law in 1990. This period marks the most progressive era in the history of deaf people. Deaf people saw upward mobility in the federal government, in education, and in self-employment. There are more deaf or hard-of-hearing superintendents and administrators at schools for the deaf than ever before.

These professional advancements in light of declining enrollment and restricted budgets present an untimely challenge for deaf administrators. The good news is that many opportunities for leadership have emerged, especially in education; the bad news is that many deaf leaders, especially in schools for the deaf, are facing challenges associated with budget reduction, limited resources, declining enrollment, mandated state and federal regulations, shifts in student profiles, and other factors. Given the circumstances, school administrators have resorted to managing programs instead of asserting themselves as visionary leaders. Teaching deaf students also is becoming more of a challenge largely because of changing student profiles as more students with special needs enroll in schools for the deaf.

PARENTS: CHANGING ROLES

Parents face more educational options than ever before for their deaf children. Truthfully, parents have the right to make decisions in the best interest of their children. In many cases, parents are not provided with a wide range of options necessary to make informed or educated decisions. Unfortunately, our destiny is within our reach, but not in our grasp. Parents, upon discovering that their child is deaf, go through shock, grief, anger, denial, and hopefully, acceptance. They are often vulnerable and in need of support. Medical professionals, audiologists, and speech and language pathologists are often the first contact for parents. The selective information provided to parents makes it difficult for them to make educated and informed decisions about their children's future. Professionals and parents are quick to consider medical "remedies" to deafness. Without considering a wide range of options, including information about the productive lives of deaf citizens, such decisions result in "life sentences" for their deaf children. Parents should consider what is best for their deaf children, rather than for themselves.

While Deaf Studies courses, particularly American Sign Language courses, have become a popular choice among hearing students, such opportunities are usually not available to deaf students in mainstream programs. Several studies have indicated that teaching pre-school children sign language will boost their vocabulary. Many deaf children do not learn sign language in spite of its popularity, but some parents introduce and use sign language as a mode of communication with their deaf children. Unfortunately, in many hearing families where members do not use sign language, deaf children generally are the ones burdened with the communication needs of the family. Often the shift on communication responsibility begins shortly after discovery of the deaf child's hearing status.

IN HINDSIGHT

Looking back in history and comparing the current trends in our history, one wonders about whether or not deaf people have progressed like other social groups. Many groups celebrated their common values and culture long before we did. For instance, women fought for the right to vote and civil rights were implemented for African Americans long before our own civil rights laws were enacted in the late 1990s. Even with recent laws for people with disabilities, we do not have the same opportunities. As in the past, self-fulfilling prophecy such as low expectations of deaf people by some hearing professionals and parents remains one of our greatest problems.

Many of the present issues mentioned here are not new. Our literacy skills have not significantly improved. In the Project HOPE study of the educational level of severely to profoundly deaf people, five percent of deaf students were college graduates, compared to 15 percent of hearing students (Blanchfield, 1999). Professional advancement has not yet occurred in other non-traditional areas of employment. Deaf culture with its language, literature, values, norms of behavior, and arts is nonexistent to many mainstream students. With such developmental gaps, some students' identities are marginalized. Low expectation is infectious in other areas, primarily in families and education. A patronizing attitude persists, along with ignorance, among medical and clinical professionals. Although there have been some social changes, in many ways, attitude barriers remain a serious obstacle in achieving equality for all people, especially deaf people.

WHAT WE CAN DO?

We began by discussing a period of enlightenment and followed with a history of constant struggles. So what do we do? This is not a question with a simple answer. All I know is that we must ask ourselves who is really in charge of our destiny, or who should be. Clearly, we must learn about our history, understand our struggles, attune ourselves with the world in which we live, prepare ourselves for rapid changes in society, and admit to ourselves that we cannot continue chasing our tails and allow injustice to continue. If the past is any indication of what we face today, then I will assume that we have not learned our lessons or taught them to the current generation of deaf adults. History repeats itself. As has been noted, much progress has been made, but many unresolved issues are still debated today with limited or no resolution. If the status quo remains, our struggles will continue unless we cut to the chase. More than ever before, we must capitalize on the momentum that has followed the passage of several laws during the past decade. So, let me briefly focus on parents, political activism, bills of rights, and education as vehicles for social change.

PARENTS OF DEAF AND HARD-OF-HEARING CHILDREN: BRIDGING THE GAP

When one reviews the history of deaf people, he or she will find that parents do not stand out. Nor do we acknowledge their role in the welfare of their children. Residential schools were one, and, in most cases, the only option for children prior to the 1970s. Deaf children who grew up in residential schools were provided with a surrogate family, peers just like themselves, access to communication, education, and co-curricular activities similar to that of hearing children with their immediate family. Residential schools are places where students develop a sense of belonging and can be a part of a group that shares common experiences, thus engaging in Deaf culture.

Today, parents face many options ranging from mainstreaming to cochlear implants to communication alternatives to residential schools. Given the present circumstances, parents are more active in determining the future of their children. Historically, parents have played a smaller role in our community and we rarely developed partnerships with them. Family is the most important social unit in our society, and parents make decisions. How can we ensure that parents are given unsolicited resources to help in making informed decisions? Consider the ideal model used in Sweden where the deaf community, professionals, and parents work together in the best interest of deaf children. We must reach out to parents; we owe that to deaf children. Parents, as a group, have a strong voice that can be used to help the deaf community promote its causes. All the resources and experts should be in a central place where parents can directly seek advice and assistance.

POLITICAL ACTIVISM: COLLABORATION

Battles can no longer be fought alone, unlike the past. NAD has tirelessly advocated for the rights for deaf people since 1880. Partnerships have been cultivated with other groups such as ASDC, CEASD, and CAID, to name a few. We should consider promoting mutual interests with non-traditional groups; for instance, other disabled or ethnic groups. The 1988 Deaf President Now movement is a model where support from the community—especially the African American community—brought about change for our cause. The African American community indicated their support by lending its historical banner displayed in the 1965 Civil Rights movement with Martin Luther King. This was an example of how networking with other groups instead of exclusively among us can bring more support for our causes. History was in the making, but, during that time, no real attempts were made to capitalize and cultivate relationships between the African American and Deaf communities. Parents, a potentially vocal group, should definitely be part of our advocacy efforts. Our legislative representatives pay attention to numerous phone calls, letters and other forms of communication. For example, in Rochester, New York, we have a very active political group made up of other disabled people from the Center for Independent Living that also advocates for the rights of deaf people. This group staged a number of protests and successfully promoted their causes. Recently, the group protested the patronizing attitude of Senator John Edwards (D–North Carolina), when he patted the head of a disabled person in a wheelchair during one of his campaign stops. The disabled community received an apology from Senator Edwards. Additionally, the National Democratic Committee is now aware of the needs of disabled citizens and is committed to work with the disabled community. The deaf community cannot remain exclusive or isolated in our struggle for justice. We should consider banding together with other groups. With larger numbers, things will happen.

BILL OF RIGHTS: A NEW HOPE

The state of New Mexico enacted a law recognizing a bill of rights for its deaf children. The Albuquerque Journal (2004) reported that it intends to raise public awareness about the unique communication needs of deaf children and to provide a template for state agencies to follow when they deal with these children. A task force in New Mexico reported that deaf and hard of hearing children do not develop effective communication and language skill and their education isolates rather than includes them (Albuquerque Journal, 2004). This is very significant! It should encourage families not to burden deaf children with the responsibility of accommodating the communication needs of their hearing family members beginning at a very young age. Siegel (2002) suggested the need for and right to communication is fundamental to the human condition. We need to collaborate to support a national agenda for the education of all deaf and hard-of-hearing children to provide an argument for a constitutional right to communication and language for deaf and hard-of-hearing children. We no longer should accept the notion of "use whatever works" as mentioned in some literature because it represents frugal efforts in the education of the deaf over the last two centuries. We need to demand more research on what really works and apply it in practice. Simply to the point, we need to encourage more research done by deaf professionals because they bring unique experiences and perspectives to the given research questions.

EDUCATION: REDEFINING THE ROLE OF NON-TRADITIONAL SCHOOLS

Education has always been an important component of our history. While we have made some strides in educating deaf children, we have a way to go before our children have full access like hearing children. A collective critical mass of deaf people is diminishing in residential schools. We are more fragmented than ever before. Holcomb (1990) reported in one of his studies that deaf students from residential schools have parallel social experiences to hearing students. He also reported that social experiences for mainstreamed deaf students are not similar to those of hearing students or to deaf students from residential schools. As stated earlier, socialization is an important developmental process, one that leads to a complete human being.

It is anticipated that mainstreaming will continue to be the future trend, which means deaf culture will not be passed on to deaf children in the traditional sense. Residential schools face some challenges with restrained budgets and declining enrollment. So what can we do to ensure that deaf children do not fall between the cracks? Residential schools can be viable resources for families and deaf children. A list of some suggestions for strengthening residential schools follows:

- Push for mandatory state budget lines to cover all operational expenses of maintaining residential and satellite mainstream programs throughout the state. The budget will fall under the direction of the residential school(s).
- Create a clearinghouse and center on deafness where information and resources can be located at several premier post-secondary institutions for the deaf with appropriate federal funding. This should be done in a spirit of collaboratation among these institutions.
- Preserve and strengthen the role of residential schools as centers of expertise and resources on deafness. All resources for mainstream support services will be centered there with satellite mainstream programs managed by the residential schools. The New Mexico School for the Deaf is a good example of this.
- Consider sending younger deaf children to mainstream programs with the intention to matriculate at a residential school at an appropriate age. This option will allow young children to remain with their families during the critical developmental years.
- Conduct infant screening and provide parents with a range of resources from a team made up of different professionals, including members from the deaf community. Parent outreach should become a critical resource in each state.
- Plan retreats for families with deaf children, and include activities where deaf children interact with one another.
- Include Deaf studies, including American Sign Language, as part of the statewide curriculum for all students in public and residen-

tial schools; ASL and English literacy should be given equal emphasis; resources should be provided for enhancing ASL skills for all
teachers of the deaf.

- Implement outreach programs targeting parents and their infants
  and preschool children with emphasis on promoting literacy skills
  among young deaf children.
- Continue to provide support to deaf students with various special
  needs including those with cochlear implants or other forms of
  amplifications.

PSYCHOSOCIAL WELL BEING

Numerous studies have repeatedly emphasized the importance of socialization, literacy, quality family dynamics, effective communication, and
positive self-identity as ingredients to healthy psychological well being.
The social experience among deaf children raises some concerns regarding gaps related to healthy development. The Swiss cheese phenomenon
represents the psychosocial and learning gaps reported in deaf children
especially those who have minimal contact with deaf role models or
access to critical incidental learning opportunities starting at home. Socialization is a critical component of psychosocial well being. For the approximately 80 percent of deaf students in mainstream programs, social
experiences for these students differ from those of their hearing peers or
deaf students in residential schools where communication barriers are
minimal or nonexistent.

With the current trend, we are seeing more students with developmental gaps compared to previous years. Some of the gaps are issues
with identity as a deaf person, psychosocial issues, misconceptions about
deaf people, and usage and understanding of ASL. Some of these students have minimal or no experience with deaf peers or adults, possess
awkward social skills, use inappropriate signs for meaning, or have no
real sense of cultural bonding. This is in no way an intention to diminish the integrity of deaf people. If a child has strong literacy skills and
healthy self-esteem, deafness does not represent a problem or a defect.

Our socialization is influenced greatly by perceptions of others
within the environment. Given many of these observations, deafness is
not the root of the problem. These deaf students generally do not have
the opportunity to involve themselves in activities with hearing students
on equal footing. The problem has to do with being raised in isolation or
having little exposure to the deaf community. This is a concern in light
of the trend towards mainstreaming without giving consideration to pro-

moting the normal development of deaf children. From a psychosocial perspective, socialization, especially with family and peers, becomes an important process for these children. School and mass media can also be agents for healthy socialization. For instance, deaf people coming from all-hearing families face challenges, especially since communication is not easily accessible and since they have no one to identify with. Quality family interaction is another critical factor when there is a deaf family member. We live in a stressed society where family quality time is becoming more sacred. Peer relationships are another important component of development for deaf children. Cultivating relationships is a skill that fosters effective communication and a sense of belonging. School is also an area where relationships with peers and adults, as well as engaging in activities are critical; lunch period is often difficult for many deaf students. Finally, the mass media can be positive in that it can provide deaf children with access to captioned educational programs. In short, communication is the key to every aspect of socialization, and we need to figure out how we can address some of the gaps. What I have discussed is just the tip of the iceberg. There is much more we need to know.

CONCLUSION

In this paper, I mentioned a range of challenges from the past and present and opportunities for the future. Marschark (1998) reported that most deaf children face significant educational and social challenges growing up and, frankly, we have not done enough to eliminate barriers. For years, we have been in the business of teaching deaf children and have made efforts to improve the standards within our community. In other words, our practice has been this approach: every educational problem requires an educational solution. Unfortunately, the resolutions have not been successful. The present trend is an indication of the past, and there is a good chance that the trend will continue if we do not address some of the persistent issues today. History repeats itself when lessons are not learned. Are we to assume that the present challenges will reflect the future? If we continue in the direction of the last two centuries, we may put ourselves in a position of "no return."

Given recent advancements in medicine, deaf people have witnessed more changes in our community. These changes divide us as deaf people. The force in the medical community is groups of scientists who have influence, power, and prestige. They may be too close to our community. Medical technology is rapidly changing especially with genetic engineering. Why has no scientist created a medicine that would change the color of a person's skin? Given the advancements in medicine, this is not far fetched. No one would dare to do that to people of color. Rightfully so; then why deaf peole? We may have begun to give scientists justifications to create medical remedies to resolve issues that persisted in the education of the deaf. Control of our destiny could blindly slip out of our hands.

We need to regroup with the goal of taking back the reins and shaping the future of our deaf children. We must broaden our horizons and think ahead. Partnerships with parents, professionals, and other social groups become even more critical now. We owe it to Clerc and Gallaudet. Their courage and bold vision for deaf people are still in our hands and will never be forgotten. It is up to us to make their vision a reality. Several decades of repeated failures are enough. It is time for us to change our endeavors and charge ahead.

REFERENCES

Baker, D. (2004, March 9). Governor Signs Bill of Rights for Deaf Children. *The Albuquerque Journal*, p. 1.

Baynton, D. (1996). *Forbidden Signs: American Culture and the Campaign against Sign Language.* Chicago: The University of Chicago Press.

Blanchfield, B., et al. (1999, October). *The Severely to Profoundly Hearing Impaired Population in the United States: Prevalence and Demographics.* Project HOPE. 1, 1, H Series.

Bochner, J. & Albertini, J. (1988). Language varieties in the deaf population and their acquisition by children and adults. In M. Strong (Ed.), *Language Learning and Deafness.* New York: Cambridge University Press.

Edwards, R. (1997). *Words Made Flesh: Nineteenth-Century Deaf Education and the Growth of Deaf Culture.* (Doctoral dissertation. University of Rochester, 1997). Dissertation Abstracts International, 58 (04), 1421A. (UMI no. 9729038).

Buchanan, B. (Ed.). (2002). *Gaillard in Deaf America: A Portrait of the Deaf Community, 1917.* Washington, DC: Gallaudet University Press.

Gallaudet Research Institute. (2000–2001). *Annual Survey of Deaf and Hard of Hearing Children and Youth.* Washington, DC: Gallaudet University, Gallaudet Research Institute.

Groce, N. (1984). *Hereditary deafness on the island of Martha's Vineyard: An ethnohistory of a genetic disorder.* (Doctoral dissertation. Brown University, 1983). Dissertation Abstracts International, 44, (07), 2190A. (UMI No. 8325981).

Holcomb, T. (1990). Deaf Students in the Mainstream: A Study in Social Assimilation. (Doctoral dissertation, University of Rochester, 1990). *Dissertation Abstracts International,* 51, (06), 1984A. (UMI No. 19032754).

Ladd, P. (2003). *Understanding Deaf Culture: In Search of Deafhood.* Clevedon, UK: Multilingual Matters Ltd.

Marschark, M. (1997). *Raising and Educating a Deaf Child.* New York: Oxford University Press.

Marschark, M. & Clark, D. (Eds.). (1998). *Psychological Perspectives on Deafness.* Mahwah, NJ: Lawrence Erlbaum Associates, Publishers.

Reefhuis, J. et al. (2003). Risk of Bacterial Meningitis in Children with Cochlear Implants. *The New England Journal of Medicine,* 349: 435–445.

Siegel, L. (2002). The Argument for a Constitutional Right to Communication and Language. *Journal of Deaf Studies and Deaf Education*, 7:3, 259–266.

Woodward, J. & Markowicz, H. (1980) Pidgin sign languages. In W. Stokoe (Ed.), *Sign and Culture*. Silver Spring, Maryland: Linstok Press.

ABOUT THE AUTHOR

 *J. Matt Searls, is a faculty member at NTID/RIT with over 26 years of experience in counseling and teaching at both NTID/RIT and Gallaudet University. Prior to his professional experience, Dr. Searls received B.A. and M.A. degrees in Social Work/Sociology and Counseling from Gallaudet University. He also earned the Doctor of Philosophy degree in Counseling and Human Development from the American University. Dr. Searls was a board member of ADARA and ASDC, and is currently on the board of the Rochester Chapter of the American Red Cross. Dr. Searls and his wife, Susan, have two deaf children, Davin and Lauren.*

"Nearer, My God, To Thee," Signed by deaf girls at the
Washington School for the Deaf; June 1911

Courtesy Gallaudet University Archives

Rhyming With Hands and Eyes: Using ASL Phonology[1] As a Language Learning Tool

ADONIA K. SMITH, M.A.

E. LYNN JACOBOWITZ, PH.D.

Adonia K. Smith is an ED.D. *candidate at Lamar University, Beaumont, Texas. E. Lynn Jacobowitz is a professor at Gallaudet University.*

HEARING CHILDREN ENJOY THE RHYMING sounds found in words as they listen to their parents sing songs, share nursery rhymes and read storybooks. In fact, this is how children acquire a vast English vocabulary—through repetitive hearing and through playing with the sounds of words. Take, for example, the classic rhyming story from Mother Goose (1916). It is full of words that rhyme with ending sounds (e.g. wool, full), repetitions of sounds (e.g. yes, sir, yes, sir) and alliteration (e.g. baa, baa, black).

Alliteration is a poetic device that refers to words starting with the same sound:

Baa, Baa Black Sheep

Baa, baa, black sheep,
Have you any wool?
Yes, sir, yes, sir,
Three bags full.

One for my master,
One for my dame,
And one for the little boy
Who lives in the lane.

Baa, baa, black sheep,
Have you any wool?
Yes, sir, yes, sir,
Three bags full.

These auditory features assist hearing children's acquisition of language, vocabulary, sentence structures, and reading skills, and even teach them about music. As hearing children develop into readers, they acquire phonemic awareness. Through alphabet books and nursery rhymes, children at approximately three years of age begin to understand spelling-to-sound correspondences of English words. Teachers in preschool and kindergarten then capitalize on hearing children's phonemic awareness and follow up with phonic instruction. In phonic instructions, children are drilled in recognizing the letter-sound correspondences, which help them "crack the code" or sound out new words (Mason and Au, 1990).

But what about deaf children who learn language visually through American Sign Language (ASL)? The auditory features of rhyming, alliteration and so on in stories do not provide the same amount of pleasure and learning because Deaf students cannot hear the sound play in those stories. This is not to say they cannot find the stories useful for studying orthographic patterns for spelling. But initially, the sound play on language is not accessible to deaf children in the same ways hearing children have access to these auditory sounds.

Teachers of deaf children may then focus on using the fingerspelled alphabet to teach beginning vocabulary. A common teaching technique for deaf children in the primary grades is to introduce the manual alphabet (fingerspelled alphabet) and teach vocabulary words based on their association with the fingerspelled alphabet. For example, using the fingerspelled handshape for the letter A, the teacher may teach the word and concept for the word *apple* or the word *ant*.

However, one of the authors of *Have You Ever Seen...? An ASL Handshape Book,* a former elementary school teacher, found that this matching manual alphabet letter-to-word technique tended to confuse her deaf students. The students would often associate the letter X with the word *apple* because the sign for APPLE was made with the X handshape. When she asked one of her students to give her a word for the letter A handshape, the deaf student responded with the word/sign LOVE, made with the A handshape. In other words, her students who could not spell yet were confused with handshapes for signs and English alphabet fingerspelling. Thus, this was an ineffectual way to teach beginning vocabulary to deaf students. The teacher then began to come up with creative ways to teach vocabulary using ASL handshapes. She also incorporated a bit of Dr. Seuss' typical nonsense-like style in her stories to make them amusing and fun for the students.

After these insights were developed, the teacher began to study how she could use the phonological formation of ASL to encourage sign play with deaf children. This led her to the question: How could teachers develop children's materials that allowed deaf children to play with and expand vocabularies and language learning through ASL handshapes?

She enlisted the assistance of an ASL teacher trainer (the second author of *Have You Ever Seen...? An ASL Handshape Book*) who had many years of experience teaching ASL literature to college students, as well being involved with the development of ASL curriculum for kindergarten through college levels. They pooled their talents to develop two DVDs/books specifically created for deaf children that would capitalize on visual awareness and knowledge of ASL handshapes in order to expand and develop deaf students' ASL lexicon.

LINGUISTIC RESEARCH

Linguists have shown that an ASL lexical sign is made up of five parameters: handshape, movement, location, palm orientation, and nonmanual signals (Valli and Lucas, 2000). The parameter of handshape has been described in books on ASL linguistics (Valli and Lucas, 2000), in sign language dictionaries (Tennant and Brown, 1998; Penn, 1992), in books, articles and videotapes on ASL poetry and poetics (Bahan, 1992; Valli, 1992; Peters, 2000; Valli, 1996, Rutherford, 1993) and instructional materials such as flashcards (Paul and Bahan, 1990).

These authors and others have demonstrated that the playing with the ASL parameter of handshape creates an ASL poem or a type of "ASL rhyme" that may give Deaf children pleasure as well as increase their ASL lexicon (vocabulary), syntax, and conceptual knowledge (Valli, 1991; 1995). Such a strong ASL base is critical if we subscribe to the theory that Deaf children can learn English by building concepts first in their first language of ASL.

The discipline of ASL phonology (cherology) may seem complex to those who have not had specialized training or coursework in ASL linguistics (Valli and Lucas, 2000). In the authors' two DVDs/books for children, they attempt to make a very complex subject comprehensible to young deaf children who are acquiring ASL as a first language. The materials are also useful for other children and adults learning ASL.

AN OVERVIEW OF TWO ASL HANDSHAPE DVD/BOOKS

The DVDs/books were created, illustrated and produced by Deaf artists. The overall purpose of the authors' project was to create two entertaining and whimsical children's DVDs/books, *Have You Ever Seen...? An ASL*

Handshape Book, and its companion activity book, *An ASL Handshape Riddle Book.* Both books were based on ASL linguistics, using Dr. Seuss' themes of nonsense and *I Spy*[2] themes of finding pictorial clues. The books also incorporate Deaf culture themes.

Traditionally, surveys of children's literature that include deaf characters have shown that most authors are hearing and/or do not depict "real" or "authentic" Deaf characters as members of the Deaf community. Instead, these authors commonly portray the Deaf characters as disabled persons who need fixing, rehabilitation, or want to be hearing (Andrews, 1996; Wilding-Diaz, 1993; Bailes, 2002). The authors' books fill that void in the field by providing children's books that authentically portray the Deaf culture. In addition, most books are written in only one language, English. While there are some children's videotapes in ASL, they often do not have corresponding written text in English. In contrast, the authors' children's books are presented in two languages: written English and ASL. Therefore, they are bilingual books for Deaf children that give them access to both languages.

The first book focuses on ASL handshape rhyme (repetition of similar handshapes in one story). The second book focuses on particular ASL handshapes. In the DVDs/books, the readers/viewers can see how easy and fun it is to make ASL handshape rhymes and also find additional signs in the riddle book using the particular ASL handshape shown on each page. Equally important is the presence of some humor in the DVDs/books for viewers/readers (Jacobowitz, 1992).

The DVDs/books are dual language children's books, curricular materials for bilingual students that deliver content in two languages to the viewers/reader, ensuring clear separation (Baker, 2001). The DVDs/ books also incorporate multimedia technology, where the text is written in English with an accompanying DVD that contains ASL short movies. The first DVD/book, *Have You Ever Seen...? An ASL Handshape Book,* is organized according to the 44 handshapes of ASL (one ASL handshape per page). While the authors recognize that there are more than 150 handshapes in ASL, they selected 44 of the most commonly used handshapes. The accompanying DVD contains ASL short movies performed by native ASL children signers between the ages of two to nine, and their parents. The DVD and book are illustrated with still-animation pictures, along with signing characters telling amusing, nonsensical stories. Each illustrated page also contains a backdrop of Deaf culture collages.

As mentioned previously, the signers in the DVD are children and parents who demonstrate each handshape and tell an amusing story. There are 12 Deaf children with Deaf parents, two CODAs, and one hearing parent. The DVD, enclosed in a pocket within the book, also contains a copy of the written text. In the DVDs/text, several curricular designs were used to maximize the information contained in the DVDs and book. Each page begins with the sentence written as a question: "*Have you ever seen...*"? This promotes the use of ASL discourse, dialogue and interactions among Deaf students. The answer is always, "*No,*" but the question and story are told in a comical, entertaining manner.

Another design feature relates to light and dark pictures. When an object or animal first makes a sign, the picture is shown in a light shade, usually indicating the topic of the sentence. When the second object or animal makes a sign, the object or animal becomes dark, usually signifying the comment part of the sentence. This light-to-dark differentiation allows the readers/viewers to see how signs are sequenced in ASL structure. Again, each page focuses on one handshape while presenting two new concepts using this same handshape. In other words, the viewer/reader is instructed to read the sentence then fill in the blanks with information provided by the authors referring to one of the 44 handshapes. For example, see Figure 1:

Figure 1: Sample page using the A handshape

The viewer/reader begins by signing, "Have you ever seen....?" Then the viewer/reader looks at the picture and reads and signs, TURTLES PAGING. In ASL, these two concepts or signs create an ASL handshape rhyme because they all begin with the same handshape: the A handshape. Each subsequent page contains a different ASL handshape rhyme told in an amusing fashion.

Each page also contains a wealth of Deaf culture information. For instance, in Figure 1, there is a poster telling of a poetry contest. Dr. Clayton

Valli was a well-known poet in the Deaf community who often presented his ASL poems at workshops and festivals. The poster illustrates a school contest where students can compose their own ASL poetry (like Valli) and compete with each other.

The use of the pager in the illustration also points to the importance of technology in the lives of Deaf people. The authors of the DVD/book continuously attempt to embed Deaf culture themes through the DVD/book. Other Deaf cultural themes seen in the book include: De'VIA art, Deaf residential schools, Deaf families, Deaf drama, etc. (Lane, Hoffmeister, and Bahan, 1996; Ladd, 2003). The authors also include a narrative description of the Deaf culture vignette on each page for viewers/readers.

At the end of the book, there is another resource where the authors present some myths about ASL that may interest the viewer/reader. Such rich Deaf cultural information that accompanies the DVD/book will make infusing Deaf culture into the curriculum easier.

The companion DVD/book, *An ASL Handshape Riddle*, is composed of the same 44 ASL handshapes as the first book (see Figure 2). The first picture, in color, is shown in the book along with a black and white outline. There is also a list of words with red numbers where the reader can check for correct answers. On the DVD, a person will sign each word.

Figure 2: Sample pages from *An ASL Handshape Riddle*

Handshape: bent V or 2

1. AUDIOLOGY
2. SPEECH
3. SKELETON
4. FAVORITE (regional sign)
5. BONE
6. CL: DOG SLEEPING
7. SQUIRREL
8. CL: MOUTH OPENING ("shocked")
9. GRASSHOPPER
10. SNAKE
11. FROG
12. BATTERY
13. DOUBT
14. GOAT
15. TRIP
16. REFEREE
17. GEORGE VEDITZ
18. CL: KNEEL
19. STRICT
20. STAIRS
21. TICKET
22. BLIND
23. HEARING AID MAKING NOISES
24. CL: GET-UP
25. VAMPIRE

In this new book, each page is organized according to the 44 ASL hand-shapes, with pictures. The student is instructed to pick out the pictures that represent the sign concept, using the particular ASL handshape assigned to each page. This format, again, is modeled after the popular *I Spy* children's riddle picture book series.

The 25 sign concepts presented on each page are designed to be orga-nized into three areas: concrete, abstract and classifiers. For an example of concrete words, in Figure 2, the handshape "bent V or 2" is represented in the pictures by GOAT and TICKET. At the abstract level, the student must interpret the pictures in order to arrive at the answers for the signs BLIND and STRICT. For the classifier of the handshape "bent V or 2," the picture depicts a DOG SLEEPING and MOUTH OPENING (shocked).

The DVD for the riddle book uses multimedia technology. Students must first guess the correct answers; if they want to check their answers, they may click on the picture onscreen, which will bring up a screen of a Deaf native signer signing the correct answer. This way, the more they play, students can easily acquire and learn more ASL vocabulary.

In the riddle book, there are also activities that capitalize on the students' knowledge and awareness of ASL handshapes. A teacher booklet provides ideas on how to use the ASL handshapes in the classroom as a teaching tool to build ASL vocabulary. For example, a typical activity for hearing preschoolers is having a letter of the week. Each week, the teacher focuses on one letter of the alphabet and uses it to expand the child's English vocabulary. A teacher of deaf students may establish a handshape of the week and build the students' ASL vocabulary by having the children focus on the handshape of the week. The teacher may also make digital pictures of the signs and display them under a picture of the handshape of the week. Teachers may also want to write the English translation of the words under each word in the handshape categories, thus stressing the bilingual skills of deaf students. For example, under the A handshape category, students would find the signs for TURTLE and PAGER. The teacher may want to write the English translations of each of these signs (e.g. turtle and pager). These are just a few of the many ideas contained in the teachers' handbook for the DVDs/books.

GAMES

Five timed computer games are provided on the DVD as extended activities for the children. Three games focus on ASL, while the other two focus on Deaf culture. For instance, at the elementary level, there are three versions available. One is the English version, where the child is to pick from multiple-choice answers. A picture of the handshape X will appear, and the child may pick from any of the following answers: CUP, BED, KEY, or FANG (the answer being, of course, KEY).

The second version is aimed at those who are younger or may not have learned the English language yet. The answers are provided in pictures (a picture of a key, for instance), instead of English. The third version is for those who may not have picked up ASL yet, with the answers being provided in signs. After the game is played, the teacher may track the children's progress by reading results from the game, which will indicate areas of strength and needed improvement. Figure 3 shows an example of games at the elementary level.

Figure 3: An example of the five games available at the elementary level

INTENDED AUDIENCES

Although the authors designed the ASL handshape DVDs/books for Deaf children acquiring ASL as a first language, they see its utility for teaching ASL as a second language to hearing children and adults at the elementary, middle school, high school and college levels. The books may be useful within different disciplines such as early childhood, early literacy, deaf education, sign language interpretation, rehabilitation, audiology and speech pathology, Deaf Studies, Deaf Literature, and ASL literature.

FUTURE PLANS AND RESEARCH

The books are the first in a series of DVD/book production, computer games and research studies that capitalize on ASL phonological parameters. We also plan to develop children's materials that use the other parameters of ASL signs such as the location, orientation, movement and nonmanual signals (Valli and Lucas, 2000)

The use of ASL handshapes in children's materials to motivate Deaf children to expand their vocabularies may be explored further in studies documenting Deaf children's acquisition of ASL signs. Comparison studies could be done comparing hearing children's use of auditory rhyme to acquire spoken words with Deaf children's use of handshape rhymes to acquire ASL signs. In addition, the authors are planning classroom studies that investigate the ASL vocabulary acquisition of deaf students using fingerspelled handshapes versus ASL handshapes.

There has consistently been a lack of materials available in ASL for children whose first language is ASL, and a lack of materials provided in both ASL and English. There is also a lack of curriculi that enable Deaf students to use artistic expression through ASL poetry, stories and plays (Jacobowitz, 2003; Valli, 1991). With expanding research showing the importance of bilingualism for both deaf and hearing children, *Have You Ever Seen...? An ASL Handshape Book* strives to begin fulfilling that need.

It is the authors' hope that books of this type will become an integral part of the design of Deaf Studies and ASL studies curriculi for Deaf children, and eventually become incorporated in these curriculi. By teaching Deaf students about ASL handshape rhyme, this may enhance not only their expressive abilities, but also their appreciation of the beauty of ASL as the natural language of the Deaf community.

ENDNOTES

1.   William C. Stokoe coined the term "cherology," as an analogue to the word, "phonology." The cherology (or phonology) of ASL refers to the smallest contrastive units of language. Stokoe proposed that signs have three parts (parameters) that combine simultaneously: *dez* or designator (handshape), *sig* or signation (movement), and *tab* or tabula (location of the sign) (Stokoe, 1960; Stokoe, Casterline & Croneberg, 1976). These three parameters were later expanded adding palm orientation and nonmanual signals (Valli & Lucas, 2000). Stokoe referred to the three parameters as cheremes, from the Greek word *cheir*, which means hands. Stokoe saw cheremes as meaningless elements that combine to form signs in the same way that phonemes combine to form words in spoken language (Valli & Lucas, 2000).

2.   *I Spy Mystery: A Book of Picture Riddles* (by Jean Marzollo, with photographs by Walter Wick) is the title of a series of children's picture books that feature a question (e.g. "where is the star?") and a second picture of a collage of overlapping pictures. The young reader is instructed to find the hidden pictures.

REFERENCES

Andrews, J. (1996). Deaf Culture Values Through Children's Literature. *Lamar University Distinguished Faculty Lecture*. Beaumont, Texas: Lamar University.

Bahan, B. (1992). ASL Literature: Inside the Story. In College for Continuing Education (Ed.), *Deaf Studies: What's Up? Conference Proceedings* (pp. 153–164).

Baker, C. (2001). *Foundations of Bilingual Education and Bilingualism*. Clevedon, England: Multilingual Matters.

Bailes, C. (2002). Mandy: A Critical Look at the Portrayal of a Deaf Character in Children's Literature. *Multicultural Perspectives*, 4(4), 3–9.

Dannis, J. (1996). A*SL Poetry: Selected Works of Clayton Valli* [Videotape]. San Diego, California: DawnSignPress.

Paul, F., & Bahan, B. (1990). *The American Sign Language Handshape Game Cards*. San Diego, California: DawnSign Press.

Jacobowitz, E. (1992). Humor and Wit in the Deaf Community. In College for Continuing Education (Ed.), *Deaf Studies: What's Up? Conference Proceedings* (pp. 187–192).

Jacobowitz, E. (2001). American Sign Language Teacher Education Programs and National Teaching Standards: State of the Art (Unpublished doctoral dissertation, Gallaudet University).

Ladd, P. (2003). *Understanding Deaf Culture: In Search of Deafhood*. Clevedon, England.

Lane, H., Hoffmeister, R., & Bahan, B. (1996). *A Journey into the DEAF-WORLD*. San Diego, CA: DawnSignPress.

Lucas, C. (Ed.). (1990). *Sign Language Research: Theoretical Issues*. Washington, DC: Gallaudet University Press.

Mason, J., & Au, K. (1990). *Reading Instruction for Today*. Glenview, Illinois: Scott, Foresman/Little Brown Higher Education.

Penn, C. (1992). *Dictionary of Southern African Signs for Communicating with the Deaf*. (Vol. 1). Human Sciences Research Council: Johannesburg, South Africa.

Peters, C. (2000). *Deaf American Literature: From Carnival to Cannon*. Washington, DC: Gallaudet University Press.

Rutherford, S. (1993). *A Study of American Deaf Folklore*. Burtonsville, MD: Linstok Press, Inc.

Stokoe, W. (1960). *Sign language Structure: An Outline of Visual Communication Systems of the American Deaf*. Studies in Linguistics, Occasional Paper. Buffalo, New York.

Stokoe, W., Casterline, D., & Croneberg, C. (1976). *A Dictionary of American Sign Language on Linguistic Principles*. Washington, DC: Gallaudet University Press.

Tennant, R. & Brown, M. (1998). *The American Sign Language Handshape Dictionary*. Washington, DC: Gallaudet University Press.

Valli, C. (1992). A Need in Deaf Education: American Sign Language Artistic Expression. In Continuing Education and Outreach (Ed.), *Deaf Studies for Educators, Conference Proceedings* (pp. 121–125).

Valli, C. & Lucas, C. (2000). *The Linguistics of American Sign Language: An Introduction* (3rd ed.). Washington, DC: Gallaudet University Press.

Wilding-Diaz, M. (1992). Deaf Characters in Children's Books: How are They Perceived? In Continuing Education and Outreach (Ed.), *Post Milan ASL and English Literacy: Issues, Trends, and Research, Conference Proceedings* (pp. 299–232).

Wright, B. (Illustrator). (1994). The Real Mother Goose. New York: Scholastic, Inc.

ABOUT THE AUTHORS

Adonia Smith is an Associate Professor in the Deaf Studies/Deaf Education at Lamar University in Beaumont, Texas. She holds a BA in Elementary Education in 1995 and a MA in Deaf Education in 1996 both at Gallaudet University. She also holds an ASLTA certification. She worked at the Alabama School for the Deaf in the elementary department for five years. She is now a doctoral student working on her dissertation and is developing a teacher-friendly ASL test for deaf children. Her dissertation was funded by the Dept of Education and by the William C. Stokoe scholarship programs. She also writes multimedia children's DVDs/books.

E. Lynn Jacobowitz, Ph.D., is an Associate Professor in the Department of ASL and Deaf Studies at Gallaudet University. She holds a professional American Sign Language Teachers Association (ASLTA) certification. She was also the 1995–1998 president of ASLTA, a national organization that certifies ASL teachers. Currently, Dr. Jacobowitz is chair of the National ASLTA ASL Curriculum Project and ASL Legislation. Dr. Jacobowitz has given numerous workshops and presentations on ASL, Deaf Culture, Deaf folklore, methods and materials for sign language teachers. She is well-known for her comedy and storytelling performances, consultations, articles, and cartoons about Deaf Culture and humor.

Deaf Students In Collegiate Mainstream Programs

JULIA A. SMITH, PH.D

Julia A. Smith is the coordinator of the Rehabilitation Counseling: Deaf program at Western Oregon University, Monmouth, Oregon.

THE RETENTION OF STUDENTS IN higher education is a major concern for students, parents, teachers, and college administrators. More than 40 percent of all college students leave without earning a degree. Of these, three-fourths drop out in the first two years of college (Tinto, 1987, 1993). These statistics are even more dire for students with hearing loss. There are approximately 468,000 Deaf and hard of hearing students currently attending college in the United States (Schroedel, Watson, and Ashmore, 2003); however, estimates for postsecondary students who are Deaf show that between two-thirds and three-quarters of those who begin their studies will never graduate (Myers and Taylor, 2000).

As colleges and universities strive to embrace diversity and provide all students an opportunity to succeed, important questions are raised: Why are Deaf students more likely to drop out than hearing students? What factors in the social and academic environment affect the adjustment process for students who are Deaf? These questions are the focus of this study.

It is important to begin with asking, what makes students in general either persist or withdraw from college? Researchers have found that persistence tends to be primarily a function of the quality of students' adjustment to the academic and social settings of an institution (Astin, 1993; Braxton, Vesper, and Hossler, 1995; Tinto, 1993). These researchers also found that students come to a particular institution with a range of background characteristics, as well as varying levels of commitment to acquiring a higher education. These characteristics include family of origin relationships, and academic, social, and emotional readiness. Background characteristics, along with commitment, influence how students will adjust to the institution's social and academic settings.

Although we have statistics on the retention and academic success of college students who are Deaf, we know very little about the perspectives that Deaf college students hold regarding their academic and social experiences in small collegiate mainstream programs. Most research in this area has been conducted at postsecondary institutions which have supportive academic and social environments already in place for 100 or more Deaf students, such as Rochester Institute of Technology, California State University at Northridge, and Gallaudet University. Due to the larger number of students at these institutions, they are better prepared to accommodate Deaf students' social and academic needs than are colleges with a small number of Deaf students (Foster, 1999).

It is important to note, however, that more than 2,300 postsecondary institutions in the United States serve students who are Deaf or hard of hearing (Lewis, Farris, and Greene, 1994) and most of these institutions report fewer than 10 Deaf students. Although researchers have provided some data on college students' experiences at larger "Deaf-friendly" college settings, we know very little about the perception of social and academic success and satisfaction of Deaf college students who attend colleges where the number of Deaf students is substantially smaller.

PURPOSE OF THIS STUDY

Deaf students leave postsecondary institutions for many reasons, some of them similar to the reasons reported by their hearing peers. These include being too far from home, having financial problems, or being unsure of goals (Stinson, Scherer, and Walter, 1997). However, past research has shown that the most prominent reasons reported by Deaf students include college preparedness issues, such as weak academic skills and inadequate emotional readiness (e.g. separation from family and friends), as well as poor adjustment to academic and social settings in their colleges. Deaf students report problems communicating with faculty, inadequate support services, and limited opportunities for social interactions with peers (Allen, 1994; Foster and Elliot, 1986).

An important goal of a college education is to obtain gainful employment. Historically, Deaf people have been underemployed (Schroedel, 1976; Welsh and Walter, 1988), although research over the past 15 years has found that a college education has made more and better jobs accessible to Deaf people (Schroedel and Geyer, 2000). Although the number of Deaf students in postsecondary schools has increased over recent years (Myers and Taylor, 2000; Schroedel and Geyer), research has not kept up with the experiences of Deaf students in collegiate mainstream programs. Knowing and understanding their experiences can provide valuable information to a variety of professionals and programs that serve clients or students who are Deaf, such as vocational rehabilitation counselors, high school transition counselors, college and university faculty and staff, and career development, outreach, and support services programs.

This information may ultimately serve to reduce the attrition rate of students who are Deaf and subsequently increase gainful employment among this population. Further, analysis of trends among this population may help us understand attrition for other groups as well.

RESEARCH QUESTIONS

On the basis of findings from the existing literature, I posed two general research questions. First, how do students who are Deaf describe their experience in a mainstream college? Second, what factors in the social and academic environment are linked to Deaf college students' perceptions of academic and social success and satisfaction with life in a mainstream college? The first question allowed the participants to comment on the overall college experiences they find the most salient, whereas the second question narrowed the focus to the more specific area of the academic and social environment and how they relate to students' readiness for college, as well as feelings of academic and social success and satisfaction.

LITERATURE REVIEW

Persistence in College. Persistence in college has been a major concern for students, parents, teachers, and college administrators, and has been studied by researchers for several decades (Astin, 1993, 1999; Braxton et al., 1995; Chickering, 1969; Foster, 1988; Gerdes and Mallinckrodt, 2001: Pantages and Creedon, 1978; Tinto, 1987, 1993). Graduation rates for students in general average 43 percent for two-year colleges (within three years of initial enrollment) and 50 percent for four-year colleges (within five years of initial enrollment) (Tinto, 1993). Individual students bring personal characteristics into their environments that affect their persistence in higher education. Two areas have been identified as having an important influence on college attrition: a) academic adjustment and integration, which includes academic abilities, motivational factors, and effective interactions with faculty in and outside the classroom; and, b) social and emotional adjustment and integration, which includes successful interpersonal relationships in the campus environment; feelings of self-worth; and issues pertaining to separation from family.

Researchers have found that personal integration into the social fabric of campus life plays a role at least as important as academic factors in student retention (Astin, 1993, 1999; Gerdes and Mallinckrodt, 2001; Youn, 1992). For instance, Astin (1999) found that environmental influences such as adequate support services and the opportunity to have social interaction with peers impact students' development and the amount of physical and psychological energy that students devote to college. His findings suggest that factors contributing to persistence also imply increased involvement, whereas factors contributing to departure from college imply limited involvement in the college experience. As pointed out, all students must deal with these factors. However, students with diverse backgrounds (e.g. cultural or ethnic minority students, or students who have disabilities) have additional struggles to overcome if they are to persist in college.

ACADEMIC, SOCIAL, AND EMOTIONAL ADJUSTMENT OF DIVERSE COLLEGE STUDENTS

The relationship between students and the college environment is seen as both reciprocal and dynamic (Bronfenbrenner, 1979, 1986; Dey and Hurtado, 1995). Tinto (1987, 1993, 1997) found that students are more likely to stay in college if the commitment and goal of college completion is reinforced by positive postsecondary experiences. This includes the college helping the student feel integrated within the institution. Negative postsecondary experiences tend to distance students from the social and academic communities of the institution and increase the likelihood that students will leave the institution and higher education altogether. Many students struggle to adjust to the academic and social environments of college, however, students from minority groups have additional hurdles to overcome.

Students of Color. Growing numbers of students from cultural and ethnic minority backgrounds are enrolling in college and most attend predominately White institutions (Ginter and Glauser; 1997; MacKay and Huh, 1994). At the same time, graduation rates for students of color at mostly White institutions have not increased in keeping with growing enrollments (Wilson, 1994). For example, Steele (1992) reported that more than two-thirds of African Americans leave predominately white campuses before graduation compared with less than 45 percent of white students (Tinto, 1987, 1993). Watson and Kuh (1996) found that adjusting to the social and academic environments seem to be central to the success of many students of color who attend predominately White institutions. They went on to report that the quality of students' relationship with peers, faculty, and administrators tend to be almost as important as individual effort to their achievement.

Other researchers, Eimers and Pike (1997) conducted a study to examine similarities and differences between minority and nonminority adjustment to college. These authors report three important findings from their study: 1) students of color had significantly lower levels of entering academic ability and subsequent achievement than nonminority students; 2) external encouragement such as support from parents was also found to be lower than among White students; and, 3) "...minority students had lower levels of academic and social integration, perceived quality, and institutional commitment than nonminority students" (p. 87). Eimers and Pike conclude that understanding adjustment differences between these two groups of students "can help campus administrators to develop retention programs that better reflect the unique and similar needs of minority and nonminority students" (p.95).

It is apparent that the academic and social environments of students of color impact their integration and adjustment to college life. Although Eimers and Pike's (1997) focus is on students from diverse cultural and ethnic background, their findings also coincide with results of research focused on retention and persistence of other minority students, i.e. those who have disabilities (Stodden and Dowrick, 2000; Thomas, 2000; Yuen and Shaughnessy, 2001).

Students with Disabilities. There are currently more students with disabilities in higher education than there ever have been (HEATH Resource Center, 1998). The HEATH Resource Center reports that nine percent of all incoming freshman reported having a disability in 1998. This increase may be the result of informed choice on the part of disabled people. Only modest effort was made in accommodating college students with disabilities in the 1970s and the 1980s. The passage of Americans with Disabilities Act (ADA) in 1990, however, has contributed to students becoming increasingly more aware of their rights to accommodation while in higher education (Thomas, 2000).

An in-depth qualitative study of college students with disabilities by Lehmann, Davies and Laurin (2000) resulted in four emergent themes:

1) students felt a lack of understanding and acceptance concerning disabilities on the part of fellow students, staff, faculty, and the general public; 2) students reported a lack of adequate services to assist them in tackling academic and nonacademic responsibilities; 3) there was a consensus that financial resources were insufficient, as well as knowledge regarding how to acquire resources to live a more self-sufficient life; and, 4) students stated that they had a lack of self-advocacy skills and training needed to live independently.

These findings support Tinto's (1987, 1993, 1997) assertion that positive postsecondary experiences in students' personal and academic environments (e.g. parental involvement and support, relationships between family, friends, and school, as well as students' feelings of academic, social, and emotional adjustment) significantly impact students' commitment to stay in college.

DEAF COLLEGE STUDENTS

Students who are Deaf are often included in discussions regarding college students with disabilities. However, students who are Deaf have their own unique struggles and challenges regarding their experiences in postsecondary education. Researchers (Schroedel, Watson, and Ashmore, 2003) estimate that during the year 2000, 468,000 Deaf or hard of hearing students were attending the nation's postsecondary institutions. This figure can be broken down to 345,000 who were hard of hearing, 115,000 who were deafened after the age of 18, and 8,000 who were deafened before the age of 18. What is a concern to many is that once these students arrived at college, most did not stay. Studies over the past few years (Rawlings, Karchmer, and DeCaro, 1991; NTID, 1997) indicate that, on average, only about 30% of Deaf students entering colleges across the country ultimately graduate. Even those institutions that are considered "Deaf-friendly," due to the high number of Deaf students in attendance, experience retention problems. At the National Technical Institute for the Deaf (NTID) for example, half of all entering students withdrew prior to graduation and almost 30 percent left prior to starting their second year of study (NTID).

These attrition rates are alarming for several reasons. Deaf people who enter the workforce without a college degree have a difficult time securing jobs in which they can compete and be successful (Welsh and MacLeod-Gallinger, 1992). Welsh and MacLeod-Gallinger found that Deaf works, in general, earn less than their hearing peers when level of education is equal. In other words, a Deaf worker with less than a bachelor's degree will earn 79 percent of what a hearing worker earns with the same degree. This gap closes with advanced degree levels. A Deaf worker with a bachelor's degree will earn 83 percent of what a hearing worker will earn, and 89 percent with a master's degree. In a more recent study, Schroedel and Geyer (2000) found that the level of college degree correlated positively with annual income among Deaf workers. They further confirmed that Deaf college graduates earned significantly less than hearing graduates at the same degree levels. Succeeding in and graduating from college is essential if Deaf individuals hope to compete and succeed in the world of work.

In recent years, studies have examined higher education attrition and persistence rates for students who are Deaf (Myers and Taylor, 2000; Stinson and Walter, 1997). One researcher in particular, Sue Foster (Foster, Long, and Snell, 1999; Foster and Walter, 1992; Foster and DeCaro, 1991: Brown and Foster, 1991; Foster, 1988), has dedicated almost two decades to understanding the mainstreamed Deaf college student; however, the majority of her research has been with students who attend the National Technical Institute for the Deaf (NTID), which is housed at Rochester Institute of Technology. In fact, most research on mainstream college students who are Deaf occurs at NTID. This is not representative of the mainstream experience in general, however, because there are over 400 Deaf students in attendance at this institution (NTID, 1997).

There has been limited research regarding Deaf students who attend mainstream postsecondary institutions with a significantly smaller number of Deaf students. What are their experiences? And, what factors relate to their persistence or withdrawal from college? Evidence points out that retention of students who are Deaf is rather dismal. Data collected in the early 1990s (Rawlings, Karchmer, DeCaro, and Allen, 1991) looked at 112 programs that serve Deaf students. This study found that two-year institutions with programs for supporting Deaf students admitted on average 12 to 14 new students each year, and graduated, on average, only three students each year, for a withdrawal rate of about 75 percent. This rate was repeated at the four-year colleges. These institutions admitted, on average, four freshman each year and graduated only one student.

An earlier study by Foster and Elliot (1986) found that lack of effective communication could determine academic difficulties and consequently student withdrawal. Their research concluded that even when interpreters were assigned to the classroom and additional support systems were in place, Deaf students complained that teachers moved through the class lecture too quickly and seemed to treat Deaf students as if they could hear. The result was students often left class feeling confused about the lecture and unsure of assignments. A later study by Franklin (1988) suggested that four factors had a significant relationship with persistence or withdrawal of Deaf students. The students who stayed in school were generally those who:

1) had better oral communication skills;
2) attended high schools that provided minimum support;
3) experienced some kind of pre-college preparation; and,
4) declared a major during the first year of college.

English (1993) had similar findings when she evaluated a model of persistence using Deaf students who attended mainstream postsecondary institutions. She found that students who reported greater interaction with faculty did better academically. English also found that those students with higher grades expressed intent to remain in college until graduation.

These studies point to the importance of the immediate and intermediate environments of the Deaf college student. Relationships with classmates, faculty, and other college staff have been shown to make a significant impact on students' retention in postsecondary education. Although the number of Deaf students who attend postsecondary institutions across the country has increased (Lewes, et al. 1994), there have been few follow-up studies to examine the experience of mainstream college students who attend smaller Deaf programs.

METHODOLOGY

The purpose of this study was to gain more understanding of how college students who are Deaf explain their perceptions of academic and social success and satisfaction in a mainstream postsecondary setting. Due to the dearth of literature in this field, this study was viewed as exploratory. The research questions and goals, as well as the lack of literature on the topic, pointed to the use of qualitative research methodology for this study. This method allowed an in-depth and naturalistic look at the topic to be studied. Lofland and Lofland (1995) state that naturalistic research "involves a close and searching description of the mundane details of everyday life. (p. 7).

The use of qualitative methods is a viable approach to research with college students who are Deaf (Foster, 1996; Mertens, 1998; Sheridan, 1996). This approach allows the uniqueness of each Deaf participant to emerge while identifying themes common to groups of college students who are Deaf in the contexts of their mainstream college environments. One of the benefits of using qualitative methods with a diverse group such as college students who are Deaf, is that it requires ongoing self-examination and reflection on the realities, values, and worldviews of the researcher, as well as the participants (Mertens).

A semi-structured interview approach was used. I developed a specific interview protocol, but participants were also able to determine the course of the discussion. Each videotaped interview took about two hours. The interviews were conducted at the student's university in a private taping room. The interviewees used a variety of communication modes, from ASL, to PSE, to spoken English. Each interview was transcribed verbatim into written English. Also, because ASL is not my first language, a Deaf language consultant was hired to review approximately 20 minutes per transcribed session to make sure the interpretation was accurate.

PARTICIPANT CHARACTERISTICS

For this study, 14 mainstream undergraduate college students who are Deaf and have completed at least one term of college at the institution where they are interviewed were selected. Participation included nine females and five males who were undergraduate students, not living with their family of origin, and not married. Students were identified from four universities in the Pacific Northwest.

Since this study focused on Deaf college students, the students had to identify themselves as being *Deaf* versus *hard of hearing* or *hearing impaired*. Individuals who identify as *hard of hearing* or *hearing impaired* often identify first as being "hearing" and second as having a hearing loss. Although Deaf and hard of hearing students are often considered together for studies, hard of hearing college students face challenges that are quite different than those of students who are Deaf. Therefore for the purpose of this study, selected students self-identified as being Deaf and received support services from their college's Office of Disability Services.

The participants were between the ages of 18 and 23. Three of these students had just completed their first fall term as a college student. Of the students interviewed, six had transferred to their current university from other colleges. Two of the participants previously attended California State University at Northridge (CSUN), two attended community colleges, one student had attended a state college as well as Galluadet University, and one had gone to Gallaudet University, a community college, and then the current university.

Most all of the students interviewed graduated from mainstream high schools. In fact, only one graduated from a residential school for the Deaf. Eight of the participants had been the only Deaf student in their high school, and six had classmates who were also Deaf. However, many of these students said that the other Deaf student in the high school often were in Deaf programs versus being in the mainstream program.

The average high school GPA for the participants was 3.58 for these students. Those grades ranged from a GPA of 2.6 to 3.93. Many of these students were extremely high achievers in their high schools. Once in college, the average GPA was 2.90, with ranges from 2.32 to 3.69. The average GPA from the four universities involved in this study is 2.95 so it seems that the Deaf students are holding their own. Again, it is important to point out that three of the students interviewed had just completed their first term in college. Research shows that during the first one to two years, students' GPA usually is lower when they are focused on their core required classes versus their major classes (Astin, 1993).

The participants reported a variety of academic majors and career goals. Four of the students are majoring in health or physical education. Two of the students are majoring in education. Two of the students are majoring in social work or psychology and the rest of the students are majoring in biology, anthropology, art and design, horticulture, and urban planning. Two of the students were still undecided about their major.

Their career goals were also quite varied. Participants had goals to become athletic recruiters or working in the health field. Two want to specifically teach other Deaf children. Two want to work with Deaf people and their families as counselors. One wants to become a medical doctor. Another student sees herself as becoming a museum curator. One wants to design video games and another a superintendent at a golf course or a landscape designer. One even has his sites set on becoming a city planner or manager.

RESULTS

After the interviews were transcribed and the characteristics of the students compiled, the analysis of the data began. Due to limited time, this section will focus only on preliminary findings. Four distinct categories emerged regarding these students: 1) the students talked about their identity and how they communicated in the world; 2) their family of origin and their relationship with each family member was also an important category; 3) the stories the students had regarding their readiness for college, or how well their high schools prepared them for college; and 4) their personal perceptions about what made them feel successful and satisfied both academically and socially at their college. Direct quotes from the interviewees are included.

Identity. In regards to identity, most students quickly said, "I am Deaf." It was interesting to hear that several of the students had been diagnosed as hard of hearing first and then later as Deaf. Many of these mainstream students had experiences both as a hard-of-hearing student and as a Deaf student. A female 22-year-old student said, "I used to be hard of hearing, but then I became Deaf. I have always felt like I was between two worlds."

Students also talked about cochlear implants (CI). Two of the students said they had an CI in early childhood. Only one of the students is currently using their CI. Three of the students said they might be interested in have a CI sometime in the future. All three said that they were too busy now to do all the training required with a new CI. Nine of the participants stated they were not interested in having a CI. Of those nine, most said they were very comfortable with who they were and saw no need for having a CI.

Communication preference was also included in the identity category. Eight of the students were comfortable using either ASL and voice or PSE and voice. Many of the students had oral training in their mainstream schools. One student did not sign at all and communicated only orally and through writing.

Family of Origin. The literature that focuses on college retention points to the importance of family support (Astin, 1993, 1999; Braxton et al., 1995). Most of the participants in this study stated that they received encouragement and support from their family members. There were a number of interesting characteristics regarding the students' family of origin. First, exactly half are first-generation college students: 50% of the students' parents did not attend college. It was interesting to note that eight out of the 14 students' parents learned sign language at the time of their child was diagnosed as Deaf; in other words, eight students began communicating effectively with their parents at an early age. Over time, five of the sets of parents have continued to sign with their child. Six sets of parents never learned sign language and have always communicated orally with their Deaf child.

The students had a variety of comments related to their families. The following quotes indicate how often the students contacted their parents' while they were in college, the changes that have taken place since they left for college, their feelings of closeness to their parents, and the importance of their parents' support:

> Mostly I talk to my mom on IM [internet-based instant messenger]. It is so easy. We don't have to go through the relay. We talk once, twice, sometimes, three times a week. We talk about what we are doing. My parents live in another state so I don't get to see them very often. (male, age 21)

> I am the closest to my dad because we are both Deaf. We have had similar experiences. He has always been there for me. (female, age 18)

> I am the only Deaf member in three generations. But my family can sign, so ASL is their second language...but I am exposed to sign language everyday (at school) and my family is a little behind in knowing the signs. So when I go home, they are sometimes confused and awkward with my new signs. (female, age 21)

College Readiness. As stated earlier, one of the areas the students focused on was their high school preparation. Preparation for college during high school is related to college retention (Gerdes and Mallinckrodt, 2001). Students in this study were asked if the perceptions they had in high school about college was found to be accurate once they arrived at college. Most of the students said they were totally overwhelmed with the amount of independence they were allowed. And many did not feel prepared for how much to study. As you can see by the following quotes, some students felt more prepared than others:

> My high school prepared me for college. I took all college level preparation courses...my teachers really encouraged me to be ready for college. (female, age 18)

> I was a high achiever in high school. I have always been a very motivated student...Nobody told me I needed to get good grades to get into college. I just did it...I want to add that a support system is imperative...I believe the people you surround yourself with will really affect you. The world is an equal playing field. If you have the right people around you, you will be fine. (male, age 21)

> I was totally overwhelmed my first year. I almost dropped out. I was so frustrated! I tried to communicate in class, but I didn't understand them and they didn't understand me...In high school every thing was there for me. If I needed help I could find it easily. (female, age 22)

ACADEMIC AND SOCIAL SUCCESS AND SATISFACTION

Academic Success and Satisfaction. There are several factors that have been found to affect the academic success and satisfaction of college students. Those include interpreters, notetakers, the amount of class participation, the relationship students have with faculty members, and the students English writing skills (English, 1993). Most students were satisfied with their interpreters. However, some students talked about their frustration with interpreters and talked about how reliant they were on the skill of their interpreter.. If the interpreter was not skilled in voicing, then the students stated that they sat back and did not participate. Voicing skills of the interpreters were one of the biggest complaints for these students and caused internal conflict for some:

> I wish interpreters were available 24/7. I don't like having to schedule two days in advance. (male, age 21)

> I feel like many interpreters don't understand that I am from a different background. I sign more English or toal communication. I feel like the interpreters expect me to fit their way of signing. (female, age 22)

> I don't trust the interpreters will voice correctly for me. Most of the time their weakest skills is voicing. I get embarrassed that if the interpreter can't voice what I am saying, then the students in the class will think I am dumb. (female, age 20)

> I am very participatory with Deaf people. I can stand up and talk about what is on my mind. With hearing people it is different. Partly because of the interpreters. I am afraid they won't understand what I am signing. I have to repeat and repeat...Sometimes I feel like I have two personalities. (female, age 20)

Students also talked about the importance of notetakers. All students said they needed to have both interpreters and notetakers to succeed in school, however, several students had complaints about their notetakers. The strongest recommendation was to have more professionally trained notetakers:

> Some of the notetakers are really sloppy. They really need to work harder on their writing because it isn't always clear. And sometimes the notes don't make sense. (female, age 18)

> Notetakers are really important and I want them available for each class. The quality of notetaking can influence my grades. I sometimes have a hard time with notetakers. (male, age 20)

Class participation and relationship with faculty has been shown to be an important part of a student's success in college (English, 1993). Students in this study said they definitely felt more comfortable in small classes or when there are small discussion groups. But most of the students stated that they often hesitated to participate in class.

One student had attended a mainstream high school and a community college where she was the only Deaf student. She transferred to her current college where there was a larger group of Deaf students. Being with other Deaf students greatly impacted her identity and confidence:

> I am participating more in classes because I have become more comfortable being Deaf. I have met so many Deaf people (since high school) and have watched how they handle things. Now I am more confident to join in. (female, age 20)

The relationship with faculty has also been shown to be important to feelings of success and satisfaction (English, 1993). Most of the students felt that technology has opened up the possibility of communication between them and their teachers:

> I email my teachers if I have any questions from class. That is the best way to communicate with them. It helps so much if teachers check and respond to their emails. (female, age 18)

> Teachers are more helpful than I thought they would be. They have worked with Deaf students before so they know how to relate to me. (male, age 18)

English writing skills also impact academic satisfaction and success (English, 1993). Out of the 14 participants, eight felt that their writing skills were equal to their hearing classmates. Six felt that their writing skills were weaker. All participants stated that they enjoyed reading, although mostly for pleasure versus assigned homework or text reading. Many of the students utilized the tutoring or writing centers at their universities. The biggest concern students had regarding the tutoring center, was making sure that either the tutor was Deaf and signed or there was a qualified interpreter was available to work with them and the tutor.

Social Success and Satisfaction. As stated earlier, the social satisfaction of college has an equally strong affect on a students' retention in college (Gerdes and Mallinckrodt, 2001). Most of the interviewees had been mainstreamed and used to socializing with other hearing students. Some said they were too busy to socialize or were more comfortable staying by themselves.

However, the vast majority of students considered themselves social people and wanted to be with others. Students at one smaller university where there was an interpreter training program and many ASL classes were thrilled with the number of hearing students who knew sign language. Most of the students stated that they are the most comfortable socializing with people who were Deaf or who could sign:

> I really love being around people and socializing. I hate being alone. I

will hang out with hearing or Deaf people. I use my voice with hearing and I sign with Deaf people. It is not a big deal. (male, age 23)

I tend to hang out with my Deaf friends everyday. I also hang out with my hearing friends who know sign language, but not everyday. I like to be with different groups of students. Sometimes I use IM with hearing people who don't know sign language and that is fine, too. (female, age 18)

Dating is an important part of the social experience in college. Most of the students said they were still "playing the field." But some had some very specific ideas about dating:

I would like to date, but I am not dating right now. It just hasn't been the right situation or the right person. Or even enough time. (female, age 21)

I would prefer to marry a Deaf man, or at least someone who can sign. Because I want good communication. I want to teach my children how to sign so they can communication with me. I don't want to feel alone again. I don't want to feel not a part of my family. But for dating, I really don't care if the hearing guy doesn't sign. If he is the right guy for me, then he will learn sign language. (female, age 22)

Feeling a part of the campus community has a strong link to a student's sense of social success and satisfaction (English, 1993; Foster and Elliot, 1986). All 14 of the students interviewed for this study were involved in extra-curricular activities at their university. Many had been involved in high school sports and continued that into college. These Deaf college students were involved in football, basketball, lacrosse, scuba diving, and intramural sports. Students were also members of fraternities or sororities, as well as being resident assistants. Students talked about being active in numerous college committees and clubs. A favorite activity for students at one university was the ASL club, which included both Deaf and hearing students, and had recently won an award for being the most active club on that particular campus.

Most students said they felt satisfied at their colleges. However, when I asked them what ideas they had to improve that satisfaction, they came up with many ideas. Most said that there should be more in-service training for both students and faculty to explain Deaf culture and Deaf students' experiences. Almost all said that there needs to be more Deaf students on campus and equal accessibility to activities:

I would be happier if there were more Deaf students at my college. (female, age 20)

I would like to see more activities accessible to Deaf students and Deaf students more involved. I think it is important to involve Deaf students in classroom activities. Sometimes I think the faculty overlook Deaf students and don't even see that we exist. (male, age 21)

All faculty should know the role of the interpreter and how to use the interpreter appropriately. There are still most teachers who look directly at the interpreter when they should be looking at me, or they tell the interpreter "tell her"...things like that. (female, age 21)

DISCUSSION

The literature regarding experiences of Deaf students in collegiate mainstream programs is very limited. It is clear, however, that approximately 70 percent of these students will not complete their college degree (Myers and Taylor, 2000). The research that has been conducted in this area has mainly focused on mainstream institutions that enroll a large number of Deaf students, such as NTID (approximately 400 students).

We know very little about college students who attend postsecondary institutions with much smaller Deaf programs. Success in college has a significant impact on future employment. Research has found that obtaining a college degree positively correlates with annual income among Deaf employees (Schroedel and Geyer, 2000). Succeeding in and graduating from college is essential if Deaf individuals hope to compete and succeed in the world of work. Positive academic and social experiences in college promote persistence for college students who are Deaf (English, 1993; Foster and Elliot, 1986).

The purpose of this qualitative study was to learn more about the experience of students who attend universities with small Deaf populations. Fourteen Deaf college students enrolled in mainstream college programs were interviewed. Students discussed their perceptions of academic and social success and satisfaction with their academic experiences. A follow-up study will be conducted in four years to see where these 14 students are academically and career-wise. This study also provides implications for future studies.

What about Deaf students in mainstream college programs who are not traditional? What is their college experience like? (The students for this study were all of traditional college ages for undergraduates.) Also, what about hard-of-hearing students? How well does school actually prepare these students for college? The students interviewed for this study said that they do not plan to drop out of college, however, the statistics say that they might. Although this was a small study and only preliminary findings are presented, I believe this research will contribute to the literature in this field and provide more information regarding college success for Deaf students, their families, vocational rehabilitation counselors, university staff, and others. I also hope this study will open the doors for more research into what can help Deaf students persist in college and so that the majority of Deaf college students can obtain their degree.

REFERENCES

Allen, T. E. (1994). *Who are the Deaf and hard of hearing students leaving high school and entering postsecondary education?* Paper submitted to Pelavin Research Institute as part of the project, A Comprehensive Evaluation of the Postsecondary Educational Opportunities for Students who are Deaf or Hard of Hearing, funded by the U. S. Office of Special Education and Rehabilitative Services.

Astin, A. W. (1993). *What Matters in College: Four Critical Years Revisited.* San Francisco: Jossey-Bass.

Astin, A. W. (1999). Student involvement: A developmental theory for higher education. *Journal of College Student Development*, 40, 519–529.

Braxton, J. M., Vesper, N., & Hossler, D. (1995). Expectations for college and student persistence. *Research in Higher Education*, 36, 595–612.

Bronfenbrenner, U. (1979). *The ecology of human development: Experiments by Nature and design.* Cambridge: Harvard University Press.

Bronfenbrenner, U. (1986). Ecology of the family as a context for human development research perspectives. *Developmental Psychology*, 22, 723–742.

Brown, P. & Foster, S. (1991). Integrating hearing and Deaf students on a college campus: Successes and barriers as perceived by hearing students. *The American Annals of the Deaf*, 136, 21–27.

Chickering, A. W. (1969). *Education and identity.* San Francisco, California: Jossey-Bass.

Dey, E. L., & Hurtado, S. (1995). College impact, student impact: A reconsideration of the role of students within American higher education. *Higher Education*, 30, 207–223.

Eimers, M. T. & Pike, G. R. (1997). Minority and nonminority adjustment to college: Differences and similarities? *Research in Higher Education*, 38, 77–97.

English, K. M. (1993). *The role of support services in the integration and retention of college students who are hearing-impaired.* Doctoral Dissertation, San Diego State University, Claremont Graduate School, University Microfilm No. 933034.

Foster, S. (1988). Life in the mainstream: Reflections of Deaf college freshmen on their experiences in the mainstream high school. *Journal of Rehabilitation of the Deaf*, 22, 27–35.

Foster, S. (1992). Accommodation of Deaf college graduates in the work place. In Foster & G. Walter (Eds.), *Deaf Students in Postsecondary Education*, London: Routledge, pp. 210–235.

Foster, S. (1996) Doing research in Deafness: some considerations and strategies. In P. Higgins and J. Nash (Eds), *Understanding Deafness Social* (2nd Edition). Springfield, Illinois: Charles C. Thomas.

Foster, S. & Brown, P. (1989). Factors influencing the academic and social integration of hearing-impaired college students. *Journal of Postsecondary Education and Disability*, 7, 78–96.

Foster, S. & DeCaro, P. (1991) An ecological model of social interaction between Deaf and hearing students within a postsecondary educational setting. *Disability, Handicap and Society*, 6, 181–201.

Foster, S. & Elliot, L. (1986). *The best of both worlds: Interviews with NTID transfer students.* Rochester, New York: Rochester Institute of Technology.

Foster, S. Long, G. and Snell, K. (1999) Inclusive instruction and learning for Deaf students in postsecondary education. *Journal of Deaf Studies and Deaf Education*, 4, 225–235.

Foster, S. & Walter, G. (1992). *Deaf Students in Postsecondary Education*. London: Routledge.

Franklin, E. L. (1988). *Attrition and retention of hearing-impaired community college students*. Unpublished dissertation. Lawrence, Kansas: University of Kansas.

Gallaudet Research Institute. (January 2003). *Regional and National Summary Report of Data from the 2001–2002 Annual Survey of Deaf and Hard of Hearing Children and Youth*. Washington, DC: GRI, Gallaudet University.

Gerdes, H. & Mallinckrodt, B. (2001). Emotional, social, and academic adjustment of college students: A longitudinal study of retention. *Journal of Counseling and Development*, 72, 281–288.

Ginter, E. J. & Glauser, A. (1997). *Instructor's manual–The right start*. New York: Addison Wesley Longman.

Lehmann, J. P., Davies, T. G., & Laurin, K. M. (2000). Listening to student voices about postsecondary education. *Teaching Exceptional Children*, 32, p. 50–65.

Lewes, L., Farris, E., & Greene, B. (1994). *Deaf and hard of hearing students in postsecondary education*. Washington, DC: U.S. Department of Education, Office of Educational Research and Improvement.

Lofland, J. & Lofland, L. H. (1995). *Analyzing social settings: A guide to qualitative observation and analysis* (3rd ed.). Belmont, California: Wadsworth.

MacKay, K. A. & Kuh, G. D. (1994). A comparison of student effort and educational gains of Caucasian and African-American students at predominantly White colleges and universities. *Journal of College Student Development*, 35, 217–223.

Mertens, D. M. (1998). *Research methods in education and psychology: Integrating diversity with quantitative and qualitative approaches*. Thousand Oaks, California: Sage.

Myers, M. J. & Taylor, E. M. (2000). Best practices for Deaf and hard of hearing student success in postsecondary education. *Journal of the American Deafness and Rehabilitation Association*, 34, 13–28.

National Technical Institute for the Deaf 1997 Annual Report. (1997). Rochester, New York: Rochester Institute of Technology.

Rawlings, B. W., Karchmer, M. A., DeCaro, J. J, & Allen, T. E. (1991). *College and career programs for deaf students*. Washington, DC: Gallaudet University and Rochester, New York: Rochester Institute of Technology.

Schroedel, J. (1976). *Variables Related to the Attainment of Occupational Status Among Deaf Adults*. Doctoral Dissertation, New York University, New York (Univ. Microfilm No.77–16447).

Schroedel, J., & Geyer, P. (2000). Long-term career attainments of Deaf and hard of hearing college graduates: Results from a 15-year follow-up study. *American Annals of the Deaf*, 145, 303–313.

Schroedel, J., Watson, D., and Ashmore, D. H. (2003). A national research agenda for postsecondary education of Deaf and hard of hearing students: A road map for the future. *American Annals of the Deaf*, 148, 67–73.

Sheridan, M. (2001). *Inner lives of Deaf children: Interviews and analysis*. Washington, DC: Gallaudet University Press.

Stinson, M. Scherer, A. & Walter, G. (1997). Improving retention for Deaf and hard of hearing students: What the research tells us. *Journal of American Deafness and Rehabilitation Association*, 30, 14–23.

Stodden, R. A. & Dowrick, P.W. (2000). Postsecondary education and employment Of adults with disabilities. *American Rehabilitation: High Quality Employment*, 1, 19–23.

Tinto, V. (1987). *Leaving college: Rethinking the causes and cures of student attrition*. Chicago, Illinois: University of Chicago Press.

Tinto, V. (1993). *Leaving college: Rethinking the causes and cures of student attrition* (2nd ed.). Chicago, IL: University of Chicago Press.

Tinto, V. (1997) Classroom as communities. *Journal of Higher Education*, 68, 659–684.

Thomas, S. B. (2000). College students and disability law. *The Journal of Special Education*, 33, 248–257.

Watson, L. W. & Kuh, G. D. (1996). The influence of dominant race environments on student involvement, perceptions, and educational gains: A look a historically Black and predominantly White liberal arts institutions. *Journal of College Student Development*, 37, 415–424.

Welsh, W. & MacLeod-Gallinger, J. (1992). Effect of college on employment and earnings. In S. Foster and G. Walter (eds.) *Deaf Students in Postsecondary Education*. New York: Routledge, 185–192.

Welsh, W. & Walter, G. (1988). The effect of postsecondary education on the occupational attainment of Deaf adults. *Journal of the American Deafness and Rehabilitation Association*, 22, 14–22.

Wilson, R. (1994). The participation of African Americans in American higher education. In M. J. Justiz et al. (ed.) *Minorities in Higher Education*, pp. 195–209. Phoenix, Arizona: Oryx Press.

Youn, D. K. (1992). Student retention: Many more ideas. *College Student Journal*, 26, 472–475.

Yuen, J. W. & Shaughnessy, B. (2001). Cultural empowerment: Tools to engage and retain postsecondary students with disabilities. *Journal of Vocational Rehabilitation*, 16, 199–20.

ABOUT THE AUTHOR

Julia Smith, Coordinator of the Rehabilitation Counseling: Deaf program, has been affiliated with Western Oregon University since 1984, first as Director of Disability Services, then as Assistant Professor. She has also worked as a mental health therapist with Deaf and hard-of-hearing individuals and couples for over 26 years. Julia's current research interest is the transition from high school to college of students who are Deaf, and her doctoral dissertation focuses on the life experiences of traditional-aged Deaf students in collegiate mainstream programs. She and her Deaf husband have been married for 25 years and have two children in college.

in/visible signs

Courtesy Emily Steinberg

in/visible signs:
The Grammars of
Translation and Film

EMILY JANE STEINBERG

Emily Steinberg is an M.A. *candidate in Deaf Studies at Gallaudet University.*

CROSSING THE FIRST THRESHOLD

THE ARCHETYPAL STORY OF ASL poetry is bound to the linguistic verity of ASL itself. Prior to William Stokoe's linguistic research in the 1960s, a poetry of ASL was as inconceivable as the notion that ASL was its own language at all. Hence modern understandings of poetry were relegated to the spheres of writing, and Deaf poets—and would-be poets—condemned to wrestle with English, a linear language ill-suited to express their multi-dimensional experiences. Poets such as Clayton Valli and Ella Mae Lentz have recounted their growth as artists in the decades following Stokoe's research and the publication of new ASL curricula.

Once ASL became a recognized language in its own right, the doors were opened for Valli, Lentz, and others to use their native language for poetic expression. This is a story of coming home to one's own language. My own story is quite the opposite, but it shares one element of the "writer's journey:" when I first came to Gallaudet, my own language abandoned me, and for me, like the poets of ASL, English didn't suffice for the creation of art.

My film *in/visible signs* is in many ways the result of that abandonment. I grew up an English speaker and writer, and it was rare if ever that I would sit down to write and feel the language fail me. Especially as a poet, I had learned how to tease apart my ideas in English, filling out the body of a poem from a single line. But in the fall of 2003 I entered Gallaudet University, and found myself trying to adapt to a new mode of being, to attune my eyes and my mind to a visual environment. I was immersed in the intricate process of rewiring my brain, training myself to think in sign and avoid that trap of the non-native, of formulating a thought in my first language and then (quick!) trying to translate it in my head. This struggle left me, for a time, something less than intimate with English, for when I would sit down to write, I would see pictures, and not words.

However, these pictures were not signs, either. So there were images, yes, but they were images of struggle, inarticulate, and illiterate. My need to express, as an artist, as an individual, as a social being, was trapped. I was caught in a liminal space between two languages: my first no longer served me, not speaking to pictures or capable of writing in signs. And I was far from grown into my second. What was I, as an artist, to do, but try and say one thing right.

My daily experience with ASL was awkward, like trying to mold a vast amount of clay, and I was taken with the impulse to create one small kernel of expression that looked right. More than looking right, that it felt right, the way a poem feels right when it expresses some essence of meaning and not just a compromise or approximation of the truth. in/visible signs became that attempt, an outgrowth of my need to express.

The poem *in/visible signs* is an original work in ASL, but it is also a translation of an English poem of mine. That poem was written in the summer of 2000, when I encountered the DEAF-WORLD for the first time. I met the DEAF-WORLD as a filmmaker and an artist, and saw it through the eyes of a(n English) poet. Early that summer, a film crew had contacted the University of Rochester, where I was a student, looking for production assistants. I volunteered and showed up the first day totally unaware that I was about to be meeting and working with Deaf people. The film was *AfterImage*, the lead actress was Terrylene.

Suddenly I was in an environment where my hometown became foreign—I couldn't communicate—and I felt it was up to me to figure out how to respond. I began studying ASL in the evenings with a few borrowed books, and during the days I would talk with Terrylene and the other Deaf people on set, gesturing, fingerspelling, writing back and forth on paper plates over meals.

Those six weeks of filmmaking left me artistically (and linguistically) awakened, and I wrote a poem at the end of the production. It was called *a language lesson*, and it marked my crossing of the first threshold into a new world. It was an attempt, in English, to express what I'd seen in ASL. Three years later at Gallaudet, that same poem became the germ for *in/visible signs*, when once again, I was living between two languages and two worlds.

FEELING-ONESELF-SIGN

Speaking, according to Derrida, has a profound effect on the identity of the Western speaker, as "self-presence" is affirmed through "hearing-oneself-speak." Dirksen Bauman writes in "Toward a Poetics of Vision, Space, and the Body" of the incomplete nature of "seeing-oneself-sign" as opposed to speaking; "Signers, unless gazing into the mirror, do not fully see themselves signify. While they may see their hands, they cannot see their own face" (317).

When I arrived at Gallaudet, to be sure, I experienced a strange sense of displacement of self. Switching gears from the mode of speaking and hearing to signing affected my sense of space, time, and memory. Remembering what someone said was no longer a matter of recalling the sounds, but the sight. My own self-presence was differently constructed as well, as I could not only not be sure of what I'd said (my own abecedarian grasp of the language ensuring that I'd sign a word differently each time anyhow), but in a sense, if I'd said it at all.

This was not a matter of doubting the language, but of reconstructing my identity to maintain continuity in a visual space. This struggle might, for some, raise the question of my impulse to make *in/visible signs*. Was my drive to create a film in ASL an unconscious attempt at reconciliation of my hearing self-presence (Derrida's "hearing-oneself-speak") with the world of sign? By creating something I could see, would I overcome what Bauman calls "the trace of nonpresence" in signing?

But while "nonpresence" was certainly a quandary I withstood as an individual, it was actually my artistic need that spurred me into the making of this film. While it may be argued that I was indeed seeking to *see* myself, as the end product of this poetic process is a film that I can watch again and again, I must submit that the creation of the film, and that of the film's poem itself, exist in somewhat separate realms. For I was not seeking to see myself sign correctly, but to *feel* myself sign.

ASL being a tactile language as well as a visual one, the experience of expression, rather than reception, became paramount to this project. In fact, after months of translating and rehearsing, the performance of the poem in studio was fulfillment enough of my desire to "feel-oneself-sign," and I have not performed the poem again since. But the editing of the film became the creation of the poem in yet another sense, and I do watch the completed film now, as I would read a poem I'd written, remembering and re-seeing the impulse and the essence.

IMPULSE IS UNIVERSAL

The question of impulse is at the center of this undertaking, but it is the expressive impulse not simply of the (adjusting) hearing person in the DEAF-WORLD, but that of the artist. Normandi Ellis writes in *Awakening Osiris*, her translation of the Egyptian spiritual text often mistakenly called the *Egyptian Book of the Dead*, "we are not just human beings; we are humans becoming." If we unpack this phrase we see that it tells us humanity is not the expression of a static state, but a process of creation. Humans "becoming" rather than "being" are humans constantly growing into new forms and expressing in new ways, that in fact, the definition of human-ity is this state of growth and change. And as we as humans grow, our medium of expression also changes.

The creative (or poetic) impulse of an artist transcends the medium they choose. That is, the inner need to create is deeper than the form of expression in which it ultimately takes its shape. To put it in formulaic terms, impulse equals universal; expression equals local.

People are driven to express in any number of different ways—writing, painting, dancing, filmmaking—and may employ one or several of these mediums to achieve their aim and the fulfillment of their poetic drive. The media themselves are channels for the impulse, not the impulse itself. This can be seen in artists' descriptions of their work, or in their search for the appropriate type of paint to use or stone to carve—one that most closely resembles the feeling-tone of that particular impulse they are striving to communicate. If poetry is art, then, language can be seen to be yet another example of medium—a channel of creation, whether it is spoken, written, or signed.

As an artist I have always tried to honor my own creative impulse, channeling it (most often) into an English poem. When I first saw ASL poetry, I saw a new medium for poetic expression, in fact a new medium (to me) of language itself. ASL poetry was doing something that written poetry could not do! In ASL poetry I saw language "in concentrate," a condensed nature of expression, similar to any written poem, but in this case, visible and embodied. In all my writing of English poetry, the end result was always a releasing, a letting-go of the poem to take on its own existence, to be read by another, often out of my presence altogether.

The goal, in writing poetry is, for me, to write it so completely that my own existence is erased and unnecessary to the life of the poem. I should not have to explain it, I should not have to attend to its reading. And although in the reading of my poems as author, a sense of owning the experience of it remains, it struck me that ASL poetry was altogether different.

The endpoint of ASL poetry is not releasing, but *becoming*, the poem. ("We are humans becoming"). When I arrived at Gallaudet and my first language—the language of my art—failed me, honoring my creative impulse (and the visual environment that surrounded me) necessitated an attempt at ASL poetry. The drive was the same, as it always is, but the quest for a new medium was kindled within me. The new medium, ASL, meant that I would attempt to experience language in concentrate in a tactile form, embodying and becoming my own poem in a way I had never before. Honoring this impulse meant risking myself, but to deny the risk would have been to deny my own becoming.

THE GRAMMAR OF TRANSLATION

A grammar is not only the rules and system of rules by which a language operates, but also a book dealing with these rules. Translation, according to Merriam-Webster, is

> "1) to change from one place, state or form to another, 2) to convey to heaven without death, 3) to turn into one's own or another language."

If I were to define a grammar of translation then, it would be a set or book of rules governing the process of translation. Making *in/visible signs* was an exercise in discovering (and writing) that grammar. Translation of poetry is a sort of alchemical process; the principles exist, but they are somewhat invisible. Ironic as it may seem, looking back at the months-long process of translation, it seemed to me that in making my first foray into ASL poetry, beginning with a poem (in English) that already expressed what I wanted to say would be easier than starting from scratch in ASL, a language I'd never tried to "write" in before. And so my first attempt at translation began.

Of all my poems, starting with *a language lesson* presented itself as the natural choice. This poem deals with language itself, with seeing and feeling ASL, and stumbling through my first few interactions. It alludes to what my raw eyes saw. It was fitting that my first attempt at ASL poetry should be about this same exchange, so that my trying-on of the medium became the message itself. But looking at the English poem, filled with metaphor and abstraction, I couldn't think of where to begin. A line-by-line transference of the poem from English to ASL would not be a translation. The metaphors would still be written concepts, not creations endemic to sign language. So that even if it did say something, it wouldn't be *in* ASL, but merely turned *towards* it. It would not enter into or embody it, existing in its "place, state, or form."

Translation involves something beyond the words of the poem. Like honoring the impulse behind the first creation, translation must transfer *meaning*, and not simply the words themselves. To arrive at the meaning, in ASL, of my English poem, I had to go back to my original impulses, unpacking the reason behind each metaphor there. For the words, as well-crafted as they may be, are still the manifestation of the impulse, and not the impulse itself. When poetry succeeds, it is because it transcends the limits of its own lines, and is a conduit to the original feeling-tone. This is what I was aiming for in my ASL poem—to translate the feeling-tone into sign.

The process took months. Reams of paper, scribbled pictures hanging on my walls, pages of free-writing to try and tap into the purest form of thought, and ultimately, the use of an entire classroom, blackboards lining every wall, so that I could write my poem, life-size, in a form of transcription I finally found workable, and see it surrounding me in the air, as the air, filled with language, surrounds me in *in/visible signs* (see Figure 1). The whole time, I worked closely with my willing friend and sign coach, fellow student Shawn Broderick, teasing apart the feelings and throwing them, and my contorted fists, into the air. This process brought up further questions, of co-authorship, directorship, and translation/creation.

There was a process of going-away-from, in following leads and abandoning them, as we experimented with metaphors and rhythms, creating a new structure and a form, that brought us closer to the destination. Jerome Rothenberg, co-editor and contributing writer in the book *Symposium of the Whole: A Range of Discourse Toward an Ethnopoetics*, writes of similar experiences translating Seneca, a language he did not know. He relied instead on a Seneca native's translation of the Seneca songs into English, and then used their translation of English to create his own. There is a constant writing and erasure that happens in translation, intercession and removal of the self-as-translator in order to journey away from, but come back to, the original.

Rothenberg writes, "the more the translator can perceive of the original—not only the language but, more basically perhaps, the living situation from which it comes... the more of it he should be able to deliver" (393). As the author of the original poem *a language lesson*, I was in a unique position to create *in/visible signs*. At least I knew the living situation that inspired those first lines! In some ways, this experience, of translating one's own work, is the only way to prove that an accurate transference has taken place. Who else but the author of the original can judge whether the translation has remained true? Perhaps because of this constant uncertainty, there is a motion in Rothenberg's writing almost towards deifying translation. It becomes an act of faith to believe that something begun with a "forced change of language" can become a successful transference of perception. But again, it is the attention to impulse that necessitates this attuning of expressions.

Looking at the two poems side by side, *in/visible signs* and *a language lesson*, one is struck by how little similarity of word and form exists between them. There are no islands in the film, no archipelago of meaning, no bodies like mirrors. (But there is air-turned-to-water, a struggle of bodies to connect, and a reflecting pool). The film is not what would conventionally be considered a translation. It is certainly not an *interpretation* of the poem, in the sense of an interpreter's rendition of it, were it read aloud. But, in another sense, it is an interpretation. The feeling of the original is there, behind the signs, and in the images that open and close the film. This is the challenge of *in/visible signs* then, that it pushes our understanding of what constitutes a true translation, what codifies the grammar of translation, and what something looks like, made new, when the goal is not to represent but to present.

WIDENING GYRES

It would be a gross oversight for me to close this discussion of language translation without acknowledging that there is a third translation of the poem in existence—the gloss of *in/visible signs* written for the interpreters to read during the second screening of the film at the Deaf Studies *Today!* conference. This gloss, when read accompanying the film, follows the rhythm of the signing, and gives a rather materialistic translation of the poem. There is an artlessness to the lines, "the air turns into water," for example, that makes the entire gloss feel something like a sieve, the essence of the poem having been drained away. And the performance of the gloss with the film becomes an interesting moment of interpreting and translating in and of itself, as the film, a "translation" of the original English poem, is accompanied by an interpreter reading an English gloss of the film, in a bizarre attempt to recoup some sense of the original impulse behind the whole project. (And for that matter, the majority of my entire presentation in Utah was fraught with this sense of intersemiotic interpretation, because I was speaking in English, about translation into film and ASL, and being interpreted back into ASL by way of interpreters. How many degrees of separation were built into that 45 minutes alone?)

But this glossed version, unlike *a language lesson* or *in/visible signs*, was never intended to stand alone. Whether it adds or detracts from the

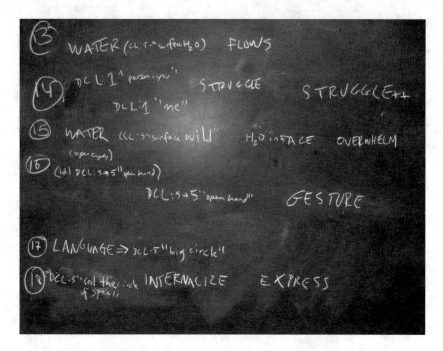

Figure 1. Translation in action

(hearing person's?) experience of seeing the film is another question. In my opinion, the gloss is not wholly successful, and I am dissatisfied with it in perhaps the same way that Rothenberg was not satisfied with the spare "factual" approach to translations of Navajo, which reproduced "the vocables exactly" but "denie[d] the musical coherence of the original and destroy[ed] the actual flow" (389).

Rothenberg's solution to this is something he calls "total translation," a phonetic representation of the Navaho vocables intercut into the English translated words. I must admit that if there is a way to perform such a total translation from ASL to English, I have not come upon it yet. Perhaps my grasp of ASL is not yet at a point that makes that possible.

And not only am I uncomfortable with the success of the glossed version, but (although the gloss is an aid to hearing viewers who do not understand the poem or are unfamiliar with ASL) I have received feedback from those who *do* know the language, and overwhelmingly it seems that the voice-over is an interruption to their sense of the flow of the film. Moreover, feedback from Deaf viewers of the film has led me to consider that the Deaf viewing experience, whilst aware of a voice interpreter speaking it—thus rendering some translation of the film inaccessible in their presence—creates a conscious disconnect in their viewing.

This is quite a reversal of the aims of the film, which presents a work of ASL and filmmaking precisely for a Deaf and/or signing audience.

I admit that I struggled, in preparing my presentation and the screening, on how to handle this matter. My decision, to show the film as-is the first time, and with interpreted voice-over the second time, was a compromise. I am not interested in captioning the film, for that, I feel, would impose the sense of linearity and English language dominance (as a recognized poetic form, and as a visible distraction from the signing itself) that I am seeking to deconstruct through the very existence of the film itself. I have considered recording myself as a voice-over, and producing a new DVD with the option for voice off or on, perhaps with the "recommendation" that the poem is best viewed in the original silent version. But I have yet to undertake this project, in part, I would hazard a guess, because I am still not satisfied with the gloss I have written.

This struggle is not unique to my film, however. It is important to realize that as the medium of ASL poetry grows, and especially as the use of film for ASL poetry, literature, and other Deaf filmmaking expands, that questions of translation, interpretation, and accessibility will become central to the field. The marriage of ASL and film can bring an awareness and appreciation of Deaf art and Deaf culture to a whole new audience, but only if the media is accessible to people on the margins of Deaf space. I have considered submitting my film to festivals. These are opportunities for a woman filmmaker to gain recognition, and ASL literature to reach new audiences. But without captioning or voice-over, will this film get programmed? Will it get seen? I may struggle for my copasetic solution, but the alternative is invisibility.

THE GRAMMAR OF FILM

The final consideration of *in/visible signs* must examine and place it within a context of visual media. Many performances have been filmed before this—ASL poetry, stories, comedy, folklore—and (with rare exception) the tapes are considered filmed performances. That is, the filming is a recording of the event, a way to preserve the telling, but it is not a writing of its own. There may have been some editing employed, but the performances existed, and could be replicated in a live space. *in/visible signs* is different.

It uses the medium of film to become film, and through the editing employed, the final result is a piece that exists only as film. The visual climax of the poem comes when the water is rising, and signs are flying hands, overwhelming my eyes. The sign used is two-handed, a closed-S handshape flicking open to an open-5 handshape, both hands bombard-ing my face. To see this performed live, one would see only the backs of my hands, my face would be covered completely, and the sign itself wouldn't convey the meaning intended. However, in the film, the "water" rises, flowing towards and away from me, and as it overtakes me, we *cut* to the hands flying not in *my* face, but in the face of the viewers, filling the screen and providing a first-person glimpse into the moment. The audience is put into my shoes and into my eyes, a situation unique to the potentials of film (see page 309).

Elsewhere, ASL has been written about as a part of the "oral" tradi-tion of non-written literature. Ethnopoetics seeks to bring discussion of oral traditions into the present discourse of the world's literature. As Rothenberg writes in the introduction to *Symposium of the Whole*, "If the recovery of the oral is crucial to the present work, it goes hand in hand with a simultaneous expansion of the idea of writing and the text, wherever and whenever found" (xiii). That assertion, and the example of *in/visible signs*, in which the shot of flying hands imbricates the poem within the filmic medium, leads us to consider film as writing and text. Not only is it a tool to record, but to create. As the pen or keyboard are the writing utensils of written languages, in this modern age, are not a digi-tal tape and camera the pen and paper of signing hands? And if so, a whole new field of inquiry opens up: the visual grammar of film itself.

The filmic qualities of ASL have been discussed. Dirksen Bauman, for instance, has analyzed the cinematic structure of Clayton Valli's poem *The Lone, Sturdy Tree* in "Re-Designing Literature: Poetics of American Sign Language Poetry." We acknowledge the way ASL recapitulates a film in storytelling, through its use of classifiers and role-shifting, resulting in an assimilation of long shots, close-ups, point-of-view, and an infinite variety of "angles" and possibilities for "editing."

There has been conjecture about the historical relationship between this facet of ASL and the technological inventions of the film industry since the early 1900s. There has been talk of using ASL stories as the shooting scripts for films, unpacking each sign and the sign's perspec-tive to determine the choreography and sequence of shooting a scene, so that the storyteller becomes the director of the film, vis-à-vis their natural signing style. These ideas begin to examine at least the way that ASL makes use of the techniques of film. But we have not yet explored the grammar of film, when applied back to ASL. Film already has its own language and varieties of expression, use of rhythm, editing, shooting, in essence, storytelling. That much is clear from even a glance at the field of film studies and the many schools of film production. How does this established grammar grow in dialogue with ASL? Or, better put, how can the grammars of film and ASL be developed together? What would a marriage of ASL and film look like that incorporated the strengths of both mediums, and was not just a still medium shot of an ASL performance with a credit roll at the end?

This has begun to happen in some places, a use of filming involving some camera movement or more frequent editing, such as in Ella Mae Lentz's videotape of poems *The Treasure,* or in some of Peter Cook's work. The tapes of performers in the *Live at SMI* series employ some editing as well, but this is mainly a composition of two or three cameras filming different (yet still standard) angles, a medium and a close-up, for example. The actual grammatical capabilities of the camera as a writing tool of ASL haven't even begun to be fully explored. It will only be through increased use of (and experimentation with) film and editing that this will take place.

For this to become commonplace, digital video, cameras, and computers must be considered standard tools for ASL writing. We cannot think of them as foreign, or the tools of "filmmakers" alone. There is a natural affinity between a visual language and a visual medium, and so ASL performers and storytellers must own that affinity, and become filmmakers themselves. By reconstructing a concept of ASL literacy and literature to include film and video, our creation and valuation of that literacy and literature can expand. If film is the writing instrument of ASL, then being literate means using that medium, experimenting and creating in it. Bauman has called film a "postmodern bardic tradition" and perhaps it is. But it is more than that. It is yet another medium for us all to honor the creative impulse, and we must seize it, and begin.

IN CLOSING

Unfortunately I cannot enclose my film within these pages, a further limit of our abilities to fit our medium with our message, but here at least is the poem which started this journey, and may provide some sense of the scope of my project. I would also like to express my thanks for those who supported the production of this film as well as my participation in the Deaf Studies *Today!* conference, especially the ASL and Deaf Studies department at Gallaudet University.

a language lesson

The first thing I looked for was the rhythm –
the body speaking like an ocean.
Infinite.
self-contained. and when still –
a deep mirror pulsing beneath skin.

Across the shifting geography of our meetings,
every now and then an accent
trips my afferent eye.

I taste the shape of silence,
weigh the space between our worlds.
Your body a series of islands.
Acronyms for life.

Testing the air in my unstudied palms,
I drop syllables like a fickle wind.

Archipelago of meanings, like so many holy tongues.

—emily jane steinberg

REFERENCES

Bauman, Dirksen. "Re-Designing Literature: Poetics of American Sign Language Poetry."
From *http://www.ubu.com/ethno/discourses/bauman_asl.html*
Bauman, Dirksen. "Toward a Poetics of Vision, Space, and the Body." *The Disabilities Studies Reader.* Ed., Lennard Davis. New York: Routledge. 1997.
Rothenberg, Diane & Jerome. *Symposium of the Whole: A Range of Discourse Toward an Ethnopoetics.* Berkeley: University of California Press. 1983.

ABOUT THE AUTHOR

Emily Steinberg is an M.A. candidate in Deaf Studies at Gallaudet University. Her undergraduate work was at the University of Rochester where she completed her B.A. in both Film Studies and Women's Studies in 2001. Her first introduction to the Deaf community came in 2000 while working on the film production of "AfterImage," starring Terrylene. Since then she has been involved in documentary and art film production and Deaf theater, working on Terrylene's play In the Now *as stage manager and produc-tion designer. Her involvement in the Deaf arts world led her to Gallaudet, where she continues her work in the intersections of film, art, and cultural studies and practice.*

About Deaf Studies at Utah Valley State College

Courses

Deaf Studies *Today!* is the creation of the American Sign Language and Deaf Studies Program at Utah Valley State College (UVSC) in Orem, Utah. The UVSC American Sign Language and Deaf Studies program is part of the Department of Foreign Languages and is home to some 320 students. From its birth as a beginning-level ASL class offered in the evening during the mid-1990s, the program has expanded to some sixty sections of ASL and Deaf Studies a year. The program administers twenty courses ranging from beginning ASL courses to advanced classes in Deaf culture, literature, ASL grammar and linguistics, interpreting, and more. The American Sign Language and Deaf Studies program also administers specialized classes for the college's approximately 40 Deaf students (taught in ASL), which teach them English literacy in preparation for entering college English.

Degrees

Currently, UVSC offers a minor in Deaf Studies. UVSC students can also use ASL as one of two areas of emphasis toward a bachelor's degree in Integrated Studies. American Sign Language and Deaf Studies faculty members are currently working on a bachelor's degree in Deaf Studies which they hope to implement in Fall 2006. Of course, many students majoring in other fields take ASL courses to fulfill the language requirements for B.A. degrees.

Information

More information about the UVSC ASL and Deaf Studies program is available at *www.uvsc.edu/asl*.